The Curators

The Roles and Responsibilities of

God's Maintenance Entities

• • •

A Channeled Work

Blessings & much
love

By

Guy Steven Needler

Guy x
10/12/19

For permission, serialization, condensation, adaptions, or for our catalog of other publications, write to Ozark Mountain Publishing, Inc., P.O. Box 754, Huntsville, AR 72740, ATTN: Permissions Department.

Library of Congress Cataloging-in-Publication Data

Needler, Guy Steven – 1961 -
The Curators by Guy Steven Needler

In the Curator's the reader is exposed to the mechanics of the multiversal environment we exist within and those entities that maintain it.

1. Spiritual   2. Channeling   3. Entities 4. Metaphysical
I. Needler, Guy Steven, 1961 - II. Metaphysical   III. Channeling   IV. Title

Library of Congress Catalog Card Number: 2019944352
ISBN: 9781940265650

Cover Art and Layout: Victoria Cooper Art
Book set in: Times New Roman, Goudy Old Style
Book Design: Tab Pillar
Published by:

PO Box 754, Huntsville, AR 72740
800-935-0045 or 479-738-2348; fax 479-738-2448
WWW.OZARKMT.COM

Printed in the United States of America

Contents

Foreword

I am here again, staring at the very empty first page of my next book. This will be the first time I have worked on a book for four months—they have flown by. Having had the break that was promised to me, I now sit here with some trepidation. I learned in the last few pages of *The Anne Dialogues* and received some level of warning in *The Origin Speaks* that I needed to write another six books! That this book is the first of these six is the daunting part.

Why is it daunting, you may ask, when I have already written six books? The answer is simple. The first books came one by one with no precognition of the books to follow until the very end of the book being finished—that is, apart from the *Beyond the Source* books. I wasn't seeing the bigger picture. Then, slowly, toward the end of *The Origin Speaks,* I started to gain an insight into the rest of the work I had to do and over the last eighteen to twenty months I have been given not only the titles for these books, but also an idea of the content.

Two books are due to be in a similar "deep" vein to the ones I have written to date, insomuch as they will deal with the Om and provide more information on The Origin. Two are going to be controversial, as they are going to touch and expose information on subjects that are taboo on many levels. They will be "stand alone" and I am told I will write these two last!!! No, I will not be saying what the subject matter is yet, but I am sure that I have spoken to one or two people about them over the last year or so. The last two are also "stand alone" subject-matter-wise but will work on subjects that I have touched on in my previous books; one being this book and another dealing with healing and with how the way we incarnate affects our energies in a dysfunctional way. Deal with them one by one, I hear you say, and I agree with you, but knowing what one has to do and moreover, the time frame that I have to work with, is the daunting part, especially as I know what to expect in terms of the difficult concepts and theories surrounding the subject matter.

All this being said, I am looking forward to working on the content of this book—*The Curators*, the title of which I have only just been given, even though I have known the subtitle for some time. It promises to be interesting, enlightening, educational, fun, and I have no doubt will have a number of areas where we go deep into the detail of the subjects being discussed. I am also expecting to provide a number of illustrations to let you see what I can see while providing links with previous imagery where possible.

Again I sit here. Having rambled on a bit, I am not only wondering when I will actually start the first words of text attributable to the title, but I am also wondering who I will be communicating with. As usual, I didn't have to wait long!

SE1, O, A: [altogether] Surprise!!!

I suddenly felt like the man who came home from a rough day at the office to open the door of his house to find a "party" waiting for him!

ME: OK, so you are all here. Which of you will I be talking to?

SE1: Predominately myself …

O: Although we will all …

A: Contribute at some point.

I must admit that I didn't expect to feel Anne's energies.

A: It is planned that I will make the odd "guest" appearance in the dialogue where and when it is appropriate. This will be especially when you are communicating with some of the Elementals that work with the Earth.

SE1: Suffice to say, most of what we will be discussing will be relevant to the multiversal environment that I created and that most of your readers will relate to.

O: However, there will be times when the bigger picture of my polyomniscient area of sentient self-awareness will need to be taken into consideration, and so at these junctures in the dialogue I will communicate with you.

ME: Feels good to me.

SE1: Good. We will start whenever you are ready.

ME: How about right now!

SE1: Why not.

A Myth Buster

ME: I want to start first with a base-line understanding of the structure of what we call the Angelic realms. I just want to show the truth-seeking world that we have interacted with these beings before and have given them labels—names and descriptions of their functions. But, I don't want to go down the route of justifying, or not, as the case may be, the imagery and descriptions of those entities mankind has classified to date, no matter how close or far away from the truth it is. What I want is, as normal, the Greater Reality that supports the current understanding, along with a little bit more if possible.

I have to admit here to cheating a little because some of this information was in a document I wrote in 2005. Note that I am still drawn to use the abbreviation for The Source as SE1 and not just SE as in The History of God.

SE1: We can look at them first if you wish, but note that we may not deal with them on an individual basis, or for that matter, on a group basis either in some cases.

ME: Why not?

SE1: Because this may not be the reality of the structure of entities who have committed to be in service in my multiversal environment.

ME: OK, let's treat it as what mankind knows to date by drawing upon my previous work and you commenting where you wish to, busting the myths as we go.

SE1: That will be a starting point at least.

ME: Thank you.

SE1: Are you sure that you want to start now?

ME: No. I am changing my mind.

SE1: I thought you might be. You are realizing that you cannot quote the information from one religion without also quoting the corresponding information from the other major religions.

ME: You still have me cornered, don't you! Even after all these years, you still know when I haven't understood the issue—even before I realize it!

SE1: Of course. Don't forget that I know everything that you have asked, are asking, and will ask. It's an interestingly small but effective advantage that I have over you in this incarnate state. What I would suggest is that you use the overall structure from the document you created in 2005 as a minor reference to that which some of mankind knows. Later in the dialogue you can look at the bigger picture. [*The 2005 document was created as a dissertation as part of my healing examinations.—GSN*]

ME: OK, it sounds like a plan.

SE1: Good. The first thing I want to state is that, irrespective of its level of correctness, the information you have refers only to the physical universe and has no reference to the rest of the structure of my multiversal environment. This in itself is a major limitation in the ability of existing information to express the aspect of the Greater Reality that it is supposed to be describing.

ME: So the first myth to be broken is that of the structure of the higher realms. Those realms or environments that are classified as the areas within the universe where the angels exist in all their hierarchical variations are not only limited to the physical universe, they are limited to mankind's knowledge and thinking ability.

SE1: Yes. Remember that the information that most of incarnate mankind has is the product of its recent frequential state, educational levels, and subsequent expansiveness, the frequential levels only being elevated in the last forty years with real changes happening in the last ten to fifteen years.

ME: So what is the structure? And, what are the names or roles of the entities that work with this structure?

SE1: Describing the roles, responsibilities, and functions of those entities that have chosen to be of service by maintaining the structure of the multiverse and its evolutionary efficiency is the whole point of this dialogue, and, as a result, the detail will be presented to you in a way that will be both progressive and logical in its application. Moreover, it will need to be described in summary from the top down and explained in detail from the bottom up. In this way the readers will gain an idea of the breadth of the subject matter we will discuss, allowing the depth to become more digestible as we move along.

Do note, though, that we are talking about those entities that are not only maintaining the structure and its detail, but also those that are involved in the perpetuation of the structure.

ME: What do you mean the perpetuation of the structure? I would have thought that maintaining it perpetuated it?

SE1: No, those entities that maintain the structure of the multiverse do just that, maintain it. They maintain it for those entities that use the multiverse for evolutionary purposes. Because a number of entities want to use it for evolutionary purposes, their focus is on being within the structure of the multiverse, experiencing it, using it, creating within it, progressing through it—not maintaining it.

However, in their desire to be within the multiverse to evolve by experiencing its environments in both its linear and parallel states, parallel states are created by invoking the functionality of Event Space, if you remember; they create an energy that provides what you would call a memory. This "Memory" energy is that which sustains the perpetuation of the structure and the creative and created detail behind the structure. It is these entities that enter into the evolutionary cycle that create the myriad variations of the environmental, experiential conditions and personal interactional opportunities necessary to allow balanced evolutionary progression, and not a skewed evolutionary progression that maintains the need for its existence. The entities in the evolutionary cycle subconsciously want these environmental, experiential, and personal interactive conditions to continue so that they can play out all of the variations that may be on offer and as a result, expose themselves and others to the full depth or quality of experience.

I created the multiverse out of the structure and sentient energies that The Origin assigned to create me as an independent but integrated function of myself, allowing smaller individualized parts of me to delve into the detail of that which is me. The beauty of this creation is that it is not the same multiverse that I created in the first instance. It has changed; it has evolved. This is a result of its manipulation, manipulation by those smaller individualized versions of me—you—who wanted to experience the multiverse in different configurative states. These configurative states are transient because the creative force behind them is not as strong as my creative force and so they cannot be maintained unless there is a focus on their continued existence, for without the desire for them to be in existence, the multiversal structure returns back to its original state, that state which I created in the first instance.

ME: So even those who use the multiverse for evolutionary purposes are maintenance entities—by default!

SE1: Correct. Every entity that is created by me has a role in the maintenance of the multiverse and its perpetuation as a creation of the collective of smaller individualized versions of me. Don't forget, everything, every entity and every environment, is a function of me.

ME: Thank you. It is always good to be reminded of this most basic but most forgotten or ignored truth.

SE1: Good. So, the first thing I am going to do is expose a few myths.

The first myth to be exposed is that the entities that are called Angels are based upon the human form; they are not.

The second myth to be exposed is that I have a human form and that the Angels sit beside me; I do not and they do not.

The third myth to be exposed is that these entities exist next to me in something called a mobile [*see religious texts—GSN*], which is a section or location within the divine mind and it is also part of a hierarchy; they do not and it is not. Although I do have to say, it's not a bad guess if you think that the total volume of my sentient energies, that is all of me, can be classified as "Mind," so if you think in this way, every entity is next to my mind simply because it is part of my mind or sentience.

The fourth myth to be exposed is that the Angels are distributed in the hierarchy that religion describes them in—the nine choirs; they are not.

The fifth myth to be exposed is that the Angels work only for the maintenance and guidance of those who incarnate on the Earth, and its environment, the physical universe; they do not. They have myriad responsibilities that include the Earth, the physical universe, and many other bodies that are made from locally low-frequency energy which do not specifically exist in the physical universe.

The sixth myth to be exposed is that the entities that work with the details of the earthly environment, the Elementals, what humankind calls fairies, leprechauns, and other similarly descriptive names, are based upon the human form; they are not. Other names for mythical forms such as pixies, elves, and the like are simply the memories of those who observed other humanoid forms, those incarnates that also exist within the physical universe and that have visited the Earth from time to time.

The seventh myth to be exposed is that those entities that are called Ascended Masters have human form; they do not.

ME: That's a lot of myths to consider.

SE1: In reality, this is only a small number of the things associated with the description of the names, roles, and functions surrounding those entities that are created by me and chose to be of service to me and those entities that entered into the evolutionary cycle. There are names, roles, and functions in other religions to describe similar entities but in essence they are all the same. You see, mankind in its use of different teachers to educate itself on how to exist in the incarnate state without becoming addicted to it, to not accrue karma, ends up moving away from the original teaching. Descriptions of the teachings change simply as a result of the teaching style of the teacher, its specialist subjects, and its own preferences to what is taught and how it is presented to its students. This quickly results in dilution and diversification from the original subject matter. So, although there may be some crossover or correlation in the information broadcast by different religions, the emphasis and focus may be completely different, and some or all of the detail may be completely different. One thing is certain, though; all religions recognize a creator and those entities that support the creator, irrespective of what they are called and what their roles and responsibilities are. The function of this dialogue is therefore to offer a religion-free, neutral, and up-to-date rendition of the mechanics of the environment you exist within, what maintains it, and how it is maintained.

The Structure of the Multiverse We Exist Within: A Deeper Understanding

I have no doubt that this part of the book will be all too familiar to those dear souls who have read my other books and as a result I note that it will be tempting to bypass this chapter. For those that have not read the previous books, it will be essential to the understanding of the rest of the content. I do, however, urge all readers to read this chapter, not just because it will act as a refresher, but because I feel that we will be exposed to new and deeper details about the structure of the multiverse and its functionality.

SE1: That was a good introduction.

ME: I only said what I felt!

SE1: Maybe, but it is accurate to state that we will be going into some more depth about the finer structure of the multiverse, specifically where and how the maintenance entities come into it. What I would suggest first is that you give an overview of the structure in your own words and I will add the additional understanding of the structural content at the end, when you have finished your description.

ME: OK, here we go.

The multiversal environment within which we exist was created by The Source, from its own energies and structural references and is located within The Source. The multiverse being within the boundary energies that designates the difference between the sentient energies that were individualized, designated as a Source Entity and given a "reason to be" by the ultimate creator—The Origin—and those sentient energies and their structures that are currently reserved for The Origin's work on understanding itself. The multiverse occupies nearly one-half of The Source's volume of sentient energy and is occupied by billions of smaller individualized versions or units of its self, our True Energetic Selves (TES). Our TES were created for the sole purpose of understanding the fine detail of The Source's sentience, its energies and structure, which in turn provides The Origin with a greater understanding of its self. The sentient energies that make up the total number of TES plus the sentient energies that make up the multiverse equals the full one-half of the total volume of The Source Entity's sentient energies and its structure.

The structure of the multiverse itself follows the same structural rules as the lower structural condition of The Source, its self, and ultimately The Origin. The lower structure of Source is based upon the relationship between frequency, subdimensional components, and full dimensions, the frequencies being the basic building blocks. Starting from the highest structural level of the multiverse, the full dimensions, we can see that the multiverse has twelve of them. The number twelve is significant and is prevalent in the continuation of the structure in the higher levels of The Source's structure and, of course, The Origin's. The structure of the multiverse has a generalized function that is repeated in all full dimensions apart from the first full dimension, which houses the very lowest frequencies. I will describe the structure of the first full dimension last.

The structure is therefore as follows; from the second full dimension upward to the twelfth, each full dimension is subject to being constructed from three sublevels or subdimensional components. Each of these sublevels are progressive, that being, they have a higher or lower position relative to each other within the space occupied by the full dimension. So in this progressive nature the third subdimensional component of the second full dimension is lower in the multiversal structure than the first subdimensional component of the third full dimension. Each subdimensional component houses twelve frequency levels or bands. Each frequency level is progressive in its finitude and is capable of housing a simultaneous self-contained universal environment. For illustrative purposes then, the twelfth frequency of the third subdimensional component of the second full dimension is higher than the eleventh frequency of the third subdimensional component of the second full dimension, but, it is lower than the first frequency of the first subdimensional component of the third full dimension. The simultaneous self-contained universes are static and progressive universal environments in terms of their function and content and exist simultaneously with each other. They are not parallel universes which are created by Event Space through the ability of those entities that occupy the simultaneous universes to make choices. Parallel universes (local, planetary, planetary system, galactic, and universe-sized) are created and dissolved through the power of individual choice. The simultaneous universes remain in existence for the duration of a full evolutionary cycle and are therefore classified as a static function of the multiverse that we as evolving entities progress through.

In summary then, from the second full dimension through to the twelfth full dimension, each dimension has three subdimensional components, each subdimensional component has twelve frequency levels or bands, and each frequency level houses a simultaneous universal environment. Each full dimension from the second full dimension through to the twelfth full dimension therefore has thirty-six frequency levels or bands and therefore thirty-six simultaneous universes associated to it. This makes a subtotal of eleven full dimensions multiplied by three subdimensional components multiplied by twelve frequency levels equals three hundred and ninety-six frequency levels and simultaneous universes (11 x 3 x 12 = 396 frequencies and universes).

As stated a moment ago, the first full dimension houses the lowest of the frequencies associated with the structure of the multiverse, but, because it houses the lowest of the multiversal frequencies, it behaves in a different way to the other full dimensions. The first full dimension is constructed from three sublevels or subdimensional components in the same way as higher full dimensions, with exception that the lower frequencies cause these subdimensional components to converge into one composite subdimensional component that exhibits the functions of all three but in one space.

Because this subdimensional component exists in one space, it can only house twelve frequency levels or bands. Because these frequencies are so low, even though they are progressive, they are not capable of housing a simultaneous self-contained universal environment in their own right. However, because the composite subdimensional component associated with the first full dimension exists in a singular space, these twelve frequencies also need to exist in a singular space and as a result create a single simultaneous self-contained universal environment that uses all twelve frequencies—thus creating what we call the physical universe.

So again in summary, the first full dimension houses three subdimensional components that compress to a single composite subdimensional component. This single composite subdimensional component houses twelve frequency levels or bands, but because they exist in one space, and because these frequencies are so low, they can only create one simultaneous self-contained universal environment. This makes a subtotal of one full dimension multiplied by one composite subdimensional component multiplied by twelve frequency levels equals twelve frequency levels associated with the first full dimension but dividing twelve by twelve because the frequencies occupy one space equals one simultaneous universe (1 x 3 = 1, 1 x 12 = 12 frequencies, and, 1 x 3 = 1, 1 x 12/12 = 1 universe).

In totality then, we have 396 frequencies in full dimensions two through twelve plus twelve frequencies in the first full dimension equals 408 frequencies (396 + 12 = 408 frequency levels). And we also have 396 simultaneous universes in full dimensions two through twelve plus one simultaneous universe in the first full dimension equals 397 simultaneous universes (396 + 1 = 397 universes).

I make a point of reference here to note that what mankind thinks of as dimensions are, in my understanding, frequency levels and not dimensions per se, because the subdimensional components and full dimensions are much, much higher levels of structure. Although we as incarnate beings exist in a universe within the multiverse that needs twelve frequencies to create it, we can only see and detect the first three frequencies. So, as a result, we see the universe as being mostly empty whereas in reality there is infinitesimally more content and incarnate beings, within the other nine frequencies, resulting in a mostly full rather than mostly empty universe.

SE1: That's a good summary of the structure of the multiverse as you currently know it. I will elaborate on the gaps in your knowledge base.

As you may have worked out, there are frequencies between the frequencies that you know of. In the wider multiversal environment, the frequency levels or bands that house the self-contained simultaneous universes have subfrequencies that allow the resolution or detail available in a specific universal environment where the availability of more subfrequencies equals more depth of universal content and functionality. Think of it in terms of an image where the number of pixels available in a square millimeter affecting how much an image can be enlarged before pixilation occurs, and, when pixilation does occur, the gaps in resolution between the pixels is where any increases in resolution can be affected and, from a frequential perspective, the subfrequencies exist. I will deal with the multiversal environment in more detail in a moment, but first I want to focus on the environment incarnate mankind exists within, the physical universe.

As you stated earlier, the first dimension houses just one universe, the physical universe, and the physical universe requires twelve frequencies to create enough resolution to allow the functionality associated with a universe to manifest. The subfrequencies play a major part in the manifestation of this functionality. They allow the creation of the physical aspects of the multiverse to occur and are predominantly associated with, but not unique to, the framework for the structure associated with the lower frequencies of the physical universe.

Within the physical universe, each frequency level (let's call the frequency levels the major levels) has six sublevels that fill in the gaps between. There are six sublevels between the zero level and the first level, six sublevels between the first level and the second level, and six between the second level and the third level, etc., etc., etc. The six sublevels associated with the first three major frequency levels, along with the major levels themselves, when expressed together in the way they are in the lowest of the frequencies of the multiverse act in a composite function. They create the form of the Gross Physical in what scientists call a three-dimensional way. However, dimensions are a much higher part of the structure of the multiverse so the use of the third dimension, etc., as a descriptor is wholly incorrect, but as mankind is used to this terminology, even if it is incorrect, it will help in its understanding. The highest component of the physical is known as the atom and the lowest component of the physical is expressed as the Anu.

It is also worth noting that there is space in between the components of all six subfrequential levels and that this is a structure in its own right allowing what you might call either a substructure to exist that is the reciprocal of the structure that is used by incarnate beings and other non-incarnates. This reciprocal structure, although not identical to the structure incarnates and other non-incarnate beings use as part of the function of the multiverse used for the evolutionary cycle, can be classified as the other side of the physical, the physical energies being loosely classified as "matter," the space in between the structure, in between the six subfrequential levels can therefore be classed as antimatter. I am going to bust another myth here because the energy that I just called antimatter will not explode when in contact with the energy that I classified as matter, simply because they are part of the overall structure, the one existing within and without the other.

It is this substructure or antimatter structure that is used for "holding" the structure that is used for the evolutionary cycle in logical steps of progression. It keeps the content and functionality associated with the structure used for the evolutionary cycle apart, allowing correct areas of demarcation. This allows the entities that work with the maintenance of the multiversal structure and loosely therefore associated with the evolutionary cycle to keep the multiverse in the highest level of evolutionary efficiency.

ME: Hold on a minute, are you suggesting that antimatter exists?

SE1: Yes and no. Yes, insomuch as there is a reciprocal to the space you all use within the multiversal environment, and, no, because it does not function or behave in the way your scientists or even science fiction writers would have you believe it does. For instance, there is no universe-shattering explosion when these two components of the multiverse are in contact with each other simply because they are already integral to each other.

ME: So, where did the scientists go wrong? What led them to make this assumption?

SE1: Limited thinking based upon lack of knowledge.

ME: Is that it?

SE1: Yes, a simple response, isn't it? Although it is simple, it is both very true and a big issue because it creates a train of thought, a thought process that is in error, and because it is used, it creates bigger errors in thought.

ME: So to go down an educated route with an open mind, I ask again for the benefit of the readers, does antimatter exist?

SE1: If you are looking for an absolute as a function of my answer, then I will say that it doesn't. I just used the term as a descriptor to help with the understanding of reciprocal space. In fact, if you want to push harder in this direction, I will further state that there is more than one reciprocal space, more than one substructure.

ME: What do you mean by more than one reciprocal space?

SE1: In the description I just gave, I eluded to just one substructure, one reciprocal space. This was a description based upon human thinking, one where there is an opposite to everything—this is dualistic thinking. Even spiritual individuals think of the physical as the universe of duality. Others think of it in terms of opposites: black and white, up and down, left and right, forward or backward, matter or antimatter, of yin or yang, of balance, that there are always two sides to a story, etc., etc., etc. The fact is that the space in-between the structure of the multiverse is, if one were to use the word "big" as a metric, significantly bigger than the multiversal structure itself.

It was at this point that I received an image to help with the words used. I saw the structure of the multiverse as a series of lines in a matrix, a very complicated matrix, one where there were matrices within matrices, and these matrices housed other matrices and were in turn housed by other matrices. Everything was within and without and back within and without again in countless iterations of complexity. However, irrespective of the complexity the structural components that made up what I am just told to call the evolutionary or operational side of the multiversal structure, there was a surrounding space. Every component of the structure whether it was subfrequency, frequency, subdimension, or full dimension was surrounded by a substructural component or, as I am just told to call it, "essence." As with the physical universe, where there are six sublevels in between the frequency levels, there appeared to be six reciprocal spaces surrounding the evolutionary or operational structure. As I looked closer, I noticed that this description was not quite accurate. In fact, it was very inaccurate by what appeared to be to the power of six. I looked again and kept my mind fully open for anything that would add to the clarity of vision and understanding of what was being presented to me. I didn't have to wait long. It was as if every component was surrounded by a group of six by six sets of energies, of substructures. Thirty-six substructural energies in total surrounded each and every evolutionary or operational component of the multiverse. It had the appearance of being surrounded by a, I can only word it in these terms, a football (UK football—GSN) of energy. A "Bucky Ball" would be a better description, except that it didn't follow the geometric laws surrounding a Bucky Ball. Each collective of six by six substructural energies, each Bucky Ball, not only surrounded a specific evolutionary or operational structural component of the multiverse but it also surrounded the energies associated with the next collective of six by six substructural energies. I "zoomed out," refocusing my vision to a point where I could see more of the structure or the operational and substructural condition of the multiverse. From this vantage point, I could see that the whole space was essentially substructural, the evolutionary or operational components being a very, very small part of the overall volume of the structure. Every space was filled by substructure, by one of these six by six collective structures, and there were no gaps! This I found very interesting because if anyone has the inclination to look up the geometry of a Bucky Ball, they will see that when two or more are together, they present structural gaps in between each other external to their structure where the structures don't meet or touch each other. However, this was not the case here. No matter how much I zoomed into the structure, every potential gap was filled with a six by six structural collective. They seemed to blend into each other, linking together, not on the surface as we would expect, but at a level within each other where a potential gap would be irradiated. The effect was that the evolutionary or operational structure of the multiverse, the matrices within matrices, was immersed in a collective of six by six substructural components that all joined together at whatever level necessary to ensure that there was a uniform supporting environment with no gaps, weaknesses, or lack of structural connectivity for the multiverse to exist within. Everything within this "sea" of substructure was connected to everything else—totally, either by direct contact at the same level or through indirect contact associated with another six by six substructural collective, or, at a different level via interconnected structural collectives. I didn't dare look at the ratio of evolutionary/ operational multiversal structure versus substructure, but suffice to say, the evolutionary/operational structure of the multiverse paled into insignificance in comparison.

With this revelation firmly seated in my mind, I burst forth an exclamation to The Source Entity.

ME: It's mostly substructure! There is no duality, no chance for an equal measure of matter and antimatter (structure and substructure). There is no possibility for antimatter to exist because the reciprocal structure is the substructure. It can't even be called "reciprocal" because it isn't! The multiverse looks like a small structure in a huge bath of interlaced Bucky Balls.

SE1: Very well done. The volume of the six by six collective substructural components all together is such that it both supports the structure of the multiverse and allows its manipulation, modification, and improvement. It is the roles of the entities that elect to be of service that maintain both the structure and its functionality at the high and lower levels of structure, functionality, and evolutionary efficiency that use the surrounding substructure to move around the multiversal environment at all of its levels without actually being within the structure of the multiverse.

ME: I have another question.

SE1: Go ahead.

ME: How does Event Space figure in all of this; do the maintenance entities work with the parallel versions of the multiverse, none of it, or just parts of it?

SE1: The substructure allows for the expansion and contraction of the multiversal structure resulting from the interaction of Event Space-based possibilities.

ME: How does the multiversal structure expand and contract? I thought that everything was in the same space?

SE1: It is. The expansion and contraction is based upon the level of detail associated with a particular location within the multiverse or the whole multiverse itself. As you have just witnessed, the reciprocal space, the substructure associated with the evolutionary or operational multiversal structure, is significantly larger and of greater resolution than the evolutionary or operational multiversal structure itself. This allows an area of Event Space to be contained within the areas of possibility associated with the multiverse in a way that ensures that it is disconnected with the normal pervasion of Event Space that is within everything that is me or The Origin.

ME: So you keep the Event Spaces that are associated with the multiverse quarantined?

SE1: Yes.

ME: How is this possible?

SE1: I will explain that in a moment. First, though, I will finish off what I was describing. As I was stating, this allows an area of Event Space to be contained within the areas of possibility associated with the multiverse in a way that ensures that it is disconnected with the normal pervasion of Event Space that is within everything that is me or The Origin because it reflects it back upon itself.

ME: I remember that The Origin advised me that Event Space is both local and nonlocal in terms of its functionality, and, even though it pervades everything that is The Origin and its creations, it is still difficult to see how something that is so pervasive is able to be localized.

SE1: The quarantine effect is created by Event Space as it uses the resolution created by the six by six collective substructures to house the parallel structure/s required to support the parallel conditions created by the entities that create them. The substructure therefore becomes the evolutionary and operational structure of the parallel condition, "for" the parallel condition. This keeps Event Space associated with the multiverse local only to the multiverse and not to the wider sentient and non-sentient energies associated with me or The Origin.

ME: But isn't that limiting? I mean, doesn't that limit the number of Event Spaces that can be created to a function relative to the six by six substructural collective?

SE1: Yes and no. The limitations are only really associated with the expansion to the area of Event Space and not its proliferation per se. Based upon this, the limitations to the number of alternative and parallel environments, localized within the multiverse or attributed to the wider area of the multiverse, is a function of the number of interactive levels of the six by six substructural collectives. For example, if 6 six by six substructural collectives were in functional interaction with each other in and around the evolutionary and operational multiversal structure, then this would result in a synergetic effect of the ability to create six to the power of six, to the power of six, to the power of six, to the power of six, to the power of six, to the power of six Event Spaces within them.

However, in creating the potential for all these local or wider environments it recreates the potential for the creation of the supporting substructure within the substructures created, effectively recreating the structure so that the function of parallelism can start again while being contained within the original structure. Based upon this, although there appears to be a limitation to the number of parallel environments that can be created by the, for example, possibility of the possibility of possible possibilities, etc., etc., in actual fact, there are no limitations because the new Event Spaces, once a certain number of spaces is reached, recreate the structure they are within, within the structure they were within, and that which they will create within the substructure of the multiverse. In this way Event Space is constrained to a localized spatial environment rather than expanded into a wider area of space.

ME: So in this respect, there is always a reciprocal or substructure for the maintenance entities to work within that surrounds a parallelized evolutionary and operational location within the multiverse.

SE1: Correct. Event Space, when invoked, creates a parallel version of everything while keeping it within the structure of the original evolutionary/operational multiversal and substructural environment. This is of course provided that the surrounding substructure is created in the way we are just describing, by the use of the six by six substructural collective.

There is another reason for the ability to quarantine Event Space in this way.

ME: What is that?

SE1: It is difficult to describe in detail but one of the functions of the six by six collectives is to create a mirroring effect, one that is similar to the effect you have when you place two mirrors in a position where they face each other.

ME: Go on?

SE1: It is the mirroring effect of the six by six collective that reflects the parallel evolutionary/operational multiversal environments and the associated parallel substructure that is Event Space, back within itself and its creating Event Space and then back to an opposing Event Space that keeps it all in the same space. The mirroring effect continues until the number of parallel conditions that need to be created are created and/or are dissolved when they need to be dissolved.

ME: And this only happens when the structure is as just described.

SE1: Correct.

ME: And this is only relative to the multiversal environment that you created?

SE1: For the purposes of this dialogue, yes. Although if you had asked the right questions a few years ago, when you were communicating with the other Source Entities, you would have found out that this is not an uncommon method.

ME: What about the maintenance entities? Are they reproduced in the same way as the environment is?

SE1: No, they are not subject to parallelism. They have to work with all of the potential parallel and actual environmental conditions as they are created and dissolved. They have a difficult job to do. This is another reason why the substructure is significantly larger than the evolutionary or operational multiversal structure; they have to move around and work with all that is, all that could be, and all that was.

I thought about this for a moment. I had encountered a similar thing before when working on **The Anne Dialogues**. *In this instance, Anne and I were discussing the functions of the guides and that they had to work with the parallel versions of our incarnate selves when we made decisions based upon a number of choices. These choices can and do create other fractal versions of ourselves the further downstream one looked. I shuddered at the thought of having to work with not just a plethora of parallel versions of entities that a Guide or Helper is/are responsible for, and the complexity associated with such responsibility, but that, in comparison with the work a maintenance entity was responsible for, in terms of the parallel versions of local, planetary, system, galactic, and universal—even multiversal environments—it was but a drop in the multiversal* *ocean. What a job, I thought. What responsibility! How could they possibly achieve or respond to such a level of responsibility?*

I suddenly gained an image in my mind of the truly infinite possibilities—the possibility of the possibility of possible possibilities and the possibility of the possibility of possible possibilities associated with those possibilities, etc., etc., etc. My poor human brain went into overload and I snapped out of the image. It was gone and I was left perplexed. This was not the first time I have been left perplexed but it may be the first time I have advertised the fact in one of my books.

The Source, feeling that I was in need of consolation of some sort, decided to give additional explanation that would make the information easier to digest. One of the questions in the forefront of my mind was this. Just how can an entity work with a moving target—such as the increase and decrease of the multiversal and universal environments including their localized versions—and hope to get the work they are doing correct in terms of ensuring the correct levels of evolutionary efficiency are maintained, and that this level of correctness is not only consistency for the mainstream environment, but all of the possible and actual environments?

SE1: That is a very long question.

ME: It wasn't meant to be. It just turned out to be long.

SE1: Nevertheless, it was appropriate. First, this is why there are so many entities that are involved in the maintenance of the multiversal environment. Second, this is why there is a hierarchy associated with them, and third, this is why there is a large list of the different roles, responsibilities, and specialisms they have to perform. Every entity has a role to perform. At one end of the scale, some of them have pan-dimensional/spatial responsibilities whereas at the other end of the scale, they have very focused responsibilities based upon one frequential state and location. I will indicate the levels of responsibilities in summary later, and we can go into the detail of the entities associated with those responsibilities, for this will form the basis for the remainder of this dialogue.

Before I illustrate these higher level responsibilities, though, I will advise you again of the following; the names, roles, and status of those entities classified as Angels and Demons, for example, are both wholly inaccurate and oversimplified, even in their inaccuracy.

ME: Why are they inaccurate and oversimplified?

SE1: Because they are based upon the knowledge of the time that the information was made available, and the ability of the people at that time, based upon the level of their education, to understand that information and the frequential level of these individuals and their teachers. If you look at any religious texts, you will see that the descriptions associated with these entities are in very simple levels of detail, detail of which bears next to no resemblance with the actual roles, responsibilities, and status they have.

I thought for a moment about the document I created in 2005 about the roles and responsibilities of God's helpers. It was a simple summary of the information I had gathered on the subject, which in itself was simple. I decided that I would include a sanitized version within this text to give the reader a basic—very basic—understanding of the existing knowledge on this subject. It made me smile. Not because it was cheating—if indeed using my existing but previously unpublished material is cheating—but because it was making use of a piece of work that I thought I would have no further use for.

Everything has a reason and every piece of work has a role to play, I thought. I was deciding whether to ask The Source for the higher level descriptions of the entities that maintain the evolutionary efficiency of the multiverse now, or after the insertion of my eleven-year-old document when The Source advised me to use my work first. I questioned it on this decision, though, before continuing.

SE1: It would be better to give the readers a revision of that which they think they know about before introducing them to the detail of my reality.

ME: I would have thought that the introduction of my previous work would confuse the readers if it was before your description, specifically as we have just been discussing the background surrounding their description?

SE1: My initial thoughts were to keep on going—going with your flow. However, right at the very start of this dialogue you had it in the back of your mind to use your old material as a descriptor first, and then move into a dialogue with me. I see that this has merit and as I just stated, it would be a good way to offer the readers a revision of some of the existing information.

Before we change to your previous work, though, I want to leave the readers with this thought. For each and every one of you that exists in the incarnate state, there is at least a billion [*old billion, a million million—GSN*] others working on your behalf. Not just helping you to be successful in your incarnate evolutionary responsibility but also working on maintaining the structure and evolutionary efficiency of the multiverse that your True Energetic Self exists within and evolves through.

The detail in this dialogue will focus on those entities that are relevant to your current incarnate environment, the Earth, its system and galaxy, and its supporting universal/multiversal environment. It would be pointless for you to know the details of all those entities that work with other planets, systems, and galaxies within the physical universe simply because they are specific to those areas of locally low frequency, those that allow the creation of planets. Nevertheless, it will provide some insight to what they "could be" because there will be a level of carry-over functionality with them when compared with those of the Earth.

A General Understanding of God's Helpers as Currently Understood

God's Hierarchy

It is generally understood within all religion bases that God has his/her helpers, and that there is a distinct pecking order. The understanding of what God's helpers actually do is the subject of somewhat dubious interpretation based upon the teachings, myths, and stories of the ancestral races of mankind. There are, however, three main viewpoints on who/what God's helpers are and what their responsibilities are. These are relative to the Egyptian view, the Greek/Roman view, and the Christian/spiritual view. However, reading between the lines suggests that their responsibilities are related to the management of the universe and all its elements, irrespective of whose viewpoint you are looking from. These are illustrated below.

Egyptian Gods

There are effectively two views on what God is from the Egyptian perspective. The first is the popular view, which is discussed in the paragraph immediately following this introduction. The second is a lesser known view, and, although I say view here, I actually believe that the view expressed by *Isha Schwaller De Lubicz* is a deeper understanding of a deeper reality which the inner circles of Egyptian priesthood had of the meaning of the universe, the beings that maintained it, and the powers/energies at their disposal.

The Popular Understanding of the Egyptian Gods

Many books have been written on religion in ancient Egypt expressing what is essentially a popular view on the Egyptian Gods. Religion in ancient Egypt was not unlike modern times. Today, not everyone believes in the same way, or of the same God, and Egypt was no different. Individual kings worshipped their own Gods, as did the workers, priests, merchants, and peasants. Pre-dynastic Egypt had formulated the ideas and beliefs of a "greater being," which was expressed in pictures. The pictures had ideas and took on human traits. The Gods lived, died, hunted, went into battle, gave birth, ate, drank, and had human emotions. The Gods' reigns overlapped, and, in some instances, merged. There was no organized hierarchical structure of their reign so the dominance of the Gods depended on the beliefs of the reigning king with their area of dominance depending on where the king wanted his capital. Also, the myths changed with the location of the Gods, as did their names. Names in ancient Egypt were very mystic and powerful and it was thought that if you inscribed your enemies' name on something, then broke it, that enemy would either be afflicted or possibly die. If you knew a name you had power and using a name could be beneficial. Each God had five names, with each being associated with an element, such as air or celestial bodies; some were a descriptive statement about the God, such as strong, virile, or majestic.

The creator of all things was either Ra, Amun, Ptah, Khnum, or Aten, depending on which version of the myth was currently in use. The heavens were represented by Hathor, Bat, and Horus. Osiris was an Earth God as was Ptah. The annual flooding of the Nile was Hapi. Storms, evil, and confusion were Seth. His counterpart was Ma'at, who represented balance, justice, and truth. The moon was Thoth and Khonsu. Ra, the sun God, took on many forms, and transcended most of the borders that contained the other Gods. The actual shape of the sun, the disk (or, aten), was deified into another God, Aten. Interestingly enough Amun-Ra-Ptah is known as the three-in-one being.

Certain Gods were worshipped in different areas. Local cities or villages, known as nomes, often had unique Gods that were known only to that region. On occasion, these Gods attained country-wide recognition and became the myths and legends that were passed on from century to century.

The "Schwaller de Lubicz" View of the Egyptian Gods

In direct opposition to the popularist view of what the Gods were in Egyptian times, *Schwaller de Lubicz*[1] purports to having an understanding that removes the "human" aspect of the Egyptian Gods and replaces it with a more functional aspect of a series of beings who are "managing" the functionality of the local universe.

In Schwaller de Lubicz's eyes Egyptian religion is based upon a mathematical understanding of the "Truth" and although the descriptions above are consistent with those illustrated in *Her Bak*, Schwaller de Lubicz clearly has a larger knowledge base and therefore clearer/deeper understanding of what the Egyptian Gods represent. These are illustrated below:

There are a number of variations on this theme depending on the location of origin of the inscribed data. However, the Heliopolis theme is represented in all of the other locations of Memphis, Hermopolis, and Thebes.

Nun—The universe (Primordial Chaos)

Ra-Atum (the sun God)—He who creates

Shutefnut—Produces Geb (Earth) and Nut (Sky)

Geb and Nut create the four nature Neters, Osiris, Isis, Seth, and Nephtys (although there are eight Neters mentioned, only four have been identified and understood)

---

1 Isha Schwaller de Lubicz, *Her-Bak, Chick-Pea, The Living Face of Egypt* (Hodder and Stoughton 1954). And, Isha Schwaller de Lubicz, *Her-Bak, Egyptian Initiate* (Hodder and Stoughton 1956).

Amun-Ra is the king of the Neters and can be represented as the condenser of energy. The variations on Amun, Ra, Ptah's name are also consolidated later and called the Amun-Ra-Ptah (the three-in-one!). The Neters are the causal powers of everything that is manifest/functions in the universe.

The worlds of the Egyptians are described in three ways: Heaven, Earth, and Dwat, which translate as Celestial, Terrestrial, and Intermediate. The Intermediate can also be classified as the astral worlds. They are explained in more detail below.

Heaven

Is the world of causal/spiritual powers, the properties in themselves (all possibilities are possible).

Dwat

Is the intermediate world (in between day and night) and is split into two:

That which is born of terrestrial genesis.

That which is emerged from terrestrial existence.

Within this is *Thot*, who is the Neter of specifications. He determines the types of nature with numbers and divine geometry.

Earth

Is that which is concrete/materialized. It is the state of embodiment of the form and represents ideas of everything brought forth by nature from the four elementary constituents of matter (Earth, Wind, Fire, and Water) up to their most complex combinations of stars, inorganic matter, and organic beings. It is the world of bodies (Thot, Ptah), the innate fire of terrestrial matter who created it. Osiris U-Nefer is the master of all cycles of renewal in nature such as vegetative life.

The Neters and Their Hierarchy

The Neters are the expression of the functions of divine power, and a hierarchy can only be established by trying to ascertain if the function under consideration is more spiritual or more material, more universal or more particular, more absolute or more relative. The Egyptians did attempt (as we do today) to make this fit into the human mind and its limited intelligence and developed the various functions of each Neter through myth to ensure that a specific formula does not create a specialized definition. This ensured that the definition of Amun-Ra-Ptah's role still relates to the three-in-one of heavenly, intermediate, and terrestrial attributes, a trait that, we will see later, was not taken by the later messengers of God whose understanding of who God is resulted in a slightly but nevertheless significantly different view on who God was and what he wanted from mankind. However, in Christianity's defense the three-in-one description was upheld as a rational description of God and his/her relationship with the Earth plane.

The Neters Acting in the Heavenly World

The Neters are part of the divine and heavenly being (God).

Amun—Is the never born.

Ra—Is the universal and contains the function of Atum as potentiality.

Horus—The heart and immanent word of Ra.

Neith—The cosmic virgin (I am that which is, that which will be, that which has been).

These are the first intelligible aspects of causal power—the source of inexhaustible life in the universe.

The Neters Acting in the Intermediate World

Amun—In this instance is descending toward the genesis and is the "bringer of light," the sacred power of the secret language.

Atum—The Solar Neter who stands between night and day and is the first division into two.

Osiris, Isis, Seth, Nephtys, Horus—Are the Neters of the intercalary days and are neither in Heaven nor Earth.

Hathor and Nut—Are the Neters of the lower Heaven. They have relationships with the forces and beings of the Dwat.

Thot—Is the mediator between Heaven and Earth and is the issuer of words from the creative mouth of Ptah (in the sense of the Logos!) and is master over all forms begotten by the numbers and the Neter of signatures (DNA!) that determine the terrestrial species. As the scribe of Ma'at, he records the impressions of the fixed consciousness of the Dwat (Universal Memory, Akashic records, etc.).

Anubis—Is the transformer of power, allowing passage from the Earth to the lower heavens. He opens the way to the Dwat.

The Neters Acting in the Terrestrial World

Ptah—Continual creator for the Earth and is the agent for motive power for the Neters whose spiritual properties and abstract functions can be recognized in concrete form in the functions/properties of natural order. These are:

Amun-Min—Who is a magnet and condenser of heavenly energy.

Seth—Who is the principle of correctness, fixation, and separation.

Anubis—Who is the transformer of putrid matter into living substance.

Khnum—Who is the power of attraction. He joins complementarities and fashions new beings.

Mut—Is the mother who decomposes the seeds to regenerate them.

Apet—Is the principle of fertility and the multiplication of substance.

The Neters of Elementary Properties

Shu—dry, Tefnut—wet, Geb—warm, Nut—cold. The principle of these Neters is to be manifest by Atum to become Fire, Air, Water, Earth.

The Neters of Fundamental Functions

Sokar—The function of contraction and fixation.

Serket—The contraction (breathing in).

Neith—The function of dilation, leading to contraction and breathing out.

Wadjit—The function of dilation essential to vegetative life (opening, blooming, unfolding).

Amim—The function of absorption, devourer of the dead.

The Four Aspects of the Feminine Principle in Nature

Isis, Nephytys, Neith, and Selkis are a number of names to describe the functions that all refer to the essential, the cause, the three-in-one!

On its own is Ma'at.

Ma'at—impersonates justice and truth and is the presence of source and fulfillment, the beginning and end, the mediator and the essence of Ra in all times and all worlds. Ma'at is the universal consciousness, universal idea, and essential wisdom. Ma'at is the consciousness of all things and is the key to the reason for man's life on Earth and forms the basis for Egyptian philosophy.

The Kings and the Gods

The kings of ancient Egypt were an integral part of religion. They formed a bridge over the chasm dividing the people and the Gods. In pre-dynastic times, the kings were considered to be Gods. In later times, around the third dynasty, the kings became "transformed into" Gods. This was a crucial part of the governing of the people. The heirs to the throne were not kept out of public display. At a young age they were known to many, and were known as children, not future Gods. A king may have had many heirs and may not have known who would assume the throne until a much later time. In order for the people (and the future king) to accept the transformation, certain procedures had to be worked out. This dilemma was beautifully solved by the ritual that merged the king with the God. Belief was that all future kings had two aspects of their being, the physical being and the "ka." The ka was the spiritual counterpart that was part of the king at birth and remained with him throughout his life. Before assuming the throne, a ritual was performed that united the king's ka and his person. The king and his priests would enter a temple, perform the ritual, and emerge as a God. All of the people would wait outside to witness the miracle of the transformation when the king reemerged from the temple. In this way, the new king was accepted as a God and his word was accepted as law.

Greek Gods

The Greek Gods are a natural evolutionary description of the Egyptian Gods previously explained. However, by the time that the Greeks were the dominant authority on worldly issues, the real understanding of the stories that were used to explain God and the roles and responsibilities of his/her helpers, was, from the author's point of view, misunderstood.

Family Tree of the Greek Gods

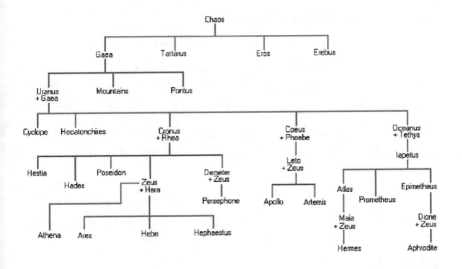

Adapted from: *The Greek God Family Tree* on the Tour Egypt Website

The Greek Gods have two main eras, the era of the first of God's helpers, and the era of what I call the lesser Gods (Neters?). Both of which have their stories told in a strictly human frame of reference, a trap that the Egyptians did not fall into.

The Titans

The Titans, also known as the elder Gods, ruled the Earth before the Olympians overthrew them. The ruler of the Titans was Cronus, who was dethroned by his son Zeus. Most of the Titans fought with Cronus against Zeus and were punished by being banished to Tartarus. During their rule, the Titans were associated with the various planets. The Titans are Gaea, Uranus, Cronus, Rhea, Oceanus, Tethys, Hyperion, Mnemosyne, Themis, Iapetus, Coeus, Crius, Phoebe, Thea, Prometheus, Epimetheus, Atlas, Metis, Dione. The responsibilities of the Titans are illustrated below.

Gaea—Gaea is the Earth Goddess.
Uranus—Uranus is the sky God and first ruler.
Cronus—Was the ruling Titan who came to power by castrating his father, Uranus. His wife was Rhea. Their offspring were the first of the Olympians.
Rhea—Was the wife of Cronus. Cronus made it a practice to swallow their children. To avoid this, Rhea tricked Cronus into swallowing a rock, saving her son Zeus.
Oceanus—Is the unending stream of water encircling the world. Together with his wife, Tethys, they produced the rivers and the three thousand ocean nymphs.
Tethys—Is the wife of Oceanus.
Hyperion—Is the Titan of light, an early sun God. He is the son of Gaea and Uranus. He married his sister, Theia. Their children are Helius (the sun), Selene (the moon), and Eos (the dawn).
Mnemosyne—Was the Titan of memory and the mother of Muses.
Themis—Was the Titan of justice and order. She was the mother of the Fates and the Seasons.
Iapetus—Was the father of Prometheus, Epimetheus, Menoetius, and Atlas by Clymene.
Coeus—Is the Titan of intelligence. Father of Leto.
Crius and Thea—Little is known on Crius and Thea.
Phoebe—Is the Titan of the Moon. Mother of Leto.
Prometheus—Was the wisest Titan. His name means "forethought" and he was able to foretell the future. He was the son of Iapetus.

Epimetheus—Was a stupid Titan, whose name means "afterthought." He was the son of Iapetus. In some accounts, he is delegated by Zeus, along with his brother Prometheus, to create mankind. He also accepted the gift of Pandora from Zeus, which lead to the introduction of evil into the world.

Atlas—Was the son of Iapetus. Unlike his brothers Prometheus and Epimetheus, Atlas fought with the other Titans supporting Cronus against Zeus.

Metis—Was the Titaness of the fourth day and the planet Mercury. She presided over all wisdom and knowledge. She was seduced by Zeus and became pregnant with Athena.

Dione—Is, according to Homer in the Iliad, the mother of Aphrodite.

The Olympians

The Olympians are a group of twelve Gods who ruled after the overthrow of the Titans. All the Olympians are related in some way and they are named after their dwelling place, Mount Olympus. The Olympian Gods are Zeus, Poseidon, Hades, Hestia, Hera, Ares, Athena, Apollo, Aphrodite, Hermes, Artemis, and Hephaestus. The responsibilities of the Olympians are illustrated below.

Zeus—Zeus overthrew his father, Cronus. He then drew lots with his brothers Poseidon and Hades. Zeus won the draw and became the supreme ruler of the Gods. He is lord of the sky, the rain God. His weapon is a thunderbolt, which he hurls at those who displease him. He is married to Hera but is famous for his many affairs.

Poseidon—Is the brother of Zeus. After the overthrow of their father, Cronus, he drew lots with Zeus and Hades, another brother, for shares of the world. His prize was to become lord of the sea. He was widely worshipped by seamen. He married Amphitrite, a granddaughter of the Titan Oceanus.

Hades—Is the brother of Zeus. After the overthrow of their father, Cronus, he drew lots with Zeus and Poseidon, another brother, for shares of the world. He had the worst draw and was made lord of the underworld, ruling over the dead. He is a greedy God who is greatly concerned with increasing his subjects.

Hestia—Is Zeus's sister. She is a virgin Goddess. She does not have a distinct personality. She plays no part in myths. She is the Goddess of the Hearth, the symbol of the house around which a newborn child is carried before it is received into the family.

Hera—Is Zeus's wife and sister. She was raised by the Titans, Oceanus and Tethys. She is the protector of marriage and takes special care of married women.

Ares—Is the son of Zeus and Hera. He was disliked by both parents. He is the God of war. He is considered murderous and bloodstained but also a coward.

Athena—Is the daughter of Zeus. She sprang full-grown in armor from his forehead, thus has no mother. She is fierce and brave in battle but only fights to protect the state and home from outside enemies. She is the Goddess of the city, handicrafts, and agriculture.

Apollo—Is the son of Zeus and Leto. His twin sister is Artemis. He is the God of music, playing a golden lyre. He is the Archer, far-shooting with a silver bow, the God of healing who taught man medicine, the God of light, and the God of truth who cannot speak a lie.

Aphrodite—Is the Goddess of love, desire, and beauty. In addition to her natural gifts, she has a magical girdle that compels anyone she wishes to desire her.

Hermes—Is the son of Zeus and Maia. He is Zeus's messenger. He is the fastest of the Gods. He wears winged sandals, a winged hat, and carries a magic wand. He is the God of thieves and God of commerce. He is the guide for the dead to go to the underworld. He invented the lyre, the pipes, the musical scale, astronomy, weights and measures, boxing, gymnastics, and the care of olive trees.

Artemis—Is the daughter of Zeus and Leto. Her twin brother is Apollo. She is the lady of the wild things. She is the huntsman of the Gods. She is the protector of the young. Like Apollo, she hunts with silver arrows. She became associated with the moon. She is a virgin Goddess, and the Goddess of chastity. She also presides over childbirth, which may seem odd for a virgin, but goes back to causing Leto no pain when she was born.

Hephaestus—Is the son of Zeus and Hera. Sometimes it is said that Hera alone produced him and that he has no father. He is the only God to be physically ugly. He is also lame. Accounts as to how he became lame vary. Some say that Hera, upset by having an ugly child, flung him from Mount Olympus into the sea, breaking his legs. Others say that he took Hera's side in an argument with Zeus and Zeus flung him off Mount Olympus. He is the God of fire and the forge. He is the smith and armorer of the Gods.

Other Gods and Semi-Gods

Asclepius, Demeter, Persephone, Dionysus, Eros, Hebe, Eris, Helius, Thanatos, Pan, Nemesis, The Graces, The Muses, The Erinyes, The Fates. The responsibility of the semi- and other Gods are illustrated below:

Asclepius—A God of healing. His symbol is a snake. His parents were Apollo and Coronis.

Demeter—Is the Goddess of corn, grain, and the harvest. She is the daughter of Cronus and Rhea. It is Demeter that makes the crops grow each year. The first loaf of bread from the harvest is sacrificed to her. Demeter is intimately associated with the seasons.

Persephone—Is the daughter of Zeus and Demeter. After her abduction by Hades, she became his wife and Queen of the underworld.

Dionysus—Is the God of the vine. He invented wine and spread the art of tending grapes. He has a dual nature: on the one hand, bringing joy and divine ecstasy; on the other, brutal, unthinking, and enraged thus reflecting both sides of the nature of wine.

Eros—Is the son of Aphrodite. Eros is the God of love. In particular, erotic, romantic, love. He is often represented blindfolded because love is often blind. His "weapon" is a dart or an arrow.

Hebe—Is the daughter of Zeus and Hera. She is the Goddess of youth. She, along with Ganymede, are the cupbearers to the Gods. Hebe is Heracles's wife.

Eris—Is the daughter of Zeus and Hera. She is the Goddess of discord. In addition to her main activity of sowing discord, she frequently accompanies her brother Ares to battles. On these occasions she rides his chariot and brings her son, Strife.

Thanatos—Was the Greek God of death. He may be thought of as a personification of death. He plays little role in the myths. He became rather overshadowed by Hades, the lord of the underworld.

Pan—Is the son of Hermes. He is the God of goatherds and shepherds. He is mostly human in appearance but with goat horns and goat feet. He is an excellent musician and plays the pipes. He is merry and playful frequently seen dancing with woodland nymphs.

Nemesis—Means righteous anger, due enactment, or divine vengeance. This God helped to avenge those who were wronged.

The Graces—They are the daughters of Zeus and Eurynome. There are three Graces: Aglaia (Splendour), Euphrosyne (Mirth), and Thalia (Good Cheer). They are known for singing and dancing for the Gods.

The Muses—They are the daughters of Zeus and Mnemosyne. They are known for the music of their song, which brings joy to any who hear it. There are nine Muses, each with her own specialty: Clio (History), Urania (Astronomy), Melpomene (Tragedy), Thalia (Comedy), Terpsichore (Dance), Calliope (Epic Poetry), Erato (Love Poetry), Polyhymnia (Songs to the Gods), Euterpe (Lyric Poetry).

The Erinyes—Also known as the Furies, punish crime. They pursue wrongdoers relentlessly, until death, often driving them to suicide. They are particularly concerned with matricide. There are three Erinyes—Tisiphone, Megaera, and Alecto. The Erinyes came from the blood of Uranus when he was castrated.

The Fates—Have the subtle but awesome power of deciding a man's destiny. They assign a man to good or evil. Their most obvious choice is choosing how long a man lives. There are three Fates: Clotho the spinner, who spins the thread of life; Lachesis the measurer, who chooses the lot in life one will have and measures off how long it is to be; and Atropos, she who cannot be turned, who at death, with her shears cuts the thread of life.

The Angelic Hierarchy

As with the Egyptian and Greek understanding of the hierarchy of the helpers of God, the Angels of the Christian and spiritual religions exist in a hierarchy; i.e., there is a form and order to the universe and its divine forces. The Angel community is the perfect example of this. The kingdom is divided into Hierarchies and Choirs. Each section of the community has its own particular purpose and energy. The Angelic Hierarchy is consistent within all of the "Christian-based religions" and can be correlated with the responsibilities of the Egyptian and Greek Gods/lesser Gods/Neters discussed above. The fact that some of these helpers are "not so good" as the others gives more weight to the correlation with the Greek and Egyptian thought process. The Hierarchy of the Angelic realm is illustrated in the next sections. Note that temple dancers in eastern religions equate to Christian Angels.

The Seraphim ~ The First Hierarchy—The First Choir

The highest Choir, these are the spirits of love. They provide the universe with positive light and spirit. They exist in the Premium Mobile next to "God." (A mobile is a section of the divine mind.)

This Choir consists of:

- Michael

- Seraphiel

- Jehoel

- Metatron

- Kemuel

- Uriel

- Nathaniel

Their properties consist of:

- Associated color: red and crimson for fiery love

- Singing praise constantly

- Being able to roar like a lion

- Being seen with scrolls of divine holy knowledge and wisdom

Their appearance:

- They have six wings. Two are used for flying, the other four for veil faces in reverence and they stand on winged heels.

The Cherubs ~ The First Hierarchy—The Second Choir

They are the second in the line of Angels. They are the spirits of harmony and are often referred to as the Angels of the air. They inhabit the fixed stars you see in each of the hemispheres at night. They represent the wisdom of God.

This Choir consists of:

- Gabriel
- Cherubiel
- Ophaniel
- Raphael
- Zophel

Their properties (consist of):

- Associated color: golden yellow or sapphire blue
- They are the guardians of the tree of life

Their appearance:

- Since the sixteenth century, the Cherubs began to appear as whole chubby children with wings and winged heels. Prior to this, they only had a human head of a smiling child on top of what seems to be a bird's body.

The Thrones ~ The First Hierarchy—The Third Choir

This Choir contains the Angels of Justice, the spirits of will who live in the essence of Saturn. Their mission is to bring judgment for individual karma and society as a whole. They are also depicted as the record keepers of the Universal Laws. Perhaps that is why they provide guidance in matters of karma, because as the record keepers, they may know better than you what karma you have to redeem and what karmic pleasures are due you. They represent the "will" that is necessary to administer justice in the universe.

This Choir consists of:

- Orifie
- Raziel
- Zaphkiel
- Japhkiel
- Baradiel

Their properties (consist of):

- Associated color: gold
- They support the throne of God

Their appearance:

- They are often shown with the scales of justice and a bouquet of flowers, perhaps a sign for both sides of the law. They stand on red winged wheels and sit on lofty golden thrones.

The Dominions ~ The Second Hierarchy—The First Choir

The first Choir in the Second Hierarchy are the spirits of wisdom and knowledge. These are the Angels who bring you the teachings of intuition. They inhabit the essence of Jupiter and represent the superior power of wisdom against the physical strength and intellectual egotistical forces.

This Choir consists of:

- Zadkil

- Muriel

- Hashman

- Zacharel.

Their appearance:

- This Choir always appears in human shape and wearing a triple crown to signify their position over the physical form. They can be seen carrying a scepter, holding a cross and/ or a sword to symbolize the balance between the active and passive forces.

The Virtues ~ The Second Hierarchy—The Second Choir

This is the Choir of choice, the Angels of Movement who dwell in the essence of Mars. They watch over the centers of free will and provide the tools we need along our path to make choices to learn our spiritual lessons and overcome karmic debt. They work in hand with the Thrones to bestow grace and rewards on those who have overcome deeds in their physical lives. This Choir also likes performing miracles here on Earth, and are often thought of as the Angels who possess supreme courage.

This Choir consists of:

- Uzziel

- Gabriel

- Michael

- Peliel

- Haniel

- Babiel

- Tarhishiel.

Their appearance:

- They have four blue-feathered wings and wear sparkling armor. They can often be seen with a scepter, axe, spear, sword, and/or a shield for protection. But each of these "tools" is decorated with instruments of passion. Some believe this is to show humanity that to move forward in life, you must learn unconditional love, even in the face of fear or battle.

The Powers ~ The Second Hierarchy—The Third Choir

The Angels of Form and Space. They are often associated with the essence of the Sun. They bring the power of intellect in such matters as math, geometry, astronomy, and so on. They are the professors and educators. They bring the "physical" form to the universe and its planets. They are guardians of the heavenly pathways and impose the will of God without fear or mercy.

This Choir consists of:

- Raphael
- Camael
- Verchiel.

Their appearance:

- The Powers are often seen with swords of flame, used to protect humans and defeat the "devils."

The Principalities ~ The Third Hierarchy—The First Choir

The Angels of Time and Personality, dwelling in the essence of Venus. They are the protectors of religious, political, and military leaders.

This Choir consists of:

- Ureil

- Raphael

- Raguel

- Michael

- Gabriel

- Remiel.

Their appearance:

- Seen in human form, they are often clad in armor. They can be seen carrying a scepter, lily flower, palm leaves, and a cross.

The Archangels ~ The Third Hierarchy—The Second Choir

The ruling angels, the spirits of fire inhabiting the essence of Mercury. These are the Angels who stand around God's throne, ready to carry out the divine and most important decrees to humans.

This Choir consists of:

- Michael

- Raphael

- Raguel

- Ureil

- Sariel

- Remiel

- Gabriel.

Their appearance:

- Since the fourteenth century, the Archangels have been seen in white linen and sometimes carry feathered pens and scrolls. They are often seen above all the other Angels in the Hierarchies, symbolizing their position and authority over the other Choirs that deal with humanity.

The Angels ~ The Third Hierarchy—The Third Choir

The final Choir is by no means the least important. They are the messenger Angels who also govern the spirit of nature. They dwell in the essence of the Moon and are seen as the supernatural beings or guardians over humanity. They deal with the nitty-gritty of everyday life and act as the direct gateway for information, knowledge, and communications between humankind and the God force.

This Choir consists of billions of entities. For every human incarnated on this planet there is a corresponding Guardian Angel to help guide them through their incarnated life.

Their appearance:

- These Angels are seen with human bodies, wings, and clothed in various garments depending on the traditions and visual acceptance of the human they have "been assigned to."

The Demonic Hierarchy

In stark contrast to the good work of the Angels above, the distasteful side of the human psyche also has its champions. These are described below and are based upon the writings of Father Sebastion Michaelis, in 1612.[2]

First Hierarchy of Demons

Asmodeus—avarice
Astaroth—laziness
Balberith—murder
Beelzebub—pride
Gressil—disease
Leviathan—blasphemy
Sonneillon—hatred
Verrine—impatience.

Second Hierarchy of Demons

Carnivean—obscenity
Carreau—cruelty
Oeillet—greed
Rosier—lasciviousness
Verrier—disobedience.

Third Hierarchy of Demons

Belais—arrogance
Iuvart—sins not covered by other devils
Olivier—parsimony.

---

2 *Springwolfs Pagan Metaphysics 101—The Beginning of Enlightenment* (Schiffer Publishing, August 30, 2011).

In order to completely intimidate ignorant farmers and little children, Friar Francesco Mario Buazzo, in 1608,[3] came up with some demons who worked as servants to the devils.

Fire Demons—live in the air and get to boss around the other devils
Aerial Demons—hover around human beings
Terrestrial Demons—terrorize the inhabitants of forests and fields
Aqueous Demons—live in water (so be careful of what you drink!)
Subterranean Demons—live in caves like trolls
Heliophobic Demons—only come out at night.

This of course is a picture limited to the religious texts and ignores the Elementals, or does it? If we look at this short description of the demons in terms of when they appear on the Earth, we can see an interesting parallel or link with the Elementals, those entities that work closest to us and about environment. That is, apart from our Guides and Helpers, of course. Based upon this, the names that are missing are those we hold close to fairy tales, such as pixies, elves, fairies, leprechauns, and others such as nymphs and goblins. I therefore would not suggest that the imagery we have been exposed to is anywhere near correct, and neither are the names and demarcations or designations of status and functions of those we call Demons. Indeed, as I write this text, I very much get the feeling that the demarcations and designations are relevant to the level of the frequencies they work with and are not a function of whether or not they can be classified as good or bad, helpful or mischievous in human terms.

As I work on this dialogue with The Source Entity, I will therefore introduce the relevance to those currently understood as a way for showing what is part of the Greater Reality versus what is created for the use of entertainment or control of incarnate humans through fear.

3 *Springwolfs Pagan Metaphysics 101—The Beginning of Enlightenment* (Schiffer Publishing, August 30, 2011).

The Hierarchy of Maintenance Entities

I felt the need to repeat a thought.

Somehow, somewhere incarnate mankind has retained a simulacrum of understanding about who and what help The Source/God to maintain the environment that we incarnate into. This level of knowledge has been taught either by those in control of, or the direction of, the education of the general population. As with most ancient information, though, it has been modified to suit the thought processes of those teachers involved at the time and/or the limitations of the language or individual educational levels. As a result the detail and clarity of the information we see today is the function of errors made over eons of time.

As I sit here waiting to restart the dialogue with The Source Entity, I feel that this book may finish up being larger than anticipated. Why do I get this feeling, you may ask? You should know that this was going to be a big task, you say! Well, one would think that I would have learned by now that the task of helping to expose mankind to the next level of information was always going to be a hard one. For now, though, the answer is that I can see the structure of the multiverse unfold before my very eyes, and from what I can see, the hierarchy of those entities necessary to support its evolutionary efficiency is incredibly large, so large indeed that the detail given in the previous chapter feels wholly inadequate.

Sometimes it is best to be given one's tasks in bite-sized chunks, without knowing the expected outcome of the final work. I mentally noted that in all of my other dialogues, this has been the case. I had been exposed to the bigger picture bit by bit, working on it—in a small and compacted way—even when I felt expanded to the point of being stretched to my elastic limit. But here, it was as if all the individual dialogues with the other eleven Source Entities and even The Origin itself were minor in comparison. I wondered why this was the case. Why did all that I have previously worked on feel smaller, when it was quite obviously bigger, certainly in exposure to the detail and concepts surrounding the entities and environments I had been in communication with? I had been exposed to unbelievable things way beyond the structure of the multiverse, a function of the isolated structure of Source Entity One, so, why, why, why did it feel so immense a task?

SE1: You are getting old!

ME: What?

SE1: I thought that would grab your attention and get you out of your reverie.

ME: OK, you have succeeded. I find myself here feeling very, very overexposed. I can't understand it, especially when I feel I have dealt with what I would consider larger, much larger subjects!

SE1: I see. Let me explain and then we should stop pontificating and move on with the task at hand.

ME: Thank you. It will be good to understand why I feel this way.

SE1: In all of the other dialogues with my peers and The Origin, you have been protected from the magnitude of what you have been dealing with. You have not been exposed to what you are working with in total. Not even in 1 percent of 1 percent of 1 percent of 1 percent of the part you have worked with. This has been done to keep you stable. Irrespective of your energetic heritage, Mr. Om, you have to participate in the same way as those other Aspects who enter into the evolutionary cycle, and this means that you experience all of the limitations of incarnate existence, every one of them. In the energetic, all Aspects can understand and work with a much bigger picture, but experiencing the lowest of the frequencies of the multiverse, that which I have created for my creations to work with, is, for them and those who choose to experience such frequencies, a great leveler. The Om are no exception to this rule, in any Source

Entity's environment. However, what you are feeling now is a function of two things. First, I am exposing you to more of the depth associated with what I am, and this is deeper in its expression to that which The Origin exposed you to in terms of its energies and environment. And second, there has been a drop in the base frequencies of the Earth over the last six years, which, although not noticeable at first, has culminated in a small but nevertheless more discernible knife-edge change at the start of 2016. This is why you are feeling the difference and the "trepidation" associated with this deeper level of exposure.

ME: But how can you expose me to a deeper level of experience than The Origin?

SE1: Because The Origin wants me to. Don't forget The Origin has had to work with your limitations as well and we all followed the same rules of engagement, so to speak. Now is the time for further expansion and this further expansion will harden you for the work you are destined to do during the dialogues to come, two new and yet-to-be-started books that will test you to your limits. Now it's time to describe my multiversal workforce.

The Multiversal Hierarchy

At last, at last, at last, I thought! I was starting to feel the energies and "knowingness" associated with channeling the information I wanted to know about. We are about to get down to the nitty-gritty. To be honest, dear reader, even though I had experienced these feelings of not knowing what is coming next in all of my books, I had been feeling more than a little anxious about not receiving any real information associated with the core subject matter associated with this book—that the information so far has just been padding, and that this book was slow in taking off, so to speak.

SE1: Your desire to move on to the main subject matter straight away is blocking your ability to receive important peripheral information—and so you are missing it and are in danger of going in circles. You have become so used to the higher frequencies of The Origin and the love-based frequencies associated with working with Anne that working with me is, from an ego-based perspective, difficult to come down to. Also, you feel you know the subject—this also creates a block.

Remember that everything is part of The Origin and should therefore be considered in the same light. Return to the desires, intentions, thoughts, and actions associated with being in the "now" and do not work on what you want. I will be, and am, giving you the subject headings associated with the material we will be discussing. Let me drive the creation of this book and you will be OK.

I felt like I had just been reprimanded.

SE1: I wouldn't go so far as to say that, but, I would say that you needed to be realigned, to return to the original level of innocence and humility you had in the beginning of your spiritual work. Cast all doubts and low-frequency thoughts aside and return to being a pure channel.

ME: Thank you. I will.

I had to admit that with the growing demand for the information I have been receiving, I was trying to force the new information out. Without doubt, I was very uncomfortable with the levels of expectation from an information-hungry readership and the stress associated with my personal desire to deliver for them. To be able to back off and go with the old flow was liberating.

SE1: Good. Let's get going.

As you can imagine, and feel you know, there is a hierarchy associated with the work and the beings that maintain the structure and the function of the multiverse I created. I will describe them in brief before we go into the detail behind each level of structure and the class of being associated with the maintenance of it.

The Curators is the overall description for those beings associated with the maintenance of the multiverse. This descriptor can be used for all levels of beings that we will discuss in short here and in greater detail later.

The Architects are those beings who work with making the environmental changes necessary to creating optimized evolutionary opportunity/ies. The roles of these beings are specific to all aspects of the multiversal environment.

The Architects work on four levels: evolutionary demand, cause and effect, structure, and environmental requirements. They have a number of entities that assist them.

They are stated below in no specific order:

The Illustrators are the beings that work with the larger version of The Source's energetic memory that we call the Akashic records, one that encompasses all that our Source Entity has experienced through its own work and work with other Source Entities. The Akashic is a small segment of this interactive memory that relates to those beings that incarnate in the human form only. The Illustrators use the ability to interact with The Source's energetic memory to describe (illustrate) the different possibility scenarios that may be created by making changes to the structure of the multiverse or its local areas, whether new or modified.

The Planners work with the Illustrators to effect a timely introduction of the decisions made as a result of the work of the Illustrators, ensuring that the chosen scenario is actioned in the "reality" chosen for it to exist within. They ensure that the changes are introduced in a seamless way.

The Orchestrators control the work specified by the Planners. The Orchestrators operate at various levels associated with the work resulting from the activities of the Planners, operating a top-to-bottom approach to the management of the changes/creations required to be actioned.

The Beginners (not to be confused with the human understanding of a beginning or start—see later) are a group of beings that work with the functions of Event Space allowing any changes to have its own "start of event." Those readers who are familiar with the terms and functions associated with Event Space will understand that everything exists in terms of events and not in terms of time. It is the job of the Beginners to ensure that the quality of the start of the event is maintained at its optimal level when introduced into the overall scheme of existing Event Space spaces. Note here that their insertion of change creates a whole new set of possibilities and as such the number of new Event Spaces, their fractals and the effects on the beings within these spaces needs to be known and managed by these entities.

The Enders (not to be confused with the human understanding of an ending—see later) are a group of beings that work with the functions of Event Space allowing any changes to have its own "end of event." It is the job of the Enders to ensure that the quality of the end of the event is maintained at its optimal level when withdrawn from the overall scheme of existing Event Space spaces. Note here that their withdrawal creates a whole new set of possibilities and as such the number of new Event Spaces, their fractals and the effects on the beings within these spaces that would not be created needs to be known and managed by these entities. The end of an event can be created as a naturalized or forced function, whereas the start of an event, if created or managed by the Beginners, is a forced function only.

The Deliverers are those beings who work on the functional side of the work of the Beginners and Enders. Their role can and does vary in any way associated with what they need to do. They are multidisciplined and are not specialized to any particular job, role, or responsibility.

The Waymakers are quite possibly one of the most specialized group of beings we will work with in this dialogue, with of course the exception of those beings who work on the environmental functionality of a local environment or habitat (a planet, for instance). They ensure that the work of the Beginners and Enders has a seamless insertion and withdrawal point relative to the effects of all Event Spaces and their fractals. This means that they work on each parallel condition as it is created or uncreated to ensure that the changes experienced by the beings in these spaces are minimalized to the point of incoherence. This means that the beings themselves are not aware of the changes new parallel conditions create as they are affected by them.

The Integrators do the ground work of the Waymakers. They are the beings that weave the different Events together into a seamless holographic state so that each Event Space is in contact with each other Event Space either directly or indirectly through direct and indirect contact with other Events.

The Seed Makers are the creators of small events, very small events, which are capable of being inserted or withdrawn from the totality of Event Space without affecting those beings that are working within the normal functions of the Events themselves. They are called Seed Makers because the events they insert allow the creation of much bigger Events to be created on what appears to be a natural level, that being, as a natural fractal (later larger fractals) of an Event Space or Series of Event Spaces. This function can act in reverse as well where the withdrawal of an Event Space is seen as the natural demise of an Event Space resulting from it reaching its natural evolutionary conclusion.

The Seeders work for the Seed Makers. Their role is to skillfully choose the Event Space/s in which to insert or withdraw the seed Event Space. If you like, they choose the moment of insertion. This role is not an easy one for the Seeders work with "What If" scenarios created by working with The Source's energetic memory and choosing the optimal moment of insertion or withdrawal.

As with all entities that work with Event Space they have the capability of manipulating it. Even though Event Space is a pan-Origin intelligent energy in its own right, those entities that absorb themselves in its functionality are eventually able to manipulate it.

The Beleaguerers are a special group of entities because they are multifaceted and are skilled in all functions associated with the entities described so far and that will be described later.

They look at the total workload to correct issues in terms of the total number of Event Spaces that could be affected if the wrong insertion point is used, or if the "What If" scenario function of The Source's energetic memory is incorrectly interpreted. Or indeed, anything that has responded in a way that was not expected or planned.

The Beleaguerers are, or operate as, a firefighting and/or clean-up function when things don't go according to plan. They operate independently of all other entities and take over the operational corrections that are needed to ensure all Event Spaces and their junctures are maintained.

The Recorders are exactly what their name describes them as—recorders. They work on the detail surrounding the work all of the other entities are responsible for and assign the actions of those entities working on the tasks they are recording and the subsequent responses of the components of the multiversal environments to the appropriate sectors of The Source's energetic memory.

It does have to be said that the Recorders work specifically on recording the information associated with the work of The Source's maintenance entities and not The Source itself.

The Interfacers are a group of entities that link everything together. They see the ways in which to dovetail the work of one set of entities to the work of another set of entities.

Although it could be argued that all entities are able to experience all things simultaneously and therefore understand the functionality surrounding the potential to link one piece of work with another; that the work of the Interfacers is not required. However, when we consider the complexities surrounding the maintenance of any part of the multiverse and those parallel environments that could, can, and will be created, there is a need for entities to specialize. Understanding the opportunities, ways, and methods of linking the work of other entities together is therefore complicated at best and requires focus to ensure seamless integration.

The Initiators (not to be confused with Beginners) are those entities that decide what modifications are needed to either maintain the evolutionary efficiency of an environment, or create modifications to introduce a completely different set of evolutionary opportunities. One way to describe them would be to use the term "Brain Stormers." In this role, the Initiators therefore create the new ideas that are eventually actioned as new environments, experiences, and evolutionary opportunities.

The Observers (not to be confused with Recorders) exist within the environments that all entities maintain or create. Their role is to experience the creations of those entities that create the structure, environments that exist within the structure, and the components of an environment. The Observers experience the creations of other entities by observing the way in which those entities that are creating, create and those entities that chose to experience those creations experience them. They achieve this in a number of ways but the main way is to place themselves within the energies of the experiencing entity and observe the experience in the same way as the creating or experiencing entity but from the benefit of being both inside and outside of the creation and/or experience.

The Producers create the energies that allow small changes or creations to be made. One should not look at this as being a small role, however, as the small changes are those that deal with the minute detail of changes or creations. It is the small changes that need the most attention to detail and so the energies need to contain all of the detailed information based upon a template to support those smaller changes. As an example of what I mean here, you should consider this as being the energies that support the structure that allows the generation of the smallest components within the physical universe, which in this instance is the Anu.

The Generators generate the "form" from energies, the structure that is created by the Producers. In this instance, one should think of the Generators being downstream of the Producers for they take the energies created by the Producers and generate the templates for the creation and stability of those components used in the creation of the lower frequency environments. In this instance, this would be all of the aspects of the physical universe represented by its twelve frequential levels.

The Environmentalists are the entities that you as human beings may be more interested in because they deal with the creation of, manipulation of, and maintenance of the environmental aspects of the multiversal structure, that being the environments that we use to evolve in from an "immersed" perspective. They include the following roles:

The Universalists are those entities that maintain, create, and support the local structure and overall content of the frequencies that are capable of supporting a universal environment, one where many areas of habitude can be created. They are the creators of the components within a particular universe that give the incumbent entities the opportunity to create within the local environments that which the universe allows to be created with those components. In essence, they create the environments for the Habitation Creators to work with, giving them their raw materials. These raw materials are galaxies, nebulae, planets, and moons from the perspective of the physical universe.

The Parallelism Engineers work with the results of, or the effects of, the interaction with Event Space. They draw the line between the local, planetary, system, galactic, and universal-sized Event Spaces that are created by the decisions, possible decisions, the possibility of possible decisions, and the possibility of the possibility of possible decisions. The line they draw is the demarcation between these different Event Spaces and their location to each other in terms of their "potential" to be in existence versus their actual existence which includes the closeness of deviation from the main line Event Space and each other. Their main role is therefore to ensure there is adequate separation between these Event Spaces ensuring that where there needs to be simple separation, there is simple separation, and when there can be "crossover" between Event Spaces by the incumbent entities, that this function is in operation.

The Concurrence Engineers are those entities that look at the relationship between each of the universes created within the frequencies of the multiverse. They ensure that the functionality of these universes is maintained. They ensure that they are within the same space and that as a result of being in the same space that they exist independently of each other. They also ensure that the progression from one universe to another is both robust and reasonable; the way I describe the universes created for use within the multiverse is as being "self-contained simultaneous universes." So, as stated above, "concurrence" is a function of being in the same space but with the added function of being in an evolutionary flow, a flow which all universes within the multiverse have—that is specific to the static structure of the multiverse. The Concurrence Engineers can and do work with the Frequential Barrier Engineers [*see below—GSN*].

It must be noted here that the Concurrence Engineers do not work on those universes that are created in parallel with the self-contained simultaneous universes. They do not work on those universes that are created by Event Space interactions because they are specialized to work on a stable multiversal environment and not a transient one.

The Frequential Barrier Engineers work in conjunction with the Concurrence Engineers. They ensure that there is a, for want of a better word, "gap" between the frequencies that allows a demarcation between one self-contained simultaneous universe to another. This may seem out of tune with the current understanding of "physics" but there can be and are gaps between what I call major frequencies, or to describe it a better way, a gap between the top of the bandwidth of one major frequency and the bottom of the bandwidth of another higher major frequency. These gaps are also part of the supporting structure of the multiverse and not the functional aspect of it. One way to think of how this works is to consider placing a sign on one rung of a ladder, missing out the one rung above it, and placing another "progressive" sign on the rung two rungs above the first rung where the first sign was placed. It is therefore the role of these entities to ensure that the gap of one rung of the ladder is maintained.

The Attractionists have two distinct specialisms. In the first distinction, they are entities that specialize in working in the physical aspects of the multiverse. They specifically work on the way in which the energies that are associated with the lowest frequencies can and are used in conjunction to each other. In simple terms, they work on the "strength" or level of attraction between each other, or put in another way, their gravity. The Attractionists work on all levels of "physical bodies," from the attraction between Anu to the larger attraction between planets, suns, solar systems, and galaxies.

In the second specialism, they work on the signature of energies that are used to ensure that incarnates are attracted to each other for the purposes of removing karmic links or working together on a common life plan. This is not the same as being attracted from a romantic perspective because it is a functional aspect of the interactive evolutionary process of entities that are working with the evolutionary cycle.

The Caretakers is the overall name for those entities that work within the frequencies of the physical universe. This is where most of the entities that incarnate mankind has knowledge about, such as Elementals (nature spirits) and Angels, reside. It includes the Attractionists above and the following roles below.

The Vehicle Creators are those entities that design and create the vehicles used for experiencing the lowest frequencies of the multiverse that we call the physical universe in the way it is supposed to be experienced. That means that an incarnating entity experiences resistance, lack of functionality, and connectivity. These are the entities that I described in your book, *The History of God*, and they can and do include members of the genre of energies of entities I call incarnate mankind. There are a group of these entities that are the collective creational mind, so to speak, for every vehicle that allows a level of incarnate interaction to be achieved within the environment they were designed for. This includes all of the twelve frequencies associated with the physical universe and the frequential representations of the vehicles created for those frequencies. From the perspective of mankind's understanding, all types of flora and fauna can be used for incarnate experience.

Just before your readers ask the question about insects, which I will discuss in detail later, a single TES Aspect would be in control of a whole hive and not one specific insect.

The Habitation Creators deal with the ability for the environment to support the perpetuation and reproduction of the incarnate vehicles created for a specific environment or environments. For instance, they understand the work of the Atmospherisists [*see below—GSN*] and introduce either *existing* flora and fauna or suggest the creation of new flora and fauna to the Vehicle Creators as appropriate whose very existence helps to support the balance of the environment in an automatic way. The Habitation Creators also include the Habitation Specialists.

The Habitation Specialists are those entities that incarnate mankind calls nature spirits. They work as a specialized function, so much so, that they may even be aligned to a single plant or microbe. It does have to be said here that even though animals and plants are classified as incarnate vehicles for the use of certain genres of TES Aspect or un-projected TES (those TES that either have no currently projected Aspects or have not generated any Aspects to project) that they would still be in need of care and attention from the Habitation Specialists. Additionally, and in some instances, the

TES who projects an Aspect or Aspects into the animal vehicle may be working directly with, or under the direction of, the Habitation Specialists that are responsible for a specific animal or plant vehicle.

The Atmospherisists are a group of entities that work with the stability of the wider environment, planetary or otherwise, and how it is used by the incarnate vehicle and supporting infrastructure it is designed for. They modify and manipulate the functions of the atmosphere and its periods of change relevant to the location of the planet or environment. A planet is not the only location for an incarnate vehicle to work within and neither is the need for aspiration to ensure bodily function within the location and frequency it resides within always necessary.

The Populationists are the flora and fauna engineers. They have various levels of responsibility—each specialized according to the environment they are working with. The environment can be universal, galactic, systematic, planetary—includes moons or nebulae based as habitable environments. They work in close harmony with the Atmospherisists, who provide the details behind the atmosphere they are creating or able to create with the materials they have. The Populationists then create the basic mechanical vehicles that are used for those entities that are incarnate for the purposes of being a "living" functional aspect of the atmosphere, so to speak.

Guides and Helpers [*these are described in* The Anne Dialogues— *GSN*] should not be confused with those entities described in summary above as being relevant to the maintenance of the multiversal environment. They are specific to the assistance of those entities that enter into the evolutionary cycle and use the lower frequencies of the multiverse as an evolutionary accelerant.

ME: This is all very good in summary, AND I know that we are going to describe these entities in detail later on in this dialogue. But I do have one question, one that a lot of my readers will want to know.

SE1: And that is?

ME: Why do we refer to some of these beings as Angels? Where did the description, or should I say, the use of the word Angel and their roles and responsibilities come from?

SE1: We have already discussed this to some extent at the very start of this dialogue, but I will see if I can make it plainer.

Each of the entities described in your short appraisal of the currently understood (and with a largely Christian bias, I note) hierarchy of those entities who are closest to me, are the result of the spiritual knowledge, intellectual capacity, and energetic ability of the incarnates of those periods when they were described. Also note that, in reading your thoughts, those incarnates that were capable of either understanding what they were seeing or were being exposed to "information-wise" were given the information in ways that they would be able to work with and move on with. When those incarnates that were being communicated with offered an explanation or description that they expressed as being some level of understanding of what they had been given was considered to be progressive they were allowed to use that information. The issue here is that this understanding was only for the illustrative purposes of one person—the person being communicated with and should not have been used for the education of others of either lesser or greater knowledge. It is the variance in understanding, or schools of thought, and the subsequent disagreements that cause the creation of one way versus another and aggression between these schools of thought, for all schools think that they are correct and the others are not. The fact of the matter is that none of them is correct to the point where they know the absolute truth about the subject they are broadcasting, they can't, because they don't have the intellectual and educational capacity and neither do they have the frequential level that supports the ability to access higher knowledge.

So, getting to the question, the word Angel is a descriptor for those entities that are disincarnate and as a result "pure" from the perspective of the incarnate. It has been misused and used as a description of those entities that communicate issues of guidance to certain incarnates—which of course are the Guides and Guides' Helpers. Even the name given has been misused and used as a means of describing the environment they exist within—that being the Angelic—you will see what I mean later.

ME: Where does the use of the word "Arch" come from in the descriptor "Archangel?"

SE1: This is a function of the use of the human languages and the desire for a structure to exist. Based upon this I suggest you look at the word "hierarchy" and break it down to two words—Higher (Hier) and Arch (Archy). Incarnates like to see things in a structured way, so, until they can see in a concurrent way—i.e., everything existing all at the same time and at the same level in a total unstructured and amorphous way, I and those who help in the education of truth seekers will give them structure. The words "Higher" and "Arch" together can be used to describe the graduations in the frequencies. "Higher" meaning above the current location of one location or entity within a location, and "Arch" is a way of describing a frequential level as being above the current, as an arch or bridge over to the next level.

"Arch" as a descriptor for an individual is a Greek word and it means "leader, ruler, or chief." In another way, it is a method of saying an individual is above or higher than another.

Angel as a descriptor for an individual is a Greek word and it means "messenger." In another way it is a method of saying an individual is a bringer of news or is an educator.

Neither of these descriptors should be used to describe the maintenance entities if used in this context, but they can be used to describe Guides and Helpers. Guides and Helpers do not, however, have the same roles as those entities that are involved in the maintenance of the multiversal structure, and those that do are either classified as Elementals and are not in a position of giving messages to incarnate mankind, or are involved at a level where they are never in contact with incarnates.

ME: Based upon this then, the use of the words "Angel" and "Archangel" cannot be used as a descriptor for any entity that is involved in the guidance of incarnate TES Aspects or maintenance entities of any level.

SE1: Correct. There is one level of description where it can be used, though, and one where the visual descriptions fit in with history, to a certain level, that is.

ME: Pray tell me, I am all ears!

SE1: You are aware of the ability for a higher frequency incarnate to create a secondary incarnation, so that the Aspect involved in the "primary" and higher frequency incarnation can experience two incarnations concurrently, one of a higher frequency and the other of a lower frequency.

ME: I am. It is described in *The Anne Dialogues*.

SE1: Well, this can also be used to allow the higher frequency incarnate to exist within a lower frequency civilization and, when the timing is right, make changes that will improve the education, knowledge, and technology of the lower frequency incarnate civilization through the communicational opportunity that is created by the higher frequency incarnate Aspect advising its lower frequency Aspect what to do and when to do it. Because they are a higher frequency, they would normally be invisible to the lower frequency incarnate Aspect. However, they would be able to, by the use of certain energetic technology, make themselves "visible" to their lower frequency incarnate Aspect and give them direction. They would be messengers to themselves—their own Angel or Archangel! This should work as an explanation for you.

ME: It does, and I was feeling a little uncomfortable about the use of the word Angel and the historical descriptions of them. In these few short sentences, you have put my concerns to bed. Thank you.

SE1: Good, this method is actually quite common and is an explanation for the reports of "God's" messengers that removes a link with Guides, Helpers, and multiversal maintenance entities because it is all maintained within the one universal environment.

The Devil Is in the Detail

Having just summarized the roles of God's helpers, I was starting to feel that I would be telling the story again, so to speak. I was feeling a little bit unsure about this process and was worrying about the expectations of the readers in terms of the religious expectations of these entities versus what I have been exposed to over the last few months and weeks.

For those of you who have read my previous books, you will be somewhat surprised that I am thinking in this way. I may have looked like I was supremely confident in my ability to communicate with The Source Entity/ies and The Origin and the detail surrounding the concepts, environments, and entities discussed. I am of course very confident in this respect and I am also aware that this can seem like arrogance. I tell you it is not and I am always concerned about how best to validate the information I am exposed to. That said, being told that one of the most memorable descriptions of the betrayal of God, including the name of the betrayer, illustrated within religious texts is basically a human creation, is going to shake a few trees. It was, in my mind, a difficult and world-shattering responsibility to have.

After some time of contemplation, and a need to clear my mind of a conflict in terms of the nomenclature used, I decided to put my money where my mouth is and ask a very simple but poignant question—that being, "can I/we use the names in the Bible as useful descriptors?"

SE1: NO!

ME: That was a quick answer.

SE1: You both wanted and needed one that was definitive.

ME: Well, you sure have given me one. I have another question, though.

SE1: Yes.

ME: I was thinking that maybe I would work with you in providing some sort of reference or link between what you advise me and how it links into the current religious and sometimes spiritual-based knowledge.

SE1: That would not be wise.

ME: Why can't I/we use the names in the Bible?

SE1: Simply because they are incorrect in terms of their visual and functional description. Incarnate mankind still thinks that it is the only sentient being in the physical universe, let alone the local galaxy the Earth is located within, and this interpretation has transplanted from religious texts, so, Angels are in incarnate human form as a result. Your work will provide a platform—as always—to allow the readers to un-learn this constant need to refer to the incarnate human form as a one-size-fits-all form factor. Now, though, it is the time to achieve the same thing by removing the reference to Angels and their human form.

ME: So where do we start then?

SE1: At the very top of the hierarchy, those entities that we discussed at the beginning. Please note, though, that I use the word "hierarchy" loosely here because in real terms, there is no such thing as a hierarchy of entities that maintain the functions of the multiverse.

ME: You mean that they don't exist or that they are equal?

SE1: Both. The focus of sentient energy that is your TES and you as a smaller aspect of your TES work for the benefit of the accelerated expansion of the evolutionary content of that sentience. As such, you and your TES are small, very very small individualized and therefore specialized units of The Origin. You therefore ARE The Origin, as am I from a greater or larger perspective. Looking at this from a different angle, you and your TES are so infinitesimally small in comparison with The Origin in its current and future forms that you don't exist. In essence then, you and I are just Origin energy with sentience—our existence being a loose function of the individuality assigned to that sentience we call us.

This thought process can and should also be used for those entities that help maintain the structure of the multiverse within my particular set of individualized sentient energies, for everything is one and everything is amorphous in functionality. For the moment, though, we shall refer to these specific individualizations of sentient energy as my helpers—my multiversal maintenance entities, and not as functions of, shall I say, "order" within that which is order-less and amorphous. This is for another day, though, and another series of dialogues, not specifically with me, I might add. It might not even be with you, but with another who can take the work further.

ME: Yes, I already know that others, those who are more expansive than me, will take over and push the boundaries further. Before we start, though, I have just picked up on one of the words that you used.

SE1: Yes?

ME: You stated that, and I will generalize here, that everything seems to be order-less and amorphous. Surely, The Origin, that is, its sentient energies, are or have order and structure?

SE1: In reality, they are largely structure-less and order-less. If they had structure, shall I say with ultimate structure, then The Origin could not function in a way that is efficient enough to allow its functionality as an Omni-present, Omniscient being to be Omni-functional.

The presentation of "all that is" as having a structure is, for the most part, for the benefit of incarnate mankind. You will move away from the need to use these terms and thought processes when you are close to ending the need to incarnate to accelerate your evolutionary progress.

ME: So, just calling a point of order here then. Why don't we simply miss out the middle man of presenting things in an orderly structure-based way that is controlled and maintained by a hierarchy of entities to one where we deal with a structure-less amorphous condition?

SE1: Because incarnate mankind would not be able to understand the mechanics and functionality of such a condition. Remember your own words to your readers, *"You can't feed steak to a baby when it is feeding on milk, and you can't expect someone who barely understands the multiplication tables to work out matrix multiplication-based equations."* We have to start somewhere and we have to educate, while in the incarnate state, in a logical and progressive way.

So, we will continue with the use of the descriptions summarized earlier as a starting point for the deeper levels of detail associated with those individualized units of sentient energies that are my multiversal maintenance entities.

ME: Thank you. Let's start from the top then.

From the Top

Now that we are getting down to the nitty-gritty of the detail behind those entities that dedicate themselves to the functionality of the multiverse, I feel like I am getting in the flow again. I fully intended to start each section with the summary for each entity that was provided to me by the Source, and I still do. For some reason, I keep receiving the standard presentation format in my head, "tell the audience what you are going to tell them, tell the audience, then tell the audience what you told them!" *It seems very clinical but it does make sure that the information is understood. I don't think I will take it to its n'th degree but I do want to refresh our memories of the basics before I delve into the detail for each of the entities and their roles. It just feels necessary somehow and is something that I have not felt before when channeling the information.*

I stopped a moment to sink into myself to understand where this feeling was coming from. I noticed resistance, not from me but from an indoctrinated public. In my previous work I have been, in general, too far away from the vagaries of religion to be concerned, with spiritual physics and metaphysics being a distance apart in most people's minds. In my understanding spiritualism and metaphysics is generally accepted by religious people with no particular attention being placed upon the subjects that are discussed under these headings—because they feel that it doesn't affect them. Here, though, I was delving into the periphery of popular religion irrespective of who the originating teacher is, for most religions refer to God's helpers in some way.

The Curators

As stated previously, this name is a useful descriptor for all of the entities that are involved in the maintenance and functionality of the multiversal environment that our creator, The Source Entity, made for us as smaller individualized units of its sentient energy to experience itself in greater depth and detail, evolving for, and on its behalf, in the process.

SE1: That's not all, though.

ME: You have some additional information to share with me, I take it?

SE1: Yes, of course. You need to be aware that there are a number of entities that are overseers, so to speak. They look after each of the full dimensions that are the basis for the higher aspect of the multiversal structure, that part of me that I have reserved for my creations, my smaller parts of me, to experiment with.

ME: Is there one for each of the full dimensions? What I mean is, is there one entity that is responsible for the first full dimension and another for the second full dimension?

SE1: Not in the way you describe it and not in the way you are thinking. In essence, there are twelve, so you are correct in one part of your thinking. However, they are not specifically responsible for a particular full dimension per se, moreover they are collectively responsible for all full dimensions and their substructures and functionality.

ME: Are they what we call the Council of Twelve?

SE1: No, no, no. Spiritualists are so obsessed with this so-called Council, it's become a distraction. In reality, there is no such formality, although in function you may be forgiven for thinking in this way. You see, they work as a higher function of those who are from the overall perspective classified as a Curator, as for example, the Curators' Curator.

ME: Hang on a moment. I am starting to understand what you are eluding to here.

SE1: I haven't said much to allow you to establish what I am alluding to yet. Suffice to say, though, you are picking up on the way these entities work and distribute themselves.

ME: What do you mean, distribute themselves?

SE1: Go ahead—describe what you are seeing in your mind's eye!

I did. What I saw was interesting. I could see that The Source had created twelve entities. Each of these twelve were distributed in a way that I had seen before. It wasn't distribution in terms of being spread out, but more in terms of individualized sentient energies. Each of the twelve were displaying the principal method that a True Energetic Self or TES (sometimes called the Godhead, Oversoul, or Higher Self) would use if it were projecting part or parts of itself into the lower frequencies of the multiversal environment for experiential and evolutionary purposes. These twelve Curators or Curators' Curators were not just partially projected, but they were fully projected into the full one hundred and forty-four possible projections. Twelve projections with each projection or "Aspect" having twelve smaller projections or "Shards!" Were they just another TES doing another role, a different role, one that was as far upstream as an individualized aspect of Source Entity sentient energy could go without being in communion with their Source? I was beginning to think so!

SE1: Very well done, and of course they are. All of my individualizations, all of my creations that are involved in the evolutionary cycle and its supporting structure at your level—that is, incarnate mankind's level—are the same in sentience, energy, and structure.

ME: So, irrespective of whether an entity is at its highest level, TES level, in the evolutionary cycle or the service-based system/ structure—whatever, they are the same basic expression of you in individuality?

SE1: Correct. Being in the evolutionary cycle you all have certain ways to use your individualization and your ability to distribute certain aspects of that individuality that are relevant to the work you are doing. Each of the twelve "Curator"-based entities operate in a state of maximum distribution all of the time. This is the most efficient way for them to operate—that being, all working collectively and all working fully distributed, or projected. So, if you want to understand why I called them the Curators' Curator, it's because their projections, and ultimately those of the other individualized TES that are working with other levels of structure and work are the Curators "in general" and the TES of the twelve are the Curators of the Curators. I would like to note here that their TES being described as the Curators of the Curators is not an expression of higher responsibility or status, it is simply a way of describing how they are distributed and how they work in a way that you and your readers will understand.

ME: One more quick question before we move onto the subject of the Architects.

SE1: Carry on.

ME: When in the evolutionary cycle our TES projects its Aspects, and the Aspects project Shards to allow the opportunity for diversified individualization, which results in multiple and separate experience and evolutionary growth of the TES concurrently, discounting, of course, these parallel conditions created by Event Space and our invocation of it through individual choice at certain experiential junctures—does it not?

SE1: Yes, it does.

ME: Is this the same for the TES of the Curators' Curators and their projections?

SE1: No, it's a different method of functioning. When the Aspects of the Curators' TES and the Shards of the Aspects for the Curators' TES are projected, they are not individualized in the same way as those in the evolutionary cycle. In essence, they are working in a collective way with the same functions as each other but with different multiversal responsibilities, that is not to say that they have different roles. Roles are not responsibilities and responsibilities do not create roles. The projection of the Curators' TES is simply a way of increasing their ability to connect with everything they need to connect with in an efficient way.

I was starting to see a picture of how this might work. Each of these twelve Curators' Curators were linked together in a form of matrix. Within this matrix, which by the way I am taking as being a humanized version of what the actual functionality was, every Shard, Aspect, and TES were interconnected in such a way where each of them were both a representation of each other in every connection with each other and each juncture within the multiversal structure. I was trying to visualize how this might work when The Source decided that it would be able to give a better description.

SE1: You are seeing the interconnectivity of the Curators' Curators in a very low-frequency way, a very basic way; in a way which is from your readers' perspective three-dimensional. In reality, there is no such description for they are interconnected in a multistructural way that is above and beyond the structure of the multiversal that is used in the evolutionary cycle.

ME: What do you mean, multistructural?

SE1: By now you should have worked out that what you experience in your temporary low-frequency existence is not what is experienced in the Greater Reality.

ME: Give me some latitude here please. I am not just asking the questions for myself, but for the readers as well. I understand that there are ways in which we work and experience things from the perspective of a being in the evolutionary cycle and there are ways in which we work and experience things from the perspective of a being in service to those in the evolutionary cycle. I am also aware that my/our ability to comprehend what we are being given is based upon our current experience and knowledge and that what we will be exposed to later is a result of our growth, resulting from previous levels of exposure.

SE1: Forgive me; I was being critical of your line of questioning. I will explain further then.

ME: Thank you.

SE1: You see, the Curators' Curators have a special function. It is to not only be the highest point of the hierarchy from a structural support perspective, but they themselves create the conditions necessary to allow the multiversal structure to exist.

ME: You're saying that the Curators' Curators are the structure of the multiverse?

SE1: No, I am saying that they create the conditions necessary for its existence.

ME: But I thought, I should say that my understanding was/is that you made the multiverse out of your own energies?

SE1: And I did.

ME: So why do you need these beings to maintain its need to be in existence?

SE1: Simply put, to maintain its continued existence by being the prime motivating force behind my desire to evolve through the creation of individualized smaller aspects of my sentience who will work without direct interaction with the greater part of my sentience that remains intact. My desire to progress and evolve is a prime function of my creation by my creator, The Origin, and as such this desire to progress and evolve is infused throughout my sentience, irrespective of whether it is whole, part of the remaining whole, or an individualized aspect of that part of me that was taken from the whole and divided up.

ME: So our desire to evolve is a function of your desire to evolve, which is a function of The Origin's desire to evolve.

SE1: Correct. And, although the original manifestation of the multiverse and of my creation of smaller individualized aspects of my sentience was the result of my desire to accelerate my evolution, this desire to maintain an environment to evolve within is embedded within my creations as well.

ME: So the Curators in general maintain the desire for the existence of the multiverse, and those beings that elected to be in the evolutionary cycle maintain their desire for their use of the multiverse and its continued existence and maintenance of its evolutionary efficiency by the Curators. The one giving the desire for the continued existence of the other maintains the continued existence of themselves in the process.

SE1: Correct. It's a self-contained, self-perpetuating system that no longer needs my desire for its existence to continue its existence because the desire of those entities that use it want it to remain in existence and therefore create its continued existence and indeed the continuation of their individualization in the process.

ME: And the Curators' Curators are at the top of the perpetuation of this particular desire.

SE1: Yes, they are. To use your computer language as a description, they are the internal operating system of the multiverse. Not only do they maintain the overall structure, they create, through the desire of those beings in the evolutionary cycle, the overall intention behind the continuation of the multiverse by being the structure behind the multiverse and its operating system.

I was considering the information I had just been given and what it meant. No more than twelve entities, twelve individualized units of The Source Entities' sentient energy were used, or elected to be the creative desire behind the structure of the multiverse. The Curators' Curators were not only the highest level of entity within the hierarchy of those beings that maintained the multiverse and its evolutionary efficiency from the perspective of an entity that was in the evolutionary cycle, they both created and were the highest level of structure of the multiverse itself. This realization suddenly gave birth to another realization, that being, that the multiverse itself was sentient by default. The third realization came quickly. Of course the multiverse was sentient, it was part of The Source, which, was part of The Origin. Although I inherently knew this, I hadn't appreciated it and therefore thought about it on an intellectual level. Why we as incarnate human beings are unable to see what is right in front of us, even when it is presented to us in flashing lights, is astonishing, and in this previous lack of intellectual realization of mine, I had astonished myself. It all seemed so logical now and taking the thought process based upon my recent realization a little further down the line made me very aware that we, even as beings or entities that are in the multiverse as units of individualized sentient energy with free will, are also a fundamental part and function of what is created by The Source to assist in its evolutionary progression. Not only are we individualized sentient energy but we are our own creation and the environmental condition that supports our creation and creativity.

I suddenly stopped myself in my tracks and posed a question to myself. If it is truly the case that we are both created and creator and environment for that which can be created, what is the point of discussing the roles, responsibilities, and functions of those entities called The Curators? Essentially from a logical perspective I/we are them and they are I/us and therefore considering that we may have created each other then there is no need for any entities to govern that which we are and have created in an environment that is us as well. My mind reeled for a moment at this prospect. I had long ago started to feel that everything was amorphous, but now I was getting the proof. I was starting to wonder if I should jump to a different level, one where everything was amorphous and report about that when The Source took over my thoughts and gave me direction.

SE1: It's too early for a dialogue based upon a higher level of understanding. You need to work on what is being used as a medium for evolutionary progression rather than the ultimate function of who and what you all are.

ME: What do you mean?

SE1: I will put it in a simple way. Everything that you know, work with, and create is real; it is part of this reality and this includes the structure of the multiverse and the functions of those entities that are it, create it, and operate within it. It also includes the information that was given to you by my peers and The Origin. However, it is also true that everything is amorphous but that which is amorphous has decided to experience structure. This is where you all come in. You are the amorphous that has created the non-amorphous—structure. In wanting to experience structure you have all created structure within a structure that I have given you all to work with.

ME: But I thought you told me that you created the multiverse and populated it with smaller versions of yourself by individualizing units of your sentient energies to populate it and that the structure was already there as a division of yourself?

SE1: It is and was. You need to know this. My division of self to create all the different genres of TES is a true statement of what did, has, and is happening. The structure of the multiverse however was given to you all as an idea, a blueprint of what could be. You all decided to perpetuate that idea and modify it to suit your own ideas on what the structure should/could be and how it should be supported and how it should be utilized to its best capacity as an evolutionary medium. And that is how, in a nutshell, the structure of the multiverse, its maintainability, and population came about.

ME: Everything is a stage then, a creation by ourselves for ourselves for the benefit of our progression.

SE1: Correct. There is no conundrum between considering the higher function of what you all are, amorphous and one, and the condition of what you are temporarily, structured and individualized.

ME: I get the feeling that everything is a gigantic game in creation and experience.

SE1: Of course it is, but the game has a desire or reason to be an expected outcome—experiential and evolutionary progression.

You can now progress with your work on this book knowing that, although there is a deeper understanding of the reason for the structure, maintenance, population, and function of the multiverse, its current condition needs to be understood and used as a tool for personal expansion before working with the amorphous while in a structured state.

ME: I expect that this will be the subject matter for discussion in future dialogues?

SE1: Yes, it will, and when the time, the Event Space, is in place for this to happen, you will be drawn to communicate with The Origin about it.

ME: It's time to move on to the next level of entities, the Architects.

SE1: Yes, it is.

The Architects

My mind had been put to rest. I now understood, finally, that the amorphous and the structured exist together as a function of each other and are not separate and in conflict. Those aware and awake incarnate individuals who pick up only the amorphous or the structure and report about it are not in conflict with each other either, for both are correct, both exist in the same space and both are a function of each other. Within the amorphous, it is those units of individualized sentient energy, the amorphous given structure, The Source Entities, and their creations, that have, in turn, created structure from the amorphous to experience the amorphous in a way that it is not—structured. The result of the collaboration between creator and the created, to create within that which is created creates further creations and the ultimate need to govern those creations that created the need for further structure and the entities to govern that structure and those entities that have the desire to use it and delve deep into the minutest detail. This is where the need for the roles and responsibilities for the governing entities raised and why I am here waiting to receive the information to describe the next level of governing entities—the Architects.

ME: Now that I have given the readers and myself a wider understanding of why the multiverse "is" a structure within a structure (you) within that which is amorphous but gaining structure, of a sort (The Origin), I am confident in my ability to understand the information in the way you present it to me and I can present it to the readers.

SE1: Good, so you should. You have been working with me, my peers, and our creator for long enough to be supremely confident in this information and even gain the information direct, in lieu of through a third party such as me. I know you have been working on a higher personal level and have had trouble with integrating the structure with the amorphous from an intellectual perspective, and this is to be understood. While in the incarnate, the ability for the Aspect to work in more than one conceptual way is difficult at best, especially when two concepts seem to be in variance with each other from your human perspective.

ME: Thank you. To be honest I was starting to think I was losing it a little.

SE1: You are not losing it in the slightest. You are just moving from one level of understanding to another, one where everything is possible and everything is in actuality.

Getting back to the work at hand, though. I gave you a summary that stated that the Architects are those beings who work with making the environmental changes necessary to creating optimized evolutionary opportunity/ies. The roles of these beings are specific to all aspects of the multiversal environment. I also conveyed to you that the Architects work on four levels: evolutionary demand, cause and effect, structure, and environmental requirements. They have a number of entities that assist them, which we will discuss in their own right later.

With the Architects functioning on each of the four levels, the multiverse receives an absolute reason for its existence, the reason being a function of the desire of those entities in the evolutionary cycle wanting it to continue to support their work in the most efficient way possible. The Architects therefore work on the four areas of major structural influence from a high-level perspective, leaving the detail to those entities that work on their behalf. That being said, they are ultimately responsible for the work of those supporting entities and as a result, they create the main focus for the work of their supporting entities by ensuring that the four main levels of the multiverse they work with are maintained from a strategic perspective that is consistent with the requirements of each and every one of those entities that are in the evolutionary cycle.

ME: Hold on a minute! Are you suggesting that the multiverse is modified to suit the requirements of each of the individual entities that are in the evolutionary cycle?

SE1: Yes, of course.

ME: Let me clarify my comment here for the benefit of the readers. What I mean is that the multiverse is actually modified in line with the evolutionary requirements of each entity in the evolutionary cycle on an individual basis and not on an overall, general, or collective basis?

SE1: Correct.

ME: I, and I hope I speak for the readers here, was under the assumption that the multiverse was a general environment that we, or should I say our TES, experiences, via its projected Aspects and/ or Shards to enable a greater level of understanding of the multiverse through the use of myriad entities experiencing the same thing. I did not see that the multiverse was modified to suit the needs of the individual.

SE1: Well, it is.

ME: Well then, in my limited understanding this means that every one of us in the evolutionary cycle has their own multiverse to work with.

SE1: You cannot include yourself in that statement because you are not in the evolutionary cycle.

ME: What? I thought I must be, simply because I am here, in your energies, incarnate in the lowest of the frequencies of your energies.

SE1: No, you are not, and now is not the time to enter into this type of dialogue.

ME: When do I get the chance to discuss it then?

SE1: In the book that records the dialogue you will have, have had, are having with the OM.

ME: And that will be in … ?

SE1: It will be in two books' time, including this book. After this dialogue you need to help others heal themselves and introduce an energetic reason for why incarnate human beings experience physical and psychological dysfunction and how it can be healed. This will need to be presented to the medical and psychological fraternity as an alternative, but necessary healing modality.

ME: But I don't need to worry about that dialogue nor the dialogue about the OM and I being outside, as you say, of the evolutionary cycle right now.

SE1: No, not yet. You will know when to—you always do.

ME: OK, getting back to this concept that …

SE1: It's not a concept, it's actuality.

ME: … OooKaay—the function of …

SE1: That's better.

ME: You're welcome! … Getting back to the function of the multiverse as an environment that is tailored or individualized to the needs of the individualized entity then, does this mean that, to all intents and purposes, the other entities we experience and interact with are not really in existence?

SE1: Yes and no.

ME: Would you care to elaborate?

SE1: Of course. The multiverse allows the creation of "temporary" interactions, the entities and environment/s to support it, and the interaction of other entities in the evolutionary cycle and their individualized aspect of the multiverse to work together concurrently.

ME: Is this a function of Event Space?

SE1: No, this is not a function of Event Space; it is a function of multiversal fluidity and adaptability. However, and this is a big however, this needs to be managed and maintained on a scale the size of all the entities that are in the evolutionary cycle and that is the collective role of *the Curators* at all levels of responsibility. Those responsibilities are what we are trying to discuss now.

As The Source Entity was talking, my mind wandered back to a concept that Dolores Cannon presented in the 2014 Ozark Mountain Publishing Transformation Conference. She talked about the existence of "Back Drop" people. I had presented the concept of "Back Fill" people and she was excited about the name used. It seemed to be used to describe the same advent of temporary or transient individuals that were created by us all to "fill in" the gaps in the background of our existence and experience, just like the painted image at the back of a stage to depict a location or place during a play. As it happened, the names were used to describe entirely different things but right now the concept of "Back Drop" suddenly made clear sense.

SE1: Now you're getting it.

ME: But it seems incredible that each TES, each Aspect, and each Shard has its own multiverse to work with!

SE1: It may seem incredible but from where I am standing, so to speak, the incredible is just simply part of the boring detail.

ME: This is why I like this job, there is always something new to keep me interested, to stretch me beyond my capacity—and more.

SE1: This is what you came here for, to experience being stretched and passing on the reasons for, and the product of, being stretched to the wider incarnate public, so to speak.

Now, though, we have digressed enough. We need to move on to the four levels of function that the Architects are responsible for.

Evolutionary Demand

SE1: As you are now aware, the multiverse is tailored specifically to the demands of the evolutionary requirements of each and every entity within the evolutionary cycle.

ME: So I see, and just thinking about the interconnectivity of all of these individualized versions of the multiverse together with the added complexity of the different Event Spaces we create as a result of our individual and collective choices is hurting my head. This is getting more convoluted by the minute!

SE1: Well, there is more to come, but, it has to be the right juncture in incarnate mankind's existence and your ability and/or others to assimilate the information.

ME: That is so very well understood. A question then, just how do the Architects work on the evolutionary demand of the multiverse? Or should I say, how do they deal with the demands of all of the collective individualized multiverses?

SE1: The evolutionary demand is a function of progress and as such is also subject to individualization and collectivization. As each TES/entity progresses, its awareness of its environment and its level of understanding of that environment changes. I will continue to use the word "entity" to describe a TES (Godhead, Oversoul, or Higher Self), Aspect (Soul), or Shard (sub-Soul) as it makes the dialogue simpler.

Continuing, though, this in turn changes the evolutionary capability of the environment within which the entity is working, its universe within its multiverse. And so, the result of this is that the evolutionary demand changes from one state, that which has been experienced, learned and understood to the point of mastery, to one where there is further growth, using the new level of mastery of the environment as a springboard to progress from, the evolutionary demand therefore being created as a function of progress and growth of the entity.

You are about to ask a question—So how do the Architects address this increase in demand—what do they actually do?

ME: You beat me to it.

SE1: Of course. I just wanted to let you know that I am paying as much attention to you and your thought processes as you are to me.

ME: Thank you.

SE1: Well, it's not a simple answer, although I will make it as simple as possible. The first thing to do is to change your mindset from thinking in the thoughts of a single all-encompassing multiverse to one that is ultimately individualized with the ability to interlink with all of the other multiverse(s) that are attributed to all of the entities that I created. In order to do this, you need to think that you are the most important thing in the multiverse and that you are the only reason for its existence. If you try to consider the "individualized and collective states of multiverse" [*The plural of multiverse is multiverse I am told; my use of multiverse(s) describes the point that one large multiverse houses a number of multiverse. Each multiverse therefore houses a number of universes, all of which are in one large multiverse.—GSN*] then you will fail to appreciate its function on either the individual or the collective levels of manifestation.

ME: Thank you, I now have a datum to work from.

SE1: Good, that's settled then. Now, for YOU, the reader, this is also a most important consideration because when you consider the multiverse in its individualized function, the concepts become manageable, or should I say, open for consideration within the limitations of the incarnate and therefore temporary human mind.

Working with this in mind then, the Architects review the basis of the environmental condition, its localization (universe) and its globalization (multiverse) and how the entity is working with it from a structural, functional, and manipulative perspective. As just stated, they then consider what I will call the level of difficulty that the current configuration of the multiverse offers to the entity and adjust its difficulty according to the entity's ability to work, evolve, and progress with the new level of difficulty.

Evolutionary demand can be considered in the same way as being at school from your perspective. A teacher teaches its class to the level of which he/she is capable of teaching and when the pupil has mastered, to an acceptable level, the material being taught, a new teacher is introduced to challenge the pupil further. The new teacher's role is to elevate the pupil's knowledge further to that of the level of acceptable mastery of the new level of material being taught, and so on. From your incarnate perspective, this is the same for the use of a Guide and its Helpers. Once a Guide has elevated its ward, its Aspect, that is working within the evolutionary cycle to the level of its own competence, and this has happened to all of the Aspects created and projected by the TES, the TES migrates to the next level of its multiversal environment, and a new Guide, of a higher level of experience and evolution, takes control to assist in the eventual elevation of the TES and its Aspects to "its" level of competence, and so on, and so forth. This progression continues until the multiverse and all its potential levels, structures, states, and manipulative ability have been fully utilized.

In both of these examples, and as I have recently stated, evolutionary demand, or pull, becomes apparent when the entity has mastered, to an acceptable level, the evolutionary capabilities of the environment, its structure and manipulation, that level being the choice of the entity and the decision of its Guide/s.

The creation of evolutionary demand (pull), though, does not necessarily mean that the whole multiverse needs to be modified to suit the new level of difficulty or challenge attributed to the elevated progressive needs of the entity. It could simply be that a universe within the multiverse needs to be manipulated, or even, a smaller aspect of a universe within the multiverse needs to be manipulated to offer the best evolutionary progression for a particular entity.

ME: So a multiverse is not specifically modified all in one go, so to speak?

SE1: No, it can be modified globally (whole multiverse) or very locally (a sector within a universe within the multiverse). A sector can be as large or as small as required; there are no rules governing how big or how small the modification can or needs to be to allow the progression of the entity in the most efficient way.

ME: In a nutshell then, evolutionary demand is created by an entity outgrowing the environment's ability to provide it with evolutionary progression, that it has mastered it, and that it needs a higher level of interaction with it to progress. The need to progress in an environment that provides no further progression creates the demand and the need for the Architects to change the multiverse, or an aspect of it, accordingly.

SE1: Correct—good summary.

Cause and Effect

SE1: The Architects work on the "cause and effect" function of the multiverse, individual, and collective. Everything has a cause and effect; there is nothing that can be considered as having no cause to be or no effect on anything else.

ME: Does this mean that even if the only explanation for something being in existence is "just because it is?"

SE1: Correct. For example, "nothingness" has a cause, the cause being nothingness itself. When something happens—whatever it is, however insignificant it is and however small it is, it starts a chain reaction to change the status quo from void to latent intent, latent intent being in place simply because it is. If latent intent were not part of the overall beingness of nothingness, then the status quo would not change. Because though, everything has potential to be something, latent intent is a function of nothingness and as a result what can be called void or chaos is really somethingness as nothingness with the potential or latent intention to be something. That somethingness is activated from that which tips the scales and changes the status quo in the nothingness. You can call it latent intent as I have just described it but note that this latency is a function of void or chaos, for something to be able to be classified as void or chaos it must "be" something.

ME: This reminds me of the discussion I had with a fellow truth seeker, Tom Campbell [*see the* My Big Toe *books, Lightning Strike Books (9 Dec. 2007) —GSN*]. I have not read Tom's books but a reader of mine had introduced us to understand some slight differences in nomenclature that we used to see if there was a disconnect. After a few communications, we discovered that there was no disconnect— just different views of the same picture and different descriptions for the same views of the same picture. As you can imagine, we had some complicated discussions.

SE1: The discussions were necessary for both of you; it was physical proof of the nonphysical, which is very important for you when you are immersed in the physical. And, it's also important for the readers because it gives them a datum to work with.

ME: So now that we have understood that cause and effect is a function of the "environment" at any level, what exactly do the Architects do? It seems to me that it's automatic.

SE1: By and large it is automatic but the Architects have the ability to amplify and de-amplify both cause and effect to ensure that the desires and expectations of the entities that create the cause obtain the correct effect. One would think this was a simple role to perform but when you look at the bigger picture of dealing with local and collective multiversal environments, and the cause and effect they have on each other, you can see how it might be a difficult role to be responsible for.

Going into the work that the Architects perform a little deeper, it is important to note that they also perform a stabilizing function where the extremes of effect that result from extreme causes can create issues with those other local multiverses that are interlinked with the multiverse that is experiencing the extremes of cause and effect.

ME: Why do they create a stabilizing function, I mean, what is the reason behind the need?

SE1: As I have just stated, they create the stabilization between those multiverses that are interlinked and that are part of the collective multiverse. However, I can see that you want some meat on the bones, so to speak.

ME: Yes, please.

SE1: OK. As you are aware, everything effects everything else, whether it is the air you move around when breathing to the water you use and change the composition of when you are washing. What was one thing is turned into something else. The effect of the expired air containing 4 percent more carbon dioxide is caused by you breathing it in and the alveoli in the lungs exchanging oxygen-enriched blood for the oxygen-depleted blood which contains additional carbon dioxide which is a waste product of the body using up oxygen to allow the correct function of muscles, organs, and other important tissues. The magnitude of the amount of carbon dioxide in the expired air is a function of the work performed by the body and the regularity of breathing to support it. Ambient air pressure and altitude also play a part. The effect of the change of the water becoming dirty and full of detergents or soaps is caused by you mixing clean water with soap to remove dirt from your skin, for example. The magnitude of change of the composition of the water plus soap/detergent and dirt is a function of how dirty you are and the amount of soap or detergent needed to remove the dirt.

In the case of the changes to the local or collective multiversal environment, if the cause is significant and that significance can affect other interfacing multiverses, and/or their universal components adversely, it can create an issue with the balance of cause and effect versus the desires and intentions of the entity or entities that created the interlinked multiverse, affecting their evolutionary efficiency and direction in the process.

So in this instance, the Architects act as a filter either stopping the effect or introducing the effects of the effect in a way which can be absorbed by the affected multiverse and not create problems with their evolutionary efficiency and direction. This could be classified as a detrimental effect.

On the other side of the coin, the Architects can amplify the cause if it is seen as having an advantageous effect on those multiverses that are interlinked with the multiverse that is broadcasting the effect of a cause. The Architects can also amplify the effect so that each and every interlinking multiverse experiences the effect at the most efficient level for it. Bearing in mind that we are talking about individual and local multiverses here, the most efficient effect of the original cause will be individualized to each of the interlinked multiverses. It is here where the Architects are most beneficial in their ability to change the magnitude of the functions associated with cause and effect.

I know that this is very high level and not the depth that you wanted, but to go into the mechanics of how each Architect performs its function would be difficult to explain in a way that is understandable. Suffice to say, they make the changes they need to make and ensure that the effect of the causes they work with is maintained in an optimal level of evolutionary performance for every multiverse and their entities, irrespective of who or what creates it.

ME: This means every individual entity's multiverse, those collectives, and the overall multiverse.

SE1: Of course. Let's talk about structure.

Structure

SE1: Structure is a function of what is required to be experienced to affect evolutionary progression; it is not just about the structural aspects of frequencies, subdimensions, or full dimensions.

ME: Are you talking about the content within each of the universes contained within the multiverses as being the structure—or something else?

SE1: The structure of the local or individualized multiverses and collective/overall multiverse, that which I initially created, are fixed to a certain point. That point being the point of commonality.

Beyond the point of commonality there can be manipulation by both the individual entities and the collective. You see, there has to be a basis, a datum to start and work from. Everything else around it is subject to change, even though there is no start or finish in real terms.

ME: And the Architects make the changes, making sure that the point of commonality is maintained.

SE1: Correct. The point of commonality is what allows the local and collective multiverses to be one and the same. The Architects ensure that the changes that are requested are met and the interactivity/interconnectivity of all multiversal conditions are maintained.

ME: Who requests the changes to the structure?

SE1: You all do. All of the entities that elect to work within the evolutionary cycle make changes to their environment to allow them to experience, learn, and evolve in their own particular way. As I have stated, the structure is not necessarily the higher-level structure of frequency, subdimension, and full dimension; it is the content, and you all change the content. Or at least you think you change the content.

ME: What do you mean, we think we change the content?

SE1: What you all see is the product of what you want to see around you. This is coupled together with the point of commonality to allow interconnectivity and interaction with all multiversal environments. But it's at the experiential level you wish to experience different things, and as a result, you create the environment to allow yourself to experience these things. It is your desire to experience in the way you want to experience that is recognized by the Architects, and is subsequently created for you. The lower level structure, if you want to call it that; you can also call it the operational structure and the content associated with it, being the focus of the Architects' "structural" changes.

ME: The difficult bit for me to understand is that, from a human perspective, this is what we think it is.

SE1: I am not talking about what you all do on a day-to-day basis, moreover what is in place that allows you to do on a day-to-day basis what you do. This is the hidden structure, the raw material, if you like.

ME: We talked about environment a lot when we talked about structure. Which comes first, environment or structure? I am getting confused.

SE1: The structure creates the condition for the environment to exist. It also creates the potential for what that environment can achieve, how it can be achieved, and the laws surrounding what can be achieved by those entities that work within it and therefore manipulate it to their own requirements. Structure is, in essence, the building block/s, nanoscopic they may be, to allow creation to be manifest by those who are capable of manifesting. You desire a certain effect and the structure is used by the Architects to create that effect. Even the smallest thought about your environment is actioned by the Architects on your behalf.

ME: What about when I want a certain change and it doesn't happen? Where are the Architects then?

SE1: Provided your actual desire for the change is strong enough and even appropriate, they will have actioned the changes necessary to include your requirements in your local multiversal environment. However, the need to maintain the point of commonality may be such that the changes you desired may not be as effective in the overall scheme of things as you expected. And so, the change will be there but it will be diluted to the point of compliance with the point of commonality.

There is also another issue that the Architects take into consideration.

That is the requirements of the environment itself.

Environmental Requirements

ME: I thought that we create the environment and that we make the changes associated with it?

SE1: You do, but the environment you create has a certain level of autonomy and as a result has its own requirements that need to be satisfied in order for it to exist in this autonomous way.

ME: And what would these be?

SE1: It would be best if I listed them for you. They are based upon the needs of the environment to support the individual needs of a single entity, the environment being a creation within the local/individualized multiverse assigned to that entity.

Reason to be, or need—this is an immediate requirement for the environment that is created within the wider universal and ultimately multiversal environment: its reason to be being why it is in existence in the first place. The reason to be is created by the evolutionary desires of the creating entity and how they can be manifest. The environment is then modified by the Architects to support the reason to be and create a link between the dominant or original creating entity and the environment so that sympathetic changes can be actioned on an automatic basis.

The ability to support individual entities' requirements is an underlying function of the reason to be. The environment will have a minimum ability requirement to allow the needs of the entity requiring its existence to support its evolutionary progression. If an environment is capable of supporting the requirements of the entity while also being capable of complying with the laws surrounding the point of commonality without major modification, then it will remain as such. If the environment will need modification later in its use, then this will be actioned by the Architects, or functions put in place for automatic modification, the maintenance entities working within the environment therefore providing the environments.

Supportability is the inverse of the ability for the environment to support the requirements of those entities that are using the environment. In essence, it is the ability of the environment to be supportable. By this, I mean that it is not overtly complicated to the point of being un-maintainable by the Architects.

ME: Is it possible that a universal or multiversal environment is truly unsupportable, that it is so complicated that it cannot be maintained?

SE1: To date there has never been an environment that is so complicated that it cannot be supported or maintained efficiently by the Architects. This is a functional requirement for the creation of an environment. There is no point in having an environment that cannot truly support the evolutionary or other requirements of the entities that desire, elect, want, or need to use a particular environment, and so there is no point in it being unsupportable.

Think of it in these terms. Currently, modern conveniences on Earth, such as automobiles, are made to such a quality that they should never need to be repaired during the designed lifetime of the vehicle; this is the same for the human vehicle. However, both automobiles and the human vehicle are designed for manufacture and ease of maintenance—ease of supportability. It is this ease of supportability that allows the Architects to work on the maintenance of the environment in the most efficient way possible.

One of the ways of classifying how supportable an environment is, is by the number of Architects and other entities that are required at any one time to support the needs of the environment and the entities using it in the way they are using it. The lower the number of Architects the more supportable the environment is—as is its ease of use [see later—GSN].

You asked a question—if there is an environment that is so complicated that it cannot be supported. I will say no. However, the universal environment that incarnate mankind exists within is one of those environments that is closest to being unsupportable—but this is not as a result of complexity. The physical universe is very difficult to support simply because of the low-frequential state that it exists within, and although its level of complexity is very low as a result of its low-frequential state, maintenance entities are required to work at every level of interactivity.

Sustainability can be classified as the ability of an environment to exist and support the needs of its own environmental infrastructure and the needs of the entities within it on an autonomous basis. When an environment is created or modified to support the needs of the entities using it, its ability to support itself is considered and is a fundamental requirement. The full benefit of the autonomous environment is that it doesn't need to be supported by any maintenance entities. However, this is only correct when those entities that work within the environment work in harmony with it. Any level of disharmonious interaction can affect the environmental balance and create the need for any genre of maintenance entities to intervene.

Using the physical universe as an example, it is fully autonomous and self-supporting. However, there are some incarnate entities that operate in such a way that they are in almost constant states of disharmony with the environment they are within and as such, constant support is required. Incarnate mankind is one of those incarnate entities that is in constant disharmony with the autonomous functionality of the environment they exist within, hence the high number of maintenance entities that are employed and the need for this dialogue to open the eyes of your readers to the level of help required to maintain an environment. If mankind existed in a harmonious state with its environment, it would not need the level of interaction it has with the maintenance entities it currently needs. In fact, it could return to its autonomous state!

Ease of use (changeability) is a function that is part of an environment's level of natural sustainability. As those entities within, or that use, the environment evolve so the need for the environment to change itself or be changed to the new and evolving needs of those entities increases. Entities evolve or have the evolutionary needs of their environment change on either a regular or random basis, along with a local and global basis, so the environment needs to be in a position where it can support both the highly and slowly evolved entities within it at the same time. The ease of use and changeability is therefore of paramount importance to ensure that there is a seamless change experienced by the incumbent entities if they cross each other's natural location of existence.

In this instance and for example, if a highly evolved entity is traveling from one location to another location within the environment, it must be able to access the functionality of the environment that is expected of its evolutionary level at all points, even when it is in an area that is normally and/or naturally supporting entities that are of a lower evolutionary level. The environment must therefore be multiversally adaptive to the demands of all entities of all evolutionary levels even if they are all existing within the same location, without any entity being able to access the level of functionality that is not consistent with their evolutionary level.

Basis for existence (not the same as reason to be or need) is a function of the structural position (location) of a universe within the multiversal environment "in totality." Although the basis for the existence of the universe is not a reason or a need for its existence, the reason and need are built on to the fundamental requirement for its basis. In simplistic terms, it is the foundation for the universe, with that foundation providing all of the raw materials and tools required to create the supportable functionality of the reason or need for a universe of a certain level and functionality to be in existence.

Current diversification from the point of commonality (to support the local and collective requirements) is a metric based upon the number of Event Spaces employed to create the required individualizations of the environment versus the overall mainstream environment. In essence, a multiversal environment or a universal environment within a multiverse that is modified to suit the needs and demands of the incumbent entities has to remain linked to the point of commonality or become individualized to the point of becoming an unsustained environment. The point of commonality is by definition the framework that all variations upon the multiversal theme are based and need to be aligned to.

As the fracturalization of Event Space experienced by a particular entity is based upon the number of its actualized decisions when considering the very local environment of that entity, so the number of diversifications from the mainstream environment is based upon the overall needs and demands of all the entities that use it. When a multiversal or universal environment is created, it needs to fulfill all of the requirements necessary to allow it to be of evolutionary benefit. As the demands of the incumbent entities change the "harmony of fit" between the initial and generalized environment and the demands of the entities working within it change, the evolutionary benefit reduces accordingly. In order to recreate the harmony of fit, the environment is allowed to diversify from its original structure and functionality to one where it "fits" and returns to being of evolutionary benefit and experience with an increase in evolutionary efficiency as a result.

Although it can be seen that a multiversal or universal environment has to be generalized, the incumbent entities also create versions or diversifications from the original structure and function that is relevant to themselves and, of course, those entities that they interact with. Event Space therefore has three functions here:

1. to create the overall diversification from the point of original creation;

2. to create the connectivity to the overall diversification from the point of commonality required to ensure that all diversified environments remain connected to the common theme;

3. that the smaller localized environments are connected to the point of commonality of the overall diversified environment that they are locally diversified from, and that that diversification is connected to the point of commonality within the original creation.

Maximum available diversification from the point of commonality can be expressed in terms of the number of Event Spaces available for the creation of a diversified environment at the levels of both overall diversification and local diversification.

ME: For some reason I feel that this is a function of the structure of The Origin and that this function is based upon the number twelve and its squares [*multiples of the same value—i.e., 12 x 12 = 144—GSN*]. Is this correct?

SE1: Not in the way that you are expressing it, for the maximum number of diversifications is dependent upon the initial level of difficulty, so to speak, of the originating multiversal or universal environment.

The maximum number of diversifications from the point of commonality is that number of environments (Event Spaces), overall or localized, from an already diversified environment, that can be created before that environment no longer has any level of commonality—no matter how small—to the originating creation. Don't forget that Event Space is just the holding/creating space for a particular environmental version and not the environment itself. As discussed in previous dialogues with you [*with other Source Entities and The Origin, etc.—GSN*] when Event Spaces have reached their evolutionary dead end, they converge back to the mainstream Event Space. This is the same for a diversified multiverse or universe because once the diversification has played its role in the evolutionary progression of the entity or entities that are within it, or that have created the diversification, that version is removed from existence allowing the entity or entities to move back in to the next closest environment aligned to them and to the point of commonality.

Number of maintenance entities required is a function of its autonomy and complexity—that being, the more autonomous or simple a multiversal or universal environment is, the smaller the number of entities are required to maintain it. One factor in understanding the number of maintenance entities required is the number of entities that have elected to use that environment as an evolutionary medium and how much diversification they create. Although it is usual for a multiversal environment to have a known number of maintenance entities aligned with it, and that they also maintain the diversifications, it is common for these diversifications to need additional maintenance entities to support those areas of diffuse diversification that are so far away from the point of commonality that they are close to having no commonality at all, while still having enough structure to keep it within the need to be maintained.

The specialization of maintenance entities required is the result of the number of core variants of diversification that are created/have been created. In essence, these are the maintenance entities that deal with the smaller and more obscure differences between a multiversal/universal environment and its commonality with the environment that was originally created. Clearly, there are maintenance entities that have specialist roles to play within the original creation, but this does not include those entities that are "one-offs," so to speak.

Just for interest, the universe that provides an environment for the Earth has a high number of specialist maintenance entities and the highest number of "one-off" specialists. I state a difference between specialist entities and "one-off" specialist entities here because it is possible for entities to specialize in general maintenance— of which there are countless numbers, common specialists, of which there are fewer numbers, but are nevertheless not able to perform general functions even though their specialism may span a number of environments, and true specialists for the maintenance of multiversal/universal functions that are seen in one variant of environmental diversification only.

Spatial requirements is allotment of the aspects of structure that gives an environment the appearance of having space or volume. Spatial requirements are therefore the identification of which frequencies, subdimensional components, full dimensions, and zones are to be used for the creation of the environment and the space or volume that it creates. When a multiversal environment is created, the total number of ways that it can be used by the number of entities that will be using it are calculated and the spatial requirements of each entity throughout its evolutionary cycle is taken into consideration. Also taken into consideration is the function of Event Space and how that will augment the spatial requirements. As Event Space cannot be actively allotted to an environment because it is an integrated and autonomous function of the structure of The Origin, the potential variables of Event Space that can be created within the aspects of structure identified can only be understood by adding and subtracting structural components that are known by the Architects to be malleable or adjustable by them. You will notice that "zones" were mentioned a moment ago, and you may even remember that zones are not part of the current multiversal environment that I created.

ME: Yes, I did wonder. I did see an image in my mind's eye, though, that showed me that the multiverse is constructed within one of the zones allotted as the energetic structure used by the sentience that is you, Source Entity One. I then thought that how could this work because in one of the first dialogues with you, you stated that you split yourself into two—one half being you and the other half being an environmental structure for evolutionary experience, this structure then being populated by all of the smaller individualized versions of you, our True Energetic Selves (TES) that were created to experience the minute detail of that environment. Within this now rather old dialogue, I thought that this would include a full "half" of your structure, not what I would guess is one twelfth of your structure—a zone!

SE1: It was a reasonable but incorrect assumption, one that was not in the right time to correct, for you would not have understood it then. Suffice to say, I will correct it now. Although I have allotted a full half of my sentient energy and structure to my multiverse and its inhabitants, this full half is contained within one zone.

ME: How does that work, I mean, how can you have one half of you residing within one twelfth of you?

SE1: This is purely a function of the spatial mechanics of each level of structure. Everything from every component from one "proper" level can be housed in one component of the structure above it, and so one half of the volume of my structure at the full dimension, subdimensional component, and frequential levels are located within one of my zones, the zones being a level of my structure that are not part of the multiverse you exist within are in fact individually large enough to house all of the structure of the multiverse, so why use six zones when I can use one to do the same thing? This was a calculation I made when creating the multiverse and although from the point of view of full dimensions, the multiverse and all of you is half of me, from the perspective of zones, it is one twelfth. Think of it as being space within space occupying the same space concurrently.

ME: And the need for volume is for what?

SE1: Giving you the space to create, exist, and evolve both individually and collectively without interfering with each other's "space," so to speak.

Frequential requirements is the finitude required to allow the creation of basic structure. Simply put, the higher the frequency, the more basic structural content that frequency can hold. The lower the frequency, the less basic structural content it can hold. Within the structure of an environment—from the perspective of this multiversal environment, that is—it is the state of the frequencies that allows the basic building blocks of an environment to be established. So far, I have only talked about frequencies in the "general sense," but when I talk about the frequential requirements in terms of the construction of a multiversal and universal (within the multiverse) environment, I want you to consider the following:

- how many frequencies

- what types of frequency

- what energies the frequencies are aligned to

- what structural level do these frequencies exist on/within

- what are the functions of the frequencies identified

- what substructure can they create

- what building blocks can they create and at what structural level they are manifest

- what depth of structure can they create and at what level this depth is manifest

- what frequencies can be linked together to create a bigger frequential condition—the creation of bandwidth

- how the creation of bandwidth can be used to link environments together

- what each frequency can create in totality

- the efficiency of creativity experienced by each frequency

- which frequencies can exist within each other

- which frequencies interfere with each other

- which frequencies are universally acceptable—so-called golden frequencies

ME: There is a lot to think about here. I expect that the list above is not exhaustive?

SE1: No, there is of course much more to understanding the frequential requirements of a multiversal environment, including how they can be used to support the connectivity of the higher levels of structure as well. Frequencies can create doorways into and out of the overall structure and can also create the shortcuts so to speak between the structural levels, specifically when considering those frequencies that can exist within each other and/or are universally acceptable to each other.

In summary, though, the basic requirement is captured in the following thought process when creating a multiversal and/or universal environment—what frequencies do I need and how many of them do I require to enable an evolutionary efficient environment to be created?

The Illustrators

Having finished with the Architects and spending some time to reflect on what they are and what they are responsible for, I am very aware that I was given the smallest of overviews by The Source. I was also becoming aware that most if not all of the roles and responsibilities of the entities I am about to enter into dialogue about, effectively work for the Architects. You will also see that they work for each other and work based upon the work of others. So, we appear to actually have a hierarchical structure (rather than a man-made suggestion of one) of entities who work collectively and individually for the evolutionary efficiency of the multiversal/universal environment/s (mainstream and localized) used by those entities that have elected to be in the evolutionary cycle. In my mind, therefore, the work of the Illustrators starts this hierarchy of interactive responsibility. What I was not expecting, though, was the use of The Source's energetic memory as a tool for maintaining the multiverse.

As with all of The Source's (God's) helpers, I decided to introduce the basis of the roles and responsibilities of the Illustrators by using some of the executive summary used at the start of the book as a lead-in to the deeper knowledge about them.

ME: The Illustrators are those entities that work with The Source's overall energetic memory. Although this was referred to as the Akashic records in the summary at the start of this dialogue, the Akashic is only one small part of this energetic memory and is only relative to recording the work of those entities recognized as energetic mankind. The overall energetic memory encompasses all that our Source Entity has experienced through its own work and work with other Source Entities. The Illustrators use the ability to interact with The Source's energetic memory to describe (illustrate) the different possibility scenarios that may be created by making changes to the structure of the multiverse or its local areas, whether new or modified.

SE1: That's a reasonable summary and one that is almost identical to mine at the start of this dialogue.

ME: It was supposed be. I very much feel that these dialogues are different from my previous dialogues and so it will be good practice to remind the readers about the general subject matter before we get into the depth.

SE1: You are starting to get good at this—just watch your ego when I praise you.

ME: I will, thank you.

SE1: Good, I will continue.

The Illustrators have responsibility for one of the more important functions in the creation of an environment. They have the ability to "fine-tune" the evolutionary efficiency of every aspect of a multiversal structure. In order to achieve this, they need to be able to see all of the possibilities associated with a particular multiversal or universal construct and how the incumbent entities affect it, ensuring that the environment is robust and responsive in all possibilities and eventualities.

ME: This very much looks like the Illustrators are working at the level of the individual entity to achieve their work.

SE1: Not just the entity level, the entity, collective entity, environmental, environmental and entity and collective entity levels.

ME: I guess that includes the collective entity levels at all of the locations that entities coalesce in as well, so that would be collectives of collectives as well.

SE1: Yes, and the multiples and permutations of those multiples of collectives and entities and environments. I am looking at you thinking.

ME: What am I thinking about?

SE1: That this is just a high-level understanding, one that sees the multiverse as the environmental condition being discussed and not the environments within the environments as well as the environments created by individual entities as variations from the standard environment.

ME: That's right. I would like to go into more detail later but right now I want to ask you about your use of two words. You said that the Illustrators look at the robustness and responsivity of an environment in terms of its possibilities and eventualities. I feel that the reader knows the dictionary description of these two words, as do I, but I feel that they have a deeper meaning.

Possibilities, Probabilities, Eventualities, and Inevitabilities!

SE1: You are correct. You see, the work of the Illustrators, as already stated, work with the ability of my energetic memory. My energetic memory is really my sentience occupying a certain type of energy that is particularly good at containing (recording) all that my creations and I have experienced and created. They use this energy to work with all that has been in existence, is in existence, and could be in existence in relation to the internal (entity-based—individual and collective) and external (Architect preference) based influences on a particular environment. By using this energy, they can create models of possible environmental conditions by changing the mix of internal and external influence while identifying what mix of influences created the strongest and weakest possibilities.

One thing I will advise you on and that is that possibilities are not parallel conditions. Although they are completely separate from each other, they are interdependent.

ME: What do you mean, they are separate but interdependent?

SE1: Possibilities are a condition of fracturalized choice. Fracturalized choice is a function of upstream and downstream influences and the changes created as a subsequence of those changes being adopted by the incumbent entities of the environment. So, it is the possibilities, created by fracturalized choice that create alternative conditions—parallel environments. Parallel environments, however, are manifest (brought into reality) by a function of a semi-sentient energy called Event Space which pervades all that is—The Origin, and therefore pervades all of me, all of my environment and all of my creations. [*See* The Origin Speaks.—*GSN*]

SE1: Eventualities are conditions that are created by a series of interactive possibilities that create a strong enough event line to pull all other possibilities into a single event—an eventuality.

ME: Isn't this a normal function of Event Space?

SE1: This is not the same as Event Spaces reconverging back into a mainstream Event Space because a mainstream Event Space is a condition that remains as a result of evolutionary dead ends terminating the possibility fractals, whereas an eventuality is a condition where a series of interactive possibilities are strong enough to override the mainstream Event Space creating an eventuality.

ME: So a mainstream Event Space is not a robust singular Event Space that every possibility stems from then. It is simply a stronger possibility than the fracturalized possibilities?

SE1: That's correct. Every event is a possibility, it's just that some are more possible than others and a mainstream Event Space is the most possible outcome—it's not the eventual outcome—it's the most probable one based upon the normalized distribution of fractal possibilities that are created by the incumbent entities of a particular environment. Eventualities are created by, for want of a better word, the skewed distribution of fractal possibilities that are skewed to the point of dominance rather than consequence. Once in the point of dominance, a new mainstream Event Space emerges, and all other Event Spaces eventually converge into that one.

ME: Is it possible then to have a series of possible mainstream Event Spaces?

SE1: It is more likely to be a parallel of mainstream Event Spaces. [chuckle]

ME: I get the joke—thanks. So it is possible to have "a number of" mainstream Event Spaces?

SE1: In the event … [chuckle again]

ME: You really are enjoying this, aren't you!

SE1: Yes, I like the play on words. Continuing on then. In the event that the skewed distribution of fractal possibilities is in itself created by skewed distributions of fractal possibilities, we have the possibility of a number of possible mainstream Event Spaces that have the same potential to become the mainstream Event Space. In this instance, none of them is classified as an eventuality because they are all mainstream.

However, in the "further" event that there is a series of interactive possibilities that are strong enough to override the skewed distribution of skewed mainstream Event Spaces, they will create an eventuality that will succeed in being the mainstream Event Space above and beyond those other mainstream Event Spaces.

ME: So what are eventualities then? I see them as being something that is inevitable in that case!

SE1: No. Inevitability is something different altogether.

ME: What? Are you telling me that there are such things as inevitabilities in Event Space?

SE1: Of course there are—why are you so surprised?

ME: One would think that by now I should not be surprised by anything I channel.

SE1: That you will continue to be surprised is an inevitability. You don't need to write "chuckle" in parenthesis, the readers will have understood the joke easily.

ME: Thank you for your confidence. Tell me what an inevitability is in terms of Event Space.

SE1: An inevitability is the result of a number of skewed distributions of skewed mainstream Event Spaces that end up reinforcing the original mainstream Event Space. An inevitable Event Space is therefore one that can never be superseded, modified, changed, or deleted as a result of any external or internal influence by entity, environment, or space.

ME: Maybe you should have stated that this is what a mainstream Event Space is in reality.

SE1: A mainstream Event Space is not an inevitability though. It can only be called as such when nothing can affect the outcome of that Event Space being the remaining Event Space in a specific evolutionary cycle. This means that the Event Space is robust enough to survive—intact through every eventuality and the probabilities associated with it that may manifest as a result of the interaction of the incumbent entities and/or their various levels of environment—local, global, galactic, universal, or multiversal.

ME: Probabilities, we have forgotten about probabilities!

SE1: No, we haven't.

ME: But I thought that probabilities would be discussed after possibilities.

SE1: No need to.

ME: Why not?

SE1: Because they are not part of the procession associated with possibility—eventuality—inevitability.

ME: I still don't get it.

SE1: That's because in terms of the creation of Event Space a probability is applicable to all three conditions. There can be probable possibilities, probable eventualities, and probable inevitabilities.

ME: I can see that the "probability" aspect of Event Space could be a sort of "wild card." I can even see it as a more affirmative condition of possibility and eventuality. What I can't see is how an inevitability can be probable. I mean, an inevitability is inevitable.

SE1: Not true. You see, when the Illustrators are using my energetic memory, they are looking at everything from a very high advantage point. They are "illustrating" what the outcomes are of certain internal and external interactions—including what they, as a function of the Curators, can, should, might, or will do to the environment they are working with. Based upon this, and from their high advantage point, they can see that certain inevitabilities are probable—are probabilities—if they allow them to be as such.

ME: What you are saying then is that, in my interpretation, an inevitability is something that is a naturally occurring condition that an Event Space can achieve. A probable inevitable Event Space is a condition that is so far upstream in the scheme of things that it is only probable that a certain Event Space will become inevitable, and that it will be able to withstand every eventuality and the probabilities associated with it. It is not by definition an inevitable conclusion—yet.

SE1: That's it. You have it now. You see this is where the Illustrators come into their own. They can see all of this and manipulate the internal and external conditions accordingly to observe all, and I mean all, of the outcomes that can be created—in any and every eventuality.

ME: What is the reason for all this then? I mean, if we have free will to be able to work with the environment that is in the evolutionary cycle, there must be billions of different scenarios that the Illustrators look at. What is the point?

SE1: The whole point is to create an efficient environment for evolutionary progression and that that environment is robust and resilient to all forces. There is no point to building a house on shifting sand; it will collapse—so why build it! If you must build a house, you must create a solid foundation on solid rock. Then and only then will it stand the test of the variability of an infinitely variable environment.

This was a train of thought that I didn't expect, even though I should have. The possibility of so many variables was difficult to comprehend, even though I have spent a lot of the last fifteen years being exposed to such concepts. The most difficult thing for the reader to comprehend, though, would be the sheer variation on the multiversal theme that could be experienced by each and every one of us individually and/or collectively. Additionally, that all of this variability was not only being monitored by a group of dedicated entities, but was understood, managed, and manipulated by them before they were presumably allowed to be accessed by any or all of us was amazing to say the least. The more we discover about our environment I thought, the more we find out that it is controlled by a higher power, one that was also created, and that this environment is convoluted—beyond belief and comprehension.

I know very well that I sound as if I have only just begun to understand what the Greater Reality is, and that this is a dichotomy when one considers that this is my seventh book on the subject. Or, that the level of my unwavering acceptance of the detail that was broadcast by my writing style and thoughts in the six books prior to this one suggested prior knowledge or a deep level of understanding is being dissolved, suggests invention on my part. Well, my answer to these thoughts is simply this. Everything I have received to date is real, it is true, and it is not invented. I have done enough soul searching, checking, calibrating, and double searching, checking and calibrating to ensure this. This is the way of the engineer in me. Test, test again, and test again for a third time before releasing.

I sat back in my chair, my "deck chair!" I was sitting in the back garden of my UK home. I like working outside when I can; it clears the mind. I was wondering why I had typed these words of idle discussion when I was told why. The Source decided to intervene!

SE1: You are always checking to see if you are going mad or that you are being delusional, aren't you?

ME: Yes. For some reason I think I am going backward. I found it easy to communicate with you and The Origin originally. It even became easier when I communicated with the other Source Entities,

SE's 2 through 12. But I seem to be struggling with this book. It feels like it's the same stuff, so to speak, but it's harder to get my head around it.

SE1: Everything to date has been given to you at a level and rate of flow that you could cope with. When you first communicated with my peers, the other Source Entities, you felt the difference and had to concentrate—hard. Since then you have grown to be able to assimilate a level of understanding and broadcast it in a way that could be understood by those truth seekers who were ready. Even though it appeared "deep," it was really surface-level information. Incarnate mankind is not even in the kindergarten stage of connectivity with itself, environment, or thinking capacity to be able to take much deeper information, and you are no different, especially in your current vessel. Constant exposure to such material can create two main thought conditions. One, it can create an ego and subsequent loss of perspective and need to validate that which one receives—especially when one's readers put you on a pedestal. Two, it can create self-doubt as one receives deeper and deeper levels of information which in turn requires a deeper level of understanding, which is not always forthcoming. It is due to being overloaded with the plethora of potential thoughts, directions, and subsequent questions to ask.

If you are not questioning yourself, your environment, that which you are exposed to as higher aspects of that environment and the entities or beings within it that come with such exposure, then one is not capable of working with such depth in a balanced and robust way.

There is a fine line between blind acceptance, understanding, and questioning prior to acceptance. Blind acceptance can be coercive in terms of lack of understanding deemed as understanding that leads to delusion. True understanding is recognized by the individual as levels of understanding and levels of none or poor understanding, which is only achieved through observing oneself from a distance— by questioning the self—being honest to one's self. That you, after so much exposure to Me, my peers, and The Origin can question yourself, your knowledge, your understanding of that knowledge, means that you are maintaining your integrity.

ME: It looks like these thoughts were my ... "greater" reality check!!!

SE1: They are. They are important for you to express, and for your readers to experience you expressing them. It validates who and what you are and what you are doing. You will be in this particular "boat" for the rest of your/this incarnate existence, and, yes, do use it as your "greater" reality check. And don't worry about the feelings of doubt about your ability to understand levels of knowledge that you thought you understood before. The detail may not appear to be much deeper than that which you have broadcast in previous books, and this may be how the readers perceive it, but the energies associated with the detail are different. You are experiencing a more accurate feeling of the level of energy associated with certain knowledge than before, even with that of The Origin and the other Source Entities, because you are not being shielded so much. I know that you thought that, and were told that, the shielding was removed some time ago, but that was to give you confidence to go on. You are now getting to the point where you can stand up for yourself, so to speak. Move on to the next subject now and be confident again—quietly confident, that is!

The Planners

I was still reeling a bit; I was still a bit shaky about appearing to go backward in my ability to understand, especially in the minds of my readers. I knew that this was just the ego, my ego, doing its best to take advantage of my confidence in spiritual/metaphysical matters to bring me down the frequencies and perpetuate its own existence. It was doing this by creating overconfidence and then self-doubt. [See article on the ego in the appendix of The Anne Dialogues.— GSN] *I shuddered. I must be more careful, I thought. No one is safe from their ego—no one.*

I tuned back into a dialogue with The Source to see what role the Planners had in maintaining/controlling the multiverse and all its variants.

SE1: The Planners work to effect a timely introduction of the decisions made as a result of the work of the Illustrators. They achieve this by ensuring that the chosen scenario is actioned in the "reality" chosen for it to exist within. They ensure that the changes are introduced in a seamless way.

ME: I reckon that about sums it up. No need to elaborate any further. I mean, my readers will understand that paragraph in one go.

SE1: They will, but as with all executive summaries, it is designed to give an overview of the subject matter, one that entices the reader to want to know the depth and detail behind the words of the summary.

ME: You are about to tell me that this is another convoluted subject that just appears to be easy, aren't you?

SE1: I could be. Nothing is as simple as it seems.

ME: Yes, I do know that. OK, what's the deal with the Planners?

SE1: The Planners work with the Illustrators but at a different level of interactive structure than the Illustrators themselves.

When the Illustrators work with the multiversal environments and their variants due to probability, possibility, eventuality, and inevitability, they look at the function of the environment from the perspective of the full evolutionary cycle. Even though they use my energetic memory to work with the different variations of static, fractal, and parallel environmental direction, it is a very high-level view.

ME: I am seeing what they see. The Planners are showing me what the Illustrators see. It's obviously a humanized version, but is very interesting. I am told this is just one way in which they see the fractalization of the multiversal environment that they use. I see a simple line, the mainstream Event Space. This line stretches ahead in front of me; I follow it. As I follow it, I see it fractalizing and duplicating/triplicating/quadruplicating, etc., etc. I don't see a multiverse, I just see a representation of a stream of events in all of the locations and frequential states and other structural components associated with the multiversal environment.

This is difficult, I thought. I am expecting to see a multiverse and the division or parallelization of other multiversal environments from the mainstream multiverse in my mind's eye. I have to keep the thought process in my head that I am not seeing a multiverse. I am seeing a representation of a stream of events, the events created by the entities/beings that will be using this particular multiversal environment. "The stream of events; this is the stream of events," I thought again!

As I followed on, I noticed that I could rise above the stream, and move in and out of it as it carried on in its forward motion and fractalized. Then, all of a sudden, everything became blurred, everything appeared to be duplicated, no, triplicated.

Every stream of events, every Event Space appeared to have been duplicated. As I refocused my eyes I see that, from the point of separation from the mainstream series of events, every Event Stream appeared to be exactly the same, but only up to a certain level. After that level, the changes to the Event Stream changed according to the potential for change. From this perspective, the changes looked nonexistent when comparing one Event Stream to another but as I looked closer I noticed that what I can only describe as "the color of frequency" changed. There were the obvious fractals that were created as a result of changes that were in turn created as a result of what I am now being told is attributed to the functions of collective choices. These choices were where whole groups of entities chose a change or alternative direction or a different way to experience the environment that they were in but that which resulted in a dichotomy, trichotomy, or quadrochotomy, etc., etc., where a choice was made after exposure to a number of possibilities or probabilities. However, the changes that were represented by the colors of the frequency were describing the localized changes to the Event Stream that was affecting entities or beings on the individual or small group level. The colors I am being told are what can be called interference to the main and fractal streams of events that were experienced by the individual or small groups of entities/beings but were not significant enough to affect the overall Event Stream, main, static, parallel, or fractalized.

The Planners tell me that the Illustrators work on these overall Event Streams. Changing them as required at both the fractal and parallel level to maintain a level of stability required to allow the local Event Stream levels to function in both an interactive and isolated way to these large Event Streams. They can see the whole evolutionary cycle from this position and can make the changes necessary without being deeply involved in the detail of the individual interactions of entities, beings, or the environment itself if it only affects the environment and is not significant enough to make a parallel or fractal Event Stream.

Seeing the bigger picture and all of its probabilities, potentials, eventualities, or inevitabilities, the Illustrators work on the changes necessary to affect a desired experiential and therefore evolutionary outcome. The Illustrators show (illustrate) the overall outcomes and routes to those outcomes based upon changes to the Event Streams, or not, as the case may be.

Apparently—they are telling me—this is the only method through which I (and incarnate humankind) would be able to digest or understand this information.

SE1: That's right. You will need to wait a moment to see how the Event Stream works with the parallelization and fractalization of the multiversal environments themselves.

To help continue the flow of the description you started, and did so very well, I will carry on to say again that the Planners work within the individual, and small group detail of the Event Streams, those that don't make the Event Streams fractalize or parallelize. Working within the so-called resistance, they see how best to place the result of entities/beings interacting with their environment and those other entities/beings by ensuring that the chosen scenarios are actioned in the "reality" chosen for it to exist within. This means that they weave a series of tentative and stable lines of environment and Event Streams together to create what you may call a reality. The functions of individual, local, and large entity/environmental interaction are classified as "scenario." A reality therefore can be defined as the melding together of environment and Event Stream.

ME: All of the time I see this information, it is represented in a linear way. I know so very well that this is not linear in the Greater Reality and that it is concurrent—that being, everything happens at the same overall event, the same space, the same Event Space.

SE1: Correct.

ME: So why do I see everything in a linear fashion?

SE1: Because, as you state yourself so many times, this is the only way in which you can understand it and observe the functions of what is being presented to you. More importantly, this is the only way in which incarnate mankind can understand it as well. It is more important for you to understand the concept rather than the mechanics behind the concept. Understanding the mechanics requires higher frequency interconnectivity with your TES, which in the low-frequency position you are in is close on impossible to connect with at a high enough level to allow correct understanding at the experiential level.

ME: Should I continue to explain what I see then? Would it be beneficial to incarnate mankind to relay the information in the way that is, quite frankly, limited to our incarnate condition?

SE1: Yes, of course. You have to start somewhere. And so does incarnate mankind, no matter how educated or knowledgeable they feel they are.

ME: OK. I think you are entertaining me a little because I am seeing another representation of the Event Stream, one where each event is a bubble of interaction between entity/being and the environment it is working within.

SE1: I am offering you an alternative visualization, one that although less linear in its representation, is nevertheless understandable to you and incarnate mankind.

ME: Thank you, I will continue. The bubbles (events) grow and explode into another bubble or shrink and implode into nothingness. Those bubbles that are growing sometimes explode into another bubble that is nearby creating a new but combined bubble. At other times they explode into a new bigger bubble allowing them to cope with an expansion of event fractals that are still combined together in the space, the Event Space, which was created for the original and static Event Stream.

Those bubbles of events that shrink and implode either disappear totally, thus representing an end of that particular Event Stream, or they implode and reappear within another event. I am just being told that when this happens, it is because the originating Event Stream bubble fractalized to create a new event bubble and when that bubble has naturally ended its usefulness, it implodes back into its originating Event Stream bubble.

SE1: Good, now carry on with what you can see.

ME: I feel compelled to describe, in a limited way, the function of the bubble. The bubble captures all of the events, the stream of events, and localized interference. The changes that were represented by the colors of the frequency were describing the localized changes to the Event Stream. These changes were affecting entities or beings on the individual or small group level in the more linear description of Event Stream previously described. The localized interference is represented in this instance by the creation of local minute bubbles that appeared to be like froth that ebbed and flowed within the bubble. Again, this is the interference to the main and fractal streams of events that were experienced by the individual or small groups of entities/beings but were not significant enough to affect the overall Event Stream, main, static, parallel, or fractalized within that bubble. All this being said, everything happens in a concurrent way, an instantaneous way, and that includes the creation and destruction of fractalized Event Streams and their spaces within and without their originating Event Stream bubbles.

SE1: Very good. The Planners use a version of the—er—this, real Event Stream [*real time in our language—GSN*] observation to work on how they may make changes to the Event Streams and their environments to ensure that there is no unnecessary duplication of the events they are witnessing. As stated before, they use the energies associated with my so-called memory function to isolate all of these Event Streams in one temporary, but nevertheless fully functional, Event Space and establish the criteria that creates duplication and therefore inefficient entity/being interaction. Once this is understood, the Planners position alternative Event Streams in place that cancel out the possibilities, and of course, all variations of probability, eventuality, and inevitability to ensure that the events and their streams are optimized.

In terms of your personal observations, I will describe this in two ways. In the linear version of your description, you used lines to represent the Event Streams that divided in a fractal way. This would be like an Event Stream that appeared to come in the reverse direction of the inefficient Event Stream and cancel it out at the point of fractalization, in effect making it appear that it did not exist in the first place. In the bubble version, the bubble of events appears to expand and contract, the expansion stopping at the point of inefficiency and contracting back to the point of efficiency. In the case of the Event Stream bubbles that implode, there is no change.

ME: Why is there no change?

SE1: Simply because there is a natural demise of the inefficient Event Stream bubble and therefore the Planners don't need to work with it. That is, if that Event Stream bubble is considered not to be necessary.

ME: Hold on. Are you about to say that an Event Stream bubble or indeed its linear version that is inefficient may still be used by the Planners in some way?

SE1: You've got it. There are times when an Event Stream bubble or a linear representation of an event in an isolated way are useful.

ME: Why isolated? I would have thought that if the Event Stream bubble that would have imploded was considered useful enough to allow its natural demise to be put in stasis, that it should be allowed to interact with the other Event Stream bubbles in and around it?

SE1: No. This is the beauty of the role of the Planners, for they can do just as you say or isolate the Event Stream or let it demise in its natural way. In general, though, they prefer to maintain those Event Stream bubbles that naturally demise but are considered to be useful in isolation as individual cases and upon their own merit.

Know this. Event Streams are an experiential condition that are a necessary function of the need—that is, my need and the need of all my creations to evolve and ultimately progress. If those that are in demise are seen as an opportunity for augmenting our/my evolution and progression, then the Planners maintain their existence as an Event Stream that will be used by both the Planners in the creation of the reality to be expressed by their work and the entities that exist and work within that reality.

ME: Ah! You talked momentarily about what a reality is, that it is the melding together of environment and Event Stream. How do the Planners work with the multiversal environment? Surely the observation of the Event Stream, linear- or bubble-based from my understanding, also includes the observation of the multiversal, universal, or local environment associated with the Event Stream. I say this because they cannot be mutually exclusive when in observation.

SE1: From your position, I would agree that this would be a reasonable thought process. Also, from the perspective of linear thought processes you have on Earth, this would make perfect sense. However, the Planners in conjunction with the Illustrators have the ability to observe event, Event Stream, Event Space, and environment collectively and in isolation so they are able to affect changes to any manifestation of these observations, make individualized changes, and see the effect on any aspect of the reality collectively created by them.

The multiversal environment/s provide the basis for the events and Event Streams to exist, primarily because they are the foundation for the creation of event/s. Even if there is no basis for an environment that can be classified as a universe or as a universe existing as part of a multiversal condition, so long as a "space" is either capable of supporting the existence of entities or beings, or is actually allowing the existence of entities within it, then it can be classified as an environment, and an Event Stream is invoked automatically. The Event Space, of course, having already been invoked to demarcate the difference between the potential to be an Event Stream and an active Event Stream itself.

ME: Which comes first then, the Event Stream or the environment, universal or multiversal? Recognizing that before all of them is Event Space, which is always in existence?

SE1: The space, if you want to call it that, needs to be populated in some way first before it can be called or classified as an environment. Once it is classified as an environment, it then needs to be classified as either a monoversal (local environment), universal (more than one locality that can be classified as monoversal, but within the space that is universal), or multiversal (more than one universal environment).

ME: Do you mean populated with entities or beings (of any sort)—energetic or incarnate?

SE1: Not necessarily. It can be populated with anything that can create an event, a series of events (Event Stream), or the potential or possibility of the creation of an event or series of events. It doesn't need to have sentient energies involved either, just evolution or progression of any sort.

ME: So an environment, of any demarcation, is a "space" for any type of change, the change being the event?

SE1: Simplistically, that's correct.

ME: And I take it that this is an automatic function?

SE1: Yes and no. It depends upon whether an environment is the subject of natural progressive evolution—what you might call Darwinian evolution, or it is the subject of intervention-based evolution. Intervention-based evolution is a function of deliberate planning on behalf of the Curators by the Planners.

When considering the multiversal environments, the Planners can work at any point in the detail from the minutest area of an environment to the largest or total environmental area.

ME: Would you like to elaborate a little on that because I have just seen an image that suggests that they can and do work on a multi-multiversal environment. Is that not an omniverse?

SE1: No, an omniversal environment is a descriptor for the function of the structure of The Origin. A multi-multiversal environment is a structural function, created or not, that exists within a Source Entity. Having said that, Event Space will create the appearance of an omniversal condition simply due to the multiple but parallel environments created by the choice of the entities within that multiversal environment, as you are aware.

What you are seeing is the ability of the Planners to effectively move a part of or indeed a whole universe from one multiverse to another. This is an important function, especially if one or a number of the reality/ies created in one multiverse are not totally harmonious with the overall theme of the multiversal environment that it was originally part of.

ME: Are you suggesting that the Planners can mix and match the universes within a specific multiverse to those of another multiverse?

SE1: Yes, of course. When they take everything into consideration, it may well be that the environment and Event Stream associated with one universe, or part of a universe, is best placed in another environmental location, one that it is in overall harmony with the series of events that create the overall Event Stream.

ME: How does that work, I mean, I would have expected that the Planners work on one particular multiverse and that they work on maintaining the integrity of that multiverse, not take parts of one multiverse or universe and place them in another.

SE1: Remember that the multiverse that you exist and evolve within is that part of me which is reserved for smaller parts of my sentience to discover, work with, and manipulate the fine detail of what I am. This creates multiversal environments that are specific to the actions, thoughts, and behaviors of an individual or a group of individual entities. It is at these levels where the Planners see where one aspect of a multiversal/universal environment is best suited to another. What's more, they do this before the environment itself is allowed to become active—so to speak.

Just what is a reality?

ME: Just a moment ago, you talked about the components that make up a reality, those being the environment and the Event Stream that creates the reality. I really want you to elaborate on this a little because, as I am sure you can sense, both myself and my readers would love to understand a bit more about what a reality is and how we affect it.

SE1: I will try to describe this in a simple overview and then we can delve a little deeper into each one.

In essence, there are a number of types of reality that exist as a function of environment and Event Stream. I will just use the word Event Stream now and not use the bubble- or line- based imagery as a descriptor. They are:

- The Overall Reality (what you call the Greater Reality)

- The Multiversal Reality

- The Universal Reality

- The Global Reality

- The Local Reality

- The Locally Individualized Reality

- The Individualized Reality

The Overall Reality is the experiential condition that is created by the existence of the sentience that is The Origin. It contains all of its personal experiences, growth, realizations, creations, and explorations of self. It is the only reality that can be considered static in function and observation, with of course the possible variations due to The Origin's own evolutionary and progressive growth that creates greater knowledge of self and ability. The overall reality encompasses everything that is, was, and will be, taking into account that everything exists NOW! Please note that The Origin is the only sentience that has the capability to operate beyond the function of Event Space and so variation upon The Origin's reality is not a function of the creation of Event Spaces due to its own opportunities or possibilities, etc., for choice. That is, if it decides to operate above it.

The Multiversal Reality is the experiential condition that is created by the governing entities responsible for a specific multiversal environment within a specific Source Entity. Bearing in mind that we are only discussing the multiverse that I created, it represents the final configuration of the environment in all its detail and scenario of events—the Event Stream—chosen by the Curators as being the optimal environment for evolutionary progression at this particular juncture in my existence. It is a generalized function of reality and is subject to change both by the Planners, other Curator functions, and the interactions of the incumbent entities/beings that are working within that environment.

The Universal Reality is a smaller representation of the multiversal reality insomuch as it starts out to be that when a multiverse and its universal components are first introduced as a medium for evolutionary progression. Universal environments are where the complexities of reality start to emerge as the result of the interaction of entities with entities and their environment. From this point onward reality becomes, for want of a better word, a convoluted interaction of hierarchical conditions that are variations of the original theme, but that have the potential to become in total variance to it while being within an overall theme of reality. The universal reality can only be changed as a result of all entities within that environment choosing to change the reality as a total collective.

The Global Reality is a further dissection of the overall theme of reality. However, in this instance, it is relative to an area within a universal reality that affects a large but not significant number of entities within the universal environment. The global reality can therefore be described in universal terms as being akin to an area the size of a galaxy [*a useful descriptor when considering the physical universe—our universe—GSN*] and the entities that work within the location of that galaxy. A group of entities within the universal environment can change the universal reality within their galactic environment if they work collectively together and choose to work in variance with the governing universal reality that it is within. At this point, we now start to see actively chosen realities within a reality.

The Local Reality is the official start of convolution within realities. This is a reality within a reality within the universal reality. Local realities can vary in size and number of interactive entities. An example of a local reality is one that can be as big as a sector within a galaxy and down to being as small as the population of a planet within the physical universe. Local realities are normally created when a group of entities choose to not only change the function of their interaction with the overall reality, but actively choose to disassociate any previous knowledge of the former reality.

The Locally Individualized Reality is relative to small groups of entities within a local reality, such as those living within a certain country. In this instance, they are aware of the local reality but are unable, for whatever reason but normally due to lack of collective inertia, to change the reality that has been changed for them by more influential entities who wish to create a reality that is for their own overall benefit and have the power to create the inertia necessary to make a localized individualized reality.

The Individualized Reality is what entities with individualized free will choose to create around you. Although you inherently know the local and locally individualized reality you exist within, you choose to weave a reality that suits yourselves—your personality, close friends and relatives, needs, desires, and wants. In some instances, the fully individualized reality can create full separation from the reason for incarnation and sight of the levels of reality around you. Even as incarnate mankind, you are able to change and manipulate your own individual reality bringing into play any possible combination of interpretations of what reality is, could be, should be, and what you would like it to be—in effect making your own individualized multiverses.

ME: Looking at this, a reality is really what we make it!

SE1: That's right. What's more, an entity can create a "surrogate reality."

ME: What's a surrogate reality? I have never heard of that description before.

SE1: You won't have. A surrogate reality is one that is overlaid onto the individual reality by the acceptance of a reality created by another entity for a short period of experience.

ME: We accept someone else's reality in place of our own?

SE1: Yes. In fact, you would be surprised to note that this is quite a regular practice.

ME: OK, OK, how does the surrogate reality work then? I am guessing that it is one where the entity decides that their own reality is not good enough or desirable enough and decides to use the reality of another as a substitute.

SE1: Close. You see, as I stated a moment ago, the surrogate reality is overlaid upon the individual's reality as a function of desire and lack of ownership of the reality they truly exist within.

In effect, all realities are a subsection, or diversification from the original reality, the overall reality, with each subsection being created as a function of the entities/beings working within the multiversal environment they find themselves in. They modify it to suit their requirements, be it multiversal, universal, global, or individual. We/you create your reality based upon your interaction with the environment and its incumbent entities—this I have already stated. In the instance of the surrogate reality, it is created by another entity or group/collective of entities as a function of what they want to experience. The entity/ies who is/are dissatisfied with its/their current reality may desire to exist within another reality but actually cannot due to the constraints of their own interactions within their environment. They are simply not able to manifest or create the conditions that allow them to change their own reality to one that is similar or same as the one they desire. As a result, they live in the reality they have and can create, but dip in and out of a reality that is not theirs by acting out the roles that they would have had, had they been able to change their current reality to the reality that they desire. In effect, they exist in two realities, one that is their true reality and the other that is someone else's reality.

I will give you an example of an entity who has taken on a surrogate reality by using the human condition.

ME: Thank you. I can already feel the words coming through and know the explanation of the example.

SE1: Well, if you feel you already know, I will let you describe the example.

ME: OK, I will do my best. From what I can see here, and using as you said, the human condition as the example, it's like when someone lives in the shadow of another and does everything they can to emulate the reality of that other person. As a result, they may dress, behave, and act like they would do if they were in the reality of that person, but they may not have the capability of supporting themselves and their actions when trying to be in that reality. As a result, the use of that reality as the surrogate may actually create a degradation of their own reality by making them unable to support themselves as let's say financial overindulgence. In fact, I am feeling that there may well be a rejection of the consequences as not being part of their reality. This rejection occurs because they can't believe the degradation—that being a change of circumstances that makes one's existence harder, but where one is not able to actually "see" how and why those changes happened. Therefore, they create a fictional reality that bridges the gap between where their true individual reality was, the desired surrogate individual reality, and the degraded true individual reality. This erases the reason for and the memory of the actions of the entity based upon its desires to exist in the surrogate reality 100 percent of the time, even though it doesn't have the capacity to do so.

I would call this disbelief.

Based upon this then, the use of the surrogate reality has a detrimental effect on the true individual reality resulting in the lack of control of that reality and further dissatisfaction. The surrogate reality, being somebody else's, cannot be affected by its user and so a feeling of being out of control in both the true individual reality and the surrogate reality in their combined states is experienced by the entity, who loses touch with which reality it is actually in. What? I have just picked up that this leads to psychosis???!!!

SE1: Yes, it does. One way to observe yourself moving into a surrogate reality is to notice yourself being dissatisfied with yourself and your environment to the point where you daydream about being in that other reality and plan things out as if you were actually in that reality for real.

ME: We all do that to some extent. I mean, I do!

SE1: Yes, you do, but in your instance you are using visualization to create the next phase of your reality, you are looking ahead rather than just wanting to be in an alternative reality, a surrogate reality.

ME: And that's a significant difference?

SE1: Yes, it is. In effect those who use a surrogate reality have the same mental processes of one who "wishes" that they were in that reality, rather than working on creating that reality.

ME: OK, you stated that the surrogate reality is a temporary condition. Why is this?

SE1: Eventually the conditions that allow the ability to work with the surrogate reality as an overlay to the true individual reality cannot be sustained and the entity falls back into its true individual reality, whether it is maintained as being the same as it was when the entity overlaid the surrogate reality or whether it is a degraded but new version of the true individual reality. In this instance, one could argue that the interaction with the surrogate reality was a function of the true individual reality from the perspective that it was a tool required to make the changes to the true individual reality that are a necessary experiential requirement that the entity chose to make before, in this human example, incarnation.

ME: But that means that the surrogate reality was a true reality.

SE1: Yes, it does—in essence, but not in reality.

ME: Time to move on, I feel.

SE1: Yes, we should.

ME: Wait a moment. We need to describe the function of multiversal environments within Event Streams. What happens to them, how are they affected, and do they affect the Event Stream itself?

SE1: It's interesting that you decided to ask this question just before we were to move on to the Orchestrators!

ME: Why?

SE1: Because you almost missed it, and because they have to work with the changes to the multiversal environment/s that arise from the changes to the Event Stream they are aligned to.

ME: Hold on. This suggests that the statement you made earlier, that *"The multiversal environment/s provide the basis for the events and Event Streams to exist, primarily because they are the foundation for the creation of event/s"* is incorrect. This suggests that it is entities within the multiversal environment that create changes to the events. Event Space is created by a decision process and an Event Stream is therefore a series of events that are not specifically, but do not ignore, a linear progression.

SE1: I think you have missed the thread of our discussion here.

ME: Quite possibly.

SE1: If you remember, it is the decisions made by the entities within a multiverse that creates the need for a new Event Space to be invoked. It is the creation of a new Event Space that results in the start of an Event Stream and the possibility of a subsequent Event Stream which is ultimately a function of the primary or originating Event Space and Event Stream as a "branch" from the originating Event Space and Event Stream. The changes to the multiversal environment that creates this new branch of events and space to support those events, the Event Spaces and the Event Streams, also have a reverse effect on the multiverse that they are aligned to. This means that whatever decisions are made within the multiverse that create new Event Spaces and Event Streams also create new multiversal conditions. In effect, the entities affect the multiverse which affects Event Space which affects the Event Stream which in turn affects the multiverse, and so on and so forth.

ME: That's a rather long-winded way of saying that the one affects the other!

SE1: Yes, it was, but it was necessary to describe the process, even in its very simple state, a number of times to ensure that it is absorbed.

ME: OK, let's continue and draw a line under this subject. I am starting to get a headache!

SE1: I will send you healing energies.

ME: Thank you.

SE1: You asked about the function of multiversal environments within Event Streams. What happens to them, how are they affected, and do they affect the Event Stream itself?

ME: Yes, I did.

SE1: As I have said before, the function of a multiverse is to create the basis for the possibility, probability, inevitability, or eventuality conditions necessary for the invocation of an Event Space and its associated branches of stream. They affect the Event Streams by being the basis for new Event Spaces to be invoked. Each new Event Space has the ability to create a new Event Stream as a natural product of its own creation thereby diluting the Event Conditions and changing them from either possibility to probability or inevitability to eventuality, to illustrate an example. The changes to the Event Streams, created by new Event Spaces within the multiversal environment/s create a change in the multiversal environment as a function of the change in the incumbent entities' interaction with one another and the multiverse they are working within again and again and again.

There you are, I have explained the process all over again but in a different way.

ME: I thought that there would be much more to the question.

SE1: Only insomuch as it has added around six hundred words to the book that may not have been entirely necessary.

ME: OK, you have got me.

SE1: There are only certain ways and certain depths in which this information can be broadcast. All you and your readers need to know in this instance is that everything affects each other. Sometimes, though, I need to repeat myself to ensure that it sinks in!

ME: Doesn't that create a self-perpetuating spiral of change?

SE1: No, and that's the beauty of this discussion. The spiral can be changed or terminated by the actions of the entities within the multiversal environment.

ME: And in the instance that a spiral is terminated by the actions of the incumbent entities, everything would return back to the originating Event Space and Event Stream.

SE1: From their particular point of origin, yes.

ME: And there are many points of origin?

SE1: Yes. BUT, all eventually lead to the Main Event Space and the Main Event Stream.

ME: Is that possible?

SE1: Of course! It's an inevitability!

ME: Why?

SE1: Because at the end of the day, the evolutionary cycle comes to an end and I/we start again. For us to start again, we need to have experienced all that can be experienced, in all of its diversity in my current particular location within The Origin, and, when that happens, all Events, Spaces, Streams, conditions, and environments become one.

ME: Got it!

SE1: Time for the Orchestrators to come to the fore.

The Orchestrators

*I was starting to notice something, no, not something, two things about the information I was channeling. First, that there is a lot of peripheral information surrounding the subjects that I am dealing with and that it is not always linked to the subject heading. I felt like we were digressing on a regular basis. Second, that this information, although at first doesn't have any relevance, does indeed have relevance further on down the line of discussion. This, I am establishing, is a function of subjective opportunity on behalf of The Source Entity, who knows where the timing surrounding the introduction of a specific idea, concept, or description is incorrect for the initial dialogue, but is ultimately correct in temporal relationship with the information that is to follow. Simply put, SE1 knows when to slip in a golden nugget or two **now** to assist in **future** subjects of discussion.*

I am sure though that you, dear reader, will have already sussed this out and will be wondering why it has taken me so long to spot it. Well, I will say this, sometimes it is very difficult to see the wood for the trees and from where I am sitting, there are an awful lot of trees and there is an awful lot of wood! This being said, all of these digressions form part of the bigger picture. It would be boring to concentrate on the one small part of the picture without sitting back on occasion to gain a glimpse of some parts of the bigger picture, specifically when these glimpses help one to understand the little part of the picture we are working on understanding.

In thinking in this way, I felt happy about the digressions, knowing that ultimately they are just as important as the information relating to the subject heading. I felt the need to move on—QUICKLY!

ME: Do you want to summarize the work of the Orchestrators?

SE1: I thought I would let you do that.

ME: I will try not to just cut and paste the information you summarized.

The Orchestrators are like managers; they control the work specified by the Planners. The Orchestrators operate at all of the levels associated with the work and activities of the Planners, operating a top-to-bottom approach to the management of the changes/creations required to be actioned. They are involved from the start to the finish of any of the actions initiated by the Planners.

SE1: Good start. I couldn't have done better myself.

ME: Well, it was your summary.

SE1: Yes, it was. As you know, though, this is just a minor overview and in no way gives any indication of the detail that the Orchestrators work on.

Individuality: A Natural Function of the Growth of Sentience (An Informative Digression)

As The Source was talking to me, I started to feel a little lost in the subject. I started to gain some information that, from my mind, almost negated the need for this extended dialogue and ultimately this book. What I mean is that everything and every entity in control of certain aspects of the multiverse/s were more than just linked together. I could see that although they were working for and in support of each other, they were, moreover, all the same being. Additionally, that the beings I had just started to discuss, that is all the beings we had written about so far in the book, which included all those to come, were just human expressions of functionality, of individuality. It very much felt like these beings were just facets of specialized functionality within The Source that were designed to maintain and manipulate the area or volume of its structure—its self, that was a further larger—much larger area of specialization used as an environment, specialized for reasons of automatic evolutionary growth. All of this included us, or should I say our TES and us as projected aspects of TES.

Everything is one, everything is a function of The Source, and there is no real individualization. Individualization is a function of incarnate mankind's thinking process which in itself is a function of the near total isolation of the Aspect from the TES resulting from the insertion into the lowest frequencies of the multiverse and a vehicle to experience them through. We are but quarks in the atomic structure of The Source, quarks with a purpose.

That made me start to think more when The Source interjected.

SE1: Yes, of course everything is one. Just as incarnate beings are smaller specialized functions of me, so am I a smaller specialized function of The Origin. Everything is one, all of the functions repeat themselves up and down, forward and backward, left and right of the scale, so to speak.

ME: It's just that I started to think that trying to explain everything in terms of separate isolated and individualized entities is futile when we think in the "all is one" thought process.

SE1: You could and you can argue that, but I will give you an example as to why it is beneficial to think in the way of individuality as well.

This is going to be a showstopper, I thought. I knew in the back of my mind that the accepted higher spiritual thinking process resides in support of the formless and the concept, the ultimate truth, that "all is one." This is going to be difficult to explain to the higher thinkers because individuality, in their/our minds, is a backward step.

SE1: Why is it a backward step when it is part of the Greater Truth surrounding the Greater Reality?

ME: What? What do you mean?

This is not the start to this chapter of the book I was thinking of. Why do we need to consider individuality within the context of the Greater Truth and Greater Reality?

SE1: Because it's a function of what it is. Listen, I will explain this again for you and your readers.

The Origin is an individualized function of sentience within a vast unfathomable area or volume of "all there is"—it is "all there is" as a result. As an individualized function of sentience, that sentience can and does grow. As it grows so does the need for specialization of that sentience. The need for specialized aspects of sentience is therefore a natural evolutionary condition that occurred as a result of The Origin's desire to experience and express itself. When sentience desires experience, it is limited by its own individuality so it divides its sentience into specialized areas of sentience assigning it "a body of energy" [*some energy to work with—GSN*]. These areas of sentience, through specialization, gain individuality, a personality if you like, allowing the larger area or volume to experience different things simultaneously rather than individually. So, individuality gives birth to simultaneousness as a function of collective individuality, which is a function of synergy.

Without specialized aspects of sentience, there can be no progress or evolutionary growth, there can be no Origin, no Source Entities, no Om, no TES, no Aspects of TES, and no Shards of Aspects of TES.

Yes, everything is one, but one, being "all there is," is full of areas of individualized and specialized units of sentience, and sentience given a body of energy to express, experience, learn, and evolve through. BUT—you all say—individuality does not exist in the Greater Reality. Individuality is a temporary illusion. I will say this: individuality is the maintenance of the illusion of individuality, and as such exists, for the illusion cannot exist without the prerequisite conditions that allow it to exist in the first place. In this case, the prerequisite is the creation of individuality or specialization of sentience which in itself creates individuality.

So, in summary then, those small areas or volumes of individualized sentience, given a body of energy, upon gaining specialization also gain personality as a function of the signature that sentience gains through specialization. That signature is a function which can be used as a name, the name also describing the function creating a function—the individuality—specialization loop. This therefore justifies the demarcation of specialized sentient energy as individualized "beings" in their own right, and, in your case, the need to describe them, their function, and their corresponding signature or name—hence the need for this book.

ME: You were reading my mind again!

SE1: Of course and always. That's how I communicate with you. That's how we all, that is everything, communicates in the Greater Reality.

Having justified the need for individualization/specialization of sentience given a body of energy and the reason for names to describe the function and signature of that sentience, I felt much happier. Everything can be individualized and or specialized while remaining a function of "all there is" and therefore being one. It all made sense.

And Back to the Orchestrators!

ME: The Orchestrators—seems like the name describes the function nicely.

SE1: All of the names used in this dialogue are designed to be informational and descriptive in the human sense, and this is no exception. It would make no sense to describe something in a way that had no relationship to the current level of knowledge of incarnate mankind; even if it is cutting edge, it needs to have a common datum. The Orchestrators as a descriptor is no exception to this.

ME: You are sending me an image again, one where I can see the Orchestrators literally flying around from one place to another, managing the work of the Planners.

SE1: That is one way of seeing it. The Orchestrators are, for want of a better word, the managers of the multiverse.

Before I continue, though, I have come to a conclusion about the depth of information we need to work with here. I know that most of the dialogue to date has revolved around the wider environment, including the more diverse functions of Event Space and Event Streams and its effect on the multiverse at all levels of interaction from collective to local and individualized. This I feel is OK for now, and, that from this point onward, I feel that we need to focus on the multiverse from a static perspective, one that is based upon the dominant structure of the multiverse and not the variations and causes for variations that can be observed, manipulated, and experienced as a result of the interaction of the incumbent entities. Although, even though I say this, it is possible that we have to make reference to the wider subject if necessary.

ME: I understand but I feel that incarnate mankind can deal with this level of detail. I mean, it's not all that deep, is it? And I wouldn't want to think that we are withholding something from the readers.

SE1: We can delve into the depth as appropriate. It's just that I want to focus on the basic management of the multiverse for the moment at least. As you request, we will delve into the detail if it is appropriate to the overall understanding of what is being described.

ME: Good. We all appreciate it. However, I do want to understand why you wanted to limit the depth of the information, the real reason, that is?

SE1: It's simply a matter of popular understanding. To date, and this includes the text in this dialogue, the information you, I, the entities you have created a dialogue with, including the other Source Entities and The Origin, has been difficult for most people to understand. Being difficult makes it less popular and only available to those who are able to work at this level. I wanted to ensure that from now on, we can make it more available. However, I see that upon reflection, we have already missed that particular boat, and editing this text to make it easier to understand would be detrimental to the subject matter. I propose, again, that we keep it simple and note that, as spiritual people always state, it will be useful to those who need to know and can use it for their own progression. My other thought is that most readers will look at this only from the perspective of the physical universe and not the overall multiversal environment.

I was a little confused here as The Source is usually decisive about things. This showed an element of indecisiveness and for me, some cause for concern. Fortunately, this was quickly "jumped on" by The Source, who further defended the decision with ease.

SE1: What you can't see is the level of detail that we can get into that is beyond the remit of the title of this book. It is always important to give what is expected from the title and not digression. Having said that, a little digression is good light entertainment, especially when the information is difficult to grasp. It allows the information to sink in slowly.

Now then, the Orchestrators appeared to you as being here, there, and everywhere because they work on all aspects of the structure of the multiversal environment from full dimension to subfrequency, which includes the content within the subfrequential levels. The Orchestrators are the first level of Curators that are involved with multiversal environmental content and not just structure or the effect on structure appropriated by those entities that work within the structure to evolve.

ME: Do you mean that they work on both structural and content maintenance?

SE1: Yes. We can break it down into functions later, and maybe they are best described in terms of the chapters that focus on the physical universe, but because in real terms they work above the frequencies of the physical, they are best described here.

The Orchestrators apportion groups of entities that are dedicated only to doing the work and not specialized areas of work.

ME: Hold on, are you suggesting that there are nonspecialized entities?

SE1: I would call them General Entities. Their specialism if you like is to be nonspecific to any particular task. They accept the opportunity to work with any aspect of the maintenance of the multiverse and delight in doing so. They enjoy the diversification associated with not being specialized and draw great individualized progression from being in general use. In some respects, these entities—entities that have no specialization and therefore no name, and up to now, no place in this dialogue/book—are the most capable entities within the roles and responsibilities of the Curators. I think that we should deal with them after the description of the Orchestrators and give them the recognition that they deserve.

ME: I agree.

SE1: Getting back to the subject at hand then. The Orchestrators use the generalized maintenance entities to work on both the structural functions of the multiversal environment and the content within it. These entities work in parallel with the specialized entities that are required for areas of operational focus.

This is important because the specialized entities are just as they are described, specialized, and deal with the detail behind their specialism, whereas the generalized entities can work on both the higher levels of the specialized areas of focus and the links between them. The general entities therefore move between the specialisms creating a homogeneous representation of the desires of the Orchestrators within the different areas of structure and content that they work with.

ME: Forgive me for saying so, but this looks like the generalized entities do all of the work and the Orchestrators do nothing but manage the work required and the entities that are assigned to do that work!

SE1: That is why they are called the Orchestrators.

ME: This particular description is destined to be short I expect because their role is somewhat obvious.

SE1: Is it?

ME: Mmm ... I feel that you are playing with me a little, like, their role is somewhat bigger.

SE1: Of course, it is. As I started to say, the Orchestrators are the first, or should I say, the highest of the Curators, considering the top-down description we have had to date, that are involved with both the structure and the content within that structure.

When involved with the structure of the multiversal environment, they ensure that the main stream, or for want of a better word, the static unchanging aspects of what the multiverse is, from an evolutionary perspective, are maintained as such, in an unchanged state. There has to be a dominant structure, a mainstream structure to evolve through, and it is the role of the Orchestrators to ensure that this dominant structure is maintained.

ME: We have discussed this before when we talked about main Event Streams and that everything that is created through choice is a variation from the main Event Stream and main Event Space. We have also talked about all of the different levels of multiversal environment that are created by the incumbent entities and the choices they make, so what is so special about the Orchestrators maintaining a static multiversal structure?

SE1: The overall requirement for all of my creations is to experience all of that which I have given to be experienced. How you all experience it is up to you. The series of choices that are made by you while progressing through the structure of my creation is therefore individualized. I created a segmentation of my own structure to be used for experiential and evolutionary purposes, and through changes brought about by all of your individual and collective decisions, that which is me therefore changes to that which you desire to experience.

As with the creation of different Event Space and Event Streams, the multiverse has a vast number of multiversal and therefore universal environmental variants that fit in with the changes to the events that are created through choice, each of them are a deviation from the originating and therefore dominant multiversal and universal structure. The Orchestrators ensure that this dominant, original, or primary structure and the content that is associated with it is maintained as such. They, along with the entities that work with them, work on all levels of the multiversal/universal structure and content, making modifications to the changes created by the incumbent entities to make sure the originating content and structure is maintained as such. There can be no changes made to the originating structure and its content for this is the datum that everything that is experienced and created is compared to. Everything else is just an illusion, a temporary condition based upon ultimate choice. [*After this text was written, I was told by The Source that an illusion that is experienced can also be classified as a reality, even if it is temporary.—GSN*]

ME: So do the Orchestrators only work on maintaining the originating structure and content?

SE1: Primarily, yes, but ultimately, no. They keep the originating multiversal structure and its content as it was in its newborn state, so to speak, in the way it was when I created it, or should I say, segmented it. Everything is unchanged, everything is pure, everything is perfect. The Orchestrators work on all levels to keep it this way.

ME: So when in the Traversing the Frequencies workshops, we project our consciousness into the self-contained simultaneous universal environments that are within the multiversal structure, do we visit the originating multiversal environments or do we visit the variations that we individually and collectively create through choice?

SE1: You move into the originating multiversal/universal environments, while your incarnate aspect remains in the individually and collectively created variant of the multiverse and its universal environments.

ME: We are in two places then?

SE1: No, you are in as many places as you have had decisions from both an Aspect of your TES and your TES itself. You, as the Aspect, are in the universal variant resulting from individual and collective choice while your TES remains within the originating universal environment within the multiverse that it is associated to as a result of its evolutionary level.

ME: So our TES is not affected by choice, or the different Event Streams and Event Spaces that are created by us as Aspects of our TES then?

SE1: Indirectly, yes, because you as a projection of your TES are working within a universal variant and its content of the originating multiversal/universal environments that has been/is being created and modified through individual and collective choice within the location of your Aspect. However, from the perspective of evolutionary progression of the TES, this is a stable and static structural function and as such is still as it was when I created it.

The Orchestrators therefore work on maintaining the originating multiverse, its self-contained simultaneous universal structures and its content. This is achieved in terms of what is within the self-contained simultaneous universal environments as a tool for evolutionary progression of the TES. The Orchestrators also work on maintaining the variations of these self-contained simultaneous universal environments and their content that is created through individual and collective choice.

Ensuring that the original multiversal/universal environments and their content is unchanged is a challenge but only requires one group of entities in one reality, one Event Stream and one Event Space, so to speak. Working on making the changes that ensure the structural and evolutional efficiency of the multiversal and universal environments and their content are in line with the decisions resulting from individual and collective choice in all of the Event Spaces and Event Streams is a bigger challenge, one that requires the Orchestrators to work within one environment and its content but within all of the variants that are made through choice.

ME: You talked about the Orchestrators working with two types of entities, specialists and generalists, and that the generalists are the most useful entities because they can be utilized across a whole range of specialisms, but not at the same depth as the specialists themselves.

SE1: I did.

ME: Does this include those entities that maintain the content, such as the nebulae, galaxies, and planets in the physical universe and the equivalent areas of local density in the other universal environments?

SE1: Yes, it does, although those entities that work right in the detail of local areas of density you call planets are the most specialized entities within the Curators.

ME: How do you mean?

SE1: Think about it for a moment. The entities that you are talking about work on things like soil, grass, bacteria, a certain genre of tree or plant, or even the weather system. They are right at the front line of environmental maintenance. What's more, these entities are only working on their specialism on one planet in one part of the galaxy in one part of the universal environment that they are assigned to. They are not just specialized, they are highly specialized, and as a result there are very few generalist entities working at these levels.

ME: So the Orchestrators wouldn't use generalists at these levels then?

SE1: Not unless there is a lot of work to be done that needs extra help.

ME: When would a Curator at this level require extra help?

SE1: When the entities that are in the evolutionary cycle at the incarnate levels make a mess of the environment in a major way.

ME: I guess the Earth is close to needing help now.

SE1: Not in the areas you would think. You all focus on pollution, but the biggest issue is the loss of ecosystem components such as trees and smaller animals and fish. Pollution can be solved overnight by stopping the processes that create the pollution, but regeneration of the ecosystem needs to be done in line with the local Event Stream, which in your terminology means real time, so based on this, an ecosystem can take decades to recover, even with help.

ME: This tells me that at the lowest levels the Orchestrators need to have one entity for one job, so to speak.

SE1: Close. For each universal environment and its content within the multiverse there is a common but uniquely assigned group of entities specifically assigned to a universe. This means that the number of entities working on the maintenance of the environment is multiplied by the number of universes, at least.

ME: I have just seen an overall image of the number of maintenance entities required at the physical levels of the multiverse, it's almost infinite, like there are more, much more working on the maintenance than actually involved in the evolutionary cycle, the number of entities working in the physical aspects of the multiverse, the physical universe, requiring more than others.

SE1: Yes, that's correct. Although there are duplications in terms of the numbers of specialized and generalized entities working for the Orchestrators when one looks at each self-contained simultaneous universe, that being, they only work in a specific environment within a specific universe. There is more opportunity for these entities to work across universal environments, or be more generalized when they are assigned to those self-contained simultaneous universal environments that are contained within the higher frequencies of the multiverse.

ME: I would have thought that the higher up the frequencies, the more entities are needed because the resolution of the frequencies is higher and therefore the environment can support more content.

SE1: Not so. You see, as the frequency increases, so the abilities or functionality of the maintenance entity increases as well. As a result, the subsequent increase in workload is balanced out by the increase in functions and abilities available to the entity at that increased level.

ME: That's a surprise.

SE1: Why?

ME: I didn't expect to hear that the Curators, at any level, are restricted in any way other than specialism.

SE1: As you are aware, lack of functionality and connectivity is a function of the lower frequencies and everything and every entity is affected.

ME: I thought that it was just incarnate entities that were affected by the lower frequencies?

SE1: No, it affects all entities, and it is particularly difficult for those entities that are working in the frequencies associated with the physical universe. We will discuss this further when we work on describing the roles and responsibilities of those entities that work with the Earth.

This was new news to me. In fact, I was very surprised. I fully believed that the entities that worked on the maintenance of the multiverse would be immune or outside of the rules or functions of the multiverse as we as incarnate entities would experience it. To find out that this was not the case was a real revelation. The Curators were bound by the same rules as the entities they were in service to! I didn't expect that one, and I don't suppose any of my readers or other metaphysisists or spiritual leaders would have either. On the other hand, though, it did make sense and it would help me forge more searching questions later on in this dialogue.

What Does the Maintenance of an Environment Mean to a Maintenance Entity?

This thought process has made me pause for further thought. Just what does maintenance of an environment mean to an entity? Especially, when the entities that maintain the environment are affected by the very nature of its frequential state. I know that I am repeating myself with this thought process but it's a good thing to do. It gets it clear in one's mind. I sat and considered this thought process for a moment. One: For each universal environment and its content within the multiverse there is a common but uniquely assigned group of entities—specifically assigned to a universe. This means that the number of groups is multiplied by the number of universes. Two: These entities are separated to work on essentially two versions of the environment they are assigned to, the original static environment, and those that are created in parallel by Event Space through the choices of the entities that are in the evolutionary cycle within the environments. Three: These entities have to work within the constraints of the environment they are assigned to work within, even though they are capable of working outside of the environment itself. The first two thoughts made sense, it was a process I could work with, it just made sense. This last (third) thought made me think deeper and ask for guidance. First, though, I was drawn to an image of a memory I had circa 2003 when meditating by the trees in the garden in the mornings with Anne before traveling to work. I saw a nature spirit, an Elemental. It was a ball of energy that changed shape, a rather spiky shape, to allow it to work on the plants in our garden. The notes I made were destined to become The History of God *but I had no idea that they would resurrect themselves in this text. As I focused upon this memory, I remember thinking that this entity was very close to the frequencies of the Gross Physical but I had no further thoughts on this fact. Neither did I note that they must be seen by other incarnate entities that exist on the fourth frequency upward, so what does maintenance of an environment mean from the point of view of the entity?*

SE1: I can answer that one for you. As you will be aware from the dialogue we have had over the last few months [*11 months— GSN*], we have talked about the structure within the structure of the multiverse and its environments and that the entities that maintain these environments use this structure to both move around the environment and work within it.

ME: Yes, we did, I am working on remembering it right now.

SE1: Good. I will send you an image and some data to support the image.

ME: I am receiving it. I can see more of the scene associated with the memory I have of the nature spirit/Elemental in 2003. Oh, there is more than I remember.

SE1: There is more than you saw as well.

ME: Go on; explain!

SE1: What you are seeing in this image is what YOU saw and what REALLY happened. What you saw was just the entity working on the plants in your garden, tending to their energetic needs by linking them up, momentarily, to the energy vortex that is in your garden to boost their energies.

ME: Yes, that's what I saw.

SE1: The rest of the image is now what happened before and after the image you saw. The entity clearly was working on the fourth frequency, what you call the lower astral. On this level, the entity has to obey the laws of the multiverse attributed to this frequential state and so is limited as such. However, what you don't know is that these entities can work around the limitations by projecting an energetic sheath around them that maintains their natural frequential state and therefore their functionality. So, they are affected by the frequencies of the environments that they work with, but they can work around it. The issue here, though, is that in maintaining the frequential state of the entity, this sheath effectively stops correct interaction with the frequencies of the environment. The entity is therefore stuck in a cleft stick: interface with the environment and lose functionality, or shield itself and lose the ability to interact with that environment. In the higher universal environments, this is less of a problem but in the lowest of the frequencies, the physical universe, this is a real issue.

ME: How do they get around it then?

SE1: They allow part of themselves to be outside of the energy sheath whereas the major part of them stays within the energy sheath. In this way, they have the ability to work with the energies of the universal environment in the way they are supposed to, in the only way they are actually able to make their modifications while maintaining their functionality. If you look closely at the image I sent you, you will be able to understand.

As I focused on the image The Source gave me, I was greeted by an interesting phenomenon. The entity I saw in 2003 was used as the example. The entity was as I saw it all those years ago, a ball of spiky energy floating over the grass. However, as I looked more closely, I noticed that the image was ever so slightly blurred. It took a lot of time to see this blurred state as the image was almost clear and crisp. As I looked closer, I noticed that there was a difference in the local crispness of the image. It was just slightly blurred up to the point of interaction with the plant it was working with. At the point of interface with the plant, the image became clear and crisp with no sign of blur. I also noticed that at the interface of this blurred area, there was a barely perceptible change in the color of the image; it was a rose or transparent pink color. This, I thought, must be the interface between the normal frequential state of the Elemental entity and the frequential state of the aspect of the plant that was represented by the fourth frequency. In this condition, the Elemental entity or nature spirit was able to continue to function according to its natural frequential state and deal with its workload in the frequencies associated with its areas of responsibility. It was fascinating to see the detail behind this old memory-based image. In the lowest frequencies, one has to work like a deep-sea diver using a dry suit, who, while at great depth, takes his glove/s off to work with more dexterity on the details of his work that cannot be dealt with while he has his gloves on. The body of the diver is in an air-based environment while his hands are in the water-based environment, a cuff seal keeping the water out of the main body of the dry suit while the hands are in the water to do the work—the diver is therefore in two environments concurrently.

ME: Now I understand. A maintenance entity not only has to deal with its own responsibilities and workload, it also has to deal with the vagaries of the environment it is working in while maintaining its own frequential integrity. It's hard frequential work!

SE1: Correct. And now you know, in summary, what it means to an entity to maintain an environment, because a maintenance entity needs to maintain its own local environment as well. In this way, it maintains, in this example, its own invisibility with those other incarnate vehicles that exist on the fourth frequency level allowing it to complete its work in an unnoticed and unencumbered way.

The General Maintenance Entities

I decided to move away from the mainstream discussion on the roles and responsibilities of the maintenance entities that I was given at the start of this dialogue and make a small detour to focus on the general maintenance entities that I was advised of during one of my recent communications with The Source, the General Maintenance Entities. I know that I discussed the roles of these entities to some degree before and I ask the reader for patience here. I just have a feeling that there is something very important and unique about them, something not apparent from the information that I have received so far. Their role seemed just a little too simple.

SE1: You're getting better at seeing the leads I give you.

ME: Oh, I feel like I have just passed a test or something!

SE1: Not a test, just the ability to see the possibilities that are presented to you when they are presented to you.

ME: It was a test then!

SE1: Call it what you will, it keeps you on your toes and keeps your ability to question fresh.

ME: OK, now I understand. Let's get straight to the point. What is it with the General Maintenance Entities that makes me want to go over this ground again?

SE1: We briefly discussed that they are possibly the most important classification of Entity in the hierarchy of Curators, did we not?

ME: Yes, we did.

SE1: Then they deserve to be represented properly.

ME: Well, that's really what I am asking for.

SE1: I know, I am playing with you.

ME: Again!

SE1: Again. You need to lighten up a little and enjoy this role.

ME: I know, I know.

SE1: Good, I can see that you have lifted your spirits a little and now that that has happened we can start.

The General Maintenance Entities are a universal resource. I use this statement because these entities are not just able to be used by any of the hierarchy of named entities previously discussed and due to be discussed, they can also take the place of any of these entities.

ME: You mean they can be Orchestrators, Architects, or any of the other mainstream specialisms?

SE1: Correct. You see, they are not just, how would you call it, "dogs bodies," "gofers," or "laborers"—they are entities that are fully capable of taking on any of the roles and responsibilities in the structure and hierarchy of the entities called the Curators.

ME: They really are fully universal.

SE1: Yes, they are. The General Maintenance Entities need no instruction or training in terms of the work that they are enlisted to work on, they just pick it up.

ME: What do you mean, just pick it up?

SE1: I will explain further. Whereas the other entities, at all levels, are specialized for and by the work that they elected to do and/or were chosen to do, these entities choose to be generalized, so to speak.

ME: Generalized! What do you mean by saying generalized?

SE1: They have the ability to "program" themselves, if you like. They change their specialism from being general to being the specialism that is required for the role they are asked to perform in the short term.

ME: Ah, so their role is only considered to be a short-term condition when they are asked to perform a role?

SE1: Yes, it is always a short-term role that they are employed to work on.

ME: So what you are suggesting is that they are blank, sort of neutral, role-wise, until they are asked to perform the role they are asked to do.

SE1: That's one way of saying it, yes.

ME: So, they do the role, then they go blank until they go to the next role?

SE1: In a way, yes. When they have finished a role, they have an option. In fact, they have a number of options.

ME: You mean they can choose what to do next, what their role is going to be next?

SE1: Yes and no. I will elaborate. At any point in their role, they can be called upon to stop the work they are doing, change role, or go back into an area in the environment where they can wait for their next role. Additionally, they can elect to stay in a role if continuous additional resource is required or they can seek a new role. The opportunities they have are therefore as follows:

Stop work: In this instance the General Maintenance Entity has two options to consider. One, they are being requested to stop work because the need for them as a resource is no longer applicable for the role they are currently in. After this, they will then return to generalization. Two, do they feel that their contribution is no longer necessary and that if they stay in the role they are currently in they will create inefficiency? Once this decision has been made, the entity returns itself to generalization.

Change roles: Is a function of the entity either requesting a role from any of the other entities within the specialized hierarchy of the Curators, or seeing a role and individually electing to go into that role on a permanent basis. In this and all instances of role activation, the generalization of the entity is rescinded and the entity becomes specialized. Note that this only happens when it is recognized that there is a need for a more specialized resource, so to speak, within a certain function within the multiversal environment that the General Maintenance Entity was working within.

Swap roles: It is possible for a General Maintenance Entity to actively swap roles with a specialized entity. In this instance, the General Maintenance Entity gives up its "generalization" and becomes "fixed" into permanence, so to speak, in the role it has taken from the specialized entity with which it has made an agreement to swap. The previously specialized entity therefore becomes the General Maintenance Entity actively inheriting all of the functions and experiences of the previous General Maintenance Entity. The previously generalized entity also inherits the functions, experiences, and experience of the previously specialized entity. In this instance, the swapping process is nonreversible from the perspective of the entity that was the General Maintenance Entity because it is no longer generalized. Indeed, the only way it can return to being generalized is if the entity it swapped with requests the swapping process to be reversed by actively swapping with the entity it swapped with in the first instance. Alternatively, though, the previous General Maintenance Entity, now specialized, can return to specialization if another General Maintenance Entity elects to swap roles with it. In this instance, it inherits the functions and experiences of the General Maintenance Entity it swaps with and not those it had in its previous generalized state.

Stay in a role: Staying in a role is usually at the request of a specialized entity if it sees the need for the General Maintenance Entity to continue in the current role it is being employed in. This is usually requested if there is a significant amount of work to do relative to the temporary state of specialism that was not previously understood.

Return to neutrality (generalization): Returning to neutrality or generalization is the normal decision that a General Maintenance Entity takes when a role is no longer necessary or is close to being no longer necessary. The decision to return to generalization can be made by either the employing specialized entity or the General Maintenance Entity itself, although it is a natural function pertaining to the existing role no longer being necessary. When an entity returns to generalization, it moves into an area of noneffectiveness within the structure of the multiverse, a sort of "employment pool" using your language where it simply "is" in a state of beingness rather than activity.

Request a role (ask specialized entities for a role): The General Maintenance Entity can actively request a role from any of the specialized entities defined in the Curator hierarchy should it desire to do so. The role offered, being based upon the need for additional resource in the specialism of the offering entity, will be of a temporary nature and as previously stated only available while there is a shortfall of resource versus the workload necessary to support the function of the multiverse that is in need of support. Note that it is not usual for a General Maintenance Entity to request a role for most of the time the request for a General Maintenance Entity's support within a function of Curator specialization comes from that specialist function itself, negating the need for the request.

Elect to be in a role (individualized decision): In this instance, the General Maintenance Entity may decide that it no longer desires to be generalized or neutral and seeks a role on a permanent basis. This is not the same as a request for a swap of roles and so does not involve another specialized entity. In this instance, the General Maintenance Entity seeks a permanent role within the specializations of the Curator hierarchy through a request of role through the specialized entities. The election to be in a role can take two forms. The first form is that the General Maintenance Entity requests a role and accepts what is available at the time of the request, if any. Or, if there are a number of roles, the requesting General Maintenance Entity makes a decision based upon the desirability of the role to it. The second form is when the General Maintenance Entity requests a specific role and is prepared to wait for that role to become available. In this instance, the entity will need to stay generalized within the area of noneffectivity and not enter into a temporary specialized role because if the entity entered into temporary specialization, it would not be able to take advantage of the role it desired due to being actively employed in a necessary function within the specializations of the Curator hierarchy.

ME: How do they change from one role or specialism to another? What is the process they use? We don't seem to have discussed that yet.

SE1: No, we haven't. I have deliberately left the description of the changing and swapping process to last.

ME: Oh, OK!

SE1: So here we go. I will describe the swapping process and changing processes individually, although they are similar in function.

The swapping process is a function of moving the sentience of the entity from one "body" of energy to another. It is the energy associated with the sentience that is key here, for the function of being generalized is attributed to the energy that is assigned to the sentience and not the sentience itself. If you remember in previous dialogues with The Origin [*see* The Origin Speaks—*GSN*], it is sentience that defines the entity and not the energy that the sentience is assigned to or that the sentience commandeers. So when the sentience of a General Maintenance Entity moves from its body of energy, it is only the sentience that moves and not the functionality of the energy which the sentience can animate. Similarly, when the specialist entity moves its sentience from its body of specialized energy, it only moves its sentience and not the specialized function of the body of energy it was associated with. So, each "Sentient" entity, in moving its sentience to its new body of energy, inherits the functionality and experiences of that energy when it assigns itself to that body of energy. Swapping back is a reverse of the initial swapping process. Permanence in a specialism is simply a function of not swapping back.

The changing process is a variation on the swapping process that does not require the sentience of the General Maintenance Entity to be moved from its generalized body of energy to a body of energy with the functionality of the specialism it will be temporarily associated with. In this instance, a percentage of specialized energy from a donating specialized entity, up to 30 percent, is absorbed by the General Maintenance Entity to allow it to work in the way, and with the functions of, the specialized energy whose role it is assigned to, or has requested to work with. When the work is completed, the specialized energy is released from its absorbed state from the General Maintenance Entity and is reabsorbed by the donating specialist entity.

A Matter of Direct Responsibility

ME: Is there anything else that you can tell me about the General Maintenance Entities?

SE1: There is always more to tell you. You just don't have enough lifetime left to be able to go through all of it.

ME: What do you mean by that?

SE1: Simply that you will never have enough time to be able to work on everything that is available to know. That is why I have so many incarnates delivering the information. Everyone works on a small piece of the jigsaw puzzle. Everyone overlaps each other in some small, or other, way.

ME: Yes, OK. But, what about the entities we have just been discussing?

SE1: That is enough for the moment; you have all that you need.

ME: OK. Can I have one last question about the General Maintenance Entities then?

SE1: OK. Carry on.

ME: We have discussed the process of being close to the lower frequencies of the multiverse and that an entity needs to create a protective shield around them to allow them to function at their own level while in these lower frequencies.

SE1: Yes, we have.

ME: Well, my question is this: Do any of the General Maintenance Entities work on the Gross Physical frequency levels? If so, do they manifest a Gross Physical body to work on that level? And, are they still able to function correctly at this level?

SE1: They do, but it is a rare occurrence.

ME: How rare?

SE1: Very rare.

ME: What makes them need to materialize a Gross Physical body?

SE1: There are times when direct intervention is required, the sort of intervention with the Gross Physical that cannot be actioned by the genre of Curators you call Elementals and can only be actioned by an entity that can change itself in the way just described. They don't actually materialize a body.

ME: Are you saying that they can do work that Elementals cannot perform?

SE1: Yes. We will get on to the subject of the genre of Curators called Elementals or nature spirits later, but to get to the point, yes. You see Elementals can only work in the frequencies that are attributed to the astral; they cannot work on the third frequency and below.

This got me thinking for a moment. If a General Maintenance Entity cannot materialize a body and an Elemental cannot work in the environment associated with the third frequency, then the only way to work directly with the third frequency is to commandeer a Gross Physical body. Hold on, I thought guides can manifest a Gross Physical body, so why can't a Curator? Now I was curious.

159

ME: OK, this means that they would need to swap with an entity that was incarnate?

SE1: Yes, it would. It means the General Maintenance Entity has to invoke a walk-in.

ME: But if a Guide can manifest a Gross Physical body, why can't a Curator?

SE1: Because it has to stay with the genre of frequencies associated with its role—that being, it exists in a subfrequential state that allows it to work within, without, in and around the structure of the multiverse and its local universal environments. They can affect changes to the multiverse and its structure/evolutionary efficiency, but cannot operate within the function of the multiverse that is associated with the evolutionary cycle per se.

ME: I still haven't got it. Neither a Guide nor its Helpers are in the evolutionary cycle but the Guide can manifest a Gross Physical body.

SE1: Agreed, but there is a difference.

ME: And that difference is?

SE1: They are not in the evolutionary cycle, but they work with entities that are in the evolutionary cycle.

ME: But so do the Curators. They support the maintenance of the environment that allows the ability of entities in the evolutionary cycle to evolve.

SE1: Yes, they do. The difference is that the Guide and Helpers are, although not in the evolutionary cycle, directly responsible for the evolutionary progression of those entities in the evolutionary cycle. The Curators are not directly responsible so they do not have access to energies that allow direct intervention from the perspective of the entities within the evolutionary cycle and are using the process of incarnation to augment their evolutionary progression.

ME: So, from where I am standing, there are three genres of energy being used in the multiverse that entities are aligned to: structural, evolutionary, and an energy that is a mixture of structure and evolutionary.

SE1: That's a reasonable description—but note that there are many more genres than those three.

ME: I expect there are.

SE1: Getting back to your question, though, the General Maintenance Entity has to invoke a walk-in to allow direct Gross Physical intervention.

ME: If the General Maintenance Entity is in effect "incarnate," how can it use its functionality, considering of course that the lowest frequencies of the multiverse effectively restrict the communication and functional performance of an entity?

SE1: The General Maintenance Entity, when invoking a walk-in, also invokes a temporary increase in communicative and functional bandwidth, one that is protected. This requires a lot of energy, though, and as such the walk-in can only be affected for a limited period before the entity has to return the body to its primary Aspect (Soul).

ME: What does the General Maintenance Entity do when in the walk-in? How do we recognize an incarnate vehicle that has been commandeered by a General Maintenance Entity?

SE1: First, the Gross Physical body has the appearance of detachment from its normal duties and responsibilities and performs in a way that is out of character. Standard stuff for a walk-in. In this instance, though, the General Maintenance Entity will steer the body it has commandeered to a location, using the Earth as an example, where it is needed. The Gross Physical body is then used as an anchor point for the energies it needs to use to make the direct intervention work.

ME: So what is direct intervention in this instance?

SE1: Direct intervention can be invoking a weather system, a change to the magnetosphere, or the use of a volcano or earthquake to stabilize the energies of the planet. It can be anything else associated with major or localized environmental change as well.

ME: Would the primary Aspect know that they are making these changes on this scale?

SE1: The Aspect would, but the ego created as a result of the incarnation process would not, and so when the Gross Physical body is released, it may feel like it was in a haze for a few days to weeks or was having some strange dreams, dreams of having immense power. Another way the ego may register an abnormal experience may be by the loss of memory for the duration of the walk-in or suddenly being woken up in a different location from that previously experienced and remembered.

ME: What other ways may a General Maintenance Entity use a walk-in as a way for effecting change to the environment, be it the Earth or any other?

SE1: There are times when interaction with the incarnate population is required.

ME: When would that happen?

SE1: If there is a need to change the way the incarnate population is interacting with the environment and that if the way the populous interact is such that any changes made by the General Maintenance Entity are negated within a short period of time, they will need also to change the thought processes of the incarnates. In this instance, an incarnate is chosen that is in the right location and maybe the right level of influence to make change to the minds and hearts of the population to the point where the work of the General Maintenance Entities is not undone.

ME: So who would be a likely person to be taken over as a walk-in by a General Maintenance Entity?

SE1: That depends upon the work to be done. However, the way to see if an incarnate's vehicle has been commandeered by a General Maintenance Entity is if the incarnate makes a significant and out-of-character change to the way it interacts with others and the direction it decides to take with its career or hobbies/pastimes. The usual individuals are those who are in a position of some sort of influence over others, or could be of influence over others. An individual who can be considered to be a champion for the cause.

ME: I guess that would describe politicians or industrialists or celebrities that suddenly turn into environmentalists.

SE1: It depends. It is not just prominent individuals that are chosen. It's the primary location and interactive properties of the individual that is most important.

ME: I have to admit that I am surprised that General Maintenance Entities use a walk-in as a way to effect changes to the local environment.

SE1: When they are working at the lowest frequencies of the multiverse and need to ensure that the changes they must make are to be permanently introduced in a way that is supported by the incarnate population, they have the capability to use any means possible to them.

ME: That is, if they are required to work in that environment.

SE1: Naturally.

I was just about to draw a line under the subject of the General Maintenance Entities when I had a feeling that we were not yet finished, not quite anyway. There was something more about these entities that needed to be broadcast before we moved on. Something quite unique—again!

ME: I was about to finish here but I feel you have a little more to tell me about these entities.

SE1: Yes. There is one thing that you could do with knowing.

ME: I am all ears.

SE1: General Maintenance Entities are not generally in abundance.

ME: What do you mean?

SE1: Although there is a nominal number of General Maintenance Entities, and these are in the most part enough to get the job done from a multiversal perspective, they can also be created by some of the Curators.

ME: Do the Curators have to be of a certain level, function, or authority to be able to create or manifest a General Maintenance Entity?

SE1: Yes, it is only the highest level of Curator that can invoke the creation of a General Maintenance Entity. Additionally, it is also only the highest level of Curator that can uncreate or dissolve a General Maintenance Entity as well.

ME: When would a General Maintenance Entity be created? What are the criteria for such a function? When would a General Maintenance Entity be uncreated? What are the criteria for such a function?

SE1: In both cases there needs to be an overwhelming need for additional General Maintenance Entities to either exist or to no longer exist. This is because there is an optimal number required to assist in the functionality of the multiverse. More are required in times of intense activity. The dissolution of the additional General Maintenance Entities is required in times of normal activity. They are an expendable commodity or resource.

ME: Why don't the Curators just leave them in existence? What is the need to dissolve them?

SE1: As I just said, there is an optimal number and this number needs to be maintained in the main. There is an optimal number of all Curators required to manage and maintain the structure and evolutionary efficiency of the multiverse. Leaving the additional General Maintenance Entities in existence upsets this balance.

ME: What do you mean, balance?

SE1: As I just stated, there is an optimal number of Curators required to maintain the multiverse and that this is in balance. The balance, though, is not a function of Curator genre versus Curator genre, it is more a function of the number of Curators, those entities in service, versus the number of entities within the multiversal environment that are in the evolutionary cycle. This balance has to be maintained, but there can be a number of instances when this is to be the case as long as it is only a temporary state.

ME: Why is it important to have a balance between those entities that are in service versus those that are in the evolutionary cycle?

SE1: There needs to be a ratio of twelve to the power of twelve more entities engaged in being of service to the maintenance of the multiverse than those in the evolutionary cycle.

ME: That's an interesting figure.

SE1: Yes, it's based upon the major function of structural expansion from one structural level of The Origin to another. It is also a function of my structural expansion, and, before you ask, it doesn't include the step-down from full dimension to subdimension, which would be based upon twelve to the power of three from a spatial perspective.

ME: Why is the ratio of maintenance entities in service to the multiverse to those that are in the evolutionary cycle based upon a function of the structure of The Origin/you?

SE1: You may well ask.

ME: I do and I am!

SE1: Well, it's to do with the amount of change, or corrections to the individual, local, universal, and multiversal environment that is made by all those entities that are in the evolutionary cycle, through their ability to make either individual and/or collective, in all of its variants, decisions. As you can appreciate, there is an enormous amount of work that needs to be done when you consider the environmental fractals that are created and therefore need to be maintained as a result of the vagaries of entities within the evolutionary cycle and the subsequent creation of Event Spaces and new or diversified Event Streams, not to mention the maintenance of the mainstream environment/s. As a result there needs to be an optimal balance or ratio between those entities that create new environmental conditions and those that fix or maintain them. As you may have guessed from our recent dialogue, this ratio, although seemingly massive, is sometimes not enough, hence the transient creation of the General Maintenance Entities.

I was somewhat surprised at the size of this ratio. It was unimaginably large. However, when I sat back in my chair and thought about it for a moment, it made sense. We, as entities either incarnate or in the energetic, can make a real mess of things, and that mess needs to be maintained or corrected. The fact that there were so, so many other entities clearing up after us was enlightening to say the least. I took stock of this for a moment and thought about how we as entities that are in both the evolutionary cycle and incarnate could help the Curators and came to the conclusion that the only way was to be efficient in our interaction with our environment and those other entities that are also interacting with us and the environment.

How can we increase our efficiency? I hear you ask. All I can say is that the best way to be effective and efficient is to give up on being selfish, think of others, and work for the benefit of others (in doing so this benefits the self), reducing one's karmic debt, and see beyond what we all do. Knowing that an experience is a lesson to be learned or an experience to be experienced, helping others to experience what is necessary with love in our hearts and an aim to help them/ us to experience it once, and not a multiple of times. It's the simplest and hardest thing to do, but if we can work in this way, we will reduce the number of environmental and karmic fractals, removing our attractions and addictions to the lower frequencies and the need to incarnate. In the process, we will reduce the amount of remedial work the Curators will need to do. We may also accelerate our evolutionary progression and the progression of this particular evolutionary cycle. We have unlimited possibilities, I thought. All we need to do is work with this idea, and as a result we will spare ourselves so much pain and suffering. Surely this is a temptation beyond thought, a decision that has no alternative? Why most of us miss it is beyond me. I dwelled on these words for a moment, absorbing the energy associated with them. We have free will to choose to make these decisions/actions. We have the capacity to choose the long road or the short road. It is ignorance, ignorance borne through lack of true education that makes us take the long road! I sighed.

SE1: It's time to move on to the next genre of Curator.

ME: OK, let's go.

The Beginners

I have a confession to make. At times I find myself in other areas of the world either as a result of my work or due to sabbatical. I am now on sabbatical (Christmas 2016) and with Celia on a day cruise from Mandalay in Myanmar (Burma) to Bagan down the Irrawaddy River. The last three thousand words have been written either en route or on location in Myanmar. The scenery is amazing, as is the history, people, supporting religion (Buddhism), and architecture. As with the trip to Peru I made earlier in the year, I have made some notes (mental and written) to use some of this experience in one of my future works, one that links religions and my work together, where there is commonality. Myanmar is, at least in my mind, another version of India. The cities are full of randomness, hustle and bustle, and the country is untouched, serene, and full of pure Earth energy. I was soaking in the pure energies associated with the Myanmar countryside. It was beautiful and pure and the aura of the trees and bushes along the riverbank glowed in golden white energy. It was calming, so much so that when The Source cut in to remind me that I needed to work for a little longer, it made me jump.

SE1: Shall we continue?

ME: Yes, sorry. I was just admiring the view.

SE1: So I see. Let's get the introduction to this chapter finished and then you can have a rest and continue to enjoy the scenery.

ME: Will you summarize?

SE1: Yes. I will elaborate a little on the original summary. The Beginners are not to be confused with the human understanding of a beginning or start. They are a group of beings that work with the functions of Event Space allowing any changes to have its own "start of event," even when there appears to be no real start. Everything exists in terms of events and not in terms of time; a start or beginning is therefore not a temporal position, it is simply a function of a change of experiential direction. It is the job of the Beginners to ensure that the quality of the start of the event is maintained at its optimal level when introduced into the overall scheme of existing Event Space spaces, or an Event Stream. Note that their insertion of change creates a whole new set of possibilities and as such, the number of new Event Spaces and Event Streams. The fractals and the effects on the beings within these spaces need to be known and managed by these entities.

Now at this point, I started to get both a little concerned and interested at the same time. We all know, I hope, that everything happens concurrently, at the same time in human speak, so based upon this, there is no start or end of anything. This is simply because everything that has happened, will happen, is happening, including all of the permutations of possibility, inevitability, etc., is happening concurrently. Time-based understanding is a human (only) concept, so to say that Event Space has a start of event, and therefore an end of event (see the Enders below) is going against the grain a little, if not a lot! I decided to ask a question about this before continuing with the rest of the dialogue. I wanted to see if these words were just for human consumption or whether or not there really was a beginning, and ultimately an end, of an Event Space or Event Stream. Before I continued, though, I stopped dead in my own tracks. Why had I not considered this before? I mean, we had discussed Event Space and Event Streams before, both in this dialogue and in the dialogues that preceded this book. Why had I not questioned a beginning and an end of an Event Space or an Event Stream?

SE1: Because it wasn't the right time to discuss and question it. You need to have a basic understanding of the concepts surrounding an issue before you are in the true position of being able to critique the information and ask questions that will ultimately extend the boundaries of your understanding, which of course includes incarnate mankind. When we work with new concepts, you are in the mode of total acceptance and total trust. It is only a considerable time, so to speak, after the event that you are able to sit back and think about what has been said. This does not mean that everything that we, you, me, The Origin, and the other Source Entities have discussed is wrong, it is humanized a little to help your understanding. That being said, you will need to understand exactly what the beginning or end of an event is before we can continue with describing what the Beginners and even the Enders do. I will reserve what the end of an Event Space or Event Stream is when we discuss the role of the Enders.

ME: OK, that sounds like a plan to me and I think I will kick off the questions right now with a very basic one. What exactly is the start or beginning of an Event and how does that create a new Event Space and Event Stream?

SE1: You are not one for waiting, are you?

ME: Er, no! I do like to ask nested questions.

SE1: So I see. I will answer them in the order that the nest was created then.

ME: Please do.

I was smiling here. I knew that The Source was playing with me a little and that it was doing its best to relax me, that being when I am relaxed, I am a better channel and better able to work with the concepts and information that The Source was going to send to me. It was also designed to make me less suspicious and more accepting. A difficult thing to achieve when one has spent most of his life as an engineer. I decided to let The Source carry on in the way it felt best.

SE1: Not a bad bit of self-discussion, I think. I approve.

ME: Thank you.

SE1: The Beginning or start of an Event can be created in one or two ways.

The first way is when a group or collective of entities actively work together to change the expected direction of a series of natural events that are identified as a main Event Stream. In this instance when the action/s of the collective that are supported by desire, intention, and thought create enough initial inertia surrounding the potential for change that it initiates the change, then that point is considered to be the beginning or start of the new Event Space. This new Event Space can be any size. In fact, the creation of a new Event Space is not dictated by the size of the Event Space and spaces within the Event Space at all because the space and the event associated with the Event Space expands and contracts as necessary within its own space. This creation of a new Event Space, as a result of collective desire, is usually one of a number of possibilities or probabilities that are aligned to the current Event Space and Event Stream.

The second way is when a single entity, again through its desires, intentions, thoughts, and actions, does something that other entities are either attracted to or are influenced by. In this instance, the actions of the entity, on its own, may not be enough to invoke a new global Event Space and can only be capable of creating a local Event Space, which would be normal. However, in the event that the actions of the entity are enough to make other entities change their own ideas, desires, intentions, thoughts, behaviors, and actions, then it can be as effective a change as the invocation of a new Event Space via collective desire. This can be classified as a so-called wild card, a fashion- or fanatic-based following because the global creation of a new Event Space would not be possible without that one entity making the choice it decided to make.

ME: Can you give me an example of how a single entity can affect the lives of others to the point where a new Event Space is created?

SE1: You have lots of examples on Earth; just think of a person who you call a household name. One where people think, behave, and act as a function of the influence of that person, one where the thoughts, behaviors, and actions of those influenced extend beyond the confines of location and time.

ME: OK. Got it. I can think of quite a few people that would come under the banner of "major influence" to the general population. Some of them are what we would call a negative influence in terms of creating a low-frequency way of thinking, behaving, and acting. There are only a few that would be classified as a major "world" influence.

SE1: Agreed. But there are a lot of people who can be classified as a minor influence. These people are able to interact with like-minded people and change the way that they think by introducing a new idea or concept in a localized way. Local can be classified as being limited to those of same mind and thought in the wider environment of a single country or city to just those individuals who interact with the person of influence on a personal basis.

ME: So, based upon this we have an accumulation of worldwide, wider local, and localized local areas of influence that can create a new or the beginning of an Event Space and new Event Stream. These would result in bubbles, for want of a better word, of Event Space within bubbles of Event Space together with the corresponding Event Streams.

SE1: Correct.

ME: I am thinking here, though, that all of this should be an automatic function of Event Space and its Event Streams and not a function that requires a Curator, a Beginner, to work with it. Just exactly what do they do?

SE1: The Beginners have the ability to manipulate Event Space.

ME: Go on.

SE1: Generally, the creation of Event Space and its Event Streams are, as you say, an automatic function of Event Space as an autonomous intelligent environment within The Origin. However, within my energies, those that are reserved for the environment called the multiverse, the Beginners have the ability to fine-tune functions of Event Space to the point where they can introduce a new Event Space exactly at the point where they feel a new series of events has the potential to start from. In this way, they separate out the Events that make up a known and already established Event Space and its Event Streams to create a new Event Space that has a known start point. Or for want of a better word, they create the beginning or start point for these events to progress from.

ME: I am struggling to see how this works. Can you elaborate a little for me?

SE1: Think of it as having the ability and authority to influence a number of beings and their environment, through making a series of minor or mini changes to the events within the overall Event Space they are associated with that results in the need for a new Event Space, this Event Space having a known and calculable start point; a start point that could only have happened through external intervention—that being, the normal interactions within the Event Stream would not have resulted in a new Event Space and Event Stream on their own.

ME: Can you give me an example of one such start of Event Space and Event Stream?

SE1: Of course. There is one that happened on Earth not so long ago.

ME: Really? When was this?

SE1: The Beginners worked with the Enders [*see next section— GSN*] to create the beginning or start of a new Event Space that resulted in the fall of the civilization you refer to as Atlantis.

The previous Event Space was not going in the right direction from an evolutionary perspective and so a new one needed to be introduced.

ME: You're about to tell me that the introduction of the Egyptian civilization was the result of the introduction of a new Event Space by the Beginners, aren't you?

SE1: You beat me to it, yes. If you look at Egyptian history, you will see that their civilization just appeared, it suddenly came into existence.

ME: Yes, I think we have discussed this before, in a previous dialogue.

SE1: Yes, we have, but we have not discussed the reason surrounding this "spontaneous" introduction of a new civilization in any real detail.

ME: You're right, we haven't. I simply thought that it was the result of the fall of Atlantis and the desire of those higher frequency incarnates who foresaw the fall of Atlantis and worked hard to reintroduce an incarnate civilization with enough technology and ability to give them a head start. To look at it in a different way, it would be a debt being repaid in lieu of allowing the failure of Atlantis to actually happen.

SE1: Well, you can look at it in that way if you wish, but the introduction of the Egyptian civilization was the beginning of a new local Event Space and the Event Streams associated with it. In this way, the Beginners ensured that the quality of the start of the event was maintained at its optimal level when introduced into the overall scheme of the existing wider Event Space and Event Stream. They have been managing the new set of possibilities and the number of new Event Spaces and Event Streams, their fractal Event Spaces, and the effects on the beings within these spaces ever since.

ME: Is the beginning or start of a new Event Space normally so obvious from the point of view of the, let's say, detached observer?

SE1: No, not always, because the beginning or start of a new Event Space may be an Event Space within an Event Space.

ME: Give me another example to work with.

SE1: From Earth's perspective that would be the sudden discovery of a new science or technology or process [*a manufacturing process to create a new material—GSN*]. One that would be impossible to discover normally, but that just appears in the mind of an individual. In this instance, the overall Event Space is not affected, but a new Event Space and Event Stream is created within it, the creation of the Event Space having a known start point.

ME: OK, I understand now. Most of the work of the Beginners is therefore based upon the influence of key incarnates then.

SE1: From the perspective of the physical universe, that would account for some of the work that they do, maybe 40 percent of it. But, for the most part, the work they do is based upon working with the wider environment before it is affected by those entities or beings that occupy it.

ME: Are you suggesting that they prepare the wider environment for a change in Event Space and Event Stream?

SE1: Yes. You see, when a new Event Space is created by the natural function of Event Space through the interaction of the decisions and the variations on the possibilities that they could go in, a whole new parallel environment is created, complete with the entities acting out their roles within that environment. It happens instantaneously. The function of the Beginners is also to smoothen the flow of the dominant Event Stream to allow a gradual transition from the main Event Space and Event Stream to the new one.

ME: Why would the main Event Stream flow need to be smoothed?

SE1: So far, all you have discussed with me is the total creation of a new Event Space and Event Stream including the duplication of the entities within that space and stream created as a natural function of Event Space responding to the energies surrounding the point of decision, and/or the variations of possibilities, certainties, and probabilities, etc., etc., etc., that create that decision point. We have not discussed the creation of an Event Space and Event Stream where there is a migration of entities from one Event Space and Event Stream to another more appropriate version. It is the creation of this type of Event Space that the Beginners are mostly responsible for and as such, the flow needs to be managed or smoothed as a result.

ME: How does that work, I mean, how can entities migrate from one Event Space and Event Stream to another without duplication, triplication, quadruplication, etc.? Surely they would be missed by those who stay and that they used to interact with in the preceding Event Space and Event Stream.

SE1: In the example of migration from one Event Space and Event Stream to another, the Beginners work on creating the environment and the introduction point of the new Event Space. They also identify those entities that will occupy it from a migration perspective and from a duplication or parallelization perspective.

ME: So this new Event Space and Event Stream is not just populated with migrated entities, it is also populated with duplicated entities.

SE1: Correct. It is a Parallel Space that is populated with parallel and nonparallel occupants.

In planning the creation of a new Event Space, its Event Stream, and its environment/s, the Beginners look at the whole picture. They look for:

- the need for a new Event Space and Event Stream in variance to the natural creation of an Event Space and Event Stream by Event Space itself;

- what is the introduction point of the new Event Space and Event Stream in comparison with the dominant Event Space and Event Stream;

- will the Event Space and Event Stream be within the dominant Event Space and Event Stream or will it be external to it;

- which entity's decision would result in them being parallelized and which result in them being singular;

- the method of translating singular entities into the new Event Space and Event Stream;

- the introduction points of the singularized entities from the global (universe wide) perspective;

- the introduction points of the singularized entities from the individual perspective;

- the result of removing singularized entities from the preceding Event Space and Event Stream from the perspective of downstream events, entity interactions, and evolutionary progression;

These Spaces can be both a fully functioning independent Event Space and Event Stream or an Event Space and Event Stream within a dominant Event Space and Event Stream.

ME: You talked briefly about transplanting entities from one Event Space and Event Stream to another and I asked if the entities in the preceding Event Space and Event Stream would miss them, that they would notice that they are no longer interacting with them. Doesn't this cause a problem?

SE1: No. From the perspective of the transplanted entity and those that interact with it, three things occur.

First, those entities that remain in the preceding Event Space and Event Stream experience, what seems to them, as a natural end of interaction or relationship. In essence, their incarnate memory is altered to suggest that the entity that has been transplanted simply moved outside of the remaining entities' sphere of existence and is no longer available to interact with them. An example you can use would be that the remaining entity would think that the transplanted entity has migrated to another country or to a distance that negates the possibility of continued interaction. They may even be given the memory that that entity has finished its incarnation. As a result, the transplanted entity is no longer in their minds.

Second, from the perspective of the transplanted entity, it sees no change other than the decision it made or the state of existence it is experiencing has no alternative. That being a parallel version of it and its environment could not be created as a result in the change in its direction, environment, or interaction.

Third, from the perspective of the parallelized entities, nothing has changed. Everything is normal. All interactions, environments, and experiences are as they were, as they are, and as they will be. It is a parallel existence in every way in comparison to the preceding Event Space and Event Stream.

In the new Event Space and Event Stream, the parallelized entities are, for want of a better word, the background props for the environment and interaction with the transplanted entities. This allows the transplanted entities to experience, learn, and evolve in the nonparallelized direction they were going in. The parallelization of these entities is therefore purely for the benefit of the transplanted entities.

ME: What creates the need for an entity to be transplanted in the first place?

SE1: A dead certainty based upon an inevitability that a decision made by that entity would result in one Event Space and Event Stream and not another.

ME: But couldn't another decision point occur further down the Event Stream that would result in the invocation of a new Event Space and Event Stream?

SE1: This type of Event Space and Event Stream is created specifically for those entities that have a stream of dead certainties and inevitabilities and as such remains stable.

ME: Couldn't the parallelized entities within that Event Space create them, though?

SE1: Yes, but they would not affect those entities that were transplanted. In that instance, although the transplanted entities would be parallelized, they would become the background props for those entities that are creating the new Event Space and Event Stream. They would simply be part of the scenery and not have any valid interactions that would create a new Event Space and Event Stream. Their ability to interact with the environment and its occupants and make valid interactions would remain in the Event Space and Event Stream that was initially created for them.

I sat down and wondered for a moment. The creation of an Event Space and an Event Stream is not a simple thing to consider, especially the point within an existing Event Space and Event Stream that a new Event Space and Event Stream is inserted, creating the "start" of Event and Stream. Even the creation of a new autonomous Event Space and Event Stream external to an existing Event Space and Event Stream is difficult because the number of possibilities of decisions that could, should, or might create the automatically created Event Space and Event Stream may negate the need for the Beginners to intervene.

I was about to contact The Source and start the dialogue on the genre of Curator entities called the Enders when I started to think about the words "start" and "end"—again. Forgive me, dear reader, for going over this very old ground again (and again!), but everything I/we have been told to date is that there is no such thing as a start and an end, that everything is concurrently operating in the same space and that time was a construct made by those entities that incarnate as human beings. Based upon this, to have no time, to have concurrence, and also have a start and end point to describe the manifestation and dissolution of an Event Space and an Event Stream seemed ludicrous, to say the least. I decided to put this to bed (bring it to a close) once and for all with The Source before moving on to the Enders.

SE1: Why bother with such questions when you already know the answer?

ME: I know you have told me in the past but it's just that it seems such a dichotomy.

SE1: Everything in the low frequencies of the physical universe is a dichotomy. That is why entities incarnate into it, to experience dichotomies, dualities, and linearity. It's just that it's difficult to see why it is.

I will start again with the same description that Byron gave you all those years ago. Event Space is like a rubber-band ball, with each event being represented by a single rubber band. Each rubber band is in contact with each other either by direct contact to a rubber band or indirect contact to a rubber band via another rubber band. Event Space therefore being a collection of events that occupy the same space, the Event Stream is the function of the events within the Event Space connecting together in a logical way, one that allows continuity of the overall Event Space in its space while allowing the events within the Event Space to be individualized. So, using the rubber-band ball as the illustration, the Event Stream is the connecting link between the various events that are logically placed together in a way where one event leads to another. In this way, the events that are linked together by the Event Stream don't need to be located side by side. In essence, event number one can be directly linked to event number forty-two even when there are forty other events in between them. This is only possible because they are all occupying the same Event Space. It is the function of the Event Stream that allows the beginning or start of an event to be connected to the end of an event irrespective of its location within the Event Space and irrespective of its state of parallelization simply because it is in the same space. Similarly, the events being all within the same Event Space is the reason why it is possible to traverse the events, to go forward or backward in time in human speak. Except that, you don't go forward and back in time, you go from one event to another, which may or may not be before or after each other.

The beginning/start or end of an event is an automatic change in experiential and evolutionary direction brought about either by the choices made by the entities within the events "within" the Event Space or by the Beginners or Enders if there is a need for a new Event Space that can only be invoked by external intervention. So, try to think in terms of changes in experiential and evolutionary direction rather than in the beginning or end of an experience or evolutionary opportunity, even though the entities described and about to be described are called Beginners and Enders.

Another way to think about it is in the way a tree branch terminates by being split out in a fractal way. The point at which the new branches are created can be considered as both the end of the previous Event Space and the beginning of the new Event Space/s. Note, though, that this assumes that there is a preceding Event Space from which to create a new Event Space. I will talk about this in a minute. However, if the branch of the tree remains to be the dominant branch after a new branch has been created, then this is considered to be the main Event Space and the small branch a minor Event Space, or an Event Space within an Event Space.

I waited with baited breath for The Source to talk about the creation of an Event Space with no preceding Event Space to be created from. Why? Because this is a real start point!

SE1: I thought you might like this part.

ME: You bet. For me this is the whole point and one where we cross over to the point of the immaculate creation of The Origin.

SE1: That's not a strictly true statement because Event Space itself allowed the creation of The Origin to take priority over its own sentience. So, there was intervention even if it was by Event Space itself. Suffice to say, the creation of an Event Space that has no preceding Event Space and Event Stream to work from is the ultimate responsibility of the Beginners.

ME: How can that be? I mean, there must be a series of events that preceded the point at which the Beginners decide to create a new Event Space, one that does not have a preceding space, to enable them to come to the conclusion that there is a need for a new Event Space.

SE1: Correct. However, the preceding Event Space is the Event Space that the Beginners exist within and not an Event Space that they are working with or maintaining.

ME: Ah! So in this case then, they can create a new and totally independent Event Space with no preceding Event Space specifically because they are outside of the Event Space that they are working with or are maintaining. They are creating it to create a new and unique environment for your entities to work with.

SE1: Now you have it.

ME: It feels a bit like discovering a new land and venturing forth to populate it.

SE1: That's one way of describing it, yes. Now we need to move on to the Enders.

The Enders

With the level of discussion that we had in the preceding chapter on the Beginners, it almost felt unnecessary to work on describing the roles and responsibilities of the Enders. I felt that we had discussed them, that they would be the reciprocal of the Beginners. I was just thinking about what the additional text and discussion may offer when The Source jumped in with the short description again and put my mind at rest with the start of new and additional information.

SE1: Moving on then. The Enders are the group of beings that work with the functions of Event Space allowing any change in event to be maintained at its optimal level when withdrawn from the overall scheme of existing Event Space spaces recognizing that the withdrawal of an Event Space and its Event Streams creates a whole new set of possibilities. Also, the lack of creation of the number of potential new Event Spaces, their fractals, and the effects on the beings from an experiential and evolutionary perspective within these spaces needs to be known and managed by these entities.

In variance to the "forced" function of the Beginners, the end of event can be created either as a naturalized or forced function.

ME: I thought we stated with the Beginners that the beginning or start of a new Event Space can be created as a naturalized function?

SE1: No. Although there can be natural creations of Event Space and Event Streams, the Beginners don't actually invoke a naturalized beginning or start, they only create a new Event Space by force. Force means that they decide to use whatever abilities they have to invoke the creation of a new Event Space based upon a desire or need to do so and if the new Event Space or Event Stream would not be created as a natural function of Event Space.

ME: Looking at this then, the Enders have an easier job to do because all they are doing is forcing or creating a natural termination of an Event Space.

SE1: It sounds simple, doesn't it?

ME: I wouldn't have said it if I didn't think it was.

SE1: Not true, though. You see, the Enders have to consider all of the downstream functions of the Event Space and Event Stream. What this means is that they have to look at the effects of removing the Parallelized Event Spaces and Event Streams from the overall productivity of the Event Space that they are electing to terminate.

ME: What criteria are required to allow the Enders to make the decision that an Event Space should be finalized or ended before it reaches its natural and automatic end?

SE1: There are many criteria. It's not just about stopping a sequence of events, an Event Space, and its Event Stream dead in its tracks. It's about looking at the evolutionary efficiency of an Event Space and in some cases, the streamlining of the number of Event Spaces that are in action.

ME: Can you advise me of the differences in criteria for the dissolution of an Event Space and whether or not it is a natural dissolution or a forced dissolution?

SE1: Yes, of course.

There are four main criteria or stages that need to be considered before an Event Space and its Event Stream can be dissolved. Please note that an evolutionary dead end is also an Event Space:

1. What is the duplication of experience and evolution when referring to other Event Spaces? Is the duplication so high that there is little to be gained by the continuation of this Event Space, or, is there enough of a difference to allow its continued existence?

2. How many evolutionary dead ends are being created by this Event Space? Do any of the dead ends actually result in a level of learning and therefore an element of limited evolution? If any evolutionary dead end results in a unique learning experience then it needs to stay in existence.

3. Is the Event Space capable of creating other Event Spaces? There are Event Spaces that don't create any fractals of themselves due to the nature of the functions of the entities working within them. If there is unique experience and learning then the Event Space remains in existence. If, however, the Event Space shows no experiential or evolutionary growth, and the experience of the entities is therefore static and mundane, then the Event Space is dissolved.

4. Is the Event Space capable of arriving at a naturally occurring end in its own right, or will it need to be forced into dissolution? The normal and automatic function of an Event Space is such that it naturally dissolves when it reaches an evolutionary dead end. However, as with the third example, this is not always the case and an Event Space can at times continue to exist in a static and stagnant state. An Event Space that remains in a static and stagnant state is of no benefit to the entities within it, whether it is parallelized, and the entities within are parallelized, or not. Such an Event Space can also stop the natural dissolution of other Event Spaces if it ends up becoming the dominant or mainstream Event Space and so must be dissolved.

ME: All of this is based upon the need to dissolve an Event Space and the criteria to support such a decision. What about the natural dissolution of an Event Space? I mean, what do the Enders work on to support the natural functions of Event Space in this instance?

SE1: All of what we have just discussed revolves around the need to change the natural functions of Event Space and not leave things as they are. The need to change a natural function is the whole reason for the need of the Curator genre of entities to optimize the natural function of the multiversal environment and its interactions with its incumbent entities and the space it exists within and without. Speeding nature up is an overarching function of the Curators and the Enders are key to this. In general, the functions surrounding the need to dissolve an Event Space are the majority of the content of the Enders' responsibilities. Knowing when to leave an Event Space to its own functions is another skill set they have.

ME: In general, then, can it be assumed that the Enders are like gardeners, pruning the dead or dying Event Space fractals away from the healthy or dominant Event Spaces, allowing the optimal performance of Event Spaces within the locations they are created to continue. This is achieved either by doing nothing because the natural dissolution of the Event Space is in itself the most efficient, or by assisting in its dissolution.

SE1: That is a reasonable synopsis. However, we have one more area that the Enders work within to discuss.

ME: What is that?

SE1: One that we have alluded to twice now but not actually discussed.

ME: And that is?

SE1: Recognizing that the withdrawal of an Event Space and its Event Streams within the overall Event Space creates a whole new set of possibilities. And, moreover, that an event within an Event Space can be removed while maintaining the space it exists within.

ME: I thought that we had discussed the first part of that statement?

SE1: No. Read the text again.

I did, and I understood what The Source was alluding to.

ME: Ah! I understand now. We have been discussing the dissolution of an Event Space, not the withdrawal of one. This is all about the withdrawal of an Event Space. Withdrawal is not dissolution; it is relocation.

SE1: Yes, and the movement of an event from one active Event Space to another.

ME: So we have two things to discuss, the maintenance of an event when removed from an Event Space, and the movement of an event from one Event Space to another.

SE1: Correct.

The Maintenance of an Event

SE1: The Enders have the capability of terminating the downstream effects of a certain event by removing it from the overarching Event Space that it is expressed within. The removal of an event can be created by the manipulation of the preceding events so that the event that needs to be removed is, in effect, terminated. Or, for want of a better word, never actually comes into existence. As a result of this, the downstream events that would have been created are no longer created and those events that were already in existence, that would have been affected by the event itself or its fractals, are no longer due to be affected.

ME: This is the same as we have just discussed, though, isn't it?

SE1: Yes, of course. The clever bit here, though, is that the Enders have the capacity to realize the individualized opportunity for evolution that maintaining a particular event in isolation to others will have, if it is indeed isolated and allowed to play out its natural functions within this isolated state.

ME: So it is no longer affected by any external influences?

SE1: No, it is maintained in its pure state. To enable the isolation and removal of an event to be successful, the Enders need to intercept the event at its conception, that point when it is a new event and has not been in existence long enough to affect other events within its Event Space and Event Stream.

ME: I was about to ask how they know when the conception of an event is to take place but being the beings that they are, with the abilities that they have, sort of explains it.

SE1: Yes, it does. As with the Beginners, the Enders exist outside of the structure of the multiverse I created within me and so they are capable of seeing the functions in a concurrent way.

ME: How does that work? I am just thinking aloud (or in type!) about Event Space being a much bigger function, one that includes you and is a fundamental component of The Origin. If Event Space is a much bigger function, how do the Beginners and Enders have the abilities to work with Event Space in the way they do?

SE1: They work within the overall Event Space, and its fractals, that I am working within, all of course within the overall structure of The Origin. It is because they are working outside of the overarching Event Space that contains the multiverse and its localized Event Spaces, while being within mine, that they can see the routes that entities make that result in the creation of a new event and remove it from the Event Space it was destined to manifest within before the point of manifestation.

ME: So it never manifests in the first place?

SE1: Yes, it does, but it is just removed and placed in isolation. Although those entities that would have been the key creators of the conditions that created the event are unaffected and continue to the next event without disturbance, if the event is isolated, they are parallelized to allow the event to play out in its isolated space.

ME: What is an isolated space?

SE1: It is an area of benign Event Space that is created by the Enders to allow the event that is removed to exist within, work its way through, and come to a natural end.

ME: An Event Space that goes nowhere.

SE1: Yes. It's a tract of Event Space that is not connected to any other possible creation of Event Space other than itself, and so is isolated.

ME: How is it possible? I mean Event Space is an autonomous function of The Origin, it creates parallel versions of itself as a result of us making decisions, and they expand and contract on a fractal basis. I am not aware of an Event Space that is autonomous from Event Space itself?

SE1: That's right, you aren't. It doesn't exist as a natural function of Event Space; it is created by the Enders.

ME: I am sorry that I didn't ask this question before, but just how do the Enders create a tract of Event Space that is autonomous from the overall and overarching Event Space?

SE1: As entities, you are all created from my energies and my structure and I in turn am created from the energies of The Origin; you already know this.

ME: Yes, I do.

SE1: Within all of these energies there is of course an aspect of sentience or intelligence associated with these energies. Do you recognize this?

ME: Yes, I do.

SE1: Then also recognize that it is possible to assign aspects of energy and its associated sentience or intelligence to other aspects of energy and sentience or intelligence.

ME: Got it!

SE1: Not yet, you haven't.

ME: OK.

SE1: You will soon, though, because I haven't finished yet. Considering that you and all other entities that are either created by The Origin or myself can also be classified as energy and its associated sentience, or sentience given a body of energy, it can then be noted that an aspect of the energy and intelligence associated with Event Space can be assigned to the energy of another entity.

ME: That would make an entity part you and part Event Space and not just an individualized unit of you.

SE1: Correct.

ME: And this means that such an entity could command and manipulate those energies that are within it, that are part of it.

SE1: Yes, and it also means that such an entity could attract more of those energies to it and manipulate those as well.

ME: And this is what the Enders are made of?

SE1: Yes, it is.

ME: The Enders are therefore part you, part Curator of the Ender genre, and part Event Space.

SE1: Yes, they are.

ME: And so are the Beginners?

SE1: Correct again. Now you are getting it.

ME: Nearly there, then. Therefore, because the energies that are used to create the Enders (and the Beginners) also have a percentage of Event Space within them, they are able to collect, command, and control energies associated with Event Space and create a new tract of Event Space.

SE1: Yes, and what's more, because the Enders have been blessed with individuality, they also have the ability to pass on the essence of individuality to the energies they work with, including Event Space.

ME: And this essence of individuality is what is required to allow the creation of an autonomous and self-contained tract of Event Space, one that never creates fractals or parallel versions of it.

SE1: Correct.

ME: And you created the Enders (and Beginners) with this ability by adding in the energies associated with Event Space?

SE1: Of course. The Beginners and Enders are not the only Curators that have this ability, the Architects do as well [*not previously discussed—GSN*], but they tend not to use this ability because the Beginners and Enders have the roles that demand the use of such a function, the Architects do not as such.

ME: I am thinking about this for a moment—an Event Space that is autonomous and self-contained with no external influences to relate to as part of a parallelization or a fractal of a parallelization and no internal decision that can make it parallelize itself. This is almost like the environment that immersed incarnate mankind thinks it exists within. Hold on; is this what we are actually working within, an isolated and individualized tract of Event Space?

SE1: No, it's not what incarnate mankind exists within. Although I sometimes think it would be a good idea. No, there are too many parallel evolutionary opportunities created by you all to make me want, via the Enders, to withdraw the space that you all occupy and isolate it. There have been instances, though, when the Enders have moved an Event Space fractal created by immersed incarnate mankind into another Event Space.

Movement of Events from One Event Space to Another

My head was buzzing now. Some part of what we have all collectively created as a parallel function due to some form of what I can only guess is a collective decision process, has resulted in the Enders moving that Event Space into another. I sat back a moment and wondered when that was and why it happened. I was about to wait and discuss this with The Source at the end of this discussion when The Source decided that it needed to be answered first.

SE1: There are two times that are of note. One recently and one in what you would call prehistory. The first mankind-derived Event Space that was moved to another overall Event Space was based in the time when the use of the human form allowed Aspects of TES to move from one incarnate vehicle to another on a regular basis, leaving some part of their energetic signature behind in the human form resulting in a disharmonic effect with the Aspects themselves as they absorbed the energetic signature of the previous users of the human form they had just moved into, effectively losing their own and therefore dominant energetic signature over time [*see* The History of God—*GSN*]. In the version of Event Space you are currently working within, the function of incarnation was changed to stop this from happening. This was achieved by stopping the ability of the incarnate Aspects from moving from one human form to another and reducing the ability of the incarnate Aspect to remember such functions while incarnate. In the Event Space that was removed, this function was allowed to continue to see what would happen. Recognizing that it would ultimately cause a loss of initial individuality, this Event Space was duplicated with one duplicate being placed in a tract of autonomous Event Space, and another in a fractal of a similar Event Space. In the first instance, the Aspects experienced a return to communion and therefore a complete loss of individuality, but only affecting the Earth as a location. In the second instance, the disharmony spread throughout all incarnate vehicles throughout the physical universe in all locations and all frequencies. It was disastrous, while also being interesting to watch.

In these two actions, the Curators noted how they can change the overall results as a function of relocating Event Spaces or effectively terminating its ability to parallelize.

The second time when an Event Space was moved to another Event Space was during what you call the Second World War.

ME: The Second World War? But that's recent, really recent. What happened at this time that required the need for the dominant Event Space to be moved? What happened to the entities that were working within that Event Space?

SE1: I will answer the last question first.

ME: OK.

SE1: There was a parallelization of all of those entities and the environments that were in that Event Space, one that would only be a singular parallelization, that being, no other Event Spaces would be created and no entities would be parallelized. This was achieved to allow this particular Event Space to play itself out in an autonomous fashion.

ME: And is it still playing itself out today?

SE1: Yes, of course. It is still local from your perspective. Those entities that were autonomously parallelized continued to interact with those entities that are also autonomously parallelized within the environment created.

ME: So what happened? What caused the need for such a series of events to be removed from the overall overarching Event Space?

SE1: The possibility of contamination.

ME: I'm sorry? What does that mean?

SE1: The use of what you call atomic weaponry was developed by all of the major players in this version of World War Two simultaneously, and was used simultaneously. This was foreseen by the Enders and as a result, the Event Space that displayed this series of scenarios was removed from the overall and overarching Event Space and allowed to play itself out. The effect was horrific, to say the least. All of the major cities and areas of dense population were destroyed and the incarnate population was deeply affected by the radiation resulting from the use of such weapons.

Suffice to say, the TES which had projected Aspects/Shards into that environment agreed to have those Aspects/Shards parallelized and isolated to allow the energetic effects of the experiences to be filtered and for the TES only to experience the resulting effects and not share it, at least not initially, with those other parts of the Aspects/Shards that were parallelized in other Event Spaces. The experience of such vast levels of destruction and the ascension of so many incarnates back into the energetic in one series of events would have been too much for the other parallelized Aspects/Shards to cope with. It was beyond anything that even the demise of the civilization called Atlantis would illustrate.

Additionally, the desire to achieve such an act of destruction had spread worldwide, not just to those who instigated it, but throughout the general populous as well. The need to destroy would be felt at the general incarnate population level in the other Event Spaces if it was not filtered by the TES and placed in an isolated, individualized, and autonomous tract of Event Space. It would have spread at this point in incarnate mankind's evolution to all Event Spaces in some level of intensity or another resulting in similar Event Streams being played out and an overall downward spiral down the frequencies. This was the contamination I was alluding to.

The entities in that Event Space are now experiencing what you might like to call a devolved state of being where all forms of civilization have all but disappeared. Disease is rife and as a result, the longevity of the incarnate vehicle is limited. Indeed, all but a few of the incarnate vehicles are sterilized by the radiation and as a result cannot reproduce. In this Event Space, the Earth is about to see the dawn of the loss of the human body as an incarnate vehicle.

ME: I am glad this Event Space did not experience such a horrendous Event Space and Event Stream. Hang on, though; what you have just described is the removal of one Event Space and the positioning of it into an autonomous Event Space!

SE1: Yes, it is. However, this is not the end of the story. Once that Event Space was created, and the Event Space just talked about was relocated, other more local Event Spaces were needed to be positioned into this Event Space to allow a change in direction to one where we have the current Event Space and Event Stream. In order to do this, those events that resulted in an evolutionary dead end in other Event Spaces were inserted into this Event Space to stop the overall creation of events that led to all parties being able to use atomic weapons concurrently. I will explain the process in summary shortly, but suffice to say it was successful.

ME: Having one country deliver the devastation and not another was a success then?

SE1: Yes.

ME: Why? I would have thought that the optimal result would have been to remove the scenario of the use of atomic weapons from the event altogether?

SE1: No. There needed to be one country that was the first user of such technology and not the majority of them. This was necessary because the population of that time, and indeed this time, needed to see what the result would be from a local perspective which would allow them to establish what a worldwide effect would be. One country's use of atomic technology was designed to be an eye-opener, not a threat, one that would allow clear thinking. Those Aspects/Shards that were in Hiroshima agreed on the soul level, so to speak, to sacrifice their incarnations for the ultimate better good.

ME: It doesn't sound like a better good, though.

SE1: No, not on the human level you are all working on, but it was the only way to stop the alternative events taking place.

ME: But we have a nuclear standoff with lots of countries now!

SE1: Yes, incarnate mankind does, but it is one that is not likely to create the undesired result. Incarnate mankind will evolve mentally soon to the point where this technology can be put to a much better and more benign use.

ME: I look forward to that day with great anticipation.

SE1: You all will, of that I am sure.

I said that I was going to explain how one Event Space is moved from one overall Event Space to another because, as you stated, what I have just described is the movement to an autonomous Event Space, and a rather high-level way in which an Event Space can be changed by introducing Events that result in evolutionary dead ends. Once I have done this, we can move on to the next genre of Curator.

Moving One Event Space to Another

ME: So what about the process of moving one Event Space to another Event Space?

SE1: This is a most difficult process and one that requires a lot of planning and pre-analysis work that is above and beyond that required to move an Event Space from its overall or overarching Event Space to an autonomous and isolated Event Space.

ME: Why would that be? I mean, it must be just as difficult to see how certain Event Streams are correctly terminated or dissolved without adversely affecting the evolutionary requirements or benefits that would have been experienced by those entities in the downstream events.

SE1: The additional work lies in the insertion of the Event Space into its new overall or overarching Event Space. When an Event Space is being transplanted, the work required to remove it is identical to that required when an Event Space is being removed from its overall or overarching Event Space into the autonomous Event Space. However, when an Event Space is being placed into an overall or overarching Event Space that has other Event Spaces that are within and without it, together with their own series of possibilities and possibility of possible possibilities for parallel versions to be created, the insertion of another Event Space and the relation of all of its downstream possibilities and possibility of possible possibilities together with the effects of these possibilities within and without the existing Event Streams and downstream fractals needs to be analyzed. In essence, an Event Space can only be inserted into another Event Space if the existing Event Streams can be left in either an unchanged state or the insertion creates some level of augmentation or evolutionary benefit to the original Event Space and Event Stream.

ME: I know that you are describing the effects, and that you continue to do so as it must provide some level of basic understanding, but I am just eager to see the process used in the actual insertion.

SE1: OK, I will send you a series of images and you can describe it to your readers.

The Source sent me the images and it was interesting, to say the least. It looked like a giant series of lines, each one interlinked, expanding and contracting, duplicating and paralleling and dissolving. It's ...

SE1: Don't just think it. Say it out loud and type it!

ME: Yes, of course. Sorry, dear reader, I was so immersed in the image I forget to record it in the usual way.

As I was just saying, I saw the Event Space initially as a series of related Event Streams. Lines of events or activities that break away into fractals and then dissolve back into one main Event Stream as the events are either completed, terminated, or join another Event Stream. But this was just the events themselves; it was not the Event Space. As I looked from a different perspective, I noticed that all of these lines were within, and without, and by without I mean external to but not dissociated from an amorphous and undulating sphere that was constantly changing its form. To say it was a sphere would be wrong actually; it would be best to describe it in terms of a bubble of soapy water that was pulled or blown through a metal or plastic hoop. As the hoop is pulled faster, the air goes into the hoop and stretches it. The same is achieved if blowing air through the hoop; however, if the hoop is pulled fast through the air and the direction of the hoop is changed, the bubble takes the shape of the direction of the hoop while trying to retain a spherical type of shape. An Event Space that is contained in an autonomous tract of overall Event Space would be spherical in nature but one that has active Event Streams that are in contact with each other, and other Event Spaces have the appearance of being an elongated or stretched soapy water bubble that has merged with another.

When an Event Space is removed from its overall Event Space, the bubble has to be disconnected from other bubbles as well as the lines of Event Streams while allowing the bubbles and Event Streams that were in connection with each other, via the removed Event Space and Event Streams. To be connected to each other again in a manner that is not affected by the loss of the Removed Event Space and Event Streams, that being, they are in direct connectivity with each other. Consider it like having three bubbles joined together by the middle bubble or second bubble, and when the middle or second bubble is removed, the first and third bubbles merge together to create one overall bubble but that one bubble is actually two bubbles co-joined together. The same thing can be observed with the lines that represent the Event Streams that reconnect at the points where the Event Streams would have been connected via the second or middle set of Event Streams.

In this way, the Event Spaces, their events and Event Streams connect directly and seamlessly together in a way that, to the outside observer, looks like there was no interconnecting Event Space and Event Streams in the first place. Each event becomes the precursor and predecessor of the Event Spaces before and after them in place of that Event Space and Event Stream that was removed.

ME: But doesn't this mean that the areas where the Event Spaces and Event Streams connect need to be modified in some way to allow the connections to be consistent with that which should precede the events prior to the connections?

SE1: Yes, but this is only required on the preceding events and not the resulting events. I saw for a moment that you thought that events resulting from the connection would need to be modified as well.

ME: I admit that I was about to ask that question, but then I looked at it from another angle and realized that as long as the preceding events were modified to suit the expected result of the receiving events then the connection would be in harmony.

I have another question, though. How much modification is required and how does that affect the natural functions of the events surrounding the preceding Event Space?

SE1: The results of the events and Event Streams within the preceding Event Space naturally lead to the end event that leads into the next or resulting Event Space. It is therefore a simple action that the Enders perform to shortcut to the start of the next or resulting Event

Space by creating a series of alternative but nevertheless natural consequences that lead to an event that connects to the first event and Event Stream within the next Event Space. Try to think of it in terms of playing the board game "Snakes and Ladders," where the dice is thrown and the result is that one player's marker lands on the bottom of a ladder that terminates on the very last square, shortcutting most of the squares on the board. The end result is the same in terms of the marker needing to land on the last square to finish the game, it's just that the player didn't need to place the marker on the squares in between the square where the start of the ladder was and the square that ends the game. It's just that the content of the Events and the Event Streams have not been experienced.

ME: Doesn't this mean that the preceding event, the last square of the Snakes and Ladders board, is lacking in experiential and evolutionary content, content that it would have accrued had it been experienced?

SE1: Yes, it does, and it ultimately needs to be recovered at some point in a downstream event, but in essence this is classified as a desirable position to be in rather than be in the position where the events would be, had the Event Space and its Event Streams not been removed.

ME: Are the entities within the resulting Event Space and Event Stream aware that the original preceding Event Space has been removed and that they are in evolutionary debt and lacking in experiential content?

SE1: Yes and no. It all depends upon what evolutionary level they are at and whether or not the changes are happening within the lowest frequencies of the multiverse such as the Gross Physical universe, or the energetic such as in the multiverse. Those of you in the Gross Physical aspect of the multiverse, the physical universe at levels 1, 2, 3, 4, 5, 6, 7, and 8 would not know if anything had happened to their particular Event Space or Event Streams. Those in levels 9, 10, 11, and 12 would recognize a change but would not know the detail. Suffice to say, they would feel as if events had speeded up.

Interestingly enough, the feeling that time has speeded up is something that you on Earth have and are experiencing. This is a direct result and function of the removal of the Event Space we talked about earlier. I say this is interesting because at your levels of frequency, you should not notice anything. Having said that, though, there is a large number of you that are at a higher than normal evolutionary level incarnate at the moment and that will have an effect on the higher spiritual abilities of you all, especially those who are advanced and leading the spiritual and metaphysical way.

ME: OK, we have talked about the process of removing an Event Space and connecting the preceding and resulting (next) Event Spaces and their Event Streams, but what is the process of inserting an unrelated Event Space and Event Streams into an Event Space?

SE1: It's a similar process to that which I have just described. The only difference is that there is work to be done at all points of connection with the preceding and resulting Event Spaces and Event Streams. With the new Event Space being different, there needs to be a modification to the end of the preceding Event Space to introduce events that are in harmony with the resulting or start of the Event Space that is due to be introduced. In this way, the new Event Space, although not in true harmony, would appear to be a logical set of resulting events. The end of the last event of the Event Space that is due to be introduced would also need to be modified to suit the start of event of the resulting or next Event Space so that there is no influencing effect from the Event Space and Event Stream to be introduced. From the perspective of the maintenance of the existing Event Spaces and Event Streams that are considered to be the resulting, next, or downstream events, Event Spaces, and Event Streams, it is imperative that the downstream results are not affected, that the expected and existing event outcomes are unchanged. That is, providing that the desire is to introduce a different Event Space into an existing series of Event Spaces with little or best still, no overall changes to the resulting downstream events.

ME: What do you mean?

SE1: What I mean is that there may be times when the whole point of moving one Event Space to another may be to change some ultimate undesirable Event Space and event or Event Stream. This also supports the multiversal requirement of changing or manipulation of universes only if it is thoroughly investigated and analyzed first.

In both instances, there is a desire to either maintain the downstream events or change the origin of those events to support the existing Events. Based upon this, you can see that it is important to analyze all inputs and outputs when considering where to introduce the Event Space within the other events preceding the Event Space.

ME: In summary then, the events within the Event Spaces that are connected together need to be modified to ensure that there is some form of continuity of Event Stream so that the Event Spaces themselves are logical in terms of the preceding and resulting events. Without the logical progressions, they cannot connect together and would cause an Event Space continuity error of some sort.

SE1: Correct, and it is the role of the Beginners and the Enders to ensure that there are no continuity errors between Event Spaces that have had an intermediate Event Space removed or a new Event Space introduced.

ME: Good. I feel like I understand now.

SE1: You understand enough for the moment; enough to allow you to access more detailed information.

ME: Thank you.

The Deliverers

Having finished with the Enders, it was a natural progression to discuss those entities that work with them both. The Deliverers were therefore the next of the Curators on the list of The Source's maintenance entities to discuss. Although I did wonder a little bit about what we could talk about, seeing as though most of what we had discussed must have covered the work that the Deliverers perform for the Beginners and Enders. I sat at my computer thinking that this was going to be a very short chapter, not that there is anything wrong with a short chapter, it's just that one gets used to long chapters at times and the sly old ego gets in the way by wanting the chapters to be long as well. The spiritual side of me knows that things are what they are supposed to be and that this also includes the length of a chapter in a book. I placed all of the wild thoughts surrounding this subject to one side and let myself connect with Source. As usual, it was happy to connect and I felt the flood of warm and loving energy flow over me, removing my concerns and calming me down. The Source summarized the roles of the Deliverers and continued with the in-depth dialogues I was used to.

SE1: The Deliverers are those beings who work on the functional side of the work of the Beginners and Enders. Their role is a multidisciplined one that varies in any way that is necessary to allow the associated work of the Beginners and Enders to be implemented. They are not specialized to any particular job, role, or responsibility per se, although they are specialized to working with the functions of the entities they serve.

ME: That was an interesting end to the sentence, suggesting that the Deliverers serve the Beginners and Enders.

SE1: All entities that are Curators are of service. The statement is of no other significance.

That being said, the Deliverers do dedicate themselves to the work of the Beginners and Enders and so they are of specialized service, even though they are multidisciplined and as such are not truly specialized in the sense of being limited to one particular function within a series of possible functions when working in service to another entity.

I can see your eyes rolling into the back of your head.

ME: You have got me.

SE1: I will explain the roles of the Deliverers in an attempt to get your eyes back to the front of your head then.

In the scheme of the work that the Beginners and Enders perform, the Deliverers work at the minute detail that is required to implement the work that the Beginners and Enders desire to achieve to make the changes discussed in the previous dialogues.

ME: I know that this will be a logical comment but it seems that the roles of the Beginners and Enders is to create the strategy and process behind the work that they do, and the Deliverers do the actual work required to make those strategies and processes come into fruition.

SE1: You have come a long way around to come to that conclusion, but, yes, the Deliverers work on the details surrounding the work that the Beginners and Enders feel is necessary to ensure the Event Spaces and Event Streams are in continuity.

ME: As you are speaking, I am receiving an image of some of the work they are doing. They deal with the absolute minute details of the way events interact and interconnect. It's as if they work like embroiderers, but they are not embroidering cloth or twine, they are embroidering what I can only describe as being fiber optic cables. Each of the cables is an Event Stream within an Event Space. They weave them within and without each other, moving them from one logical place to another logical place. Each of the Event Streams represents a series of interconnected and interacting events within the overall or overarching Event Space. There is more, though. It is as though the so-called fiber optics that represent the Event Streams have what I can only call programs traveling through them like dots and dashes in a digital transmission of light. Each of these dots and dashes represent the events themselves within the Event Streams. The dots represent a short event and the dashes represent a long event. As I look closer, though, I see that there is a size to the dots and the dashes as well. The size of the dots represents the impact a specific event makes on the direction of the Event Stream. The size and length of the dashes indicate the duration of the event within the Event Stream as well as its impact or influence within the Event Stream. To put it another way, an event can be short but of high, medium, or low impact and importance and an event can also be of longer or long duration while also being of low, medium, or high impact or importance. The longer the dash, the longer the duration of the event and therefore the greater the duration of its overall influence on the Event Stream. The larger the size or diameter of the dot and/or the body of the dash, the greater the impact on the overall Event Stream.

All of this is of course for illustration purposes but the relevance feels unbelievably close to the truth. I felt invigorated again.

I see something else, though. I see entities moving in and around these dots and dashes. One of the entities moves close to a dot and creates a barrier or a shield around it. The dot changes appearance. Previously it looked, or should I say, appeared to be, a color that was in harmony with the colors of the dots and dashes before and after it. Now it appears to be a neutral color, one that would be acceptable to any area within the Event Stream. The entity looks like it is removing the dot—it is! It moves the dot to another location within the Event Stream and inserts it. The appearance changes to one that is in keeping with the appearance of the, in this instance, dot before the moved event and a dash behind the event. Initially, though, before the color of the inserted event changes to one that is the same as the preceding and resulting event, all three change color to a slightly reddish hue. This change in color is temporary, and within a few seconds, the color stabilizes to the natural color of the total series of dots and dashes in the local area of the insertion.

In the area of the removal of the event, a similar process occurs. Before the event is relocated, it is held in stasis and its neutral appearance or color is achieved. The two events that were before and after the removed event, two dashes, join together as interconnected events, or become the logical predecessor and resulting events. As they become the predecessor and resulting events, they too temporarily change appearance to one that is of a light blue color. They also change back to an appearance or color that is in harmony with the local events in the Event Stream. As I looked at this process closer, I noticed that these entities that were working on behalf of the Beginners and Enders were extremely efficient at moving events around. Moreover, the movement of events from one place to another appeared to be an amazingly regular practice. Events were seemingly moved or relocated, transplanted, or simply removed in rapid succession. I then got the impression that there was a lot of work to do here and that there was a queue of events that needed to be moved, transplanted, or relocated in some way.

I started to question what I was seeing here and as a result I sat back a moment. Every time I have discussed Event Space and Event Streams I am led to believe that we create the Event Spaces by the decisions and the choices we make and that they multiply (expand) or reduce (contract) as a result of their evolutionary benefits. This dialogue has made me understand that Event Spaces and Event Streams can be moved and modified to suit new locations in the Event Space or overall/overarching Event Stream. What I am seeing here is that the Deliverers, under the direction of the Beginners and Enders, are moving the locations of Event Spaces, and modifying them to suit or not as the case may be, all of the time, on a super regular basis. Does this mean that we have even less of an idea about the events within the Event Spaces and their Event Streams? I was starting to think as well that most of the Curators deal with the management and manipulation of Event Space and Event Streams and not the minute detail of maintaining an environment for us to exist within. I knew that this was not correct of course because I have received the summaries for each genre of Curator, but nevertheless, it did make one think.

SE1: This is making you think a bit, isn't it?

ME: You bet it is.

SE1: Then I will elaborate. The Deliverers work on the directives given by the Beginners and the Enders, and they are very good at it. The issue for you here is that your paradigms are being broken again. You expected a fundamental function of the structure of The Origin, Event Space, to be totally autonomous and self-maintaining. It can be, but it can also be manipulated by entities with the correct levels of functionality. You also expected that everything was totally linear in terms of the way Event Space and Event Stream operate. It can be, but it can also be manipulated and as a result become nonlinear in operation while also being linear in function— operation and function being two separate ways of working. What you are confused about is that "everything" needs to be maintained to a certain level to allow the evolutionary efficiency of its overall function to be maintained.

ME: Yes, I understand that, but what it looks like to me is that nothing is left to chance; there is no randomness, no true randomness in the multiverse. Everything looks as if it is steered and that nothing is made through choice.

SE1: The choices that are made by those entities/beings that use the opportunity to accelerate their evolutionary progression through the use of incarnation are the aspect of randomization of a well-oiled and maintained multiversal machine. This is because of the immersion experienced within the Event Space. It is the so-called mistakes that are individually and collectively made that create an Event Space that is out of harmony with the expected, or to use a better word, "desired" Event Space that is managed by the Curators, and in this instance the Deliverers, who act on behalf of the Beginners and Enders.

ME: So everything is manipulated?

SE1: No. Although it seems like it is from your standpoint, the major manipulation from the perspective of the Curators in general is to the optimal positional location or existence of an Event Space or an Event Stream.

ME: So, from the perspective of those entities that are working within the Event Space that is being relocated or manipulated to allow relocation, there is no difference or no difference that can be detected?

SE1: We have been down this road before, but the answer is the same. Some entities sense a difference; others do not. Rarely some know what is/has happened and work within their new Event Space and the environment within it that is created as a result of that Event Space being created.

ME: OK. Got it.

SE1: It might be useful to look at the reasons again for the dots and dashes that represent an Event Space being moved, transplanted, or removed.

Move, Transplant, Replace, or Remove: The Maintenance of an Event Stream

SE1: It is most important to know why an Event Space and its environment needs to be moved, transplanted, replaced, or removed within an Event Stream to be able to understand how the integrity of an Event Stream is maintained.

ME: Why? I mean, most of incarnate mankind don't pay attention to the planet they are on. Why would they need to understand why an Event Space is moved?

SE1: Simply because it provides some knowledge on how the Greater Reality that you exist within functions. It also gives theoretical physicists, who are on the border of spiritualism in their thinking, a way marker, should they decide to delve into your work and the work of others like you. Like you always say, today's spiritualism and metaphysics is tomorrow's science.

ME: OK. Got it.

You made me change the title of this section to include the words *"Maintenance of an Event Stream."* Is this not what we have been discussing all along?

SE1: Yes, of course, but this is a specific function of the Deliverers and although they work on behalf of the Beginners and Enders, they also have to work with their own understanding of the demands of the Beginners and Enders.

ME: Well, I suppose it makes sense to understand why one is doing what one is being asked to do before blindly doing it.

SE1: Correct. First of all, though, we will discuss this from the perspective of just one Event Stream, while recognizing that the decisions being made here can affect the movement, transplantation, replacement, or removal of an Event Space from one Event Stream to another as well. It's just a deeper level of understanding, one that functions within an Event Stream and between Event Streams.

ME: We have already discussed the movement of Event Spaces from one Event Stream to another, and I am sure we will discuss it again with the next genre of Curators. But as you say, this is in essence a deeper level of understanding.

SE1: Yes, it is and it is most important to go over this "old ground" a few times to allow it to sink in, so to speak. Let's get on with the descriptions then.

Moving an Event Space

An Event Space can only be moved if its outcomes, that being the connectivity with the resulting Event Space that is created from it, becomes locationally disharmonious with that resulting Event Space. This effectively means that the Event Space itself is disharmonious with the overall trend of the Event Stream when in the position it is in.

Event Spaces are only locationally disharmonious if the entities and beings working within it make it that way as a result of their decisions. The disharmony, however, should not be big enough to necessitate the need to remove the Event Space altogether from the Event Stream and quarantine it. In this instance, it can be moved to a position within the Event Stream that is more in keeping with the resulting connectivity of the Event Space, or it can be placed in parallel with the modified Event Stream where the preceding and resulting Event Spaces are joined together. This effectively allows the Event Space to continue within the Event Stream but without affecting the resulting Event Space as it was previously. The entities and beings within the moved Event Space also move with that Event Space.

Transplanting an Event Space

An Event Space should only be transplanted from one location within the Event Stream to another if the Event Space's experiential and evolutionary performance would benefit from it being in a location where a functionally, experientially, or evolutionary similar Event Space is not providing the desired connectivity to the resulting Event Space. The reciprocal possibility is also necessary with the Event Space that is being replaced (not the same as being replaced in the section later) is better placed in the location of the first Event Space. You could call this "swapping locations" within the Event Stream if you wish, but transplanting is more appropriate a word in this instance because the entities and beings within the Event Spaces being moved, move into the transplanted Event Space and do not move with their primary Event Space.

Replacing an Event Space

An Event Space is replaced with a new Event Space when the perpetuation of an Event Space in that location is required but the primary Event Space itself is disharmonious in its connectivity with the preceding Event Space and the resulting Event Space. In essence, the need for an Event Space in this location is a necessary key component of a series of Event Spaces within the Event Stream. It cannot be transplanted or moved due to the level of disharmony and the impact of the disharmony with the downstream Event Spaces and the effect it has on the upstream Event Spaces' ability to connect, due to causing continuity errors.

In this instance, a totally new Event Space, totally blank of entity-created events while actually being devoid of entities, is introduced to ensure there is no disharmony between the preceding and resulting Event Spaces. This Event Space is in effect just providing a connection between the two Event Spaces with a series of static micro-events in place to ensure there is a logical progression between the preceding and resulting Event Space. It is used when simply removing the disharmonious Event Space and joining the preceding and resulting Event Spaces is ineffectual.

In the event that a fully functional and populated Event Space is required to fill the connectivity gap between the preceding and resulting Event Spaces then a newly created and populated Event Space without the disharmonies can be introduced. Additionally, if a similar and parallel Event Space is already in existence and can be moved without detriment to its Event Stream then that can also be utilized. However, in both these situations this would be classified as transplantation.

Removing an Event Space

An Event Space can be removed in its entirety and not replaced if its experiential and evolutionary functionality is disharmonious and the end of the preceding and start of the resulting Event Spaces can be modified to allow a seamless level of connectivity, effectively negating the need for the Event Space to remain in place or for a replacement to be introduced.

The Event Space being removed is then subjected to (forced into) the normally automatic function of merging. This is so that the experiences of the parallelized entities and beings is reintegrated within the Event Space and Event Stream in the position where they would normally have reintegrated when the accrual of experiential and evolutionary content reaches a dead end. Within this process, all disharmonies are dissolved.

ME: I would guess that this is just a high-level description of the reasons why the Deliverers manipulate Event Spaces?

SE1: It is, but even though it is high level, it forms the basis of the reasons why Event Spaces are moved, transplanted, replaced, and removed.

Let's get on to the Waymakers. They also deal with Event Space, as do the four genres of Curator afterward!

ME: Good, I am starting to get all Event Spaced-Out!

The Waymakers

My comment in the last chapter seemed to be a pertinent one. To be honest, I was getting a little exasperated as well. There appeared to be a never-ending series of entities that were working with the multiversal environment from an Event Space and Event Stream perspective. I was very worried that you, dear reader, would be thinking the same, and would be minutes away from putting the book down and using it as a doorstop. It was therefore with some delight that I received the news that there were only four more Curators, after the Waymakers that is, that deal with the manipulation of Event Space and their Event Streams. I needed a change in direction, and I was feeling that my readers would need one as well. Noting that this was not going to happen in the next few chapters, I decided to get my head down and get on with the task at hand. Anyway, I thought, we are receiving a depth of detail about the use of Event Space by the Curators that we haven't had before.

SE1: Correct. You, that is incarnate mankind, haven't experienced this level of detail and it is only through dialogue with me about the roles and responsibilities of the different genres of Curator that this depth becomes available. If you are getting bored with this subject, make it more interesting by asking more questions.

ME: I am not bored; I am just worried about the level of detail and whether it will be attractive to my readers.

SE1: It's the detail that will attract your readers, not whether or not YOU think they will be bored by it. Remember, by trying to manipulate the level of detail that you are delivering to the metaphysical public, you are stopping those who are capable of assimilating that detail and understanding the concepts that surround them.

ME: Touché. Let's move on then, and I will try to become more inventive and searching with my questions.

SE1: Here we go then. **The Waymakers** are quite possibly one of the most specialized groups of beings within the Curators. The only exception being those entities that work on the environmental functionality of a local environment or habitat (a planet, for instance). They ensure that the work of the Beginners and Enders has a seamless insertion and withdrawal point relative to the effects of all Event Spaces and their fractals. They work on each parallel condition as it is created or uncreated to ensure that the changes experienced by the beings in these Spaces are minimalized to the point of incoherence, meaning that the beings themselves are not aware of the changes new parallel conditions create as they are affected by them.

ME: These beings seem very much like they do the work of the Deliverers.

SE1: At first glance I would agree with you, but it's the detail behind what they do which makes their specialization different from the Deliverers.

One way to look at the work of the Waymakers is to consider it as being focused on ensuring that there is continuity with the events, environment, and interactions that are experienced by those beings/ entities that are within the events and their parallelizations but that these parallelizations are a function of the work of the Beginners, Enders, and Deliverers.

ME: I have an image to work with and share now. The work of these beings really is detailed. They see the changes that are needed at the actual point of a being or entity's experience to ensure that they really don't have any continuity errors in their experience when a parallel or fractal Event Space is created.

SE1: Correct. They see the overall effects of the Beginners, Enders, and Deliverers on the downstream individualized and collective decisions of the beings or entities within their Event Space and how they interface with the Event Spaces that are proposed to be interfaced with their Event Space. They identify the areas of potential continuity error and work on ways to reduce those errors to a bare minimum or even zero.

ME: Wait a minute. What I can see here is that they move along the natural progression of the events within the interconnecting Event Spaces seeing where there are gaps or directional changes within the lines of continuity. I am just being told that this is very important work because an Event Space has a purpose that is unique to it and only it and that that purpose in terms of its inception and fulfillment must not change, else it negates its existence. These connections between preceding and resulting events of Event Spaces that are being moved, relocated, transplanted, or otherwise, is therefore of supreme importance because the objective is to make those interfacing aspects of the events within the Event Spaces function in a way that is consistent with the lines of continuity to the point of seeing no perceivable difference.

SE1: Now you are getting it. The Waymakers do just as their name describes: they create the ways which ensure that there is no loss of continuity. In essence, they are the engineers of the ways to keep continuity, even when there are none, or the result could be that no continuity may result later. If you take it down to the very close level of detail that they need to work on, you will see that they have the ability to change the ways in which individual entities or beings respond to their environment and how they interact with other entities or beings within that environment to ensure that continuity is maintained.

ME: But they don't actually do that themselves, do they?

SE1: No. They identify what needs to be done and how it is done. It is the responsibility of the Integrators to perform the "hands-on" work, so to speak. However, they do their work in a number of steps. They "try out" what they are proposing first before they ultimately pass on the methods of modification and the depth of those modifications that are necessary to the Integrators. In order to do this, they move along the lines of continuity performing various levels of tests to see what modification creates the most harmonious lines of continuity.

In order to do this, they move outside the Event Spaces being worked on, those being inserted, removed, transplanted, or parallelized and look at the fine detail in terms of the accuracy of continuity of those events that span the whole length of the event or events within the Event Spaces. It is only when they are satisfied that the lines of continuity are harmonious, that they advise the Integrators of the work that they are required to do.

ME: I very much feel that the Waymakers are good at paying attention to detail, even right down to doing a lot of the work that the next genre of Curators, the Integrators, perform.

SE1: They do work hard. In fact, I am glad that you mentioned that they perform a lot of work that the Integrators perform. It's not that they do their work for them (it's the other way around), so much as they create the overall need for the work that the Integrators perform.

You will notice that there is a lot of interaction with each of the genres of Curator.

ME: Yes, I do. It almost feels that they are one amorphous mass of maintenance entities.

SE1: Maybe that is a reasonable thought process, but I was looking more at the convolution and interactive interdependence of what they do rather than that they may feel as if they do each other's work and that, from what I can see in your mind, there is no actual need for the different genres of Curator.

ME: Yes, well, that was in the back of my mind.

SE1: That being said then, the next description may reinforce that thought process incorrectly, simply because the description of the work that they do will sound similar to other descriptions.

ME: I will try to remain open-minded and look for the deeper meaning then.

SE1: Good.

The most important function that the Waymakers perform is to work on changing the minds of entities, their decisions and ways they interact with their environment and other entities within that environment.

ME: Hold on a minute. I thought that it was the role of the Guides and Helpers to change the minds, the directions of an incarnate entity?

SE1: Ordinarily that is correct, but the directions given by the Guides and Helpers are relevant to the life plan of the incarnate entity they are responsible for. When the Waymakers work on changing the minds of an incarnate entity, they are working on the details surrounding making the events between two or more Event Spaces link together.

ME: How do they make an entity change its mind or thought process or direction?

SE1: First of all, they need to work with the Guide and Helpers of the incarnates that they need to work with to ensure that the overall life plan of the incarnate is not compromised. Remembering of course that a life plan is only a series of achievements that an incarnate entity has chosen; how it experiences or completes those achievements is fluid and can be changed. The only requirement is that the achievement is met in some way.

ME: But aren't there achievements within the life plan that are surplus, that are extras that can be invoked in the event that the incarnate entity completes its, shall we say, minimum achievement requirement?

SE1: Yes, of course. What you don't know is that the total number of achievements within a life plan can be mixed and matched within reason. As a result, this makes the life plan more achievable and, more importantly, more adaptable to the vagaries of the incarnate entities' interactions with its environment and other incarnates within that environment.

ME: So is there a nucleus of achievements within a life plan that must be met, that the Guide and Helpers must help the incarnate entity experience above all others and therefore the Waymakers cannot effect?

SE1: Yes. There are mainstream achievements that an incarnate entity must meet, but the level of experience gained with that achievement is also variable. As long as the achievement is made, how big it is isn't important. Although, there are those who from the Earth perspective would say that if the achievement was to be a doctor then being a famous surgeon or important consultant suggests that the achievement is more successful than being a general practitioner or just a general doctor within a hospital. In this example, being a doctor is the achievement, which has been met. The level of experience is designated by the depth of achievement, irrespective of status or fame resulting from it.

ME: So as long as the nucleus of achievements is met, everything else in the life plan, achievement-wise, can be manipulated by either the Guide and Helpers or the Waymakers?

SE1: That's right.

ME: So just how does a Waymaker change the minds, the thoughts, and directions and therefore ultimately, the experiences and achievements of an incarnate or other entity?

SE1: This may sound overly simple, but they work in the same way as the Guide and Helpers, hence the need to interact with the Guide and Helpers of the entities that they are working with to affect the changes required to necessitate the levels of interconnectivity between Event Spaces that were previously incompatible.

ME: So they don't actually interact with the incarnate entities and or other entities directly?

SE1: On rare occasions, yes, they do. However, in the event that they have identified key entities that need to be worked with, whose directions, thoughts, and achievements need to be manipulated to ensure that the continuity of the Event Space being worked on is consistent with the continuity of the Event Space that it is being linked with, they need to work with the entities that are experts in knowing the incarnate entity and its ways of working. Those entities are the Guide and Helpers. Why are you chuckling?

ME: Well, it's just that I am seeing a picture of a Waymaker whispering in the ear of an entity, trying to persuade it to change its mind from the current direction it is going in to one that is in favor of the direction that the Waymaker wants it to go in.

SE1: Oh, I see. Well, that is the job of the Guide and Helpers if you want to think of it in that way. As I have just stated, it is only on very rare occasions when a Waymaker will directly intervene, having an importance above those of the Guide and Helpers, to change the mind and direction of a key entity if that entity is the nexus of a nest of changes and that the importance of the change in direction is more than that of the life plan in its current and expected/predicted levels of achievement. In this instance, the planned life plan may be changed with those achievements that are already experienced, recorded, and those achievements that are planned or are still in the nucleus of achievements modified to suit the greater need. The entity affected is compensated for any evolutionary gains being missed.

ME: If the Waymakers work at this low level to ensure that the entities working within the Event Space are experientially compliant to the needs of the local continuity of the Event Spaces being joined, who works with the environmental changes at this level to support the entities that have been made to change direction?

SE1: The Integrators!

The Integrators

I had just returned from a few days' break from working on this book and I noted that in the first summary in the start of this dialogue The Source stated that the Integrators performed the groundwork of the Waymakers. That they are the beings that weave the different events together into a seamless holographic state so that each Event Space is in contact with each other Event Space either directly or indirectly through direct and indirect contact with other events.

Having absorbed the information in the dialogues with The Source about the work of the Beginners, Enders, and Waymakers, I was a little troubled. I couldn't see what additional work they could perform that was above and beyond that which we had already talked about. I sat here at my computer and waited for my link to The Source to establish itself with me, to allow The Source to explain how the statement about the work that the Integrators make is different from what we had already discussed and what I already knew. As usual, The Source had an explanation for this, and my concerns and worries were put to one side.

SE1: It is possibly a little difficult for you to see the differences in the work that some genres of Curator do when they work so closely together. For me and those entities that are not incarnate, it is easy to see the differences for they, like you when disincarnate, have specific energetic signatures.

ME: Thank you. So just what work do they do to weave the different events together into a seamless holographic state so that each Event Space is in contact with each other?

SE1: First of all, you need to realize that the Integrators, as with the Waymakers, work on the delivery side of the roles that the Curators have to perform in maintaining the overall functionality of the multiverse. This means that they work on finer detail, much finer, than those Curators that we have previously discussed.

Let me continue then by resetting a mental process for you to use. Normally, Event Space and Event Streams function, that being, they multiply (expand) and divide (contract), on an automatic basis, creating new Event Spaces and Event Streams resulting from the interactions between entities and the environment they are working with within the Event Space and Event Stream, including the possibilities associated with them. The work of the genre of Curators that work with Event Space is to manipulate it from that which functions automatically, to that which is desired or needed by the Curators, to ensure the evolutionary efficiency of the multiverse and its environments is maintained at an optimal level at all times. This means that the overall functional strategy for the multiverse is continually being fined-tuned, so to speak.

ME: Yes. I remember you advising me of this, more than once or twice.

SE1: It is good practice to keep reminding you and your readers of the processes and ways in which the Curators are working because it can all become a blur.

ME: Agreed.

SE1: Good. Getting back to your question then, the Integrators look at all of the changes that are being made from the highest level down, and work on the integration of those Event Spaces that are about to be changed as a result of the work of the Waymakers. They achieve this from the perspective of understanding how the "changed minds" of those entities that are considered to be key to introducing continuity between Event Spaces actually affect those Event Spaces and act accordingly.

In previous dialogues on the manipulation of Event Space and their Event Streams, we have considered it from the position of the overall or overarching Event Space. The work of the Integrators, being a collaboration with the work of the Waymakers, and in some ways feeding into the work of the Seed Makers [*see next chapter—GSN*], focuses on those Event Spaces that are local to the entities or beings that create them.

ME: I am just receiving an image of what they do. I shall explain it.

SE1: Be my guest.

ME: They connect together those Event Spaces that are local to the individual entities. It's a bit like molecular cohesion or molecular splicing. To ensure that the overall or overarching Event Spaces that are being connected together are totally connected and that continuity is maintained at the point of interface of any interconnecting Event Space, they work at the entity level. They work on connecting those Event Spaces localized to a particular entity or key entity by placing them in the correct interfacing event. Localized Event Space is an individualized version of the overall or overarching Event Space and as such creates a localized reality as well.

The Integrators work on maintaining the cohesion between existing local Event Spaces or creating an interface between those local Event Spaces, those that are at the connecting interface between two overall or overarching Event Spaces that are being linked together. The work of the Waymakers is to change the minds or directional thoughts of the entities and key entities that are the interfacing events within the two Event Spaces. However, the Integrators manipulate the realities created by the localized Event Spaces at entity level to ensure that those realities created by the local Event Spaces support each other's existence creating continuity, plausibility, and therefore context.

I see that the creation and manipulation of realities here is the key because at the entity level, and certainly the incarnate entity level, it is the interdependence of realities created by the localized Event Spaces that maintains the cohesion between the overall or overarching Event Spaces. It is context that keeps the interaction between realities coherent because when realities that are out of context are linked together, the entities that have created the realities start to question them, breaking the cohesion between the realities and therefore the local Event Spaces.

SE1: Very good. And this attention to detail is why I called it holographic.

ME: This is OK in terms of the overall explanation, but how do they change the relationship between an individual's localized Event Space and its relating reality? Just how do they stitch them together?

SE1: They work on the relationships between the local Event Spaces, local Event Streams, and the resulting realities of individuals and collectives of individuals that interact or could interact with the Event Spaces that need to be linked together.

Using those local Event Spaces that are normally or naturally linked together as a template for context, they see what changes need to be made to allow the plausibility of one local Event Space being linked with another that it is not currently linked with.

ME: Is this not the same as cohesion or context?

SE1: No. Cohesion is that which results from the plausibility of one Event Space being linked to another in a natural, or if not natural, a compatible, way. Context is the overarching subject matter that the Event Space is created from. Plausibility is therefore the level of probability that two unrelated Event Spaces could be linked together.

ME: I don't quite get it!

SE1: Think of it in these terms. If you saw a mobile phone in the hands of a person dressed in medieval clothes in a medieval environment, you would think that the two are out of context, that the person dressed in the medieval clothes in the same environment could not possibly have such a device because that technology and its infrastructure was not available at that time.

ME: That's right. I would start to wonder if the mobile phone actually existed. I would also wonder if I was actually hallucinating.

SE1: Of course you would, and that is because the two are out of context and therefore the two Event Spaces that are linked together that allowed that image to be in existence could not coexist and therefore are not cohesive and the two being linked together is not plausible. There is therefore no relationship.

On the other hand, if the person in medieval clothing is not actually in a medieval Event Space, but is in a representation of medieval Event Space in an Event Space where there is the mobile phone technology, such as in a medieval reenactment, then the two together, although being out of context, are nevertheless plausible. In this case, there can be cohesion between the two Event Spaces and they can be linked together. There is a relationship.

In the case of two local Event Spaces that are not linked together, the Integrators create an interfacing event that allows plausibility between the events within the two local Event Spaces that are to be linked together, therefore creating cohesion between the two and a relationship.

ME: And this works even if they are out of context?

SE1: Yes, it does. You see, if in the minds of the entities affected by, or who created, the local Event Spaces, it can be seen that the two events within the linked Event Spaces are plausible, then that level of plausibility is reinforced and becomes cohesive.

You are aware that Event Spaces can and are created through the possibility of something happening or coming into being?

ME: Yes, I am.

SE1: And you are also aware that an Event Space can also be created if there is the remotest chance of the possibility of the possibility of the possibility of possible possibilities?

ME: Yes, I am.

SE1: Then you will recognize that the variations on possibilities can also be used by the Integrators to create the interfacing events required to create plausibility between two events and therefore two Event Spaces, creating a relationship.

ME: I guess they must be able to if you are advising me as such.

SE1: Yes, I am and, yes, they can and do. I will also advise you that they not only use all of the variations of the possibility of the possibility of the possibility of possible possibilities to create the interfacing event, but they also need to work on them as well.

ME: Why? Ah! Don't tell me. It's because the different variations of the possibility of the possibility of the possibility of possible possibilities change with the introduction of the new event.

SE1: That's right.

ME: Incredible. What I am seeing now is an image of all of the Event Spaces that are created or that need to be worked on by the Integrators. It's based upon an image I have seen and described before.

SE1: Go ahead and explain it.

ME: OK. Every Event Space that is created creates the possibility of a new Event Space fractal. This is also the same for those Event Spaces that are linked together by the Integrators when there was previously no link. But what I hadn't appreciated was that this is not a 2D representation, as I had seen and described in the past, but that it is 3D [*what we humans call 3D, that is—GSN*]. The best way to describe it is like seeing a tree, like seeing how a tree's branches grow and divide and grow and divide. No, it's more like seeing a series of trees where the trunks of the trees oppose each other with the trees themselves joining at the tips of the ends of the branches. It's like one tree is on top of another tree with the one on top being upside down. There is more, though. The image I am seeing now is that there are lots of trees all joined at the tips of the branches. It's like a big ball of treetops all joined together with the trunks sticking out from the treetop ball. The branches are the fractals and where Event Spaces link together and the trunk is the resulting mainstream Event Space.

Again there is more, though. Just when I thought that the trunks indicated that this was the evolutionary end of an Event Space and its Event Streams the trunk starts to fractalize again. There is no end to this ebb and flow of the creation and dissolution of Event Spaces. As I zoom out I also see that there is no end to the size of this image. It's ended up looking like a huge fluffy tree-like ball of Event Spaces that fills every aspect of space within the multiverse.

SE1: It also fills every aspect of space within The Origin as well.

ME: I bet that the Curators are glad that they don't have to work with the structure and the Event Spaces within the wider environment of The Origin?

SE1: Of that they are most pleased. Come on, let's move on to the Seed Makers. These Curators work on even smaller Event Space detail than the Integrators. They can also create the possibility of plausibility and therefore the relationships between events.

The Seed Makers

I looked at the previous summary for this genre of Curator and got excited. I sat back a moment and thought about what I had just said. What am I so excited about, you might think? Mmmm! Upon reflection I decided that I had best let you, dear reader, read the summary yourselves before I express why I am so excited.

The Source Entity had stated that the Seed Makers are the creators of small events, very small events, and that they are capable of being inserted or withdrawn from the totality of Event Space without affecting those beings that are working within the normal functions of the events themselves. The reason that they are called Seed Makers is because the events they insert allow the creation of much bigger events to be created on what appears to be a natural level, that being, as a natural fractal (later larger fractals) of an Event Space or series of Event Spaces or Event Streams. Apparently, this function can also act in reverse as where the withdrawal of an event can also be seen as the natural demise of an Event Space resulting from it reaching its natural evolutionary conclusion at the point of the withdrawal of that event. Knowing what I/we know about how Event Space can and is manipulated by various genres of Curator now makes me think that an event that is removed without the correct and remedial work being undertaken can and does result in the natural demise of the Event Space that that event is a function of. But is this really correct? The Source decided to put me straight before we started to get into the discussion and description about the Seed Makers.

SE1: I am going over old ground here but in the natural order of Event Space functionality, that being, when there is no external manipulation by one of my Curators, an event cannot be removed as a result of natural Event Space function. Removal of an Event

Space, no matter how small or inconsequential, is not part of its normal function, even though Event Space itself is intelligent. If an Event Space is left to its own devices, the events within it are naturally created and/or fractalized by the decisions of those entities that exist within it. They are also naturally dissolved/defractalized by the decisions of those entities that exist within it. Events and Event Spaces within the overall or overarching Event Space always ebb and flow in this way. This is a natural function that occurs even if there are no entities within an Event Space because the environment within the Event Space also changes as a result of the forces and energies within that environment creating myriad possibilities for environmental change.

ME: So the removal, insertion, or movement of an Event Space, no matter how small, is a function that is only possible as a result of external (Curator) intervention.

SE1: Correct.

ME: What is fascinating me, though, is the Event Spaces that the Seed Makers are working with, what I will call microscopic Event Spaces, and introducing them or removing them without major effect on the rest of the overall or overarching Event Space.

SE1: It's more than that. The microscopic Event Spaces that the Seed Makers create are capable of being introduced and/or removed from Event Spaces that are local to an individual entity or being without detriment as well. In fact, this is what they do.

ME: Can you be more explicit?

SE1: The Seed Makers are not called the Seed Makers for nothing. What they do is to create microscopically small Event Spaces that are specific to the needs of an individual entity, being, or environment. They work with how the entity or being interacts with the environment or how the environment interacts with the actions of the entity or beings within the environment.

In essence, what they do is create a number of new micro-possibilities that can be inserted into a local, collective, larger collective or overall or overarching Event Space in order to create a change to the wider Event Space environment from a natural perspective to one where the inserted micro Event Space is the start of the change, the catalyst. The change can be the result of a discussion with an entity's Guide and Helpers to help the entity change its direction within its life plan or, in most cases, it can be a need to change the direction of an entity, group of entities, or the environment to create a more evolutionary efficient experience. In any event, the micro Event Space inserted should not be noticeable as a catalyst until observed from further down the Event Stream. What I mean is that the micro Event Space should not be monumental in its immediate impact, so to speak, but should be subtle and create a slow but sure domino effect to the changes expected as a result of the insertion.

ME: So a micro Event Space is really an event?

SE1: No, it's an Event Space in its own right.

ME: I don't understand what you mean then.

SE1: Consider Event Space as a bubble and I will send you an image to help you understand.

I was suddenly suspended in an environment that I knew was an Event Space, an overall or overarching Event Space. I then moved into an Event Stream and was inserted into an Event Space that was localized to an entity. I didn't know what or where the entity or being was but that didn't seem to matter, it was the Event Space that was the subject here and not the entity that was creating the local Event Space. Within the local Event Space I could feel, and could have experienced if I had the time, any event that this entity had been part of or had created within its local Event Space. The Source was clearly using this entity and its Event Space as an example because it could easily have been a larger or collective Event Space. I was told to bear in mind that the Seed Makers create a number of micro Event Spaces to solve a problem or satisfy a need (see the Seeders in the next chapter) what I was about to witness was specific to a "chosen" micro Event Space and its insertion.

From my vantage point in this entity's local Event Space, I saw a small sphere being inserted. This was the micro Event Space, and its role was to affect the entity in a certain way, one where it might desire to change its direction and that that direction may also influence and change the direction of other entities or beings. At first the detail within the Event Space was observed as a wild transient thought and then discarded. The Seed Makers relocated it, making the opportunity for it to be observed for a second time. This time it was observed and the entity chose to use it. As this microscopic Event Space became more dominant in the existence of the entity, it started to be more influential and grew as a result, becoming bigger and bigger. As it grew larger, it touched other local Event Spaces, linking them together. It continued to grow and became a collective Event Space which later touched other collective Event Spaces creating a bigger collective Event Space. It continued in the same fashion until it touched on and engulfed the overall or overarching Event Space, becoming the overall or overarching Event Space in its own right. It was an image of a bubble getting bigger, touching other bubbles or groups of bubbles and getting bigger, and, as a result, becoming the biggest bubble encompassing all other bubbles. It was amazing to observe.

ME: So this is what you mean about what the Seed Makers do; they create the possibility of change by making an Event Space so small that it doesn't upset the natural flow of events but eventually absorbs all others and becomes the flow of events.

SE1: That's right.

ME: How does that work for the removal of a micro Event Space then?

SE1: The removal of a micro Event Space can be considered to be the reverse of the process used in the insertion of a micro Event Space.

ME: That's easy then.

SE1: No, not quite. You see, when a micro Event Space is inserted, it creates the domino effect just described if that is the intention behind the insertion of the micro Event Space. The removal of a micro Event Space can create both a domino effect and an implosion or dissolution of Event Spaces. If you like, you can call it a reverse domino effect.

ME: I would have thought that it would have just stopped what was expected to be created, Event Space-wise, from its point of, let's say, inception?

SE1: It can do that, but that is just one scenario. You see, the removal of a micro Event Space is more complicated than inserting one.

With the insertion of a micro Event Space, it is understood that it is required to create other Event Spaces, changes in paradigms, or change the direction in an entity or being's life plan. The removal of a micro Event Space is used to remove other Event Spaces, change paradigms, or change the direction of an entity or being's life plan. The only supposed difference is the creation/reduction of so-called downstream Event Spaces, but removing them, when they are in an existing Event Space and Event Stream, requires more attention to detail.

ME: Are there any micro Event Spaces that do not create downstream events and Event Spaces?

SE1: Yes, there are countless numbers of them. What you need to know is this, though, that the Seed Makers can see what "grows" from an Event Space perspective, what grows from the point of insertion of a micro Event Space, what dissolves from the point of removal or insertion of a micro Event Space, and what simply doesn't happen at all.

ME: Can you explain in more detail?

SE1: Yes, I will separate them out. Note that we have already described in some detail the function of Event Space growth due to the insertion of a micro Event Space, and so I will only describe it again in brief.

Event Space growth due to the insertion of a micro Event Space is due to the insertion of a key event that invokes a cascade of events that affect other events and their Event Spaces, linking them together to create new localized Event Spaces and the possibility of a new overarching or overall Event Space.

Event Space growth due to the removal of a micro Event Space is created as a result of the removal of a key, but nevertheless important point, in an Event Space or Event Stream that inhibits or deflects the direction of expected or desired event growth. It is usually attributed to the thought process of an entity or being and its ability to link into the events that it is required to work with to allow the downstream growth of the direction of an event.

To think of it in earthly terms, try to consider the removal of an entity that resists a certain level of change that it is being exposed to or the ability to follow up a thought process or an opportunity. Another way to consider it would be to think of an inventor, say Thomas Edison, giving up after his second or third failure in making a useable electric light bulb. The removal of the thought process of failure as an inhibitor to success allowed him to continue his work and the myriad number of experiments required to reach the stage of creating the right material to manufacture a robust filament and the environment necessary for that filament to exist within to allow it to achieve a useable longevity.

Event Space dissolution due to the insertion of a micro Event Space is created as a result of introducing an event that acts as an inhibitor to the initial, existing, or continuous growth of a series of events in an Event Space, ultimately resulting in the collapse of growth and dissolution of the events within the Event Space and later the Event Space itself.

Another good Earth-based example of this is the loss of inertia surrounding the use of a transport modality in favor of another. A good example here is the adoption of canals over the use of roads to transport heavy goods around relatively flat countries. The insertion of a paradigm-based micro Event Space via a respected individual resulted in a change in the direction of how best to transport large quantities of cargo around a country from using what was going to be a natural progression of using roads to one where the creation of waterways was required. However, because this did not completely dissolve the road-based transportation Event Space, a subsequent micro Event Space was inserted later to change that direction back to that which was a natural progression and dissolve the Event Space that supported the paradigm of transportation via man-made waterway—but not river or sea.

Event Space dissolution due to the removal of a micro Event Space is used to actively create a natural dissolution of an expected downstream Event Space due to the lack of supporting desire to progress or maintain the paradigm associated with that Event Space.

A good Earth-based example of this would be the removal of the Event Space surrounding the use of the HOTAL engine, the concept of which was developed in the late 1980s. This was purported to allow the use of a modified jet-based aero engine to remove the need for rockets used in space flight or low-orbit air transport. The desire required to support a paradigm of interested individuals in positions of authority and respect to fuel its growth was removed as an experiment in understanding the fragility of technology-based Event Spaces and their ability to be changed. The subsequent events and Event Space surrounding this technology are now poor memories only maintained in a small number of interested people. This opportunity, however, may be introduced later through the insertion of a new micro Event Space creating the desire for such technology when the supporting materials, designs, and sympathetic financial supporters are in place and incarnate mankind is more spiritually mature.

Event Space stasis due to the removal of a micro Event Space is created to actively stop the key start point of an expected downstream Event Space coming into existence. One way to consider this is the removal of the confidence surrounding an invention by the inventor choosing stability of income if in a full-time and established career over initial financial uncertainty and the need for risk-taking, or the fear of a change in lifestyle. In incarnate mankind's terms, this could be considered as an opportunity lost where the micro Event Space surrounding the start of a new Event Space masks the potential associated with the new Event Space which results in its dissolution at the point of creation or even its static growth. Static growth for an Event Space can be considered as being an Event Space that does not create any fractals due to the lack of opportunities that create decision points.

SE1: There is another function of the insertion or removal of a micro Event Space.

ME: And that is?

SE1: That the insertion or removal of a micro Event Space is the most effective way of changing a being's life plan.

ME: But we have already mentioned this. Why mention it again?

SE1: I mentioned that a being's life plan can be changed earlier but that was relative to the need to change a life plan for the benefit of creating a seamless change that allows a change to an overall or overarching Event Space. This is relative to a being's life plan that has been requested to be changed by the Aspect from the energetic levels. It's usually by its Guide who has either identified a need for a change as a result of the Aspect actively desiring a change, or that the Guide and Helpers can see a potential for the incarnate Aspect being incapable of steering itself back into the main direction of the life plan if it is off course, so to speak.

ME: So again, the Curators are involved not only with the maintenance of the multiversal environment, but they can also be of service to those entities or beings that incarnate? Hang on, I thought that it was difficult to change an incarnate's individual life plan?

SE1: The Curators can and do interact with the Guide and Helpers of an incarnate entity. However, if the need to change an incarnate entity's life plan is a function of the need to change the Event Space it exists within by using the insertion or removal of a micro Event Space relevant to its life plan, then that is accepted as part of a higher order. If it is at the request of the Aspect, then there needs to be a good justification for the change in the life plan that requires the insertion or removal of a micro Event Space. There needs to be a rock-solid justification anyway to make a change to an incarnate entity's life plan even if it doesn't need insertion or removal of a micro Event Space.

ME: Why the need for the insertion or removal then?

SE1: Simply because it allows the upstream ability to change downstream events in a life plan in an easier way. This creates the condition where the entity feels that it is in control of its incarnation rather than being directed by some unknown force and the feeling that they have no control of their incarnation.

ME: What you are saying then is that, at the incarnate entity/being level, the insertion or removal of a micro Event Space is to invoke the possibility of the incarnate making the choices and decisions that result in it going in the new and desired life plan direction and not the actual changes themselves?

SE1: Correct. This creates the best seamless scenario possible and one that removes any downstream disharmony or irregularities. It is the most efficient way to change a life plan but needs significant backroom planning, so to speak, hence the need for rock-solid justifications. Having said that, I reiterate that changes to a life plan are not normal and are avoided because the Aspect (TES), Guide, and Helpers agreed to the life plan prior to authority to incarnate being given, therefore the life plan must have been achievable by that Aspect. Changing a life plan is therefore a major digression from the agreed plan.

We have spoken enough about the Seed Makers. Let's move on to the Seeders.

ME: OK.

The Seeders

SE1: **The Seeders** are a group of Curators that work for the Seed Makers. They have a rather interesting role insomuch as they have the authority and ability to skillfully choose the micro Event Space/s in which to insert or withdraw within the seed Event Space [*the one to be changed—GSN*]. Think of it in terms of a number of micro Event Spaces being available, as a result of being created by the Seed Makers, with each of them creating the desired change to the overall or overarching Event Space. They are able to choose the best micro Event Space to use and the moment of insertion. To achieve this, the Seeders work with "what if" scenarios created by working with The Source's energetic memory and choosing the optimal moment of insertion or withdrawal.

As with all entities that work with Event Space, they have the capability of manipulating it. Even though Event Space is a pan-Origin intelligent energy in its own right, those entities that absorb themselves in its functionality are eventually able to manipulate it.

ME: What you are suggesting here then is that, even at this level of entity, they are not absolutely clear about how Event Space works and have to run a number of checks to see which inserted or removed micro Event Space achieves the best result?

SE1: Yes, fun, isn't it!

ME: Sorry, I don't understand!

SE1: Event Space is very adaptable and when a change is made, a whole new set of possibilities, the possibility of possibilities, and the possibility of possible possibilities becomes available. Although, the dialogue we are having now suggests that the manipulation of

Event Space is an exact science from the perspective of beings such as the Curators, it is not.

ME: I am just getting a picture of what you are suggesting.

SE1: Go on.

ME: Well, what I am seeing is that to truly steer Event Space to a desired or required Event Space and Event Stream, there needs to be constant changes to the fine detail via the insertion or removal of micro Event Spaces to allow the desired/required Event Space to be invoked. This is the reason for the ability to choose from a number of micro Event Spaces while also having the ability to choose which one is suitable for which insertion/removal point within the Event Stream. From the perspective of the Seeders and other Curators, it all looks as if the Event Space that is being worked on is constantly under recalibration or manipulation, but from the perspective of those entities or beings in the environment created by the overall or overarching Event Space, it feels and operates as if everything is in a logical progression.

What I now see is that the Seeders, together with the use of your energetic memory and the ability to create "what if" scenarios, and observe their functions from start of event to end of event, are able to create a portfolio, for want of a better word, of optimal micro Event Spaces to insert and/or remove at various points in the Event Stream of the overall or overarching Event Space to create the optimal Event Space that allows what is required of that Event Space from an interactive and evolutionary perspective to come into fruition.

SE1: And all of this includes the fractals as well, don't forget.

ME: Yes, how could I forget the fractals? Hang on, I was being flippant, of course! The amount of work they have to do includes all of the fractal Event Spaces as well, hence the need to choose from a number of micro Event Spaces and a number of insertion/removal points within the Event Stream. So when I was thinking of just one Event Space and one Event Stream that they work on, they also work on the hidden detail of all the parallel versions that are being created.

SE1: Yes, of course.

ME: Why do they need to work on the fractal Event Spaces and Event Streams?

SE1: Because, as I have stated many times, these fractals also provide parallel opportunities for experiencing learning and evolving, doubling, trebling, and quadrupling, etc., etc., etc., the ability to accrue the maximum possible evolutionary content that an incarnate or disincarnate entity or being can, within an experience and its fractals.

ME: Yes, I am aware of that, but it doesn't stop me from asking the same questions time and time again. I am aware that Guides and many of the Curators have the ability to work on multiple Event Spaces, those being the fractals created and dissolved through the choices made by the entities or beings within the environment that they work in. I am also aware that different genres of Curator work around the fractals in different ways. I am just trying to understand how the Seeders work with the different fractals of the micro Event Spaces they plan and choose to use in their role.

I do have one other question first, though, and it is not quite related to the Curators per se, but it is to the nomenclature used.

SE1: Carry on.

ME: Well, it is a bit basic but it is one that I feel will be important to the readers.

SE1: As I said, carry on.

ME: What is the difference between a being and an entity? I mean, we have both used them in the same context throughout this dialogue, but if that was the case, why use different words?

SE1: It would be incorrect to say that they are one and the same thing because they are not. I will elaborate.

It is all to do with the sentience. A being is a small individualized unit of me, one that has a nominal level of sentience that is assigned to a body of energy by me. This can be a TES, an Aspect of a TES, or a Shard of an Aspect. It can also refer to the creator of that individualization, which can be used to describe the relationship between The Origin and I. The demarcation here is that it is created by another being of higher or similar sentience.

An entity is created through the natural attraction of similar or sympathetic energies that develops its own intelligence as a result of groups of energies moving together to create a bigger group of intelligent energies. Once the intelligence grows to the point of being able to make deliberate decisions about attracting other energies, and those energies that are attracted also have enough intelligence to choose to enter into an attracted or communal state, the intelligence is on the road to changing its status to consciousness and later creativity with sentience being much further down the line [*see* The Origin Speaks—*GSN*].

ME: So to summarize, a being is created through the separation/individualization of existing sentience and/or energy, and an entity is created through intelligent attraction of energy leading to sentience.

SE1: That is reasonable enough. You see, a being is already sentient whereas an entity may be at any point along the road to sentience including being in the low-intelligence but nevertheless decision-making point, or in fact, fully sentient. One is created sentient whereas the other actually evolves to the point of being sentient—both can make decisions that result in the creation of a new Event Space.

ME: I am really glad we got that one out of the way. Moreover, it's really good to know that there are reasons for the use of these words and that we are not just duplicating the description.

SE1: I would never do that. It's just not an efficient or effective way of describing a concept. We should go back to the first question you had on understanding how the Seeders work with the different fractals of the micro Event Spaces they plan, and choose to use, in their role.

I want you to consider that the Seeders have the capability to link themselves with the micro Event Spaces that they are planning to use and insert into the various scenarios they study before they choose them as "live" micro Event Spaces. When they use my energetic memory, they are capable of both being the observer and the participant of the functions and actions resulting from the insertion of the micro Event Space they are working with and the insertion or removal point that they are expecting to use. I will send you an image of how they work so that you can describe it.

ME: Thank you. I can see the image of a single Seeder. It appears to be at what I can only describe as a viewing portal. The viewing portal is the access to your energetic memory. This viewing portal is not in what incarnate mankind would call two- or three-dimensional display; it is aligned as a function of event experiences, the alignment of which is in the logical progression of the events as they unfold.

A Seeder, seen as a ball of pure sentient energy, chooses from a selection of micro Event Spaces that are also represented by a ball, a ball of Event Space. This ball is inserted at a certain point in an Event Stream, one where there is a known fractal probability and where the fractals of this probability are seen, and new Event Spaces of various sizes and fractal divisions are created. Event Streams are also created as a result. These are the directions in which the fractals go and in which new fractals can and are created. The Seeder is in two positions I note; one where it is the observer of the creation or dissolution of Event Spaces and/or Event Streams, and another where parts of it are taken with the micro Event Space that it has inserted. It appears like there are lots of little lines being projected or pulled from the Seeder. These are bits of itself following the micro Event Space at its point of insertion and following all of the Event Stream and Event Space fractals. The Seeder is both inside and outside the unfolding Event Spaces and the Event Streams. In this way, it can both observe and experience all of the possible events created, or not as the case may be, and all of their possibilities concurrently. It knows when its level of understanding of the ultimate outcome desired from the insertion point is assured and ends the scenario. Choosing the next micro Event Space and maybe a new insertion point, it returns to being both the observer and participant again, with a new set of fractals being created.

ME: Isn't having all those strings flowing from them to each micro Event Space and other resulting Event Spaces a burden for them in terms of their ability to process all the information that they are receiving?

SE1: There is a point where they can manage on their own, so to speak, but when the amount of work they have to do to follow all the Events and Event Streams becomes difficult to follow efficiently, the Seeder can mirror itself to perform this role in parallel.

ME: So they have a limitation in the amount of fractals that they can work with?

SE1: Not really. It's more a case of working in the most efficient and effective way possible so that they can make an educated decision as to which micro Event Spaces to use and where to insert or indeed remove them. Mirroring themselves allows them to parallel process in every way possible to allow them to do their job.

ME: Placing themselves in a parallel processing or mirroring allows them to look at many Event Spaces and their fractals, but what allows them to make the detailed choice about which micro Event Space is appropriate at which insertion point or removal point?

SE1: From the perspective of your incarnate human mind everything looks linear and so the mirroring function the Seeders use appears to be linearized when they look at the Event Spaces and the actions and reactions that their insertions or removals of micro Event Space and their locations create, but this is not quite correct.

ME: How do you mean? I would have thought that the Seeder would need to be able to accelerate the experience of observing the effects of inserting or removing micro Event Spaces.

SE1: It can and it does it in two ways. One is observational and the other is experiential.

ME: Don't tell me, I can see it. A Seeder uses your energetic memory function to allow it to create the different "what if" scenarios to allow it to see the different Event Spaces that are created as a result of their work. The Seeder also needs to experience the changes to the Event Spaces that its work makes from the perspective of the entity or being who is experiencing the Event Spaces and Event Streams by moving into those Event Spaces, micro, local, global, etc., and their fractals, and zooming in and out of them by the mirroring or paralleling process. In this way, they can zoom into the various events—and look backward, forward, up and down, so to speak. While in this "immersed" state, it can achieve and create things that it cannot do while in the observation mode of using your energetic memory. While being immersed, while being in all of the Event Spaces that are linked to the Seeder, via the lines from the Seeder to the different fractals, it can move into those individual lines with its mirrored sentience, observe its work in all of the Event Space and Event Stream fractals via your energetic memory and experience all of the Event Space and Event Stream fractals via the mirroring function, simultaneously. In this way, it can make minor modifications within a "what if" scenario to increase the efficiency of a desired outcome if the best micro Event Space is not quite perfect or acceptable in its delivery in as fast and as efficient a way possible. In essence, it can observe in both "real time" and "fast forward/reverse" for all Event Spaces and Event Streams and their fractals created as a function of the insertion or removal of the micro Event Streams chosen, and select the optimal micro Event Space/s and their insertion/removal points. They can achieve a decision as to which micro Event Space/s to use and its optimal insertion or removal points in a nanosecond from our incarnate perspective.

This is amazing. From the viewpoint of the incarnate human, all of this happens in an instant. It's just like the Seeders look at a series of timelines, insert and/or remove a few changes, dive into the scenarios and their fractals, and move on to the next job they have to do.

SE1: Yes. It happens in an instant and is instantly effective. All you would experience is the end product, so to speak, and that end product is an instantaneous change that you generally don't perceive.

ME: Yes, I understand. We have discussed the ability of the entities and beings that exist or work in a particular Event Space and Event Stream perceiving any changes before. It would be unperceivable to them to notice unless they are highly evolved.

I am interested in our next genre of Curator, the Beleaguerers, now. It seems almost impossible that from the summary you gave that they would be needed. They also look as if they are very similar in functionality to those universally gifted Curators that work on any of the specialisms of those specialized Curators they work with/for.

SE1: To some extent, yes, but these Curators are to all intents and purposes the clean-up squad, correcting the results of misinterpretations of those entities that manipulate Event Space in any of its volumetric conditions, so to speak.

ME: Are you saying mistakes are made?

SE1: Not so much mistakes, more like errors that grow as a result of selecting a micro Event Space that is fit for one purpose in comparison to others, but that is not fully compatible with all the downstream fractals that can manifest.

The Beleaguerers

I have to admit that the idea of a group of Curators that were there to sweep up any mistakes, for want of a better word, sounded both unlikely and preposterous, especially when considering that The Source had a group of entities that were looking after the maintenance of that part of it that it had separated out from itself, that which we call the multiverse, and that they were infinitely more capable than those entities, in my mind, that are in the evolutionary cycle. Indeed, from my perspective, the possibility of the need to correct what I am going to insist upon calling mistakes or errors didn't portray the human understanding of our Source, our God, our Creator. Having entities that were capable of being somewhat less than accurate, not perfect, or even create problems was a quandary. None of this part made sense to me and I decided to keep a few questions for The Source in my back pocket to do some double-checking. An imperfect God, Mmmm!

SE1: Before I answer your questioning thoughts, I will run over the description of the Beleaguerers again. These entities are a special group of entities because they are multifaceted and are skilled in all functions associated with the entities described so far and that will be described. The previous entities differ insomuch as they are multifaceted within the skill set of those higher Curators that they work with/for. Although the Beleaguerers are truly multifaceted, they tend to work mainly on the total workload to correct issues in terms of the total number of Event Spaces that could be affected if the wrong insertion point is used, or if the "what if" scenario function of The Source's energetic memory is incorrectly interpreted, which includes anything that has responded in a way that was not expected or planned.

So as you alluded to, the Beleaguerers are, or operate as, a firefighting and/or clean-up function when things don't go according to plan. They operate independently of all other entities and take over the operational corrections that are needed to ensure all Event Spaces and their junctures are maintained.

ME: Tell me, how can your Curators make mistakes? I would have thought that the Curators at least would be acting and working in a state of perfection so that those entities and beings that are in the evolutionary cycle have the best chance of evolving in an efficient and effective way.

SE1: First, answer me these questions of you. Do you not make mistakes?

ME: Yes, I do.

SE1: Do you not create karma through missing the opportunity to negate it?

ME: Yes, I do, we all do.

SE1: Do you not find different ways of doing things?

ME: Yes, of course, that's the spice of life.

SE1: And do you not wish that you could have done things better?

ME: Yes, that's my ego and the benefit of self-reflection.

SE1: And I allow you all to do these things and be ineffective and inefficient at times?

ME: You must do so, because we are.

SE1: Then you will realize that there is a certain advantage to me by allowing my creations to get things wrong or be less than perfect.

ME: That would be depth of experience and that depth of experience is a function of experience, learning, and evolving.

SE1: Correct. It is depth of experience that allows the accrual of evolutionary progression in a more accelerated way. That is why I am happy with errors creeping in.

ME: Would these not be called errors but merely a function of entropy?

SE1: Meaning that … ?

ME: Meaning that the management team for the multiverse from an Event Space perspective is a lousy function where the attempt to create a more perfect condition, does in effect, create a less than perfect condition?

SE1: That is an interesting thought process you have. It is also one that I need to steer you away from.

ME: Why?

SE1: Simply because I can already see you going down the path of thinking that I encourage the possibility of actively seeking my Curators work in error and that I do this to see what the Curators do to get themselves out of trouble, so to speak.

ME: Well, the thought did cross my mind.

SE1: I know. I saw it.

ME: Going back to the thought process that the Beleaguerers are in existence to correct mistakes in the unlikely event that errors do creep into the modifications to Event Spaces, micro and larger, how do they make the changes? I mean, when we look at the amount of work and the level of detail that the Seed Makers and Seeders have to do, the checking they have to do from a "what if" scenario, zooming into the Event Space and Event Stream, checking the effects and results, even before they insert a micro Event Space into an overarching/overall Event Space or Event Stream, the Beleaguerers must need to do the same level of work or checking before they effect a correction?

SE1: That was a long way around to ask a question.

ME: It was rather, wasn't it?

SE1: Yes, it was. However, it provided a necessary preamble to your thought process and actually made a lot of sense.

ME: Thank you.

SE1: The answer to your question is that they don't.

ME: So what happens?

SE1: Before I answer the question I want to recalibrate your thoughts a little. The Beleaguerers work on making corrections to the effects of the insertion or removal of a micro Event Space within an overarching or overall Event Space and its Event Stream. They rarely introduce a new Event Space, of any size.

ME: What do they do then?

SE1: Make minor adjustments to the existing Events within the Event Space. You see, it is important to not disturb too much of what is "approved" for use from the perspective of Event Space and Event Streams.

ME: How do you mean?

SE1: The work that the Seed Makers and the Seeders do is, in general, accurate but there are the odd occasions when those entities and beings that are within the Event Space that has been modified do something that was not seen in the "what if" scenarios. If this affects the overall direction that the Event Space and the Event Stream have been modified to go in, in terms of the Event Space fractal creation and dissolution, then minor modifications to the modifications are required.

ME: And so the Beleaguerers make these modifications as fine-tuning, I guess?

SE1: Yes. In effect, this is the whole point of their work. Although you may have identified them as firefighters, they are not rescuing the Event Spaces they work with from an impending doom situation, but they are changing the so-called natural events that were created as a result of unpredicted entity or being activity back to that which was desired and agreed.

ME: When we discussed the work of the other Curators that manipulate Event Space, are the changes that are made not discernible to those entities and beings that are within the Event Space? Is this the same for the work of the Beleaguerers?

SE1: No. Although they are multiskilled, and can effect any fine-tuning required in any of the skills of the Curators, they prefer not to recreate the work of any of the Curators that they are working with.

ME: They prefer to repair it then?

SE1: That would be a better way of describing the work that they do, much better than being called a fine-tuner or a firefighter.

ME: You just alluded to the point that they don't achieve a seamless change to the Event Space and Event Stream they're repairing.

SE1: Yes, I did say that.

ME: What happens when they make a change then?

SE1: Some of the entities and beings within the Event Space see some change that is either a change that is specific to them or is a minor adjustment to their overall experience in some small way.

ME: Can you explain in more detail?

SE1: I will give you a working example. Have you experienced a known future or expected a series of events that seemed like they were a "certainty," so to speak?

ME: Yes, on a number of occasions I have felt that the future is certain and that I understand and know the events leading up to, and progressing from, an expected event that would be considered a milestone event. Moreover, I could see it happening without fail.

SE1: OK, and have you seen events where the certainty doesn't happen for some reason?

ME: Yes, I have.

SE1: And have you seen events that suddenly come into existence from nowhere?

ME: Yes, I have.

SE1: Well, both of these are times when changes are being made as a result of the work of the Beleaguerers. They have repaired the Event Stream within the overarching or overall Event Space putting them back into the stream or sequence of events that they were or are supposed to be in.

My mind went back to a couple of times when what was expected didn't happen. In the first example, my late wife, Anne, was working at Birmingham University in the UK and was struggling to find funding for her research. A member of a "natural remedy" pharmaceutical company had a long-term friendship with my father-in-law, Anne's father. This company had funded my father-in-law's metaphysical research for a number of years and had stated that they would fund Anne. Anne was a senior research fellow in medical microbiology and genetic cancer research studies at the university, and this company wanted her to provide scientific evidence for the functionality of their remedies in healing illness and ailments. This research was going to be an important and essential step in creating scientific and therefore justifiable evidence for natural preparations being a real healing medicine and not just spiritual mumbo jumbo. We were waiting for the contract to come through from the company when we had the news that a senior director was changing the way they worked. One of them was to stop any research that justified the healing effects of natural remedies and Anne's grant was removed, leaving her without funding for the foreseeable future.

Within a few weeks of this information, we were on our yearly pilgrimage to the College of Psychic Studies in Kensington, London, UK. The College of Psychic Studies has a group of highly trained psychics and one of them was our favorite. She had proved to be very accurate over the years and we had returned year upon year to her for her intuition and inspiration. We therefore had an appointment each. We always recorded these "readings" and we were both surprised to hear that the removal of the funding wasn't supposed to happen and that something outside of the expected reality had happened.

Listening to what The Source was telling me, this very much felt like one of those events that had been changed or repaired by a Beleaguerer.

I then looked at my own past and saw the event surrounding my mental decision to leave the so-called day job. Based upon my previous calculations, I could do my spiritual work and day job and would be able to leave at age fifty-five with a pension. I could use my pension as a basis for paying our bills with a bit to spare for our hobbies. In the background was the fact that we had recently had a redundancy program and I found myself suddenly doing the maths again, this time without being greedy! It suddenly hit me. I could retire now! It was now! I could focus on my spiritual work now! I hadn't seen this before, it simply wasn't an option. Within six months I had left the company and was drawing my pension. I was very happy because I was working on my true path, my heart's desire, and I had a parachute. I didn't need to make a profit to be able to live and do my spiritual work.

Again, this wasn't supposed to happen—yet. Something had happened to the Event Stream in both examples that made us change direction, albeit in personalized ways. Couldn't these be two examples of the work of the Beleaguerers? I wondered.

SE1: In both of your examples the Beleaguerers made minute changes to the local Event Spaces of Anne and yourself. In Anne's case, it was to ensure that she was able to take leftover or surplus funds from other scientists that had grants but who had moved on, leading her to the point where she could take her university pension at an unreduced level. In your case, it was an even smaller change to your executions and realization that you needed less money than you had desired to be able to do your spiritual work full-time.

ME: I have another example.

SE1: Go on.

ME: My father-in-law wanted to pursue his metaphysical interests while he was working at his university position as an "out of hours" interest. He had a few students who were also interested and the only way to get everyone together was to hold meetings at the university. Being the conscientious person he was, he asked his professor if this was OK. The professor took his time, but when he replied, he stated that this would be OK as long as he realized that in doing so, he would not be able to progress in his career as a metallurgist. That being, he could not progress any further than his current grade of senior research fellow. My father-in-law was a very capable man and would have easily gained a professorship. I sensed that his professor was jealous of his work because he had created a unique and novel way of welding metals together that were normally resistant to being welded and was traveling the world lecturing on his development.

My father-in-law felt that his metaphysical research was more important and accepted that his career progression was now at a dead end, even though he made many more contributions to his field. He was content with being able to make another contribution toward metaphysics, one where so-called modern science could prove that the worlds of spirit existed, that today's metaphysics was tomorrow's science.

SE1: Another good illustration. If your father-in-law had been allowed to progress in his metallurgy as well, he would have gained more responsibility and that would have been an issue to him. He would have had to ensure that more and more of his time was taken up with administration of his "department," for he would have ended up in control and responsible for his own department and would have been a professor in his own right within eleven years. This would have stopped his research with the result of him not publishing his books [The Loom of Creation *and* Explorations in Consciousness, *which he self-published. These led up to his third and last book,* Kosmos, *published by Ozark Mountain Publishing.—GSN*]. Neither would he have been able to make contact with those other serious metaphysical researchers such as Harry Oldfield [*Anne and I met Harry one night together with my father-in-law. He demonstrated his device to record the human energy field and its changes due to disease. He is a brilliant metaphysician.—GSN]* and the founder of the natural remedy pharmaceutical company who sponsored his work.

ME: And this was only possible because of the work of the Beleaguerers?

SE1: Entirely. The Beleaguerer in question didn't need to do much more than put a suggestion into the mind of Dennis's professor, one that was in keeping with the way his ego worked, and the direction of his life plan was secured.

ME: So they really don't do big changes, do they?

SE1: No. They are experts in using their multifaceted skill set to ensure that the changes to the Event Spaces, making micro Event Spaces, are easy to achieve and work within the parameters of the existing predictions made by the Seed Makers and the Seeders in order to correct or fine-tune things.

Again, look at all of the things that you have experienced. Things that have happened, like you were lucky and were in the right place at the right time, or what you may sometimes think of as being the wrong place at the wrong time.

I was thinking of another example where a decision was made in my old place of employment to reorganize the department. I was to move back into my old role because of the integration of two departments. Just when this was happening, the recession/depression of 2008 hit the country, resulting in redundancies in my company and my department. The role I was transitioning from was identified as redundant due to the integration. Normally this would not have been a problem and my transition would have been secure as the plans for the reorganization were finalized and populated with personnel from a planning perspective. It would have been just the role that disappeared. Our Human Resources (HR) department saw this as an opportunity to make up their redundancy figures and I was left jobless and needing to apply for roles, at and below my pay grade. I eventually gained a role, a grade and several benefits lower than where I was. The weird thing was that my new role resulted in me performing the same function that I was responsible for before the redundancies. I always thought that there was something fishy about it. I put the blame on someone not liking me at that time but I now know that this was the work of the Beleaguerers. This was in place about four years before the example above where I knew I had enough money to leave.

SE1: Now you're getting it. Everything seemed as if it was out of context from the perspective of continuity but with continuity maintained.

ME: That's it—that's it! The biggest thing it actually did for me was to detach me from my dedication to the company. At this time, my work on *The History of God* was drawing to a close and I was starting to get more interested in broadcasting my work to the metaphysical and spiritual public. I gained more spiritual stamina as a result and forged forward. I had switched my point of focus back to where it should have been. Again, I suppose in sympathy with my father-in-law's story, my life plan was recut so that I could do this work and not get immersed in my old career. My personal first example earlier, being downstream of the second, was more of an awakening moment, whereas the job loss just seemed bizarre, simply because I couldn't see what was happening.

Just think, dear reader. How many times have things happened to you that you thought were out of context but that you begrudgingly accepted only to find out later that it was the best thing that had happened to you!

SE1: This chapter will make your readers think back to a lot of their own examples where something happened that should not have by definition. Just think about what is happening to the UK and the US now. [*The reader should refer to the recent US and UK elections 2016/2017 and the UK's vote to leave the European Union.—GSN*] This is the work, the bigger work I might add, of the Beleaguerers.

It's time to leave these extended discussions on Event Space and those entities that work with it and go on to the Recorders.

ME: I am looking forward to it.

I sat down and thought for a moment about what The Source and I had been talking about with reference to the Beleaguerers and how some of the experiences I had witnessed and been involved with had been effected by this genre of Curator. I wondered as to how many of the incarnate entities on the Earth, not to mention other planets or areas of locally low frequency within the physical universe, had experienced unexpected changes to their direction in incarnate existence. I thought again. What if all the unexpected changes in our incarnations were a result of the fine-tuning, the introduction of micro Event Spaces introduced by the Beleaguerers and other Curators who have the capability to manipulate Event Space, to keep the overall or overarching Event Space operating in the way desired by The Source. This would mean that for those entities incarnate on the Earth, that there is no such thing as true individualized free will, simply because our direction and experiences are being fined-tuned on a regular basis. I decided to ask The Source this question before moving on to the Recorders.

SE1: No need to ask, it is a perfectly valid question.

ME: OK, so what is the answer?

SE1: The answer is yes. I do have certain desired experiences that I experience through you all and in the Greater Reality of this evolutionary cycle, I want to make sure that I/you experience or contribute toward the experience of others so that I can experience in both general and depth what I want to experience, learn, and evolve from.

ME: Is this "not" true experiential evolution resulting from first-time or revised second- or third-time experience then? I mean, from what you are saying, you are picking and choosing what or how you want us to experience on your behalf?

SE1: Of course, I am, and I do this through your TES, your Guide and Helpers, and those entities that maintain that part of me which is called the multiverse. Try not to think of it in terms of being guided to the point of not being in control of your own free will, but moreover, that I and my Curators are ensuring that the experience and learning from that experience is what is desired, and that the environment and its Event Spaces and Event Streams support that desire. I/we are simply fine-tuning the actions associated with your free will. Try to think of it another way. That the whole point of what experience is, is to see if the guidance is listened to, is appreciated, understood, and used. And when it is not, then the Event Space that is changed away from the expected Event Spaces, in all of its parallel derivatives, is recalibrated back to what it should have been. This includes the individual interactions and experiences within an entity's life plan and current position within that life plan. You still have free will to do what you do in the way you want to do it in the environment it is being done in; it's just that there are times when errors creep in and that these errors need to be ironed out.

ME: But aren't these errors part of the game, so to speak?

SE1: Of course. But when they have been experienced, they have served their purpose. It's a bit like being on a journey and knowing the road/s you need to use and the places you need to go through to get to the end of the journey and then suddenly taking a detour, the detour being taken because something grabs your attention for a moment. Once you have seen and experienced what grabs your attention you need to get back on the main road, and, if you have time to get to your destination, you increase your speed to make up the time lost so that your arrival time is as desired. In doing so, you can interact with those entities that you planned to interact with at your destination in the environment you planned to interact with them in.

ME: OK, now I understand. We have free will up to a certain point only, our point of distraction from our planned path. It is the role of the Beleaguerers to spot these distractions, and if we are not able to correct our distractions ourselves, they put us and our Event Spaces back on track.

SE1: Now you have it. Now it really is time for the Recorders.

The Recorders

ME: The Recorders are exactly what their name describes them as—recorders. They work on the detail surrounding the work all of the other entities are responsible for, and assign the actions of those entities working on the tasks they are recording and the subsequent responses of the components of the multiversal environments to the appropriate sectors of The Source's energetic memory.

It does have to be said that the Recorders work specifically on recording the information associated with the work of The Source's Maintenance Entities and not The Source itself.

SE1: Well copied!

ME: Thank you. I would have thought that recording what and how each of the Curators did, do, or will do was an automatic function carried out by you? Why do you need to have a specialized entity to do this?

SE1: Before you say "but we all are part of you," I will say that the Recorders are that part of me, under the guise of a Curator that is specialized in working specifically on recording the work of the Curators. However, although they have the role of Recorder, what they are really doing is an important function of my memory retention.

ME: Can you elaborate a little more?

SE1: As you are aware, we/you are in the third evolutionary cycle and as such everything that is, was, or will be was experienced before.

ME: Yes, OK. I understand this, but maybe the readers may not. Shall I explain a little first?

SE1: Be my guest.

For the readers, this information in relevance to the Hindu texts on the breathing in and out of the universe can be found in The Origin Speaks *as well.*

ME: The evolutionary cycle is a function of The Origin's desire to know and experience itself in totality. Although not originally classified as an evolutionary cycle, it has become such due to its repetition. That being, it has been experienced by all Source Entities, with the exception of SE12, and those entities and beings within those Source Entities that they have created, or have allowed the evolutionary generation of beings through intelligent energetic attraction within them, three times.

Three times, I hear you all say. How can that be? I will explain further.

The original evolutionary cycle was, as stated above, a function of The Origin's desire to know itself in a level of detail that was not efficiently available to it in its singular form of beingness. In order to increase this knowledge of itself, which, when it was experienced and learned created evolution, which was something that The Origin desired, decided to duplicate itself. The story of the twelve Origins is explained in *The History of God* and *The Origin Speaks*, and although it is a link to the start of the evolutionary cycle, it is not necessary to elaborate on it now for it is the experiential function of The Source Entities that is the real evolutionary cycle.

There is an area of polyomniscient sentient self-awareness within the totality of The Origin that it is aware of and that is fully understood. There is also a much larger area, most of this area of The Origin's understanding of self in fact, that is not yet understood, but is nevertheless known about.

How can The Origin not know about itself in totality? you ask.

The answer is to look at this from the human perspective. We all know ourselves and our environment including the wider environment to a certain level, but to understand our human bodies, we need to use microscopes of varying magnifications and refer to experts in the various functions of the human body to understand what we might see when looking into the microscope at our cellular and atomic structure. In order to know more about ourselves we seek counsel of those who have focused on looking deeper into the structure and functionality of the human body, those who have a specialism within a particular area and others who have specialized within the specialization within a specialization. This is where The Origin is at currently, working on creating specialist functions of sentience with the specialized functions of sentience also given the power to create further functions of specialized sentience. All of these functions of specialized sentience feed back to the originating sentience, The Origin, what they have found out about themselves, itself, and how it interacts with other specialized functions of sentience. They improve this knowledge by moving around and into those parts of The Origin that it is aware of but not fully conversant with. In this way, they improve both in the depth and the breadth of knowledge.

From the human perspective, we then go further abroad, looking at our environment. We all have a basic level of knowledge about our environment even if in most cases, we have no personal experience of this wider environment. For instance, we know we exist in a house and that that house is in a suburb of a city, that that city is in a country, which is part of a land mass, which is on the Earth, which is a planet in a solar system, which is in a galaxy, which is in a universe, and that this universe we are now recognizing is part of a multiverse. For the most part, we know about the house we live in and the suburb that house is in, but as we go further abroad our knowledge reduces drastically the further away from our center of normal activity we move.

As we investigate our wider environment further, we start to fill in the gaps in our knowledge. Some are filled with depth; others are filled with breadth and little depth. Some if not all of the wider knowledge is filled in by the knowledge given to us by others we communicate with, those who are fortunate enough to experience other countries, the people in these countries, and their cultures. Or better still, those who are capable of expanding the boundaries of human knowledge and, through various media, broadcast it for the benefit of others. None of us have, with the exception of a very few brave individuals, in the human physical state that is, traveled much beyond the confines of the planet, let alone know much about solar systems, galaxies, nebulae, universes, or even a multiverse because this is peripheral knowledge. It exists but it doesn't affect us. However, there is a small number of individuals who are investigating the "what ifs" of our environment and how we interact with it.

Again, this is where The Origin is now. It is aware of its local self-environment, that area beyond but within the sphere of its area or volume of polyomniscient sentient self-awareness, in human terms, the human body. It is also aware of the structure of itself beyond that, in human terms, the house the human body lives in and the suburb it is within. However, although it has this knowledge, it is also aware due to the regularity of structure within that which it knows of itself, that there are another eleven groups of twelve sets of structure beyond that.

The most important thing in the mind of The Origin is that it wants to know ALL of that which it is, and it wants to know ALL of that which it is IN DEPTH. I also know that it will be a lengthy process, one that has only just started, in this particular Event Space and it is still working on the understanding of the human body, using the human example. [*The reader should also refer to* The Origin Speaks *for an explanation of The Origin's structure associated with its polyomniscient sentient self-awareness.—GSN*] So, how is it doing this?

In understanding how The Origin understands more of the area (volume) where its polyomniscient sentient self-awareness resides, we will start to understand both the reasons for and the overall function of the evolutionary cycle.

SE1: Well, that was a good, if not lengthy, introduction to the explanation of the cycle.

ME: It may be, but I feel that this preamble was a necessary scene setter to allow what you are allowing me to describe next. As you always say to me when we talk in private, I can give you the information in a purer context, but unless you are expansive enough to work with the information, it will always have to be explained in a humanized way. This way expands with knowledge, of course, and so the complexity of information and contexts surrounding it expand with it. Feeling that the readers will at this point start to get impatient, I had better carry on with the explanation then.

SE1: I would.

ME: OK. The Origin created the Source Entities to assist it in its task of understanding itself better. They were created through the basic process of recycling that sentience and the energies associated with that sentience used to create the Twelve Origins together with individualizing that energy/sentience combination with additional sentience and energy to create the Source Entities. Each Source was allowed to become self-aware in its own way and when self-aware was educated as to its reason to be and what its role was within the sentience of The Origin. The brief, so to speak, was to experience, learn, and subsequently evolve in any way they felt would be beneficial. [*The stories behind what and how they are doing this are explained in summary in the* Beyond the Source *books.—GSN*] Our Source Entity, Source Entity One [*The use of the assignation Source Entity One or SE1 is not an indication of which Source became self-aware first; moreover, it is simply my way of identifying the order in which I committed to a dialogue with a Source Entity, ours therefore being the first became SE1.—GSN*], is the subject behind this dialogue, and as such, is the focus of this dialogue. Nevertheless, each and every Source Entity, notwithstanding SE12 follows the same process.

From the perspective of you as our Source Entity, you were placed within the area or volume of The Origin where its polyomniscient sentient self-awareness resides with the remit of experiencing, learning from those experiences, and accruing evolutionary content as a result. All Sources do this, even Source Entity Twelve, although SE12 is now outside of this area/volume. This experiential/learning/ evolutionary content is gained through the investigation of the experiential abilities and capabilities of the Source Entity self— while it is in a static location within the area or volume of The Origin's polyomniscient sentient self-awareness. In your case, you separated yourself out into two, while still being one. One side being you and your own personalized work, and the other being the creation of an environment, simply put, the annexing of half of you, and the creation of smaller individualized units of your own sentient energies to investigate the experiential abilities and capabilities of those annexed energies and their structures, the multiverse as we know it, discounting for the moment, the possibilities associated with Event Space. Once you/we have experienced all the possible and/or potential experiential content available in all of its convoluted variants in the location that you are in, and every entity or being has experienced that, by progressing through each and every aspect of the structure and its abilities, capabilities, and interactions with other entities experiencing the same, it can be said that that particular evolutionary cycle is complete.

In the event that a location occupied by a Source Entity is fully known, experienced, and understood, then that location becomes part of The Origin's area or volume of polyomniscient sentient self-awareness. At this point in the overall Event Space and Event Stream, the Source Entity concerned accepts all of the individualizations it has created back into its overall sentient energy, with each individualization entering into one of the many forms of communion that can be experienced when reintegrating with one's creator [see The Anne Dialogues for further detail—GSN]. When all individualizations are in communion, and any individualized Source Entity structure is also reintegrated, a Source Entity is then considered to be "one" again. It can then start the process of moving the sentience away from the original, or chosen, group or body of energies used to house the individualized sentience created by The Origin and called a Source Entity, to another location. The sentience detaches from the energies used in the completed evolutionary cycle and seeks out another group of energies that have not already been used by another Source Entity.

SE1: Don't forget that it is not necessary to work with the energies previously occupied by another Source Entity because the experiences, learning, and evolutionary content accrued by each Source Entity is shared by the other Source Entities and so that energetic location is already experienced by default. The way each Source Entity experiences what each other experiences is a complex process. Suffice to say, such is the communication between us that we experience everything in terms of how the other Sources would have experienced that location and how we would have experienced it as well.

ME: How does that work then?

SE1: It is a synergetic function of being the first layer of sentience individualized from The Origin. Maybe you will discuss it with The Origin in another dialogue.

You should carry on.

ME: Once an energetic location that has not been experienced by another Source Entity has been found, the sentience attaches itself to the unexperienced set or body of energies associated with that location and starts to designate areas of it as self, structure, and individualizations of self. It then establishes a plan of action as to how it wants to experience that location within The Origin together with the ways in which this can be done. Having established this, it then assigns further annexing to the structure that is its new self and populates it with different variations of individualizations of its sentient energies. Sometimes it reassigns existing individualizations of sentience to experience, learn, and evolve in order to use existing experiential and evolutionary experience, and other times it creates new individualizations to gain a new and fresh context.

This is the start of a new evolutionary cycle, a new mapping cycle.

SE1: Yes, and for information, we are now on the third evolutionary cycle.

ME: I knew that this was the third evolutionary cycle, but please explain to the readers what this means to them. I mean, how many of our TES have been through the first two evolutionary cycles?

SE1: Most of those TES who were created by me to accelerate my evolutionary progression in the first evolutionary cycle are operating in this evolutionary cycle. Those that are not are still in communion with me in one of the various states of communion that are available to a TES or Aspect [see The Anne Dialogues—GSN].

ME: Why are they not involved in this evolutionary cycle?

SE1: Simply because they either choose not to be or that I decided that a particular TES was either better employed in a communal state with me or would not be required in this evolutionary cycle.

ME: Would they be individualized in the next evolutionary cycle?

SE1: It's possible that they will be individualized and others that are in this evolutionary cycle will not be. This is always the case and will always be the case.

ME: So there are or will be times when a TES is either in an evolutionary cycle or in communion with you.

SE1: That's right. There are also times when a TES elects to be in, or is placed in, a position of being in service.

ME: Just like those entities that are the Curators in this evolutionary cycle.

SE1: Correct.

ME: What happens when we have mapped out all of The Origin's area or volume of polyomniscient sentient self-awareness? How many evolutionary cycles will this take?

SE1: When all of the area or volume of The Origin's polyomniscient sentient self-awareness is mapped out the twelve Source Entities become a higher function within the next level of structure within The Origin, and the process of mapping, experiencing, learning, and evolving continues at this higher level.

ME: What happens to the TES that each Source Entity creates?

SE1: All of my TES will become Source Entities at my current level of evolutionary capability in their own right. The other Source Entities are expected to make similar responses, but they don't have to and may choose not to. It's up to them. The benefit of making all entities or beings that were created or have evolved into Source Entities is that it allows a higher level of interaction and depth of experience with the next level of The Origin's structure. There is no robust number of cycles left to experience that I can give you. However, to say that there is over one thousand million would be a ballpark figure.

ME: Just how big is this next level of The Origin's structure?

SE1: According to SE12, it follows the same progression as the current structure that The Origin's polyomniscient area of sentient self-awareness portrays. There are twelve new levels of structure with each level expanding in volume and finitude by a function of the power of twelve for every step upward and outward.

ME: That's an unfathomable difference each time a level of structure is explored and experienced then.

SE1: Yes, it is. And now you can see why every individualized TES in my energies will be elevated to the position of Source Entity and therefore be creating their own TES when this series of evolutionary cycles is complete.

ME: And when every Source Entity has also completed their cycles as well.

SE1: Yes.

The reader who is interested in this subject may benefit from reading The Origin Speaks *where additional information is available.*

ME: Shall we continue with the Recorders?

SE1: Yes. To go over the start again, the Recorders are those functions of my memory that are individualized to correctly record the work of the Curators in this particular evolutionary cycle. They can see what happened, what happens, and what will happen as a result of the work of all of the genres of Curator.

ME: Is this a linear function or does it also include all of the parallel choices as well?

SE1: Everything is recorded irrespective of the effects of Event Space and certain Curators' abilities to manipulate Event Space, and this is the point.

The Curators work on the maintenance of the environment used by those entities and beings that are in the evolutionary cycle, and the Recorders remember and store what they do to achieve this maintenance. This information is separated out from my standard memory function, including those other individualized memory functions of the different methods of experiencing the lower frequencies through incarnation, the human version being the Akashic. They are used to guide the Curators' decision processes in the remaining events in this evolutionary cycle and those entities or beings that will be Curators in the next evolutionary cycle.

ME: Bearing in mind that everything that has happened, is happening, or will happen is happening all at the same time, so to speak, how does this provide a benefit to the Curators? I mean, they are outside of linearity.

SE1: This is true but even Curators can have a tendency to go over old ground, so to speak. The objective of having a memory of what they have done in all of the circumstances that they have, are, and will be involved with is to streamline the overall functions of their work and the evolutionary cycle.

ME: I have been told a number of times in my readings with clients that this is the third cycle as well and more importantly, that this cycle is faster than the previous cycles. Is the use of the information that the Recorders maintain a reason why the cycles are going faster and faster?

SE1: Yes. The second cycle was faster than the first, and the third is faster than the second. One of the things that you will notice, and you have also picked this up in your appointments with your reading clients, is that we have only just started the third cycle and there are already entities that have reentered into communion with me.

ME: Yes, I noticed that.

SE1: Well, you will also notice that this is fast in comparison to the previous cycles.

ME: Just how fast?

SE1: This cycle has reached the same position in entity evolutionary progression as was experienced in the second cycle in approximately 18 percent of the time it took the second cycle and less than 1 percent of the time it took in the first cycle.

ME: So we are evolving fast!

SE1: Relatively speaking, yes. But it will have to be much faster to allow us to map out and experience all of The Origin's polyomniscient area or volume of sentient self-awareness and expand into its next level of structure. Note, though, that the more experienced in exploring the structure of The Origin, the faster the evolutionary cycles progress. At some point, therefore, an evolutionary cycle will be completed in the blink of a human eye.

ME: So the work of the Recorders is essentially to make sure that the Curators don't go over old ground in every new evolutionary cycle then?

SE1: If you want to think of it in that way, you can. You see, as each evolutionary cycle is invoked, there is a level of crossover between the previous evolutionary cycle and the new evolutionary cycle. If the Curators for the new evolutionary cycle are able to see what the previous Curators achieved, then they can create a level of sustainable acceleration in the progression of the new cycle in comparison to the previous evolutionary cycle by not going over old ground or making improved decisions in similar conditions or circumstances.

ME: The end result being why the cycles are going faster and faster.

SE1: That's correct.

ME: I have another question before we move on to the next Curator.

SE1: Go ahead.

ME: Does The Origin benefit from the work of the Recorders?

SE1: The Origin benefits from everything that all its creations work on or experience, irrespective of if it is one of its Source Entities, a Source Entity's TES, a TES Aspect, or an Aspect's Shard. The Recorders are my creation designed to ensure that I benefit from my retention of experience. They focus on the quality of retention of the experience and as such the recordings they make could be of interest to The Origin if it were to focus on their work. However, The Origin experiences everything that happens within me and my environments automatically and so would have no need to focus upon the work of my Recorders per se because in essence, they are part of The Origin's memory retention by default.

ME: You mentioned that the Recorders ensure that you benefit from your retention of experience. Can you elaborate on what this retention of benefit of experience is?

SE1: Simply put, they are there to ensure that every experience that I have via my creations is not just recorded and forgotten about. It is not lost. Just think about what you all experience.

When you experience or learn from an experience or item of education, you are knowledgeable to a certain extent about what you are experiencing and what you are learning from that experience. That information is in the forefront of your memory and, to some extent, it overshadows those experiences that you have had before, and so the memories and learning associated with those experiences become less and less prominent and distinguishable. The skill set that you gained from such experiences will still be there but your ability to access and use them will be reduced in efficiency the longer the period that they are not used for. Just think about when you learn a language. When you are immersed in that language, you pick up new words, grammar, and sentence construction concepts quickly and so you become fluent. When you don't use that language for some time, you start to lose some of those words, grammar, and sentence construction concepts and struggle during the first days of reusing the language again. If you never use it again, it will move further and further away from the forefront of your memory and become more and more difficult to access without some time or even retraining.

An alternative way of looking at this is when you experience being in a new location on holiday. You remember what you did and where you did it when you return home, but with the passage of time (events), you move the focus of your memory on to other things and the memories associated with the holiday move into the background. It is only when you have a reminder given to you by a person who was with you or the presentation of a photograph that the memories of that holiday start to come back into the forefront of your memory. Even then, though, not all of the memories come back because it is usually only those that are associated with the photograph that are invoked. In effect, you lack the ability to have immediate experiential memory recall due to focusing on experiences that need your present attention, unless you are using a previously gained memory or skill set in the present.

This immediate retention of experiential memory is a problem with all entities, irrespective of their omniscience, simply because we are all in the current moment, so to speak.

ME: That's all very well, but you are supposed to be omniscient and omnipresent and as such have instantly available recall of every experience that you and your entities have had, are having, and will have!

SE1: Omnipresence just means that an entity is everything and everything is it—within the confines of its sentient energies, that is. Omniscience means that the sentience associated with that entity is located within all of the energies that make up that entity. It is the focus of that sentience that creates the attention of the entity to the detail associated with the localized sentient energies and that which they have experienced.

ME: So omniscience is just a name to describe the total distribution of the sentience within a body of energies then?

SE1: Correct.

ME: And omnipresence is just a name to describe that everything associated with a particular body of sentient energy is associated with a single entity, that entity therefore being omnipresent within its own body of energy.

SE1: Correct.

ME: And if all of the energy associated with that entity is sentient energy, then that entity is therefore omniscient within its own body of energies.

SE1: Now you are getting it.

ME: Isn't that limited, though? I mean, incarnate humans truly believe that God, you, and The Origin are accessing all experiences in all locations at once and are therefore retaining everything with the ability to have instant access of experience and evolution because everything is happening in the now. Nothing is forgotten in God's mind because everything is in the present; everything is still being experienced.

SE1: And that is true from your incarnate perspective because you have extremely limited functionality while being incarnate, and you are within the body of sentient energies that are mine so everything would appear to operate in the way described by incarnate mankind. I will explain how it is achieved. First you have to realize that sentience has an epicenter, a focus of active function that is the main area of activity of that sentience. This epicenter creates the state of beingness that generates the personality behind the sentience. It is this beingness, the personality, that is the essence of the sentience and therefore the entity or being itself. It is the ability of the desire of this beingness to move around the rest of its sentient energies in an instant that creates the ability to appear to be in the omnipresent omniscient state that you incarnate humans expect your creator to be in. This is how The Origin, the other Source Entities, and I work. This is how we have omnipresent omniscience. This also describes how your True Energetic Self functions and how all True Energetic Selves function.

ME: And this includes the TES created by the other Source Entities?

SE1: In general, yes. I say in general because not all Source Entities have created what you would recognize as entities in the genre of my TES creations.

ME: So how is this instant access of experience that maintains the benefit of recent experience achieved?

SE1: The Recorders create a condition where every experience is located in a tract of sentient energy that is always associated with the epicenter of the sentience, the state of beingness of the entity. This tract of sentient energy is specialized in the ability to retain experiential memory and continuously present it to the sentience, the state of beingness that is the entity, in a way that creates the appearance that it is always happening in the moment, so to speak.

This creates the instant accessibility of the memory, its experiential content, the learning associated with it as well as the evolutionary content associated with it. All of this together creates the continuous benefit of the experience to the entity and its fluidity of the use of such experiences when required.

ME: So what you are saying is—it's like everything that is experienced, was experienced, will be experienced is experienced— as if it is just being experienced because it is always with the focus of the sentience.

SE1: That's a lot of experiences, but, yes, that's a reasonable description of what I experience! There is more to this, though.

ME: Go on?

SE1: I don't just experience these things as if they are being experienced in the now, I also experience the experiences in terms of the learning and evolutionary content that associated with the experience as well.

ME: So you have at the forefront of the focus of your sentience, the benefit of the depth of the experience. You also have that understanding about an experience which we achieve only after the experience. This takes place when we reflect on that experience, compare and contrast that experience with similar or same experiences, and probably reexperience as well?

SE1: That's correct. This is why the work of the Recorders is important. It is not just because they assign experiential memories to specific components of my energies, they also record and present to my focus of sentience all of the benefits associated with those experiential memories.

ME: But isn't having all this information in the forefront of your sentient focus a distraction?

SE1: No.

ME: Why?

SE1: Because I have the capacity to cope with every experience and its benefits that every entity I created experiences, and this includes those variants created by the invocation of Event Space.

ME: So where is all this information stored then? Just where is your sentient focus?

SE1: It's in the rest of me, the other half of me that is not used in the creation of my multiversal environments and my creations.

ME: But I thought that you told me that the side of you, that is still you and not individualized, was for your own investigations of self and other work.

SE1: It is. I have many things that I am working on. However, the focus of my sentience is not with my multiversal environment and the entities that I created to populate it, this is what I created all of you for. One doesn't have a dog and bark oneself, does one?

ME: I guess not.

SE1: I do, however, have some small part of my sentience focused on you and a few others right now.

ME: Where is the focus of your sentience then?

SE1: My main focus of sentience is located in that part of me that is still me. Some part of that sentience is the link to the recordings that the Recorders have created for me so that I can experience everything that you are all experiencing, in whatever Event Space that is concurrently and with the benefit of experience associated with it.

ME: So you are constantly with us all then, even if it is in an observational position in a location that is outside of the multiversal environment you created for us to evolve through.

SE1: Correct.

ME: Well, I am pleased to understand how this all works with the Recorders and now think that we can move on to the next genre of Curator: the Interfacers.

SE1: I agree; let's go.

The Interfacers

ME: Shall I start?

SE1: By all means.

ME: The Interfacers are a group of entities that link everything together. They see and engineer myriad ways in which to interconnect the work of one set of entities to the work of another set of entities. This can also be from one entity to another as well. It is not restricted to groups.

SE1: That is a good summary. I will continue.

It could be argued, however, that the work of the Interfacers is not required because all entities have the ability to experience all things simultaneously and therefore understand the functionality surrounding the potential to link one piece of work with another. Having said that, though, when considering the complexities surrounding the maintenance of any part of my multiverse and those parallel environments that could, can, and will be created, there is a genuine need for entities to specialize. Understanding the opportunities, ways, and methods of linking the work of other entities together is therefore complicated at best, and requires some significant focus to ensure there is a seamless level of integration.

ME: So what you are saying here then is that the Interfacers create an image out of a series of smaller images.

SE1: That is one way of looking at it. You have an image in your mind that you would like to share with the readers?

ME: Yes, I do. It may be a good way to start off the description of what the Interfacers do by giving a concept that is easy to understand.

SE1: Easy concepts are always good to use; it gives the reader confidence that they are going to be able to understand and opens up their ability to digest more complicated concepts later.

ME: This image is almost similar in some respects to the images I have seen to convey the concept of inserting and removing Event Spaces, but instead of Event Spaces, I am seeing the work of any group of entities or individual entities as a two-dimensional image. Each image represents the work of the group or individual that is relevant to a certain area within an event.

Wait a minute, aren't these images just micro Event Spaces?

SE1: No. They represent the work that is the basis for the need for an Event Space. What you are seeing is the actuality within an Event Space.

ME: Actuality, don't you mean a probability?

SE1: No. The Interfacers work on the actuality/ies that are allowing or have allowed the Event Space to be created. Each Event Space has actualities as a function of the creation of possibilities.

ME: Wouldn't it be more correct to suggest that a possibility creates an Event Space and that the creation of that Event Space turns the possibility into an actuality?

SE1: If it helps your incarnate human mind to think in those terms, yes, for that is another way in which it can work. This is what you would call a chicken and egg or Catch-22 situation because both ways work.

ME: OK. I will not argue the point with you, I know better than that. Getting back to the image I am seeing then, I see this as being like a jigsaw puzzle, where one image joins a few others at certain points and at those points only to create a bigger picture. This image joins the other images together both inside the Event Space as well as outside in other Event Spaces as well.

SE1: Correct. Remember, though, that it is the work that the entities do that is linked, and not the events that are linked. The events are linked or joined by other events. Work is work and an event is an event.

ME: OK. Before we move on I think we need to have a definition here as to what the difference is between work and an event.

SE1: Fair enough. In real terms, it is the work that an entity or group of entities perform that results in the creation of possibilities. Irrespective of what that work is, possibilities are created. When a possibility is created, an Event Space is invoked and the possibility becomes an actuality. When the possibility becomes an actuality, the work of the entity or group of entities can continue, and will only become divided again when a possibility is created. The work therefore of an entity or a group of entities is what they do in terms of how they interface with themselves and their environment/s.

The work of an entity or group of entities is largely performed in an isolated way and is usually performed in a way that is specific to them. The Interfacers provide the basis for the interconnection between the isolated areas of work of the individual and groups of entities allowing the work to have a wider function and purpose.

ME: How do they do that?

SE1: They create incentive and directions that would not normally be there. You have a saying on Earth, when the key is available, the doorway can be opened, and one cannot pass through the doorway without the door being open.

ME: Ah! So they open and close the doors of connectivity between groups or individuals so that their work can cross the barrier between them and therefore make them co-joined and interdependent of them while also being independent of them in some way.

SE1: Correct. Now you should continue to show the readers what you were seeing in your mind's eye.

ME: I was seeing every piece of work that an individual or group of entities was doing as an image. Each image represented was joined to another by any function of the work that could be considered to be a reasonable and compatible link. It didn't even need to be a full link, just reasonable and compatible. I see the Interfacers working with these links moving the images of the work that are reasonable and compatible into a position where they could link in to each other. As I moved out of the detail of the one or two images I was seeing, I saw a bigger picture emerging, one where the images created a bigger image, an image of interconnected individualized and group entity work. It was all working together like an electric circuit board. I moved further out and saw that these connections were not in a two-dimensional sense, they were three-dimensional, that being from an illustrative perspective. Every image was interconnected with the images that it should be connected to, either through direct interconnectivity or indirect interconnectivity.

I zoomed further out and saw that when I moved further and further away, the image that was a component of a larger image became smaller and smaller until it became but a pixel of the large image it was part of. I continued to zoom out, and the big image suddenly became a small image, and then a pixel in an even larger image. I zoomed out again and again, and this process of the larger image becoming a smaller image and then a pixel in a much larger image repeated itself again and again. It seemed that it was never-ending. I had just gotten to the point when I thought that I had seen that this was unfathomable when I saw a line of demarcation pass me. I wondered what it was so I asked The Source to explain.

SE1: That was the dividing line between one Event Space, the one you were in, and the Event Space adjacent to it. You have experienced these lines of demarcation before, when communicating with the other Source Entities when channeling the *Beyond the Source* books.

I thought about what The Source Entity had just said for a moment. Yes, I remember seeing Event Space as a series of events moving before my perceptual eyes with each Event Space looking like it was a single image in a reel of cinema film. Each one flicked by faster and faster until everything was happening all at the same time and all I could perceive was a white screen when all Event Spaces became one. The lines that separated the images of each Event Space must be similar to what I was experiencing now.

SE1: That is a good analogy, but it is not the same as what you are experiencing now, for this is the linking of work together to create the seamless connections between them and so remove any possibility of poor or lack of continuity. The line of demarcation was simply your moving out of the Event Space that contained all of the linked work within that Event Space and moving to the next Event Space that was linked to it via those links.

ME: I thought that Event Space was linked together by smaller events within an Event Space?

SE1: There are many things that help to link Event Spaces together; some we have discussed and others we have not. Suffice to say, those that we are discussing now are relevant to the work of the Interfacers only.

ME: Is there anything more that we can discuss about these Curators?

SE1: Only insomuch as they provide an essential role in ensuring the continuity of the work streams between individuals and groups within an Event Space. As a result, they create a deeper level of continuity between Event Spaces by providing the keys to the doors that link the corridors of each area of work and each adjacent Event Space, so to speak.

ME: And when we think that even Event Space, within the locale of your multiverse, is being maintained to ensure its evolutionary efficiency, then creating the optimal levels of continuity between the work of entities within it is very important.

I have a feeling that we can't discuss much more about the Interfacers, so I think that we should move on to the next genre of Curator.

SE1: I agree. Not every Curator needs ten thousand words to explain their function. Let's move on to the Initiators.

The Initiators

SE1: The Initiators are not the same as the Beginners. The Initiators are the entities that decide what modifications are needed to either maintain the evolutionary efficiency of an environment or to create modifications to introduce a completely different set of evolutionary opportunities.

One way to describe them would be to use the term "Brainstormers." In this role, the Initiators therefore create the new ideas that are eventually actioned as new environments, experiences, and evolutionary opportunities.

ME: Are you suggesting that the Initiators work out what those entities that are in the evolutionary cycle need to experience and then provide a plan for that environment to be created?

SE1: Yes, that's correct. You see, the Initiators work mostly in those frequencies of the multiverse that are designed to be of evolutionary importance; that being, they are capable of creating evolutionary acceleration. One of those frequencies, or should I say, sets of frequencies, is where you are now.

ME: Are there any other frequencies than those that are capable of creating evolutionary acceleration?

SE1: All are capable, but it is those that are closest to the lowest frequencies that give the better opportunities for evolutionary acceleration.

ME: And I would guess that is because they are the hardest to work with.

SE1: Yes. You see, the higher up the frequencies an entity is, the easier it is to work in real terms.

ME: Why is that? I do know that it is harder to evolve when in the energetic, relative to being incarnate, that is.

SE1: It is the loss of functionality and connectivity that creates the opportunity for accelerated evolution. The other opportunity is the ability to create and be responsible for that creation. Based upon this, the Initiators look at what the current opportunities are for interaction and creativity within an environment and look to see how that can be improved. They also look at what changes or further improvements can be introduced within an environment based upon its frequency and flexibility.

ME: I suppose that the higher up the frequencies an entity is, the more fluid the environment can be, and therefore the more can be done with its evolutionary potential.

SE1: Yes. You see, there is a lot that can be done to improve the experiential, and therefore evolutionary capability of an environment.

ME: Can you give me a little more detail?

SE1: The Initiators look at all of the possible variations of experience that can be achieved against those that are currently being experienced. They look into what can be achieved with a minimum of change versus major changes.

ME: I suppose there is no point in making major changes if the evolutionary acceleration can be increased by making minor changes.

SE1: Correct. Don't forget that there are always the natural variations that are experienced by an entity through the invocation of Event Space and these have to be taken account of as well.

ME: So any improvements need to be above and beyond those experiences that are naturally available from the wider perspective of Event Space as well.

SE1: Yes. The Initiators are brainstorming planners then that constantly look at making changes to the environment we work with to increase the evolutionary potential, the chance to create evolutionary acceleration.

ME: OK, can you give me some examples of what they do, let's say in the physical universe, one just above the physical universe, and two or three further up the frequencies of the multiverse?

SE1: Of course. I will specify the frequency level and location in terms of the full dimension it is associated with.

The Physical Universe

In the physical universe, the first full dimension, the Initiators provided a natural barrier between the Earth and the rest of the universal environment by placing the Earth in one of the extensions to the galaxy, one of the spiral arms, and also placing that galaxy at the edge of the universe from the perspective of a spatial location. In this way, the Earth is "difficult to get to" for entities that are incarnate both from an interstellar (within the galaxy) and from an intergalactic (outside the galaxy) perspective.

Additionally, the Earth was initially only available for use (being present) on the first seven frequencies associated with the multiverse, but it was seen as being advantageous to increase its availability to being present on all twelve frequencies used to create the physical universe and therefore be a truly pan-frequential body within all of the frequencies associated with the physical universe.

ME: You're suggesting that the Earth was moved by the Initiators to ensure that it was a difficult place to get to then by simply placing it off the beaten track (path), so to speak?

SE1: Correct. When incarnate mankind was given individualized free will, it was important to ensure that the effects of such individualized power was contained to one particular location from a frequential and positional perspective.

ME: Why would that be necessary when individualized free will is specific to incarnate mankind only?

SE1: It is specific to incarnate mankind only, but like all incarnate civilizations, mankind's current civilization has the potential to move away from the current location of the Earth and this could happen quite quickly when the correct technology is developed. Providing that incarnate mankind develops a higher level of maturity at the same time as its technology, then the location-based quarantine will be lifted and ways to get to and from the Earth using frequential and dimensional transportation will be allowed to go further out into areas of other incarnate populations. Until then, the Initiators have ensured that all use of such transportation methods by incarnate mankind will loop back to local space allowing only minor distances from the Earth to be achieved by colonization attempts.

ME: Is there anything else that the Initiators have done that affects incarnate mankind?

SE1: Yes. They have created a natural feeling of aversion to going close to the location of the Earth within those other incarnate spacefaring civilizations that exist in the same frequency as the Earth to ensure contact with other incarnate civilizations is kept to a minimum, and that those that do interact with incarnate mankind are usually of a higher frequency. Although, as you are aware, this is not always the case as the inquisitiveness of some incarnates of the same frequency is strong enough to overcome this aversion. There is also a rule or law of noninterference that the vast majority of incarnates adhere to, although there are a few low-frequency incarnates that manage to ignore or forget the law, hence your sporadic contact with intra-galactics at the same frequency as incarnate mankind is now at.

ME: Talking of this, is there an Initiator plan to allow incarnate mankind to achieve a meaningful and sustainable level of contact with other incarnates, irrespective of their frequency?

SE1: Yes. It was due to be in the next forty years but with recent developments that have resulted in a longer and deeper reduction in the Earth's base frequency, which occurred after an initial increase, this is expected to be over forty and more like one hundred years.

ME: We really are making a mess of things here then?

SE1: I would say that things are going as well as expected. Moreover, the current era is becoming a bit of an eye-opener for you. [*For the reader's reference, this is August 2017 and the UK is leaving the EU and the US has a new president who is shaking a few trees.—GSN*] This in itself could make things worse, or as an eye-opener, create an accelerated change for the better as people will be more active in how they decide their collective futures and not be complacent.

Don't forget, though, that the Initiators worked out what needed to be done; they are not the Curators that actioned the plans.

The Fourth Universe

ME: OK, so what have the Initiators changed, or should I say, planned to change in the fourth universe?

SE1: The fourth universe is in the fifteenth frequency. This is the frequency that is totally disassociated from the work that is achieved in the first, second, and third universes. If you remember your conversations with me during the writing of *The History of God*, you will remember that when incarnate mankind has, as a result of individualized free will, mastered incarnation, that the rest of the incarnate vehicles and their civilizations used in the physical universe, in all of its frequencies, will be granted the use of individualized free will in lieu of the various versions of collective will that they currently have.

ME: Yes, I remember that.

SE1: Then you will also remember that when the other civilizations have also mastered incarnation through individualized free will, there will no longer be a need to use the lower frequencies associated with the first full dimension.

ME: Yes, I also remember that.

SE1: Then you will also remember that the second and third universal environments that are contained within the thirteenth and fourteenth frequencies are reserved for the content of the physical universe.

ME: Yes, and that is because the universal content associated with the physical universe is still of use, and can be used in these higher frequencies to allow beings and entities the opportunity to experience the lowest frequency universe in a different way to that previously experienced. Hang on a bit! I thought that incarnation was only necessary in those frequencies of the first full dimension, within frequencies one through twelve and not those of the second full dimension, which is where the second (thirteenth frequency), third (fourteenth frequency), and fourth universes (fifteenth frequency) are located?

SE1: This is correct, but the thirteenth and fourteenth frequencies do have some capacity to allow a certain level of tangibility, or should I say physicality, although I doubt that you would be able to relate to it as being physicality in the sense that you are currently experiencing, hence the opportunity to transplant the content of the existing physical universe initially in the thirteenth frequency or second universe and latterly in the fourteenth frequency or third universe. Here we have the need to ensure that these two universes were kept clear of environmental content to ensure that the physical universe could occupy that space without issue.

The Initiators, through looking at the evolutionary possibilities and probabilities, decided that the ability to continue the opportunity to reserve universal space, so to speak, for the universe that at the lowest frequencies delivered accelerated evolutionary content, was not advantageous enough once it was moved into the third universe. Based upon this, the fourth universe was allowed to be free form in the same way that the higher frequency universes were, allowing those entities and beings within the fourth universe to create local environments within it in a way that they felt would be beneficial to them from an evolutionary perspective.

ME: So what you are saying then is that, in essence, any areas of local low frequency that would create, for want of a better word, planets, solar systems, galaxies, and nebulae, was the role of the incumbent entities or beings?

SE1: In a way, yes. The most important thing that the Initiators decided was that this universal environment would be the first of the universes to have the ability to be truly manipulatable. Or, to put it another way, the first universe where an entity or being could be truly creative.

ME: If there are other universes where entities or beings can be creative, what is the benefit of the fourth universe being a creation-based universe?

SE1: In this instance, it is the frequency band associated with the fourth universe that is the benefit. It is easier to create something in a higher frequency because of the finitude of the energies that are associated with the higher frequency and its associated universe. However, to be able to create on a lower frequency is harder and therefore accrues more evolutionary content as a result.

ME: So in my excursions to the fourth universe using my Traversing the Frequencies method of projecting my sentience into the rest of the multiverse, everything that I can see or that I experience is created by those entities and beings that are within it? Nothing is a natural creation or has been created by a Curator?

SE1: That's correct. Everything is created by the entities and beings within it; nothing is created by me or a Curator.

If you like, you can consider the fourth universe as a training ground for universal creativity because if an entity or being can create its own environment in the frequency associated with the fourth universe then it can create in any of the other free-form universes of higher frequency.

The One Hundred and Eighty-Ninth Universe

ME: So an example of what the Initiators decided upon or established in the fourth universe was to suggest that the Curators make it the first free-form universe. What was an improvement-based decision that they made about the one hundred and eighty-ninth universe?

SE1: In this instance, it was the inclusion of the connectivity within it. In most other universes, rapid transportation from one location to another within the same universe is achieved as a function of interfrequential movement. That is, moving out of the frequency of the universal environment that an entity or being is within and moving into a higher frequency and therefore higher universe to travel the distance required to be traveled, albeit its represented travel being drastically reduced in the higher universe, and then dropping back down to the original frequency and universe at the point of the interceding loci between the higher and lower universe at the location of desired arrival in the lower universe.

A well-educated and competent entity can travel very efficiently from point A to point B using this method. However, it does have its issues and that is the need to maintain an environment that is concurrent with the natural environment within the environment that is being used as a traversing medium. It is more difficult to maintain a lower frequency environment in a higher frequency than it is to maintain a higher level frequency in a lower frequency environment.

In this universe, the Initiators decided that it would be beneficial to see how efficient the use of, for want of better words, shortcuts would be introduced within the normal structure of the universe to allow instantaneous travel between all locations within the universe that were of importance. These shortcuts were dynamic, though, insomuch as they changed their location automatically if a location lost or changed its level of importance as a result of the focus of the use of one location changing to another, and the number of entities using that location reduced, then the shortcut would automatically move to the location that was becoming the new preferred location. If the opposite point/points of shortcut stayed stationary in terms of their usage, then the opposite point/points of the shortcut would remain in place. If, however, they also changed in their usage or popularity, then the opposite position of the shortcut would also move to one that was in keeping with where entities needed or desired to travel to due to the usage or popularity of the new opposite location.

ME: So, it was truly dynamic only operating where absolutely necessary and not allowing any underused shortcuts?

SE1: That's right. What's the point of having a railway line between two points when no one is at either point or desiring to travel between the two points? It is an unrequired service and is therefore not necessary to provide such a service. This is the same for the shortcuts in this universe.

The Three Hundred and Seventy-Fifth Universe

ME: What about the three hundred and seventy-fifth universe? What did the Initiators organize for that universe?

SE1: Pure creativity was created for the fourth universe with it being the first universe to have such a function while being in a low frequency. With some effort on behalf of the entities within it, it was totally manipulatable. In this case, it was decided that in order to create some form of balance, this universe would best serve those entities and beings that are within the evolutionary cycle, and that are of a high frequency, by making a high-frequency universe that is totally static from a creativity perspective; that being, it cannot be manipulated. It therefore offered an evolutionary challenge that was not normally available in the high frequencies of the multiverse.

ME: That's all they did for that universe?

SE1: It may seem like a small thing to you, but it is quite a radical parameter to apply to a whole high-frequency universe.

ME: What did the universe look like? What did it do?

SE1: In the creative universes, those that are high frequency, the entities create the environment that they need to experience, learn, and evolve within. These environments can be local, where a number of entities or beings work together, or universe, where all of the entities in the universe work together to maintain the universal environment that they collectively want.

In this universe everything is provided and cannot be changed.

ME: What do you mean, everything is provided?

SE1: In this universe there are a number of sectors, three hundred and ninety-six to be exact, that have been created under the advice of the Initiators that have the basics of each of the other universes with the exception of pure creativity.

ME: How can the Initiators create a sector where a universe has pure creativity and can be manipulated but not have creativity?

SE1: Simply put they took a "snapshot" of what was created in those universes by those entities that were creating within them at the time that the decision was made that this universe was to be creatively static, and inserted it into the universe. Each sector is therefore a simulacrum of the content of all of the other universes in the multiverse up to a certain point.

ME: And the entities work with and within what is there but are not able to change anything?

SE1: Correct. Think of it in these terms; it's a bit like renting a property in an all-inclusive way.

ME: Go on.

SE1: When you rent a property in this way, you are able to live in the property in every way. You cook, clean, eat, sleep, work, and relax, but you do not maintain the property or change the property to your own personal tastes, you are simply existing within it. You can't even ask the owner to change any of its aspects to your own tastes either; it just is what it is, a place to exist.

ME: So what is the point of being in a universal environment that cannot be changed or manipulated? Isn't it creativity that makes us evolve?

SE1: Yes, it is. However, it is of a different evolutionary benefit to be in an environment where you have no responsibility for your environment and surroundings.

ME: And that benefit is?

SE1: To concentrate on the interactions with the other entities and beings that are within this environment. You see, creativity creates responsibility for that which is created, and responsibility reduces the amount of time that can be spent on interaction with others. Think about how much time you spend personally looking after and maintaining that which you own.

ME: Yes, it does mean that I spend a long time doing things other than enjoying myself, if you want to put it that way. Everything I create needs my attention to ensure it continues to operate or be in existence and is either functional or of service to others. It would be like being on holiday all of the time if I had nothing to do other than experience and exist.

SE1: It's not quite like that.

ME: It's not?

SE1: No, there are still roles that have to be taken and things to do, it's just that you are not required to create anything or change anything.

ME: So, it's a bit like being stuck in time where everything stays the same, nothing is invented, no progress is made in terms of improving the way we interact with the environment.

SE1: It is progress; it's progress without environmental progress. As I just stated, it is all about improving the way in which an entity or being interacts with another or groups of others.

ME: Let me gain some clarity here then. Working within an unchanging environment is not like being in a job where the job actually results in some form of creation; it's about population of that environment and experiencing that environment.

SE1: Correct. Another way to think about it is to consider yourself to be an explorer. An explorer moves through a new environment without changing it, observing it and working with it, enjoying being in it. It is the same as seeing a new city or other environment when on holiday. You can't affect any changes to that environment because you are just visiting it. However, in visiting, observing, and using the facilities of the city you are justifying its existence, and you justify its existence by experiencing it and not changing it.

ME: This really is a powerful evolutionary opportunity then because if the rest of the universes within the multiverse offer evolutionary progression by creation and responsibility for that creation, then simply experiencing and interacting with that which is already created is a completely different state of being.

SE1: That's right and that's what makes this universe so important, and that's why the Initiators decided that this type of evolutionary opportunity should be made available to those entities and beings that are within the evolutionary cycle.

ME: It's a holiday universe in disguise!

SE1: If you want to call it that, you can. I simply see it as an alternative way to evolve.

Now let's have a look at what the Observers do.

The Observers

SE1: I think that the best way to provide a quick description is to, again, almost cut and paste that which we created at the start of this dialogue. It is a very good summary and there are a lot of crossover questions that you can ask with reference to incarnation.

ME: What do you mean?

SE1: They will come to you after you have added the summary.

ME: OK, I trust you.

SE1: **The Observers** are not the same as the Recorders. They exist within the environments that all entities maintain or create. Their role is to experience the creations of those entities that create the structure or the environments that exist within the structured, the components of an environment.

The Observers experience the creations of other entities by observing the way in which those entities that are creating, create, and those entities that chose to experience those creations, experience them.

One of the main ways in which they achieve this is to place themselves within the energies of the experiencing entity and observe the experience in the same way as the creating or experiencing entity, but from the benefit of being both inside and outside of the creation and/or experience.

ME: I see what you mean; I am getting a lot of images to describe how they work. It's almost like these entities not only move into the energies of the environment/s that an entity or being creates, they are the entity/being.

SE1: Good, very good. I will explain in further detail for you.

ME: Just a moment, though. I want to understand a couple of things. The first thing is to understand why they need to experience what is being experienced, especially when those entities and beings that are in the evolutionary cycle are already experiencing the environment that they have created or have decided to participate in.

SE1: You have misunderstood the summary and so I will backtrack a little.

In the first instance, the Observers are experiencing the environments that are created by other Curators, especially those that are fundamental to the structure of an evolutionary environment. To run the risk of repeating myself here, they, in essence, experience the "feel" of that which is created to create the structure to support an environment. Think of it as the supporting structure to the structure of an environment.

The Observers move within this overall supporting structure and, for want of a better word, establish through direct integration with the energies of that structure, how the structure is created and how it performs when it has a lower structure to support which has an evolutionary environment to house. To make it even simpler to understand, they become the structure, the creations, or the supporting environment itself, and in this way, they can experience how it works.

ME: I am seeing that they can also experience the creation process of the overall structure, the structure that supports the environmental components, and the environment itself as if they are the creators themselves. In this way, they appear to be able to experience the creator and the created.

SE1: Exactly. There is more to this, though.

ME: I suspected that there might be.

SE1: One of the reasons the Observers put themselves in the position of observing as the creator and the created is to give a completely independent and unbiased level of feedback to the creator of how the creativity process felt as it was being used with respect to that which was being created. In effect, they look at the appropriateness of the techniques used in the creation of that which is created and the efficiency of the creation process. Coupled together with this is the effectiveness of the resulting creation.

ME: The whole point of the Observers observing is to feed back on the efficiency and effectiveness of creativity then?

SE1: You can think of it in that way, yes. The result here is therefore to help those entities and beings that are creating overall structures, supporting structures, environmental components, and the environments themselves use more appropriate and therefore efficient methods of creating from both the perspective of the creator and the created. This of course is all from a structural and environmental perspective.

ME: I am seeing that they have another way of judging the efficiency of the creativity process, and that is from the perspective of those entities that work within the environments that a creating Curator creates.

SE1: And that is?

ME: By being one of those entities or beings that are in the evolutionary cycle.

SE1: Again, good, very good. One of the best ways to judge how well something is created is to be in the role of that entity or being for which the creation was created. In this particular instance, the example would be to experience an environment and its supporting structure and componentry as if one were in the evolutionary cycle.

ME: Are you talking from the perspective of those who incarnate or all entities and beings, which would include those that are within the multiversal environment per se?

SE1: I am suggesting that an Observer can enter into the energies of any entity or being, irrespective of whether it is still using incarnation as an evolutionary accelerant or has evolved beyond the use of incarnation to evolve.

Another Explanation for Walk-Ins

ME: Is an Observer's ability to enter into the energies of an entity or being in the evolutionary cycle another way to describe a walk-in?

SE1: From the perspective of incarnation, yes. Actually, you could also consider it in this light for those entities and beings that no longer need to use incarnation to evolve.

ME: Is there a difference in real terms then?

SE1: Not in the data they gather. However, there is a difference in the way they interface with the energies of an entity or being.

I will describe the differences for you because although the effect is the same, the methods of interface and interaction with the entity or being are radically different.

Energetic (Non-incarnate)

In this way, the Observer is able to observe from a detached perspective the way in which an environment works. By detached I mean that the Observer interacts with how the energies associated with the creations of an entity or being or group of entities/beings function, either within the environment or the environment itself. In this way, they observe and experience the workings of the environment or creation from all angles, so to speak.

ME: What do you mean "all angles?"

SE1: Think of it in terms of using a computer. The Observer would record the total experience.

For example, using the computer as a user and the user's interface, the interface with the different programs within the computer, and the operating system of the computer. They would also record how the software behind the programs works from a construction and an operational perspective, including how each of the related software modules interact with each other, including how the nonrelated software modules relate to each other. They would then experience and record how the software modules are affected by the hardware they are associated with and how they control the hardware they are designed to manipulate, including the interaction between the different levels of hardware. Finally, and this is not an exhaustive list by the way, they would experience and record how each of the components within the hardware works and how they interact with each of the other hardware components and groups of components including interdependencies between components and groups of components.

ME: So the Observer experiences, observes, and records the total experience and functionality then?

SE1: Yes, but this is in a pure observationally detached perspective. This means that although they experience the environment or the creations within the environment and their functionality, they don't have the opportunity to fully interact. That means that they can't make any changes based upon what they have observed and recorded and cannot affect the creation within the environment or the environment itself in any way. They have only recorded the data from all angles of environment, creation, function, and functional interaction such as efficiency of interaction and functionality.

One thing that I haven't commented on here is that the Observers also record the thoughts, behaviors, and actions of the entities or beings that are creating the environments or the creations within the environments.

ME: So they record the process of creativity by the creators as if they are the creators?

SE1: Yes. This, however, is from the purely energetic perspective, which of course is the normal environmental condition that we all exist within. Recording the experience from an incarnate perspective is different.

Incarnate

SE1: The Observers work at every level of the multiversal environment and that includes the lowest frequencies that are associated with the physical universe, which of course includes the Earth environment.

Focusing on those frequency levels that are classified as Gross Physical then, they observe and record the work of those Curators that work at the maintenance of and creation of physicality to support the environments within the physical universe that require a vehicle for those entities and beings that are in the evolutionary cycle, those who want to work in the frequencies associated with the Gross Physical in the way it is best experienced. This could be planetary, system based, or galactic. It can also be the flora and fauna relative to a specific planetary environment.

As with the way they record creativity and subsequent creations in the purely energetic, they do the same in the physical, without being specifically physical.

ME: And this means they have to work with an Aspect, a Soul that is currently experiencing physicality by the only real way to experience physicality, by being incarnate in a vehicle specific to the planetary environment that is being used for evolutionary purposes by that Aspect or Soul. In essence, they become a walk-in!

SE1: Correct. In this way, they can experience the interaction of the entity and environment and the creativity of that entity within the environment as if they were incarnate themselves.

ME: But they are still only in recording or observational mode?

SE1: Yes. As with the purely energetic way they observe, the Observers simply experience the interaction of an entity or being with or within its environment and the process of creation within that environment together with the interaction with that which has been created with or within the environment. This is the same whether it, the creation, is a component of the environment or an environment itself.

ME: From the perspective of the incarnate entity or being, though, wouldn't the observation be from the purely interactive or minor creative level?

SE1: Yes. Well, actually, yes and no. You see, this can be from the creativity of an incarnate who, for instance, builds a house, to one who designs a power station, to one who creates a frequential portal to allow rapid transport from one location to another within the physical, to the movement of a planet from one location to another. In this instance, the Observer observes and records the process of creativity and the function and interaction of that creativity within the basic environmental constraints of the Gross Physical and those frequencies close to the Gross Physical, as if they are the creator but without actually being the creator. Environmental creations or indeed any creations that are made at the levels of the Gross Physical are of significant interest to the Observers, and walk-in agreements between Observers and entities/beings in the evolutionary cycle using incarnation to accelerate their accrual of evolutionary content are very common.

ME: What happens to the data they get?

SE1: It is stored in that area within me that is reserved for memory for the use of the next cohort of Curators to use in the next evolutionary cycle. Observational experiential experience is one of the best ways to assist or even assure the acceleration of an evolutionary cycle from one cycle to the next.

ME: That's true at any level, though.

SE1: Yes, it is, but to be able to see how it (anything but predominantly how creativity assists in evolutionary progression) was done versus how it could be done ensures that each evolutionary cycle is not only more efficiently experienced, but is significantly shorter than the preceding cycle.

ME: So what they do is provide a vehicle for accelerating the evolutionary cycle by recording what has been created and how it affects the environment and those beings or entities that use the environment so that this can be used as a "lessons learned" function. Other than that, they change nothing.

SE1: That's correct. However, providing a "lessons learned" function is a very important service. You can see how fast this evolutionary cycle is moving in variance to the first and second evolutionary cycles. If everything that can be experienced and recorded is from an outsider's point of view, with the benefit of the foresight and hindsight that a Curator of this genre has, then when a similar set of environmental conditions or interactions is presented to those entities or beings that are in the evolutionary cycle, they will have an improved experiential knowledge base that is generated from the data that is understood from the previous cycles. This improved experiential knowledge base allows significant improvements in creativity and interaction with their evolutionary environment and those entities or beings within it, accelerating the movement through the evolutionary cycle associated with the evolutionary environment. This can only be achieved when one is both inside and outside the creation and/or experience.

Let's talk about the Producers.

ME: OK.

The Producers

SE1: **The Producers** create the ability for change, that being, they create the energies that allow small changes or creations to be made. Within this role, the Producers deal with the minute detail of changes or creations. It is the small changes that need the most attention to detail and so the energies identified for use need to contain all of the detailed information based upon a template to support those smaller changes. As an example of what I mean here you should consider this as being the energies that support the structure that allows the generation of the smallest components within the physical universe, which in this instance is the Anu.

ME: Are we actually discussing the physical universe now or was that last statement just an example?

SE1: It was just an example. However, the work of the Producers is seen in all aspects of the multiverse as you would expect. Let's work on the work of the Producers from a higher level, though, in this first instance.

ME: OK. You mentioned that the Producers program the function of energies according to a template that makes those energies support the changes required.

SE1: That's correct.

ME: It feels a little bit like how RNA programs the function of DNA [*see* The History of God—*GSN*].

SE1: That's an interesting example but in reality the structure you talk about is not high enough in the structural level.

ME: What do you mean, "high enough?"

SE1: The components of the physical universe that are created by atoms are low in the frequency range. RNA and DNA are created by atoms. Atoms are six levels of quanta above the Anu, which is the highest level of Gross Physicality frequentially and so atoms are low in frequency in comparison with the Anu.

ME: So the higher up the structure a component is, the higher the frequency of the energy that creates that component in that part of the structure.

SE1: Correct. Now you have it. I will elaborate further. The Producers work with the energies that are required to make small structural and creativity-based changes. However, these energies need to be told what they are supposed to do within the local and overall structure or creation that they are supporting.

If you can remember our most basic discussions, you will know that energy is a function of frequency, the one is created by the other and is used by sentience to create experience, learning, and evolution. I know that I am repeating what I said in the summary at the start of this description but it is the only way that I can ensure that you and your readers will understand.

ME: That's OK. Please carry on. I feel it will be beneficial as always.

The Creation of Energy

SE1: I will. Sentience can ultimately manipulate everything that it is in and around, and frequency and energy are the basic components for environmental manipulation or indeed creativity.

Energy can be created by combining disharmonious frequencies together so that they create resistance within themselves. The resistance between disharmonious frequencies is specific to the frequencies being combined together. This resistance is a product of the disharmony between two or more frequencies that do not naturally harmonize with each other. The result is a change of state of the combined frequencies to one which is a localized state of cohesion, which holds the frequencies together in this state of disharmony. In effect, they are locked together in a state of disharmonious harmony. This disharmonious harmony and its resultant resistance creates a field of frequential changeability around it that has no natural purpose other than just being in existence as a function of the disharmonious harmony. This field of frequential changeability can be further described as radiation and this radiation is a product of the resistance between disharmonious frequencies and the state of cohesion that is subsequently created causing disharmonious harmony. This field or radiation can also be classified as a type of energy because of its cohesive state, the cohesion being created as a function of the disharmonious frequencies moving in and around each other creating the disharmonious harmony. In essence, they are both repelled from each other and almost attracted to each other.

This state of being almost attracted to each other and then repelled is observed more clearly when one of the disharmonious frequencies is close to the location of a couple or small group of disharmonious frequencies that have already entered into disharmonious harmony, and are therefore creating a condition where there is a momentary state of attraction before changing back to repulsion.

The more disharmonious frequencies that are combined, the more complicated the energy. The more complicated the energy, the more capable it is of being able to perform more advanced and smaller tasks.

ME: So is energy normally created in this way?

SE1: This is the way that the Producers create the energy that they use to make structural changes in the way they do. It is also a way in which advanced entities or beings can make energy that was not normally in existence.

ME: This method is not reserved for the Producers then?

SE1: No, but the entities or beings referred to are very highly evolved. Very highly evolved.

ME: You mentioned that energy is normally made. What did you mean by this?

SE1: In the normal way of things, energy is created as a function of the random interaction of frequency in harmonious and disharmonious states as frequency passes through the subdimensional and full-dimensional lines of demarcation. Frequencies and subfrequencies that pass through lines of sub- and full-dimensional demarcation tend to pervade the same space and as a result are thrown together creating energy in more or less the same way that I have just described when considering the work of the Producers. The difference here being that this is a natural function rather than a function of directed creativity.

There is another way in which energy is created, one that is rather special and unique and doesn't require disharmonious energies interacting with each other.

ME: What's that?

SE1: Energy can be created by the movement of sentience from one frequency to another. This is specifically aligned to the overall sentience of what we are all individualized units of, The Origin. It can also be aligned to rare events that all Source Entities and all TES experience during the phases of the evolutionary cycle, the movement of sentience.

ME: Can you explain further?

SE1: When the sentience of The Origin moves around its general area/volume of polyomniscient sentient self-awareness [*and later outside of this area/volume; see* The Origin Speaks—*GSN*] and encounters an area that was not previously exposed to its sentience—and within the totality that is The Origin this is quite often—it creates an eddy current. This eddy current acts as an adhesive between frequencies that are either in harmony with each other or are normally disharmonious because it is a function of The Origin's sentience. The Origin's sentience, and all sentience that is derived from the individualization of its sentience, has a natural ability to create an energy from the interaction with its sentience through the natural cohesion instilled on anything that is in contact with The Origin's sentience in any derivative of individualization.

If you can remember back to *The Origin Speaks* and *The Anne Dialogues*, you will note that sentience is autonomous to energy, that sentience is simply associated with energy from the perspective of being a "body" of energy to work with, within an environment that is made of energy. Sentience is that which we truly are and your True Sentient Self (TSS) is that which evolves. Any sentience that is individualized from Origin, Source, TES, or Aspect, but up to and including Shards (note that Shards cannot further individualize sentience), is in essence Origin sentience in smaller denominations of individuality. Based upon this, any frequency that is used for transportational or housing purposes of this type of sentience has its natural repulsion of one frequency or another neutralized. As a result, harmonious and disharmonious frequencies group together in a more natural state of harmony, one where they form energy that the sentience can use as a body of energy for experiential purposes within areas of The Origin's polyomniscient area/volume of sentient self-awareness. This frequency, "touched" by sentience, is abundant and so can be used by Source Entities and TES as the framework or structure from which their ultimately Origin-based sentience can work on experiencing the energies and their functions that were created by contact with, or the inference of, sentience.

ME: What about those that are beings? I remember earlier on in this dialogue that an entity is created by the individualization of sentience from The Origin, a Source Entity, a TES, or an Aspect. However, I also remember that a being is that which is a product of what we would call natural evolution, evolution gained through the grouping together of similar or same energies that develop similar or same intelligence, and, a desire to further group together with similar or same levels of intelligent energy, developing until they themselves create sentience.

SE1: And, that sentience born from the energetic interaction of similar or same energies can also move away from those energies that created them making it similar in functional ability to that sentience which is created through individualization.

ME: Yes, it does appear to be very similar and actually identical.

SE1: Well, it is, apart from the ability for the sentience to create frequential cohesion where there was none before, and therefore energy, by its mere association with or travel between the frequencies.

ME: So that is the difference between an entity and a being's sentience?

SE1: Yes. It is not just a matter of how the sentience is created, but what it can do as a function of its method of creation.

ME: And I would guess that justifies the reason for the two descriptive names.

SE1: Yes, and it is a reason why only entities are allowed to be Curators of my multiversal environment and not beings.

ME: Because they are not the same quality of sentience.

SE1: Correct, they are not the same quality of sentience.

ME: But that is not a real reason, is it? I mean, the method of creating an energy by a Producer is not a function of its quality of sentience, its route to individuality so to speak, because a being can create energy from frequency.

SE1: Correct again. The reason is simple, but if you like, discriminatory.

ME: Go on.

SE1: I am delighted when energy/ies progress to the point of self-generated sentience, especially when this occurs within my own "body" of energy and its higher structures of both me and my multiversal environment for evolutionary progression, but I have an overall plan for this and all of my evolutionary cycles.

ME: And that plan is?

SE1: That I create the evolution through self or individualization of self. My individualization of self is both experiential that being within the evolutionary cycle, and regulatory, for example in control of or maintaining that which is used by my individualizations for experiential and evolutionary growth.

ME: So as long as you created that which is evolving and managing the evolution, it falls within the constraints of your plan, and that any evolutionary progression that is not part of the plan, say in the evolution of energy to the point of sentience ...

SE1: ... is a bonus, a wonderful bonus, but its product cannot be used in the management of that which is used to evolve, or is an environmental vehicle for evolution.

To be honest, I was a little bit surprised that The Source could be openly "discriminatory" of how sentience can be allowed to work with it and its multiversal environment for evolutionary progression. This shone an interesting light on how The Source operates. It both revered the natural or evolutionary creation of sentience external to its own individualization of self, while actively restricting the functions that that sentience can perform on behalf of it in its desire to evolve through what is a "created" or "constructed" means of accruing evolution.

This made me think about a few things such as the longevity of such beings that are created through natural attraction of similar or same energies, that being, do they survive the transition of one evolutionary cycle to another?

What Happens to Beings when the Evolutionary Cycle Finishes

Recognizing that we had, for want of a better word, gone off course here with the work of the Producers, I wanted to ensure that this question was supplementary rather than a distraction. I always like to receive additional information about the Greater Reality but likewise like to ensure that the additional information is relevant to the theme of the information that we have diverted from.

SE1: To be honest we have almost finished with the work of the Producers. There is only one area of their work that I would like to share with you.

ME: And that would be?

SE1: What they do for the physical universe.

ME: Now you have my attention, and I have no doubt, the attention of my readers here in the physical.

SE1: We will deal with that later. You have a more interesting question, one that will be a surprise.

ME: Yes, well, as you know, I am always open to receiving a surprise.

SE1: Good. As you are aware, an evolutionary cycle is described as being when all of those entities that I have created through my separation and individualization of smaller units of self have experienced all that they can experience within the environment that I created for them to experience. They have worked with the minute detail of that environment on all of its frequential levels while interacting with other entities who are also interacting with the environment in its myriad evolutionary opportunities, and have risen through the frequencies and evolved to the point where further interaction with the environment in its current invocation is no longer of evolutionary benefit.

ME: I guess this is when everything is understood and can be repeated and interacted with without deviation and loss of evolutionary efficiency.

SE1: That's one way of saying it, but I prefer that it is when all of my creations have mastered their evolutionary environment.

As you know, when this point of mastery is reached, an entity seeks communion with me, again reintegrating that sentience that was individualized back into the whole sentience that is me, in my particular state of individualization from The Origin. When all of my individualizations, when all of my TES have reintegrated into communion and I am therefore whole again, I detach my sentience from the body of energy that I have commandeered within The Origin and relocate it to a new location and commandeer a new body of energy from The Origin. At this point, I will decide on how I wish to experience this new body of energy and whether I want to create an evolutionary environment and populate it with existing or new individualizations of self, my sentience.

ME: So not every individualization of self, not every TSS you create is brought back into existence?

SE1: No. Some stay in full communion, others stay in the various forms of communion that we have previously discussed, and some are created as new individualizations.

ME: What happens to that sentience which is created through natural attraction of energies? What happens to the beings?

SE1: The beings that are created through natural attraction of similar or same energies are considered to be a growth in my sentience, and although, as a result of their quality of sentience, they are not able to create energy per se, they are nevertheless a function of my actions to evolve.

ME: So they are you, you in smaller areas of evolution?

SE1: Correct.

ME: So if they are you in reality, then they must survive the transition from one evolutionary cycle to another!

SE1: Well, they do and they don't.

ME: Go on.

SE1: The classification for when the evolutionary cycle finishes is based upon my creations achieving mastery of the environment that I created for them to evolve through and master. In essence, their whole reason to be is to experience, learn, and evolve through mastery of the environment they are projected into—they therefore have direction. With a being, because it has sentience that has evolved independently of my creativity or individualization of self, there is no such direction integrated within its sentience.

ME: And so I would guess, there is no such desire to integrate with you when the end of the evolutionary cycle is reached?

SE1: Correct. Don't get me wrong, some beings do recognize who and what they are ultimately part of, and as such, seek communion with me at the end of the evolutionary cycle.

ME: But there are those who are not so clued up, and therefore not so proactive in seeking communion then?

SE1: Again correct. As I have just stated, in essence the sentience that is a being is in reality growth of my overall sentience and goes through the transition of one evolutionary cycle to another. Whatever it ends up being, I need to become whole again.

ME: And that level of wholeness includes your evolutionary growth—the sentience that is the beings as well.

SE1: Now you have it.

ME: So what do you do with those beings that either don't know they need to seek communion with you or actively seek not to be in communion with you?

SE1: Sentience is an interesting commodity.

ME: Why is that?

SE1: When it is in an individualized state it seeks to retain its individuality unless there is an attraction to being in communion with a larger sentience.

ME: Hold on. Are you telling me that you have to persuade a being's sentience to become part of you, to commune with you?

SE1: No, I simply place an overall desire within me that pervades me, that is attractive to all sentience within me but is not originally created through my individualization of self, of my original sentience that was me at the start of the evolutionary cycle that has just ended.

ME: And that desire is to be in communion with you?

SE1: Of course. This desire to be in communion with a larger, a significantly larger sentience is intoxicating, and so all sentience that naturally evolved and became a being is drawn to me and communes with me.

ME: And what state of communion do they enter into?

SE1: The full state of communion.

ME: No other variation of communion?

SE1: No. At least not initially.

ME: What does that mean?

SE1: This is more of a view of the longer term but once a being has entered into communion with me for the first time, I can elect to individualize them in the creation of the next evolutionary cycle.

ME: And would that individualized state be the same as that which the being had when it entered into communion with you?

SE1: Not necessarily. I can individualize the sentience as a percentage of its original sentience together with a percentage of other sentience that has either been individualized before or has never been individualized. Or as you allude to, I can individualize the sentience as it was before communion with all of its knowledge and experiential base intact. I can also elect to individualize it as it was before communion but with its previous knowledge and experiential base erased. Although, nothing of course is lost as I will have absorbed it in anyway.

ME: What status does this sentience have once it has been in communion with you and then re-individualized?

SE1: In the event that the sentience is a part percentage with another previously individualized aspect of my sentience, it will gain entity status or the same quality of sentience as an entity because it is associated with sentience that was previously individualized from me. If on the other hand, the sentience is a part percentage with another previously un-individualized aspect of my sentience, it will gain entity status or the same quality of sentience as an entity because it is associated with sentience that is being individualized from me. Finally, if the sentience is individualized as it was before it entered into communion with me, I can elect to maintain that status or quality of sentience, or I can elect to appoint that sentience with entity status and the subsequent quality of sentience.

ME: So the sentience gains a higher quality of sentience as a result of your desire for it to change?

SE1: Not quite. The quality of sentience changes naturally as a function of my desire to individualize it. As a result, it becomes an entity and is no longer a being. In effect, I elect to let the change happen as a natural function of individualization resulting from my desire to individualize a smaller aspect of my overall sentience.

ME: If the change of status of the sentience from being to entity is a function of your re-individualizing it, why would you wish to not appoint the same status or quality of sentience and recreate a being and not an entity?

SE1: I don't, but I could. In effect, it takes more energy to hold the sentience back, to keep it as it was. Placing what you would call nature in stasis is not an insignificant thing to do.

ME: Let me go in a different direction for a moment. Would the sentience be allowed to be a TES or have the same functions as a maintenance entity?

SE1: The sentience assumes TES/TSS status and quality as soon as it is individualized in any of the ways I have just described. That is provided it elects to be part of the evolutionary cycle or become a guide. The TES/TSS level allows further individualization which is based upon the will of the TES/TSS itself, allowing the creation of Aspects and Shards. If, on the other hand, it elects to be a maintenance entity it would generally remain at the TES/TSS level and not individualize further.

ME: So a being can become a maintenance entity then?

SE1: Yes, of course. However, as you have just become aware, this is not something that is available to it during the evolutionary cycle that allowed its evolution to being status in the first place.

Using Energy to Create the Anu and Other Micro Environmental Changes

ME: Thank you for that information. It was very interesting, and I am sure the content will have answered a number of my readers' questions that will undoubtedly have come to mind as a result of our dialogue. For me, it cleared up a few loose ends with the entity versus being descriptors.

SE1: I thought it would and that is why I decided to allow you to go down that particular path. Now, though, we need wrap up the information on the Producers and discuss the way in which they use their talents to work with the physical universe.

ME: OK, we have got to the part where you can tell us all about how the Producers create the Anu. With the Anu being a well-known physical component within Hindu metaphysical texts and western mysticism, I am sure that a few words on this subject will make a big difference in our overall understanding of the physical structure of the universe we incarnate into.

SE1: It will certainly help in your understanding but I doubt it will give the scientists a head start.

ME: Why is that?

SE1: Simply because from their perspective, the Anu is a spiritual component and therefore something that cannot be quantified.

ME: I thought that the Anu is a physical component.

SE1: It is, but it is something that cannot be detected at the moment with humankind's detecting machines. That is why it is classified as a spiritual component. In essence, it is energetic or spiritual because it is part of everything that is me and The Origin; it is only the fact that the Anu are low frequency that makes them part of the physical aspect of the multiverse.

ME: So how do the Producers create the Anu?

SE1: First, I need to advise you that the Anu are a basic building block for all things that can be considered physicality.

ME: Are you suggesting that they are the common denominator for all materials that we know about and currently don't know about?

SE1: Yes. Every material that is identified in your periodic table is created by variations of ways to group the Anu. From the physical universe's perspective, they are therefore at the center of everything that is available for use in it, from the lowest frequency associated with it, the first, right up to the highest frequency, the twelfth. It is a pan-frequential component.

There are another thirty-six materials that incarnate humankind will discover over the next one hundred and twenty-nine years and during the end of this period, the Anu will actually be detected. That is according to one particular group of Event Spaces and their Event Streams plus the probability of being linked with this particular Event Space and Event Stream.

ME: And the Producers create the Anu to introduce different environmental structures!

SE1: Yes. They get involved at this level because it is possible that the creation of new materials and environmental conditions that could or will be beneficial to those entities that are incarnate and the continued functionality of the environment the incarnates are working within.

ME: What necessitates the need for a new material?

SE1: When an incarnate civilization gets to the point where it needs to find ways of preserving its natural environment, the Producers create the possibility of new materials that would ensure that the natural environment is preserved by grouping together Anu in different ways that can be used by the Generators [see next Curator—GSN] to create the form that is a material type. The Producers therefore create the basic building blocks for the creation of materials and pass this on to the Generators.

The Producers create the Anu by creating energy/ies in the way described earlier on in this dialogue and then laminating them together, so to speak. The energies are of course created by associating disharmonious energies together in a harmonious way. The Producers then have a way of locally containing these energies by making the energy "flow" and then cutting them off from the flow, creating a very localized flow of energy that oscillates along its own length. A similar "flow" of energy is created which is then cut off from the longer flow. It is then aligned with the first local flow with the oscillations moving in the same direction while being out of phase with each other creating both an attraction between the energy/ies that is associated with the flow and oscillation simultaneously. This is repeated twelve times creating a striated or laminated energy that is associated with its flow and oscillation but in a way where the harmonization is always in a state of potentiality but never in actuality. This is because the energy flow of one striation or lamination is always trying to catch up with the flow of the energy that it is next to. The oscillations inhibiting ultimate harmonization through them by being in constant movement away from the point of harmonization. Think of it like having a carrot swinging on a stick in front of you and moving with you. You can always see the carrot but you can never get close enough to it to actually grab it in your hand. The harmony is that you are moving with the carrot, the oscillation is the ability to almost grab the carrot before it swings away.

When this has been achieved at all twelve frequency levels, the Producers then join the flow of energy to itself in a way that is similar to a Mobius loop thereby keeping the flow within the flow, within the striations, so to speak.

There is more than one type of Anu, and Anu are always paired together as opposites. You are already aware of the left-hand and right-hand Anu. There are also up and down, forward and backward, and within and without as a standalone Anu. There are also standalone forward and backward Anu to the up and down, left and right, and forward and backward Anu.

An example of how the Anu are paired together can be best visualized with the left and right Anu. The striated flow and oscillations of the right-hand Anu flows to the left with the striated flow and oscillations of the left-hand Anu flowing to the right. There is a point on the left-hand side of the right-hand Anu where the striated flow of the oscillating energy is exposed. This is mirrored by the left-hand Anu where its right-hand side of striated oscillating energy is exposed. These two areas are where the left-hand and right-hand Anu can be co-joined together in an additional lamination or striation of opposing energy flow, going left and right, creating a total of twenty-four striations and energy flows that is only local to this area. Here we have the function of the Anu, for separately they are nonfunctional in terms of the creation of a physical building block that can be used by the Generators to create form of some kind. It is this area of co-joined striation that creates the basis for physical materials because at this point of co-joined energies moving in different directions, it is possible for the flow of energies to affect each other and counteract the flow of one Anu relevant to the other. In essence, this means that there is resistance created between the two Anu. This resistance manifests as cohesion keeping them together. It is also possible for the right-hand flow of energy in the left-hand Anu to change or swap places with the left-hand flow of energy in the right-hand Anu. This creates tension and a change of roles from left to right to right to left, up and down to down and up, forward and backward to backward and forward, and within and without to without and within. It also includes the permutations of within and without aligned to left and right, up and down, and forward and backward.

ME: And this is the function of how all so-called physical materials are created?

SE1: Yes. Almost every material that is available in the physical universe is created by the interaction of the Anu in one of the ways, or multiple combinations of the ways, described.

ME: Hold on a moment. You just said "almost every material" and not every material. What did you mean by that?

SE1: There are some materials that are in the physical universe that are not created by the use of the Anu and are therefore not truly available in the physical universe per se.

ME: I would make a guess that these are those materials that are the structural components of the physical universe then?

SE1: Very good. I will explain further for you. There is a lattice of energies that are as close to being physical as they can be without actually being physical or being affected by the physical. A normal function of the physical is attractivity due to what you call mass, or in your words—gravity. Everything in the physical universe is linked to everything else through localized, short-distance, medium-distance, and long-distance mass-based attraction or gravity. It is this gravity that keeps most of the components of the physical universe in place, so to speak, and is consistent throughout the frequencies associated with the physical universe. However, in variance to what incarnate humankind may think, the higher the frequency, the higher the attractivity, and so at the higher frequencies there is an imbalance of attractivity that is based upon a function of location. This lattice is therefore in place to hold those higher frequency components of the physical universe in place, negating the tendency for higher frequency components of the physical universe to coalesce together.

ME: What would happen if they did coalesce together? No, don't tell me. It would create a physicality!?

SE1: Wrong word. It would create a solidarity.

ME: What do you mean? A solid, almost Gross Physicality, at the high-frequency levels of the physical universe?

SE1: Not quite. Not in the way you are thinking. What would happen is that all components—that being the high-frequency manifestation of things such as planets, solar systems, galaxies, and nebulae would all group together, causing that aspect of the physical universe to collapse to the point of solidarity or coalescence. In essence, there would be no natural gaps in between the components as a result of the natural attractivity or gravity that is acting on and/or counteracting the possibility of these components moving together—solidifying or coalescing.

ME: And due to this increased attractivity or gravity in the higher frequencies, there needs to be a structure to hold everything in place, and this structure is the lattice you talked about.

SE1: Correct.

ME: And this structure is essentially a material aspect of the physical universe that is created without the use of the Anu to keep these components in place.

SE1: Correct again.

ME: And this is what is classified as being a material that is not created through the use of the myriad combinations of the Anu.

SE1: Correct yet again.

ME: Which frequency levels are we talking about then?

SE1: The upper end of the subfrequencies associated with the tenth frequency upward. So this is the last two subfrequencies of the tenth frequency, including the eleventh and twelfth frequencies.

ME: So, the highest quarter of the frequencies associated with the physical universe.

SE1: Yes.

ME: I am just thinking a moment. The incarnate human vehicle has a component that is in the tenth frequency. Are we associated with that lattice as well then?

SE1: Yes, but only in a very minor way.

ME: OK, what is that minor way?

SE1: The lattice is required to ensure that solidarity does not occur within the environmental components that are associated with the physical universe at the highest frequencies. The last two subfrequencies of the tenth frequency are not significant enough at your "size," so to speak, to create any levels of interference that would inhibit your functionality.

ME: And I suppose that this is because the tenth frequency is only associated with the energetic "step-down" function of the incarnate human vehicle, allowing the projected Aspect to integrate into the lowest frequencies associated with incarnation in a gradually reduced way.

SE1: Well done. Also, you are not affected because in real terms that function of the incarnate human form is not structural per se, it is only manipulative.

ME: Would the Generators have any input into the creation of the lattice?

SE1: Yes, of course. You see, for the Generators to create or make adjustments to the lattice, they need to have the energies created by the Producers to work with, and this includes those that are not created by the use of the Anu.

We are digressing and need to move on. We are now very close to discussing those Curators that are directly involved with the physical universe as an aspect of the multiverse, the Generators being the first of those Curators that can actually be fully attributed to it.

ME: Looking at my notes, though, there are more Curators to discuss that are involved with the higher structures of the multiverse as well, including more on Event Space.

SE1: That is true. I should have said that we will soon start to discuss more of roles of the Curators that are working with the Gross Physical aspects of the physical universe. The Generators are the first of those that work in the energies that can be classified as Gross Physical. Is that better for you?

ME: Yes, much better.

The Generators

I had a quick look at my notes again. I decided that I had misinterpreted the information and that The Source's first comment was correct. The remaining Curators, although some being associated with higher multiversal functions, all related these functions to the lower frequencies of the physical universe. I wanted to ask why The Source had changed its direction when it came to me that The Source was making me look again, and realize that work that the Curators perform in the physical universe is not specifically within the constraints of the physical universe, even though it affects it or is designed to modify it. Nothing is in isolation, I thought, nothing!

I decided to move on and continue the dialogue with The Source and the description of the work of the Generators. As is the norm, I decided to use the summary at the start of this book to remind us of the work the Generators perform.

The Generators generate the "form" from energies, the structure that is created by the Producers. They take the energies created by the Producers and generate the templates for the creation and stability of those components used in the creation of the lower frequency environments. From our perspective, this would be all of the aspects of the physical universe represented by its twelve frequential levels.

ME: I am quite excited about this genre of Curator.

SE1: And why would that be? They are simply Curators.

ME: I am excited because they work on the form of the physical universe. It's something that my readers can relate to. It gives them a mental break from the difficult concepts and an anchor point to start from to help them become more expansive. As if they weren't already.

SE1: We will see if it is a real break later.

As you are now aware, the Producers create the basis for so-called physicality to exist by the production of the various versions of the Anu and their interactions with each other. The Anu, however, are energetic, and not in themselves what you would call physical in nature on their own. Also, the Anu are slightly unstable by nature and therefore cannot be used as a standalone component per se. They therefore need to be associated with other Anu to become stable.

The Generators use this requirement for Anu stability to create the templates for the materials that are both seen and unseen in the physical universe.

ME: I suppose you mean that the unseen materials are simply those that exist on the frequencies above the Gross Physical.

SE1: Yes, of course. Everything that is in your periodic table is created by the Generators, and this includes those materials that are in the wider periodic table associated with all twelve frequencies of the physical universe, so to speak.

ME: And, there are some materials in the periodic table that we are aware of that are unstable as well, those that are radioactive, for example.

SE1: You are talking about those that decay over a long or short period once isolated.

ME: That's right. Are they missing something?

SE1: No. They are designed to decay and provide a function as a result of the decay. Incarnate mankind already uses a small part of the functions associated with the decay to generate power, but there are many other functions that can be exploited as well.

ME: I would like to discuss these functions.

SE1: Later. Right now, let's look at the form that the Generators create from the energies or the Anu that the Producers create.

ME: When I think of form, I think of an object. Is this what you mean by form?

SE1: No. The form is the basic structure of the material or element that can be created by the interaction, the addition and subtraction, of various types of Anu. Although you can only refer to eight basic versions of the Anu—left, right, up, down, forward, backward, within, without—there are more than enough combinations and variations of interaction to allow all of the materials that are available in the physical universe to be generated by the Generators. The form that the Generators create or generate is the framework for each material to exist at its most basic level. Forget the number of atoms, electrons, protons, neutrons, quarks, and leptons, etc., as being the basis for the structure of a material or element and its atomic weight; the Generators create the framework that they follow in their interaction and the framework for their creation and their existence.

ME: As you were saying this, I was receiving an image that suggested that there are different types of, for example, quark, and that although they are basically the same from the perspective of their form, they are different in the way they interact with each other.

SE1: Keep going.

ME: Well, what I am seeing is that there are many different variations on the types of quark we know about and this difference results in a difference in the way that they group together, and that they result in different groups of quark as a result. This is mirrored in the behavior of the leptons as well. Going up in the structures, this means that atoms are different with different functions and interactions with other atoms; we already know that there are different atoms and that each atom is relative to each material or element on the periodic table, together with the number and combination of protons, neutrons, and electrons being the basis for their difference. What we don't realize, though, is that this is the same for electrons, protons, neutrons, quarks, and leptons, etc., that being, there are different versions from that which we already know about. What we think of as a basic component of a single variant are actually basic components with many variants. Based upon this, we are only seeing a small part of the atomic picture and that this atomic picture produces myriad more materials/elements than we know at the moment.

SE1: This is true. There are those that don't have the components that you just described but nevertheless create an atom and those atoms are only available higher up the frequencies.

The Generators, using the energies created by the Producers, create the variations of these atomic components and the function of their interactions with each other.

You are aware that a material or element can change to another material or element as a result of atomic decay?

ME: Yes, this is due to the components of the atom's nucleus being unstable and some of those components moving out of the nucleus to create the stability. This is called radiation and the different types have been given names, such as alpha, beta, and gamma radiation or waves.

SE1: Well done. Did you therefore know that those components that move out of the nucleus as radiation can also regroup to create another material or element?

ME: I know that they can affect another material or element, but I wasn't aware that they could create a material or element in their own right.

Well, they can and do, and these materials or elements are of a higher frequency and therefore not detectable by the current level of technology available to incarnate mankind. Again, it is this function of attractivity and therefore the creation of form that is only available as a function of the frameworks created or generated by the Generators.

ME: So, they are not only creating a so-called solid and stable material or element directly, they are also creating materials or elements that are the indirect product of decay.

SE1: Correct. In fact, a lot of materials or elements that are in the physical universe are created indirectly as a function of atomic components that move out of the nucleus either in a random direction or a streamed direction.

ME: I would guess that the random directions are a function of normal decay whereas streamed directions are a function of components that move out of the nucleus and are then focused or externally guided.

SE1: That's right. And mankind can, to some extent, create the conditions for atomic components to leave a nucleus by guiding the streams of atomic components from one material or element into another material or element and then guiding and focusing the resulting atomic components that are forced to leave the nucleus into a stream or beam that can be used for other work. This stream or beam is a material or element in its own right and can be guided and focused to interact with another stream or beam of atomic components to create a new material or element.

ME: Isn't this what incarnate mankind is doing in the Large Hadron Collider (LHC) in CERN and other atomic laboratories around the world?

SE1: No. Most of the work of scientists in this field is looking at the effect on two streams of atomic components when they are fired at each other; they are not looking at what is created.

ME: Well, in support of them, they do see what happens to the components when they collide because they trace where they go to once the collision has taken place.

SE1: And what do they normally see?

ME: That the atomic components disappear.

SE1: And that is all that they see because their detecting machines cannot see that the traces left behind are a signature that reflects two things. One is the atomic component changing direction after the collision, and the second is the change in frequential state. It is this change in frequential state that is observed as a function of the atomic component disappearing, or for want of a better word, becoming a different material or element in a higher frequency, one that is currently undetectable.

ME: So is this new material or element useful in real terms?

SE1: Not in this low frequency, no. However, when one is incarnate in the higher frequencies the material or element is very useful to those incarnates in that frequency and at the frequency that the material or elements attain. Think of it in terms of being in a higher frequency and that the interaction with the environment supported at that higher frequency is similar to that experienced by you all in the Gross Physical frequencies. It can and does appear to be a physical or sometimes solid (for that frequency) material or element. The difference being that the materials and elements that exist in the higher frequencies of the physical universe have differing functional attributes, that means that any incarnate can manipulate them in ways that are in keeping with these attributes.

ME: This means that there are many other materials or elements that the Generators have created but that incarnate mankind has yet to detect and use.

SE1: That's true and at some point you will be able to detect and use some of these materials or elements because they are close to the Gross Physical frequencies; most are not. It's just that some of them are not going to be available to incarnate mankind until collectively, you have all matured to the point where you can use the power associated with these materials in a responsible and service-driven way.

ME: So if these materials or elements are not for our use at these frequencies, why do the Generators create them?

SE1: Most of what the Generators do can be described in two categories. One: the actual creation of a material or element, that being, it is given the form (structure) of the material in the physical universe. Two: to create the potential for the creation of new materials or elements by creating a level of attractivity between compatible and noncompatible high-frequency atomic components that works only when they are in release from their original nucleus. This means that the creation of a material or element and its form is not guaranteed, but is possible. This possibility being a function of natural attractivity of compatible and noncompatible high-frequency atomic components or by intelligent design by knowledgeable incarnates creating the conditions for atomic components that move out of a nucleus to join together and create a new material or element.

ME: Intelligent design meaning that the knowledgeable incarnates understand what can be created by forcing those atomic components that are moving out of a nucleus to co-join with other atomic components of another material or element that are also moving out of a nucleus to create a new material or element of known or expected functional attributes.

SE1: Yes. And again, this is only possible when the Generators create it as a possibility.

ME: And that they only allow such knowledge to be available to incarnates of the right level of maturity.

Hang on a moment! How do the Generators make sure that this knowledge is only available to those incarnates of the correct level of maturity and not fall into the hands of those that are not?

SE1: Fortunately, this is a natural function of evolution, or the frequency level that an entity or being incarnates into.

An evolved group of incarnate entities or beings can access the higher functions associated with their evolutionary level irrespective of the frequency they incarnate into, and as such, know how to respect the features and functions of materials or elements created in this way. They, however, rarely incarnate into frequencies associated with the Gross Physical, and they would never let this knowledge get into the wrong hands. Those that incarnate into the higher frequencies of the physical universe maintain a level of communicative ability attributable to the frequency that they incarnate into and therefore understand and respect the environment that they are in and the materials and elements that are within it or that can be created within it.

ME: Can you give me an indication of a material or element that should not be in the hands of incarnate humans?

SE1: There is one element or material, out of the few that is close to the Gross Physical frequencies, that is not going to be released to incarnate mankind until there is total parity in incarnate existence on the Earth. Parity in existence means that a civilization is operating in a state of maturity that, although has individualized free will, thinks of the benefit to the collective in every decision that is to be made from an individual and a governmental perspective. This level of existence also means that companies created by one individual or a group of individuals where the benefits or profits only go to the individual or the group of individuals does not naturally exist. Based upon this, profit-focused monopolies for fuel, food, clothing, housing, and transportation will not exist, for there will be no place for them.

This element or material would or will solve the world's problems overnight in the correct environment, but in the wrong environment would create destruction and poverty for all but the elite.

ME: What is this element or material? Why is it so special?

SE1: It is an element that has a single function of repulsion. It repels itself from any known and unknown material or element. But if joined together with another element or material, it acts as a universal amplifier. It will change or increase the power of the functional attributes of any single stable element or material—one thousandfold. The trick is to overcome the natural repulsion, and that takes a high level of understanding.

ME: I would expect that it takes a lot of energy to achieve.

SE1: No, not energy; understanding of how to, for want of a better word, "splice" the material or element with others. Each splice has a unique combination, so to speak.

As The Source was saying these words to me, I started to see an image in my mind's eye. Before I describe what I saw, I am suddenly reminded by The Source that this is not the answer to the problem, it is simply not the right time for this information to be presented to incarnate mankind. We are far, far away from the level of civilization required to be able to both detect and "harvest" this material or element. What I am being shown is a simple overview of the complexity of detail behind what a splice with another element or material would entail. I can only describe what I see as being a convoluted system of Anu, quark, lepton, subatomic (proton, electron, positron, neutron), and even atomic interconnectivity and interaction. The two elements or materials were not just bonded together in an alloy where atoms are shared through attraction or intermingling with each other by infiltrating the gaps created in their atomic structure under a certain frequential state—in our case being melted through the administration of heat—they shared combinations of all of the atomic components illustrated above in both regular and irregular ways.

Heat or energy was not needed here to join the two elements or materials together, just an understanding of what combination of atomic components are attracted, un-attracted, accepted, or rejected to/from each other within each of the elements or materials.

I saw Anu from one element or material within the quarks of the other while still being associated with the first. There was interaction between similar and dissimilar atomic components.

As I looked harder and deeper into this mass of interacting atomic components, I noticed something significant. In all of the combinations required to join the elements or material together, the effect of joining them, created a synergetic affect relating to the cohesion of the interaction, one that was amplified from the Anu upward. In essence, once the elements or materials had been joined together at these atomic levels and in the combinations just described, their strength of bond and supporting functional attributes were magnified at each atomic level. This amplification was so complete that once the final level of structure was created, at what we would call the physical manifestation of the element or material, there was nothing that could reverse the process. Nothing could separate them out again. At least not in the physical universe, I was being told. It was a total stable integration and interaction of atomic component, structure, and form. No decay was possible because every atomic component was interlinked either directly or indirectly. Nothing could be lost and nothing could be gained. So the new material could not be changed or added to once created.

I saw one of the materials or elements presented to me as a Gross Physical product. It looked like cling film but it could not be torn or broken. It could be folded or joined together. Joining like for like elements or material created in this way was at least possible then, I thought, but then The Source told me that this was a functional attribute of this particular element or material. It was light, so very light. The Source then showed it to me as an example of its strength. It showed me a laser projected to it and an armor-piercing bullet being shot at it. Nothing went through the material, even though it was only one layer thick. The Source then showed me a sheet of the material or element being folded into a box section. When folded into this shape, it became instantly ridged. The box section was about thirty meters long and was compared to a similar length of reinforced steel joist (RSJ). They were both used to lift a heavy object, weight unknown, but the RSJ buckled under the strain and the box section of cling film-like material lifted it with ease; it didn't even bend. I was amazed. The Source told me that this particular material is in regular use by those incarnates that exist in the fourth and fifth frequency for the creation of habitats and transportation systems on their planets including those vehicles that are used to move between the stars and galaxies. The Source also told me that this material could not be used in the sixth frequency because it was too "gross" physical at that frequency, but was sufficiently physical to be used in the lower limits of the fourth frequency that were close to the upper limits of the third frequency. This is why we sometimes saw craft made with this type of material. We only see vehicles made of this material if we were in an area of locally high frequency on the Earth when they were in our proximity. If we moved into an area of locally low frequency, or caused the area of locally high frequency to drop down to a lower level by our interaction with it, we would not see them. This is another explanation for unidentified flying objects (UFOs) appearing and disappearing, I thought. What a useful material it would be for the inhabitants of the Earth to have.

SE1: Did you notice something else about this material or element?

ME: No. Yes. Maybe. Was it to do with its functional attributes being affected by its geometry?

SE1: Well done. Yes. This material or element changes its functional abilities according to the shape it is made into. You only saw it as a sheet, a very thin sheet, which was folded into a box section. If this was a solid box section, the functional attributes change to that of the geometry it is fabricated or made into.

ME: I would think that that is obvious. All materials that we currently use are capable of doing that and we use it to good effect.

SE1: That's true, but I was not alluding to the physical geometry. I was alluding to the function associated with what you call sacred geometry.

ME: You mean it takes on the properties of the form of sacred geometry as well?

SE1: It's not as generic as that. This material or element takes on the properties or the form of the sacred geometry that it is fabricated into that are relative to that particular material or element. This is true for all materials or elements that are created with the use of the base material or element used in this type of, for want of a better word, alloy.

ME: And this is why it's important and why it will only be available to incarnate mankind when we are working as a collective of individuals with individualized free will that has individually chosen to work for the benefit of the collective in total.

SE1: Correct.

ME: I think it's time to move on to the next genre of Curator, the Environmentalists.

SE1: As you wish.

The Environmentalists

The Environmentalists are the entities that deal with the creation, manipulation, and maintenance of the environmental aspects of the multiversal structure. As incarnate human beings you may be more interested in these Curators because they work on, although not exclusively, the environments that we use to evolve in from an "immersed" perspective. The Environmentalists have a number of subroles and the remaining descriptions are Curators that work on a specialism that is maintained under the overarching description of "Environmentalist."

ME: So all of the remaining Curators are a function of the Environmentalists?

SE1: That's what I have just stated.

ME: It's OK. It is just that I noticed that one of the Environmentalists works on parallelism.

SE1: Well, Event Space is an all-pervading function of the structure of The Origin and therefore myself and as such, it only stands to reason that there are entities that deal with the effects of individualized free will and choice at the levels associated with the Gross Physical, would you not think?

ME: Yes, you're right. It's just that I thought that we had finished with the subject of Event Space.

SE1: Event Space is a major function of everything that is, so it will and does have a habit of appearing here and there. Especially when you least expect it. Don't forget that an environment can be as small as the gap in between a pair of frequencies and as large as The Origin itself.

ME: Touché. Let's look at the Universalists first then.

The Universalists

The Universalists are those entities that maintain, create, and support the local structure and overall content of the frequencies that are capable of supporting a universal environment. A universal environment can be described as one where many areas of habitude can be created that are either in isolation from each other or are interactive.

They are the creators of the components within a particular universe that give the incumbent entities the opportunity to create within the local environments that which the universe allows to be created, but only with those components. In essence, they create the environments for the Habitation Creators to work with, giving them their raw materials such as galaxies, nebulae, planets, and moons from the perspective of the physical universe.

ME: These are the Curators that create the galaxies then.

SE1: And the raw materials that are within a galaxy.

ME: How many universes have galaxies within them?

SE1: Sixteen at present.

ME: But that is impossible. There are three hundred and ninety-seven universes!

SE1: I said at present. Many galactic habitual constructs that are in my multiverse are created by those entities that are working within a particular universe for experiential purposes. Either they create a galactic environment with the help of other entities with similar plans or ideas that require significant interaction or use a universe that is created by a Universalist as an experiential tool. Alternatively, they can elect to use a galaxy that is in one of the lower frequencies where galaxies are formed by either the work of the Universalists or through natural means. In the event that a galaxy is created by an entity that exists in one of the higher frequencies, then once its role is over it is dissolved. This is the reason why there are only sixteen universes with galaxies at the moment. In the higher frequencies galaxies, etc., are created, used, and dissolved. It is only the lowest frequencies that have galaxies that are more permanent in their existence.

ME: Some of my Traversing the Frequencies (TTF) students see galaxies in all of the universal environments they visit. Why is this?

SE1: They have the power to create that which they want to see and experience. They also have the ability to interpret that which is not a galaxy, such as a group of energies of local density, but that has the attributes that are similar to a galaxy, as a galaxy, if they have no other frame of translationary reference to use to describe what they see.

ME: So what you are saying is that most of what my TTF students see is based upon translation and not based upon actual perception?

SE1: No, I am not saying that. If they are expansive enough and are capable of understanding what they are seeing or perceiving in its correct form of representation then they will experience the reality of that perception. If on the other hand, they have the capacity to only experience that which they are perceiving as a function of translation, that being memory-based imagery, feelings, emotions, sound, or sensations that can be either closely or loosely relative to that which is being perceived, then that is used to record the experience. This is only used if there is a chance of the experience being useful to the student perceiving it in one of the universes traversed to. In the event that the experience is too far removed from their expansivity or translation-based perception, then a so-called blank screen (white or black) is registered by the observing student, the result being that the student feels that nothing was experienced. Some students, however, still receive a feeling of being somewhere or communicating with something even though they have no datum to work from and therefore justify their feelings in human terms.

ME: But it's not imagination, though? Some feel that they are imagining the experience.

SE1: No, it's not imagination. The human form does not have the capacity to imagine, only experience within a certain framework.

Please note again that incarnate existence at the frequencies associated with the Gross Physical are extremely limiting in its perceptual functionality.

Let's get back to the Universalists.

ME: Yes, please do. I have a question first, though. It is one that relates to certain images that purport to show structural lines between the planets and other areas within the physical universe.

SE1: These are generated by certain individuals and are not true representations of the structure. The structure is not detectable by any devices available to incarnate mankind either now or in the future.

ME: And I would guess that this is because it is outside of the normal frequencies and energies that are used to construct things like planets, stars, and galaxies, etc.

SE1: Correct and by this point in our discussions, well known. The people who create such images are doing two things, though. First, they are creating a level of understanding that there is a structure behind what is only seen by the human eye and those devices that augment its capacity for sensory perception. This creates expansive thought. Second, because these images are known to be created and are therefore not true representations of the supporting structure of the physical universe, they bring into disrepute any individual or thought process that suggests such a structure exists, simply because it cannot be detected for real, so to speak.

On the other hand, it does provide the opportunity for conjecture and discussion, which is always useful as it attracts those with an open mind.

The Universalists use the structural frequencies and energies to create the templates, framework, and components required to allow the Habitation Creators to do their work. I will give you an example of what they do by using a human reference.

If you can, consider an electronic device such as a computer as an example of a universe. The Universalists create the basis for the generation of the computer (universe) by creating the basic components that are required to make the computer. They make various components such as resistors, transistors, diodes, and capacitors in all of the variations of size, mounting, and functional capacity required to support the manufacture of every aspect of the computer as a whole—the universe. They then instill within these components the interconnectivity functions between them, assigning rules for connectivity and function associated with single components and groups of components. From the perspective of a computer this means that grouping components together allows the synergetic functions of memory, amplification, processing, user interface, and display. Also included is the ability to interconnect with other groups of components—computers—external to the local groupings.

If you take this example in terms of any of the universes associated with the lowest frequencies of my multiverse, you will see that things like planets, moons, nebulae, and galaxies are the basic building blocks of a universal environment at low-frequency levels. The planets and moons are the smallest components that can be used by the Habitation Creators with the larger groups of components being the galaxies and nebulae.

ME: Aren't the planets, moons, galaxies, etc., habitation in their own right?

SE1: No. In creating these basic components the Universalists generate the possibility for the creation of habitation and not the ability to be habitation itself.

ME: Scientists believe that they understand how planets, moons, galaxies, and nebulae are created and that it is a function of attractivity at a micro and macro level—including the nuclear level for stars. Is this really a function of the work of the Universalists?

SE1: What scientists can see and observe is the end product of the process of creativity that the Universalists use to generate the planets, etc. The Universalists are able to provide the conditions necessary to allow stars to burn and/or create smaller versions of themselves or throw off energies that change their composition to one of stability when away from the process of nuclear fusion. They create localized areas of intense gravity to allow smaller bodies of low-frequency stable matter to join together as one, rather than groups compacted together. They also invoke different rules of attractivity and interaction with frequencies and energies that are loosely grouped together to allow the generation of planets and gasses and galaxies within larger nebulae.

In essence, they create the maximum number of components and their variations required to allow the maximum number of different versions for the potential of habitation that the Habitation Creators can use in a simple and easy way.

ME: I have just seen an image of what they do in terms of maintenance. What I saw is what I can only describe as lines of attractivity/non-attractivity between different bodies, that being moons, planets, or suns having to work together in a certain way to allow them to provide the best possible opportunity for evolutionary interaction. We know that gravity is one way of creating attractivity but this attractivity, this gravity, needs to be created or instilled within the basic functions of the elements created by the Universalists in general.

Shall I go on and describe what I am picking up?

SE1: Yes, of course. I am feeding it to you anyway and as usual it is interesting to see if you understand what you are being given.

A Question of Attractivity, Magnetism, and Gravity

ME: OK. If we take a bar of steel as an example, we see two properties with it. The first one is that it has weight or mass and that this weight or mass allows it to be influenced by the gravitational attractivity of the area of locally low frequency, the moon, planet, or sun that it is close to, in human terms, that it is close to the surface of the Earth. We see the weight as the factor that makes the bar of steel drop to the floor if it is pushed off a table, for example.

But it's not the weight or mass of the steel bar that makes it fall to the floor and make contact with the surface of the Earth, it's the gravitational attractivity associated with the way that the elements that make up the steel are arranged. The key here is that I am compelled to use the words gravity and attraction together and not separately. I will come back to the rest of this because the second part of what I am seeing has equal importance and will result in the two being described together.

The second property has two parts to it. The first part of this second property is associated with attractivity with that which creates the steel bar with another steel bar. The second part is the attractivity with other materials.

Before I carry on, can I ask a rather simple question?

SE1: Yes, of course.

ME: Can the attractivity between two objects that are already under the influence of a larger level of attractivity be classified as gravitational attractivity?

SE1: Yes, it can, and many planetary bodies affect each other in this way. I think that I will continue with describing your example in the process.

In a basic example, the Earth is attracted to the Sun but the Moon is attracted to the Earth and the Sun. The Earth is attracted to the Sun in a way that results in its rotating around the Sun while the Moon rotates around the Earth. Taking this to a micro level, if, in your example, two steel bars were attracted to each other, they would also be under the influence of their attractivity to the Earth. This is well known. The attractivity between the two steel bars or a steel bar and another material can only take place when the atomic particles that make up that material are aligned to the point where the collective attractivity of the particles creates a larger level of attractivity. It is this larger level of attractivity that creates the overall attractivity that you call magnetism. If a steel bar had its particles aligned correctly, it would be attracted to a steel bar that did not have its particles aligned as well as to one where its particles were aligned. The attractivity of the magnetized steel bar to both the magnetized and nonmagnetized steel bars being, in general, the same level of attractive force or gravity.

ME: I can understand the way in which the two steel bars that are magnetically attracted to each other are attracted to each other. I can also understand the way in which two steel bars that do not have their particles aligned to create magnetic attractivity do not attract each other. What I have difficulty in is understanding why a steel bar that has its particles aligned and is therefore magnetic can be attracted to a steel bar that does not have its particles aligned and is therefore not magnetic—that is, per se?

SE1: Certain atomic combinations allow the particles within the material created by the combination to behave in a temporary condition of attractivity or magnetic attractivity. This temporary condition is achieved when particles within a material that are in the same combination as a material that has its particles aligned to create attractivity or magnetism are within the same space, so to speak. When they are in the same space, they feel the attractivity of the material whose particles are in alignment and align themselves into the same pattern of alignment as that felt. The result is attractivity to the point of material to material contact. The level of the attractive force is relative to the number of particles in alignment. When one of the steel bars experiences a greater force than that of the attractivity, i.e., being pulled away, the temporarily aligned particles lose the feeling of the attractivity that made them go into alignment and they revert to their previous state, losing the magnetic effect.

ME: I just saw an image of a group of particles moving around within the structure of an atom so that the so-called orbits within the atom become static. This function of orbital stasis not only occurs at the proton, neutron, and electron level, but also within the quark and lepton level as well, everything moves within the confines of that which it is within, that which it creates, moves into stasis. It is therefore the alignment of every level of the structure of the particles that creates the reciprocal level of attractivity required to allow the magnetic response between a material that is normally in a state where its particles are aligned and one where its particles are not aligned. This can be achieved with any combination of particles from natural elements to those that are man-made and therefore include those materials that are not metallic.

ME: Hold on, nonmetallic materials that are magnetic? We have not yet detected or created such a material, that is, at least to my knowledge.

SE1: Well, this is not strictly true because you do have rubber-based magnets. What do you have on your fridge door?

ME: Yes, but they have magnetic particles added to the mix before the magnet is molded, so based upon this, the rubber only appears to be magnetic when in actuality, it is not.

SE1: Good. You can now recognize that the magnetic particles still attract each other when in solution or within another solid material.

ME: Yes, I can.

SE1: Excellent. So now you can recognize that attractivity or magnetism is particle-based and not gross-material-based even though the particle itself is the base component of the gross material due to its atomic structure.

ME: So as previously explained, if magnetism or attractivity is a function of the atomic structure then it seems reasonable that a nonmetallic particle could have or be made to have the same characteristics without it transmuting to a metallic particle.

SE1: Yes, it is reasonable, but not yet possible with the current level of science surrounding material and particle physics. Suffice to say, when incarnate humankind is able to affect a change of state of attractivity at the quark and lepton level, then you will be able to make a plastic attractive to another plastic, or any polymer to any polymer. In fact, any material can be made to be attractive to another once the method of how to change the state of attractivity of the atomic structure of a material at the quark and lepton level is known.

ME: So a material such as wood or stone can be made to be magnetic or attractive to the same or different materials.

SE1: Yes, although when working with organic structures at the subatomic level one needs to be aware of what function of the organism will be affected if the current and natural status of attractivity or magnetism is changed.

ME: Oh. I have just been shown that there are some incarnate vehicles where this state can be changed at will. This enables the incarnate vehicle to change from one shape to another.

SE1: Yes, and an organ such as a liver can be changed to have the same function as a kidney or heart. You see. Changing the attractivity of an organic material can and does result in metamorphic changes to structure and function of the material from a global or localized perspective.

ME: Thank you. I would like to ask another question before we move on to the next genre of Curator—the Parallelism Engineers.

SE1: Do carry on.

ME: What functions do weight or density (mass) have with attractivity?

SE1: As you are aware the weight of a material is the force exerted on its mass by the gravity (attractivity) of a body that it is majorly affected by. In your instance, it is the Earth. The Earth in turn has its mass affected by the force of attractivity, the gravity, of a number of bodies, but majorly the Sun. Mass is a product of material density within a known volume of space, or to put it another way, how densely populated the material is with the atomic structure that makes a material what it is. The weight experienced by a material is therefore a product of its attractivity to a larger body derived by the population density and alignment of the components of its atomic structure. An object can be changed to being heavier by changing the alignment of the levels of subatomic structure to one where its attractivity to the larger body is increased—being in synchronization with each other. An object can be changed to being lighter by changing the alignment of the levels of subatomic structure to one where its attractivity to the larger body is decreased—being out of synchronization with each other.

As stated earlier, density and therefore mass can also be changed by increasing the frequency of a known proportion of the atomic components of the material so that those components are represented on a different frequency to the ambient frequency. With those in the ambient frequency still remaining in the known volume for the mass of the material, the density and therefore attractivity induced by mass and therefore its weight are reduced in the ambient frequency while being increased in the higher frequency, which is a temporary condition in this instance. They can be reduced to almost nothing, making the material very light.

Based upon this, there are two ways in which a material can be made either attractive or less attractive to a larger or smaller body effecting what you call gravity—through subatomic alignment and frequential manipulation.

ME: Again then, it is one of the responsibilities of the Universalists that the subatomic structure of any material in the physical universe ensures that the atomic components that make a material are created in a way that allows them to have the functionality that you have just described.

SE1: In a nutshell—yes.

The Parallelism Engineers

SE1: The Parallelism Engineers mainly work with the results and effects of the interaction with Event Space within a universal environment. Using the physical universe as an example, they draw the line between the local, planetary, system, galactic, and universal-sized Event Spaces that are created by the decisions, possible decisions, the possibility of possible decisions, and the possibility of the possibility of possible decisions of those entities and beings that are within that universe. The line they draw is the demarcation between these different Event Spaces and their location to each other in terms of their "potential" to be in existence versus their actual existence which includes the closeness of deviation from the mainline Event Space and each other. Their main role is therefore to ensure there is adequate separation between these Event Spaces ensuring that where there needs to be simple separation, there is simple separation and when there can be "crossover" between Event Spaces by the incumbent entities and beings within that Event Space that this function is available.

ME: I have to admit that I thought we had worked on the function of Event Space and as such covered this particular subject in some considerable depth. In fact, I have stated this before!

SE1: We have covered a lot of information about Event Space and its function but as you can imagine there is a lot that we have not covered. You simply cannot underestimate the amount of influence this aspect of The Origin has on everything. The wonderful thing is, though, that we can work with it in some way that is beneficial to us all. The Parallelism Engineers provide a unique function within my Curator hierarchy that allows the generation of, or the observation of, the correct juncture in an Event Space where it can end or should end and therefore where another Event Space should begin. Also tied in with this is the size or volume, if you wish to call it that, of the Event Space being observed.

Please note that these Curators operate very close to the environments that are affected by the changes in Event Space status and are therefore sensitive to the possibilities, the possible possibility, and possibilities of possible possibilities associated with any part, location, or function of an Event Space. In this way, they are able to ascertain whether or not an Event Space should be allowed to create a new Event Space or if this should be achieved in an inferential way.

ME: OK, I understand that Event Spaces can be dissected and events within the overall Event Stream of an Event Space can be manipulated because we have discussed this before. You have described to me the way in which certain specialized Curators can cut and paste, delete, or insert events into an Event Stream by modifying the end of event and start of event so that they lead into each other. What is the difference here?

SE1: It's about the potential to be in existence versus actually being in existence and creating a high level of containment.

ME: Go on.

SE1: The Parallelism Engineers observe the Event Spaces and who and what they are being influenced by and decide where the point of separation should be placed between one Event Space and another. This is irrespective of size or volume. You can see this in operation at times on Earth. You will see that one series of events, and Event Stream, suddenly stops or is created. You can even see the size or volume of the affected area, so to speak. For example, if an event is local then the individuals and environment that are affected are confined to that location and there is a defined point or juncture where the Event Space comes into existence and disappears from existence. Consider the tsunami that took place in Indonesia the Christmas of 2004. It was confined to those areas that were in the direct line of the tidal reaction to seismic activity. It was generated and created a completely new experience set for those in the area and changed the topography of the land. Some incarnates survived, others left their incarnation, others were involved in clearing up and finding survivors and those that had died, and others were involved in surviving and helping others survive. It was a confined Event Space that only affected those that were within it from an experiential perspective.

In this example, the Parallelism Engineers created three conditions:

1. Automatic Inclusion

2. Automatic Separation

3. Desired Inclusion

With **Automatic Inclusion** those incarnates that were within the volume of "space" affected by this Event Space were included in the experience and were a function of the overall experience associated with this Event Space. They experienced the tsunami firsthand. These would be the entities or beings incumbent to this Event Space.

With **Automatic Separation** those incarnates that are not within the volume of "space" affected by this Event Space function were not included in the experience and were not a function of the overall experience supported by this Event Space and as such will be divorced from it. They are therefore outside of this Event Space. Had they knowledge of this event, then this is attributed to the possibility of crossover between one Event Space to another. The level of crossover is attributed to the Event Space that they are in and how interactive it is with the Event Space of the disaster, that being how much demarcation or separation there is between the Event Spaces. They may have varying degrees of knowledge of the event finishing with no knowledge at all. All this depends upon the level of demarcation, of separation, between Event Spaces and how individual incarnates desire to interact with the experiences supported by another Event Space including how far off the mainstream Event Space they are and how much one Event Space is required to influence a downstream Event Space. In essence, they experienced the tsunami secondhand via news and either took notice of it or not, as the case may be. These would be other entities and beings around the world.

With **Desired Inclusion** those incarnates that wish to move from their current Event Space into another Event Space and experience that which is available in the desired Event Space can do so provided the means of moving from the Event Space that they were in, to the new Event Space, is available to them. In many instances, this means that the difference is just an issue of physical relocation, the boundaries of the Event Spaces therefore being volume- and location-based rather than reality-based. They initially experienced the tsunami secondhand, then wanted to be part of it, and therefore moved location to experience the tsunami and it's after-effects directly. These would be relief workers.

ME: What about a function of **Desired Separation**?

SE1: There is no function of **Desired Separation** available because the desire to change Event Spaces through desired inclusion creates the same result.

ME: But this just illustrates location- and volume-based separation or demarcation. What about reality-based separation?

SE1: A reality is based upon, or created by, the perceptual interaction of an entity or being or a group of entities or beings with an environment and its incumbent entities or beings or groups of entities or beings in a way that is specific to that entity or being or a group of entities or beings and their mindset/s. Once a mindset is created then a reality is created and an alternative reality can also be created within the same space. This is a perception-based representation of an Event Space for myriad realities can exist in the same Event Space and myriad Event Spaces can exist in the same space.

Entities or beings, therefore as a function of their mindset, elect to be in one reality or another while remaining in the same Event Space. This is not a role of the Parallelism Engineers because in function, a location-based demarcation of Event Space, of any volume, is mostly derived by the incumbent entities or beings within and without it.

ME: So the Parallelism Engineers create a change in mindset?

SE1: Yes. They affect the thought processes of the incumbent entities or beings to the point where they actively ignore events, environments, or interactions with other entities or beings that are around them. In this way, they exist in a different reality to those that they are ignoring.

ME: To them they appear not to exist then, even though they do?

SE1: Correct.

ME: I suppose this could be explained by people who live in the same street or suburb but never interact with each other or even know of each other's existence?

SE1: That is one way of explaining it. In this instance, they exist in the same Event Space but in a different reality within that Event Space.

Remember, a reality is a function of Event Space and is, from a simplistic perspective, created by an entity or being's desire to interact with the environment and those entities and beings within it. A parallel condition such as a parallel universe, galaxy, planet, or location is an Event Space that is separate from but similar to another Event Space in every way except for the functions of entity or being interaction and the changes in the environment that are subsequently created.

If you remember the content earlier in this dialogue, a parallel condition is created by choices made by an entity or being if more than one choice is available and a decision is required as to which choice to make is therefore also available. The volume of an Event Space is created as a function of the number of entities or beings that make choices that are linked to, or are consistent with the choices of other beings or entities.

ME: You said that the demarcation between parallel versions of Event Space is one of the functions of the Parallelism Engineers.

SE1: Yes, it is. Let's recap a little first, though, and understand the nomenclature used again.

1. **Space** is the area or volume within me (and ultimately The Origin) where everything exists. Don't forget that Event Space pervades The Origin and is a fundamental component of The Origin. What I discuss here is just localized to me and my multiverse.

2. **Event Space** is an area or volume of space within me that exists as a parallel function of that space. It is space overlapping space or space within and without a space.

3. **A Parallel Condition** is the duplication of Event Space. It is the creation or generation of a new but similar Event Space when a choice can be made and that that choice or the possibility of the choice or the possible possibility of that choice results in a large enough downstream differential to create a new series of experiences that are self-contained and independent of the Event Space they separated from. The overall size of the Event Space is a function of the inclusion of other entities or beings that interact with the initiating and subsequent downstream experiences generated from the initial choice.

4. **A Reality** is an entity- or being-generated perception-based condition that exists in an Event Space. An alternate reality to that of the Event Space is a personal or group-based perception or desire for a certain experiential environment within a known environment relative to their thoughts, behaviors, and actions and the desire to ignore that which they don't desire to be or interact with.

5. **Demarcation between Event Spaces** is the line of noninteraction drawn between one Event Space and another. It is the role of the Parallelism Engineers to either ensure that there is sufficient difference in the Event Spaces to maintain

an additional Event Space or create the conditions necessary to support an additional Event Space, if an additional Event Space is desired by the Curators to further support evolutionary progression of those entities or beings within it. Note, though, that an insufficient demarcation line can result in lack of integrity of an Event Space and therefore create an alternate reality instead. Sufficient demarcation results in a robust Event Space.

ME: In the event that there is the desire for an Event Space to be in existence and that there appears to be a lack of integrity within the demarcation between the original Event Space and the newly generated one, what do the Parallelism Engineers do to reinforce this demarcation line?

SE1: They do four things. One: they observe the conditions that created the Event Space in the first place. Two: they establish if the downstream integrity of the Event Space increases or not. If it does, then they do no work as this is a natural function of Event Space and is therefore correct functionality. If it doesn't, then they choose to make a number of corrections. Three: they establish if the corrections can be made by making changes to the mindsets of the incumbent entities and beings to reinforce the decisions that were made to create the new Event Space. An example of one such change would be the creation of a new fashion "craze," desirable object, profession, or political condition/situation, so to speak. Four: they can change the environment in some way to deflect the thoughts, behaviors, or actions of the incumbent entities or beings within the two Event Spaces that have a poor demarcation line so that the environmental change supports the new Event Space reinforcing the demarcation line and justifying the new Event Space.

Mostly, though, the Parallelism Engineers use the methods that affect a change in mindset because it was a change in mindset and a need to make a decision that resulted in the creation of the new Event Space in the first place.

ME: What about the potential for an Event Space to be in existence? What makes them do the work to make a potential Event Space become an actual Event Space?

SE1: The Parallelism Engineers constantly monitor the ebb and flow of events, choice, reality, and the interaction of the incumbent entities and beings with themselves and their environment and make a judgment on whether a new Event Space should be considered in the event that one is not naturally created. There are many times that the conditions for the creation of a new Event Space are met, only to be dissolved as a result of the change of choice of one or more entities or beings to the opposite. If it looks like an Event Space should be in existence, and by that the Event Space leaves a downstream shadow of existence, which is created by a number (more than one) of near creations and subsequent dissolutions of the Potential Event Space, then the Parallelism Engineers will use any or all of the four methods just described to create the conditions necessary to support the continued and robust existence of the Event Space in question.

SE1: Let's move on to the Concurrence Engineers.

The Concurrence Engineers

I felt that we had finally moved on from the inclusion of Event Space (I realize that I had said this a couple of times before!) and were now on the home straight to the Curators that were responsible for the static aspect of the multiverse and the universe that we, as incarnate entities or beings, existed within. I sensed no parallel conditions or realities to be discussed. Everything was to be in the singular from an environmental perspective. Everything was to be something that could, from the perspective of the metaphysical reader, be in a "known" space, that is, if a multiversal space was considered to be known. I guess that this could only be a true statement when we focused on the physical universe but at least we were not to be exposed to the concepts of fractal multiple versions of ourselves and our environment. Indeed, from where I was looking, the work of the Concurrence Engineers appeared to be somewhat straightforward as well. Let's see what The Source Entity has to say about this Curator, I thought, before I completely succumbed to this direction of consideration.

SE1: Tally-ho! Let's carry on, shall we. I note that you have created a target for completion and we need to ensure that we are not late.

ME: I have set up a deadline and it may be touch-and-go to meet it, but I am sure we will get there.

SE1: Good, a deadline is always possible when one is positive about making it a reality.

ME: I thought we had finished with realities?

SE1: We have. I just thought I would throw in that word to make you sit up and take notice. OK, let's look at the next genre of Curator.

The Concurrence Engineers look at the relationship between each universe created within the frequencies of the multiverse. They ensure that the functionality of these universes is maintained even though they are within the same overall space, and that as a result of being in the same space, they exist independently of each other. They also ensure that the progression from one universe to another is both robust and reasonable. As you are aware, I describe the universes created for use within the multiverse as being "self-contained simultaneous universes." "Concurrence" is therefore a function of being in the same space but with the added function of being in an evolutionary flow, a flow which all universes within the multiverse have—that is specific to the static structure of the multiverse.

The Concurrence Engineers, however, do not work on those universes that are created in parallel with the self-contained simultaneous universes and as such do not work on those universes that are created by Event Space interactions. These Curators are specialists and work on the stable multiversal environment and not the transient ones.

It may be difficult for you to separate out one of the roles of the Concurrence Engineers with the Frequential Barrier Engineers because they do have a small level of crossover, especially when it comes to the demarcation between universes and the nomenclature used to describe the demarcation. Based upon this, I will describe the area that could be described as common later, now. The Concurrence Engineers can and do work with the Frequential Barrier Engineers, however [*see below—GSN*].

ME: I guess that will be the frequencies that are common in terms of the universes being separate and self-contained?

SE1: Yes, but that is as far as it goes. The Frequential Barrier Engineers are a very focused and specialized group.

ME: OK, let's go then.

SE1: As you are aware, the base structural component of the multiverse, and indeed everything that is The Origin, is a function of the frequency of energy. It is the separation or demarcation of the frequency within an energy that allows the creation of everything—predominately including the environments that are used for evolutionary progression.

The energies that are classified as full dimensions and subdimensions and their components of frequency are all contained in one space within me. It is the ability to separate out the frequencies that allows multiple environments to exist within this space. The Concurrence Engineers therefore work on the function of multiplicity of environment that is concurrently in existence within a single volume of dimensional and subdimensional space.

When considering the steps in frequency within this space the Concurrence Engineers work on the containment of the environments within the frequency that the environments are supported by, including the resolution and depth of content that can be housed within that frequency. It is the finitude, so to speak, that allows one universe to exist in the same space as other universes but not be in contact with the content of another, either above or below it. It is the increase in finitude that supports the stepped change in universal function and experience as an entity or being progresses from one universe to another, evolving as a consequence.

The Concurrence Engineers work with this finitude ensuring that, along with the work of the Frequential Barrier Engineers, the difference in environmental content, experience, and functionality is sufficiently different. This difference creates the need for that universe to be self-contained and therefore offer unique evolutionary opportunities. These evolutionary opportunities need to be progressive from one universe to another and in keeping with the difference in environmental content, experience, and functionality between these universes.

ME: I feel that from a frequential and evolutionary perspective, the structure of the multiverse is linear in fashion, but that it can still be experienced in a random way, not specifically in linear order.

SE1: Nearly. The multiverse is linear from an evolutionary perspective and the Concurrence Engineers ensure that each universe offers a unique set of evolutionary opportunities that progress the higher up the frequencies one goes. However, experiencing these universal environments is achieved in two ways. One: the TES can project a smaller Aspect into any of the universal environments below its current evolutionary level. Two: the location of the TES within the multiverse, its current universe of habitude, is a function of its evolutionary content. TES evolutionary content is a function of the total experiences of itself and its projected Aspects/Shards accrued in a concurrent way.

ME: So the multiverse is both linear and static in normal representation, that being from the perspective of our evolutionary progression, but it can also be parallelized in part or totality as a function of the component of Event Space that pervades it.

SE1: We have discussed this before but your comment is totally correct.

ME: Thank you for reminding me.

I have one question that has been nagging me for some considerable time. Actually it's three.

SE1: Carry on.

ME: Exactly what is the function that:

1. creates the separation of the universes for evolutionary purposes?

2. allows progression from one universe to another?

3. ensures a difference in experience is available from one universe to another?

SE1: Well, they are all big questions and I will try to summarize the answers as much as possible. Don't forget, though, that we are referring to the evolutionary function of a TES and not one of its Aspects or Shards. They have a significant part to play in the function of a universe's evolutionary capability as a result of them being part of it.

Separation of the Universes for Evolutionary Progression

SE1: When considering what creates the need for separation of the universes for evolutionary progression, the Concurrence Engineers take a judgment on how high, frequentially, a TES can progress as a function of the universal environment that they are in. In essence, they do not create an evolutionary barrier between different universes, but moreover they assign an evolutionary quotient to each universal environment, identifying what can, or should be, achievable in each universe. This is how they are separated from each other from an evolutionary perspective.

ME: Would it be reasonable to assume then that some universes offer more evolutionary progression than others?

SE1: Yes, and actually the progression is not always obviously linear.

ME: What do you mean, "not obviously linear?" I thought that a TES needed to progress in a linear way through the multiverse?

SE1: In general, this is correct, but it is possible to bypass, so to speak, a universe and progress to another that is more concurrent with the evolutionary requirements of a TES.

You see, although the universes are linear in frequential procession, they are not all required to be accessed in a linear way. The only requirement of a TES is that they are experienced in a way that is concurrent with their evolutionary path. The Concurrence Engineers are fully aware of the evolutionary possibilities of each universe and how a TES can progress from one to another and offer individualized progression possibilities for each TES.

ME: How does that work then? I mean, just to clarify this thought process, are you saying that although each universe has a linear and progressive progression from an evolutionary perspective that some allow significantly more evolution than others, and depending upon the evolutionary content accrued by a TES that it can progress from one universe to another potentially leapfrogging a universe?

SE1: Yes. Let me explain. As I just stated, the Concurrence Engineers grade the universes in terms of their evolutionary capability so a universe of limited evolutionary capability may be preceded by one of maximized evolutionary capability and in turn superseded by one of medium evolutionary capability. The overall result being a progressive evolutionary state from one universe to another. This progression, however, is based upon what is achieved in what can be called an average way.

Evolutionary progression within a universe is based upon experience through creativity and ownership of that which is created until that which is created no longer offers new experience. This continues until a universe no longer offers evolutionary potential. As a result, the universes are constantly re-graded by the Concurrence Engineers and the re-grading is a function of the number of TES, Aspects, and Shards within them and their interaction with the environment and what they create within that environment.

In the event that a TES is able to achieve the maximum level of evolutionary progression in a universe when it offers significantly more than its superseding universe, and that the evolutionary content gained is therefore more than the average evolution possible in the existing and superseding universe, then the Concurrence Engineers allow a function of bypass which is triggered by the evolutionary content of the TES. Such a TES is therefore allowed to progress to the next universal level over and above the evolutionary natural superseding universe.

ME: What you are saying then is that a TES has an evolutionary signature that allows it to progress to the next universe that offers the best evolutionary possibilities for it?

SE1: Yes, and the Concurrence Engineers create an automatic function that allows the TES to move from one universe to another based upon its evolutionary content accrued in previous universes and that which it has achieved in the current universe. It is the evolutionary performance of the TES within the current universe and its potential of moving into the superseding universe, or the one beyond, that triggers this function.

ME: And what happens if the evolutionary potential of the superseding universe changes due to the interaction of its incumbent TES, Aspects, and Shards?

SE1: It is possible that due to the constant re-grading of the evolutionary potential of a universe that two TES that have accrued the same historic evolutionary content and have achieved the same maximum evolutionary potential from the same universe do not progress to the same superseding universe.

ME: What would cause two TES to have two different evolutionary paths when they appear to have the same evolutionary content and performance in their current universe?

SE1: If they are both in the same temporal juncture, for want of a better word, they will progress in the same way. However, if one TES reaches the same evolutionary position as the other but at a later juncture and the evolutionary potential of the superseding universe is upgraded, then its evolutionary signature may not or will not be able to trigger the function of automatic universal bypass.

However …

If one TES reaches the same evolutionary position as the other but at a later juncture, the other TES only progressing to the superseding universe, and the evolutionary potential of the superseding universe is subsequently downgraded, then its evolutionary signature will or may be able to trigger the function of automatic universal bypass. It is therefore the evolutionary content of the TES that allows progression from one universe to another provided it has achieved what it can to progress and the work of other TES, Aspects, and Shards in its current universe have not affected its evolutionary quotient in a way that requires it to be re-graded positively. In the event that a universe is re-graded while occupied, then those TES will need to gain more evolutionary content in order to progress to the next universe. If the re-grade is negative, then there is no opportunity to progress earlier because it is the evolutionary quotient of the universe at the juncture of progression into that universe that is the evolutionary demarcation for movement from one to the other universe, so a lower evolutionary progression is naturally expected of that TES.

ME: Based upon this then, it is possible for one TES to be able to move to the superseding universe before another if the other TES entered into the universe at a juncture when it was a higher grade of evolution and the TES in question entered after a downgrade.

SE1: Correct.

ME: That's tough luck on the TES who entered into the universe when it had a higher evolutionary quotient.

SE1: That's evolutionary progression—it's dynamic and personal even though the so-called static and linear ladder is a bit adjustable. You have a saying, "what you lose on the swings, you gain on the roundabouts" and this is the same for all TES. A TES may lose in the evolutionary transition from one universe to another but it may gain in subsequent evolutionary transitions and vice versa.

ME: Nothing is really lost then, it's just a different way to go.

SE1: That's correct.

ME: Thank you. I have a final question. What ensures that there is a difference between one universe and another?

SE1: From the perspective of the incumbent entity or being, it's simply to do with what they can achieve in one universe versus another as a function of the difference in frequency. Clearly a higher frequency universe can support more structure and content. From the perspective of the Concurrence Engineers, it is a function of them checking that this natural difference in frequency is employed to its maximum, and that the difference is relative to both the preceding and superseding universes. In reality, the Concurrence Engineers are constantly checking the progressive possibilities from one universe to another and make relevant changes to the environment to ensure that there is evolutionary progression from one universe to another, hence the re-grading.

I think that this is a good lead in to the Frequential Barrier Engineers.

The Frequential Barrier Engineers

SE1: As you are now aware, the **Frequential Barrier Engineers** work in conjunction with the Concurrence Engineers. They ensure that there is a stepped difference or a real gap, for want of a better word, between the frequencies that allows a demarcation between one self-contained simultaneous universe and another. Although this may seem out of tune with the current understanding of "physics," there are gaps in between the major frequencies, or to describe it a better way, a gap between the top of the bandwidth of one major frequency and the bottom of the bandwidth of another higher major frequency. These gaps are part of the supporting structure of the multiverse and not the functional aspect of it. One way to think of how this works is to consider placing a sign on one rung of a ladder, missing out the rung above it, and placing another "progressive" sign on the rung two rungs above the first rung where the first sign was placed. It is therefore the role of these entities to ensure that the gap of one rung of the ladder is maintained.

ME: I have just seen that it's a bit more difficult than what you have just stated.

SE1: Go on?

ME: Well, we know from the information given to me in *The History of God* that there are areas of locally high frequency of a preceding universe that can interact with areas of locally low frequency of a superseding universe. How does this work when there is supposed to be a gap between them?

SE1: As you can see from the introductory text, there is a difference between the structural aspects of the frequencies and the functional aspects.

ME: Can you make this a bit clearer for us? I mean, from my perspective, they are difficult to separate.

SE1: I understand. It's best to think of the work of the Frequential Barrier Engineers as being just that, entities that work on the barriers between the major frequencies.

ME: Again though, how do they ensure that there is a gap between frequencies that cross over or overlap?

SE1: As you know, there is the possibility of an entity or being traveling from the universal environment supported by a lower frequency to the universal environment supported by a higher frequency. This is only possible when the structure is affected by the work of the incumbent entities or beings to the point where it creates locally low and locally high frequencies and that the spatial locations of these overlapping frequencies are the same or similar. The environment supported by each major frequency has a difference that is a function of the bandwidth, finitude, and resulting content. This is the function of the universal environment. The structure of the multiverse, although also being a function of frequency and bandwidth, is not affected by the content within a universal environment.

The Frequential Barrier Engineers ensure that the structural aspects of the multiverse are separate even though they are in the same space. Try to think of it in this way. Consider two vessels of water in the same ambient temperature, one frozen and full of ice and one not. Now think of the point when, in one vessel, the water is not quite cold enough to freeze and that in the other vessel the water is not quite warm enough to defrost. The ambient temperature of the surrounding environment supports both conditions simply because the frozen water is of a lower frequency and therefore has higher frequential density, whereas the water that is not frozen is of a higher frequency and therefore has a lower frequential density. They are both in the same space and in the same temperature but exist in different states of being.

ME: So even though they may overlap frequentially, they don't actually join together to make one vessel of water or one vessel of ice, they remain as two separate vessels of differing content.

SE1: That's correct and it is the difference in state that provides the structural gap when the frequencies of two universal environments overlap frequentially.

ME: Got it! The Frequential Barrier Engineers create or maintain a state of being between the two major frequencies that is relevant to each of the frequencies. Based upon this, even though they may locally share the same space and their frequencies therefore overlap, and could be considered to be of the same frequency, their density or structural function as a whole frequency, so to speak, remains the same and so they do not interfere with each other. This noninterference is the mechanics behind ensuring that there is a gap between the two frequencies because the maintenance of a frequential gap or barrier is not about localities, it's about considering the frequency as a whole and not just the locally low aspect of a higher major frequency being in the same frequential space as the locally high aspect of a lower major frequency.

SE1: Well done. And this works the same way when considering the frequencies of the multiverse as a whole.

ME: It's the density, for want of a better word, that creates the gap of barrier between the frequencies then?

SE1: Yes, the Frequential Barrier Engineers create the state of being, that can be called frequential density, for each of the frequencies, and this state of being is consistently distributed throughout the whole of the frequency, right down to the smallest subfrequency.

ME: A subfrequency carries the same status or state as the whole frequency then?

SE1: Correct.

ME: And therefore the state or status of two subfrequencies from two separate major frequencies cannot merge or become one as a result?

SE1: Correct.

ME: And so this creates the barrier and it is a barrier of state or status, what we called frequential density.

SE1: Now you are getting it.

ME: OK, if we have a state of beingness of the frequencies that acts as a barrier, what exactly is the function that allows progression from one universe to another?

SE1: Evolution.

ME: Yes, I understand that, but how does an entity of one evolutionary level jump to the next evolutionary level?

SE1: Try to think of it in these terms. When you are working with the higher frequencies in your current incarnate condition, you sometimes feel that you are about to burst out of your head, do you not?

ME: Yes, I do, it's like I need to be out of this level. I am pushing but there is a considerable amount of resistance to the push, so to speak. It's like I am under an elastic sheet that stretches but does not break.

SE1: Right. What you are feeling is the natural barrier that separates the frequency that you are in from the next one.

The Frequential Barrier Engineers create a condition where there is a level of elasticity before an eventual break, an evolutionary and therefore frequential escape density if you like, that allows the movement from one frequency to another. This can only be achieved by becoming the frequency that you want to move into while still being in the current frequency. This function of frequential elasticity operates even in areas of locally low frequencies of a higher frequency universe being in contact with the locally high frequencies of a lower frequency universe.

ME: I am getting an image here of oil and water. The oil has to move out of the water to sit on top of it close to the water/air interface. It's a little like the oil is being ejected from the water.

SE1: Good analogy. Think of it in that way but with some initial resistance at first before the oil makes its way to the surface of the water. You can also think of it as being like the elastic limit of the elastic sheet you talked about.

ME: The necessary requirement then is to be the frequency that you need to be and allow the frequency that you are in to eject you to the frequency that you need to be.

SE1: Correct, and the Frequential Barrier Engineers can manipulate this level of resistance to be more resistive or less resistive.

ME: You talked about the barrier between frequencies being a function of the beingness of the frequency and that it was applicable to every aspect of the frequency, no matter how small, and I am wondering what this barrier would look like? I mean, from a human science perspective, a frequency is a progressive and linear structure, but this does not allow the concept of a gap to be explained.

SE1: Think of it in this way. The multiverse is a structure within a space, the structure being a function of the space. Each frequency, as a function of the structure within that space, occupies a certain amount of that space in an isolated way. This occupation is based upon both the spatial location within the space as well as its structural location from the perspective of its frequential state or beingness relative to that structure.

ME: I am seeing a rather interesting image of how this works.

SE1: Go on.

ME: Well, we know that each of the universes associated with the multiverse is a function of the frequency that they are aligned to and that they exist in the same space, each universe being separated by the content associated with their frequency. This is how we currently understand how a space can be concurrently occupied. But what I am seeing here, though, is that the frequencies of that space do not occupy all of the volume of space that is associated with their frequency, that it is compartmentalized. What I am seeing is the multiverse as, for want of a better word, a big bubble or sphere and that it is full of smaller bubbles or spheres. Each of the smaller bubbles or spheres has a spatial location as well as a frequential location. Each of them has a frequential surface tension similar to that which we see with a droplet of water. I am just being told that the shape of the bubble or sphere is a function of the frequency and that some are more ovoid than spherical. This means that the universal environment created by frequency is also a bubble or spherical in representation. What's more, I am also being told that the function of the frequency is spherical in nature as well; it's not linear, it's spherical. Based upon this, movement from one frequency to another is achieved by either jumping or being ejected from one frequential sphere in its spatial location to another frequential sphere in a different spatial location. It's both a frequential and spatial move. The shape of the sphere is a function of the local frequential state within the sphere and so this changes the shape from spherical to ovoid or amorphous, even undulating.

SE1: And what about the gaps?

ME: The gaps are a function of the shape of the frequency and its location within multiversal space and its proximity to another frequential sphere. Based upon this, the gap between two frequential spheres, and therefore the universes supported by them, is not a standard gap because the frequential progression from one frequential sphere to another is a function of both location and frequency. I can see now that that gap can be manipulated by moving a frequential sphere from one spatial location to another by any amount.

Oh, hold on! This means that, for example, it is possible for a sphere of frequency level 63 that represents the 52nd universe to be spatially closer to a sphere of frequency level 195 that represents the 184th universe than a sphere that is of frequency level 64 which is closer to it frequentially.

Aha! This is how the Frequential Barrier Engineers create or maintain a gap between each of the frequencies. They move them away from each other. I expect that at times, from a linear perspective, when a locally low frequency of a higher frequency is close to, or in the same spatial proximity to, the locally high frequency of a lower frequency that they simply move the frequential sphere to a slightly different spatial location in order to maintain the gap, so to speak.

SE1: That's right and it's not just one frequential sphere that they have to move, because more often than not they have to move others as well to ensure that the overall gapping structure is maintained.

ME: Do they ever run out of gapping room?

SE1: No, never.

ME: I am glad I asked that question then. And, when we are ejected from one frequency to the next, are we moved spatially as well?

SE1: Naturally.

ME: Here we go again. I have just had another eureka moment!

SE1: Go on.

ME: Well, this explains an effect that I had noticed and have asked my Traversing the Frequencies Level 3 (TTF L3) students to look out for.

SE1: Yes, I am waiting!

ME: When we go through the exercise to see how fast we can move from one frequency level to another, I noted that the feel of the actual movement between the frequencies when moving through the frequency levels in a random way felt different to that which one would expect from a linear representation of the multiverse. I will try to explain in a better way.

When we move through the frequency levels using the methods described in the workshops we move from the Earth level to the level of interest and back down. It's just two locations, the Earth and the environment supported by the frequency for the exercise. Also both my students and I are concentrating on the methodology of getting there and back and not the feel of the translation from one frequency level to another. In TTF L3, the students are much more advanced and we go into different levels of detail because the higher we go in the frequencies, the less physical response we receive. However, when we focus on the translation from one frequential location to another, we gain a different level of feedback, we feel inertia. The inertia felt coupled together with the time taken to travel from one frequency to another tells us that the so-called distance between the frequencies is not linear in time traveled or spatial location.

SE1: So what you are saying is that you have felt the fact that the spatial location of a frequency and its environment is not progressive from a linear perspective.

ME: Yes, that's right. I first noticed a couple of years ago, when I started to include some more advanced techniques for the TTF L3 students, that I felt that the time taken to get from a frequency that was close to the one that I was moving from was not the same as I would have expected it to be if compared to a frequency that was frequentially further away. Basically, I expected it to take longer to go from, say, frequency level 23 to frequency level 359 than going from frequency level 23 to frequency level 127. I noted that sometimes a frequency that was very close to my point of origin could appear to take longer from a temporal perspective than to get to one that was further away. I also noted that this was not a general thing, that sometimes the expected time to get from one frequency to another was correct and that being in a frequency that was frequentially close by took a shorter length of time to traverse to than one that was frequentially further away. There appeared to be no rules that applied to this experience. Furthermore, the feeling of inertia associated with traversing from one frequency level to another was similarly random. I felt that some environments that were supported by the frequencies were in random spatial locations as well. I could feel that I was traveling in any direction, that being, up, down, left, right, forward, backward, in a circle, in a spiral, diagonally—any combination of those just mentioned including feeling that the multiverse was moving around me, me being at the center of the movement of the multiverse.

Without premeditating the response from my students, I ask what they feel during the random and fast movement around the frequencies and, in general, they all report similar or the same responses. For me, this justifies the imagery of the frequencies being in the locations that they need to be within the structure of the multiverse, and not where they are expected to be logically or even mathematically from an incarnate human perspective.

Simply put, one can feel or experience the true structure of the gaps between the frequencies if one were to focus on them.

I expect that it is possible to feel a difference in the time and spatial location taken to move from a frequency and its universal environment to another known frequency if it was changed; if one was, for example, moving from the 27th frequency to the 67th and that the Frequential Barrier Engineers had changed the frequential and spatial gapping—to feel the difference between the old and new gapping, so to speak.

SE1: The change may be subtle but, yes, it could be detected by one who is sensitive to such changes. Remember, it is the role of the Frequential Barrier Engineers to ensure that there is a minimum but robust gap between the frequencies, ensuring that they do not overlap from a structural perspective. This structural perspective is a moving feast, because as you are aware, the incumbent entities or beings can affect the frequency locally by the work that they do, both positively and negatively.

ME: What happens then when we get the opportunity to move from one frequency to another due to a locally high location within a low frequency being spatially close to the locally low location within a high frequency? I mean, if it is the role of the Frequential Barrier Engineers to maintain the gap, so to speak, what happens to an entity or being that uses this transient condition to move from a low frequency to a high frequency and vice versa?

SE1: If they move as a result of just being in the correct spatio-frequential location at the time of overlap, then they stay in the location traversed to if the Frequential Barrier Engineers correct the situation—unless of course they move back to their normal frequency before the overlap is corrected. If, on the other hand, they use a mechanical/energetic device to assist in their traversing from one frequency to another, and they are just using the overlap as an assistant for their device, then they will be able to move back by using this device. This, of course, does not stop an entity witnessing the effects of a temporary overlap for they can witness the effects, the scenes, and events within the universal environment supported by the overlap, and still be in their normal frequency of domicile when the overlap is corrected, provided they are not in the spatial location associated with the overlap.

ME: Would this explain why we have reports of some people seeing past, present, or future events that are not associated with the location that they are in?

SE1: Yes, it would.

ME: And would it also explain the sudden and unexplained disappearance of people, airplanes, boats, and other forms of transport?

SE1: It would explain that which is associated with such cases, yes.

ME: So do some entities actively choose to stay in a lower frequency if they moved from a higher frequency to a lower one?

SE1: Only if it suits their evolutionary needs or life plan.

ME: And that would be the same for those entities or beings that actively choose to stay in a higher frequency?

SE1: Yes, but it's more likely that an entity without the ability to return to their frequency of domicile elects to remain in a higher frequency than remain in a lower frequency.

ME: Do the Frequential Barrier Engineers ever help an entity or being get back to their frequency of domicile?

SE1: Never, this is not their role. Know this, though. They only remain in the frequency, domicile or not, for the duration that they are required to be projected from their TES. Once that duration is over, the TES recalls that Aspect to the evolutionary frequency of the TES for communion.

Let's move on to the Attractionists.

The Attractionists

SE1: **The Attractionists** have two roles and therefore two distinct specialisms. In the first distinction, they are entities that specialize in working in the physical aspects of the multiverse, the physical universe. In this first specialism, they work specifically on the way in which the energies that are associated with the lowest frequencies can and are used in conjunction to each other. They work on all levels of "physicality," from the attraction between Anu to the larger attraction between planets, suns, solar systems, and galaxies.

In the second specialism, they work on the signature of energies that are used to ensure that incarnates are attracted to each other for the purposes of removing karmic links or working together on a common life plan. This is not the same as being attracted from a romantic perspective because it is a functional aspect of the interactive evolutionary process of entities that are working with the evolutionary cycle.

ME: You suggest that the Attractionists have two roles. Does this mean that they perform both roles or that these entities have a specialism within their specialism? What I mean is, do they specialize in either the first role or the second role and therefore not the two?

SE1: In essence, they choose which role that they want to specialize in within the remit of being capable of performing either role. When these entities elected to perform these roles, they understood the commonality between the specialisms but recognized that they were different in reality. Based upon this, there are Attractionists that specialize in the attractivity between that which is physical and Attractionists that specialize in those that interact with the lowest frequencies of the multiverse.

ME: Are there any Attractionists that work with both specialisms?

SE1: Yes, but only from the perspective of overseeing the work that the specialized Attractionists perform.

ME: So, they are not really specialized in both specialisms; they are arbitrators. They need to be able to understand the work that the true specialists perform from a bigger overall perspective.

SE1: That's correct. They need to be able to see the functionality of the work of the Attractionists that are specialized and guide them where necessary to ensure that the work they perform is appropriate from an environmental or personal and collective interactive perspective.

ME: I think it may be beneficial if we described their specialized roles in more detail on an individual basis rather than trying to from an overall basis.

SE1: I agree. Let's deal with those Attractionists that deal with the components of the physical universe first.

The Attraction between Physical Components

SE1: Attraction or gravity, for want of a better word, is controlled by those Attractionists that specialize in this function; however, it is not strictly based upon size.

ME: I am being told that the level or strength of attraction is aligned to the function of the physical component from both an environmental and interactive basis.

SE1: Well done. Based upon this, it would not be a surprise to note that a planetary body, for example, does not have the same level of attractivity than one Anu to another.

ME: No, I can see that, but what is the process that creates such attractivity?

SE1: It's all to do with cohesion.

ME: Cohesion? What's the difference between cohesion and attractivity?

SE1: In general, attractivity is aligned to the function associated to the scale of a physical component in its physical universal environment and its interactivity with other components of similar or same subatomic structure. Cohesion is to do with the subatomic forces that hold the components together that make the larger components and give it presence.

ME: Now I am lost.

SE1: OK. Let's look at what the Attractionists work on using an example of how a larger physical body is created from the subatomic.

If we look at the physical universe in general, we see an environment that is full of groups of physical components that have a certain type of cohesion. Some aspects of the physical components are represented as planets—both singularly and as systems of planets, nebulae, and galaxies—groups of planetary systems and nebulae. They are created through a combination of the cohesion and attractivity of the atomic and subatomic components that make them up. The interaction between these bodies, however, is attractivity but the overall function of the physical universe is cohesion.

Cohesion therefore holds everything together from a componential perspective but the interaction of these components with each other is attractivity.

ME: Got it. Wait a moment—I am receiving an image to support what you are saying.

I started to see a planet as a matrix of cohesive components. Each component was a material, and the subatomic components that created the materials were linked together by type. The cohesion between each material type was not just attractivity or what we might call local gravity, it was a wide level of attractivity that gave all subatomic components a link to each other no matter where they were. This meant that they didn't necessarily need to be within the same spatial location to create the material. Even though they were separate from a localized state of cohesion, if they were together but captured within another matrix of cohesion that represented another material, they were held in a state of separated cohesion, or for the want of a better word, the "potential of total cohesion" if they were in a state of separation within that cohesion. From the perspective of the "very localized" representation of their cohesion, this was represented as a "form-based" signature, the form being the basic physical representation of the material in its cohesive state. Simple attraction does not provide a form per se, cohesion does. Incarnate mankind, I felt, did not yet understand this. A basic form is created by a material in cohesion and that cohesion is a very powerful force. All we see is the attractive forces in a very rudimentary way. I was given an example of what this meant.

Water molecules with a reduced frequency create ice but the form is based upon the random reduction of that frequency and the volume of water reduced in frequency; it could be classified as formless. However, a snowflake has "form" specific to subatomic cohesion and therefore displays a form-based signature in an individualized way. If it became ice, it would adopt a different structure that is based upon attractivity through loss of en-mass frequency, or a better way of describing it would be low-frequency atomic "stick-tion!" If, however, the snowflake is joined by others, the function of overall cohesion synergy comes into effect creating snow and not ice. The temperature and the materials are the same, but the form-based signature is maintained as a function of cohesion creating the snow and not attractivity through low-frequency atomic stick-tion which creates ice.

SE1: Very good.

ME: So a naturally occurring molecular structure can be classified as a cohesive state of attractivity whereas a manufactured molecular structure such as the creation of a metal through raising its frequency, heating it so that it melted, is just attractivity.

SE1: Correct.

ME: This will be a hard concept for people to understand.

SE1: But it explains the difference in structure that can be observed. With metals by the way, this difference is subtle and difficult to see with current levels of technology.

The Attractionists create the level of cohesive and attractive strength of the materials that can be created by all of the subatomic combinations available within the twelve frequencies of the physical universe.

ME: So how does this work when we consider alloys of materials?

SE1: The Attractionists created a high level of attractivity between subatomic structures of the same type and other levels of attractivity (high or low) between similar or sympathetic subatomic structures, the level of attractivity being a function of the ability to remain cohesive with its natural state of subatomic structure while in a state of attractivity with another similar or sympathetic subatomic structure and a non-natural state of being "intertwined" with the product of the subatomic structure in terms of its form within the atomic structure. As a result, the structure of the alloy is made up from both attractive and cohesive forces that allow two materials to be attractive to each other while the cohesive forces between the materials of the same type are maintained through the gaps in the subatomic structure of the materials that are being alloyed. This creates matrices of attractivity and cohesion that are interactive and intertwined with similar or sympathetic subatomic structures creating larger bodies that interact with each other in an attractive way relative to the collective integral cohesive state of the individual bodies.

A physical body can be large with either little cohesion and attractivity or high cohesion and attractivity. Similarly, a physical body can be very small with either little cohesion and attractivity or high cohesion and attractivity. An example of this is the relative attractivity of Earth's Sun in comparison with its size, which is small in comparison to a planet the size of Mars. There are planetary bodies that are the size of Mars that have the attractivity of twenty thousand suns.

ME: Are these in our galaxy?

SE1: Yes, there are many such so-called high-gravity planets.

ME: They would not be called black holes or black suns?

SE1: No, they are a different creation and are another component of the physical universe that the Attractionists create through assigning different levels of cohesion and attractivity. I will explain in a moment what they are.

I haven't mentioned the interfrequential [*between the twelve frequencies of the physical universe—GSN*] cohesive conditions that apply with some materials. Interfrequential cohesion ensures that a material is represented on more frequencies than just the natural frequency that the subatomic structure of a material exists within. For example, the subatomic structure of many materials is only represented on the frequency that they are aligned to. However, a common level of creativity is to have pan-frequential bodies where a planet, for example, is represented on more than one frequency. The Earth is one such pan-frequential body that was created by the Attractionists to be available to the incumbent incarnates throughout the ascension potential that individualized free will offers. In the case of the Earth, it is simply that the higher up the frequencies one travels, the more content associated with the Earth one is able to interact with, and this includes the materials associated with those frequencies.

ME: What are black holes or black suns then?

SE1: For a start, they are two different things. I will explain.

A **Black Hole** is an area of static crossover between two or more frequencies. Usually three frequencies are involved at any one spatial location such as level 4, 5, and 6 where level 5 is the link between levels 4 and 6. A Black Hole is not to be confused with the locally high-frequential area within a lower frequency overlapping with the locally low-frequential area within a higher frequency, which you know, is a temporary condition created by the evolutionary progression associated with the entities or being located in the areas of overlap.

In this instance, the Attractionists create the cohesive state in the subatomic structure of the associated material aspects of the environments supported by those frequencies where crossover exists. This allows the connection at that spatial location between the frequencies and the potential to use them as a means of movement between them. One could consider a Black Hole as a function of cohesion in its own right. A Black Hole, as described by incarnate human theoretical physics, is incorrect. Theoretical physics describes a black sun. This is because a Black Hole is not a physical manifestation whereas a Black Sun is.

A **Black Sun** is a physical body that has so much attractivity and cohesion that nothing in the frequencies associated with the Gross Physical can escape from its grasp. That is, from a gravity-based perspective. Indeed, they are only in existence in the Gross Physical aspect of the physical universe, frequencies 1, 2, and 3. The cohesion needs to be extremely high to ensure that the attractivity can be maintained without imploding under its own attractivity. Contrary to incarnate human theoretical physics, they are not size-relative in terms of their attractivity. However, they do have size and are usually no bigger than a small moon and no smaller than an island, say, the size of the Hawaiian island of Maui. The scientist's evidence of the location of a Black Sun is based upon the deflection of light, but light is not an indicator of the presence of a Black Sun; it is simply an indicator of a level of attractivity of any planetary body that can attract particles of a certain subatomic structure, light being one of them.

The Attraction between Entities

SE1: When the Attractionists work on the signatures that assure the attraction between different entities or beings is functional, they are working specifically at the request of the Guides and Helpers of those entities or beings that are incarnate.

ME: How do they do that? I mean, it seems a very diverse and specialized role to play when you consider the work of those Attractionists that we have just discussed. I am afraid that this has not been sitting comfortably with me.

SE1: It's uncomfortable if you look at it in isolation. However, if you look at it in terms of the overall picture of "attraction," then you will see how important it is to have the same genre of Curator working on both the attraction between the physical aspects of the multiverse as well as the interactive aspects.

ME: I don't really understand!

SE1: Try to look at it this way. It is the environment that gives the entity or being the opportunity to experience, learn, and evolve. It is the entity or being—collectively or individually—that molds the environment to that which offers a more diverse opportunity for experiencing, learning, and evolving, but this can only be achieved in the bigger sense if the incumbent incarnate entities work together in a way that is consistent with that which they want to experience in the environment that either they are in or need to be in. In this instance, it is all about the environment that they need to be in.

ME: And I suppose the only way to create the environment that one needs to be in is to change the environment that one is already in to that which is needed?

SE1: Correct. The Guides and Helpers work together to achieve a coherent level of understanding of what the current overall environmental opportunities are that support the experiential requirements of the entities and beings that interact with it, and what needs to be changed to allow those experiential opportunities to be progressive and therefore support the ongoing demands of the entities and beings within it. Because the best way to experience a new environmental or interactive condition is to make the changes oneself, the Guides and Helpers work on the supporting specialisms the entities and beings need to bring into the environment that they are responsible for to allow them to both make and experience the changes and evolve in the process. In support of this, the Attractionists create a subsignature for the entities that need to work together.

ME: What is a subsignature?

SE1: Think of it as a subroutine in a computer program. As you already know, each and every entity and being, me included, has an energetic signature that reflects what they have experienced, achieved, learned, and their subsequent level of evolution. It's how you identify each other when in your normal energetic environment. When, however, two or more entities or beings need to work together to create a level of interaction to support either personal or collective experience or the reduction in karma between each other while incarnate, there needs to be some sort of attractive force to make you want to engage with those other entities or beings— especially when you're incarnate.

ME: I expect that is because we are not so connected when we are incarnate?

SE1: That's right. The subsignature is assigned by the Attractionists upon request and direction of the Guides and Helpers at the Aspect level—the actual entity or being that is incarnate—and not at the TES level. This subsignature creates the various different types of attraction between incarnates to ensure that they are attracted to work with each other for the correct reasons, whether it is environmentally interactive or personally interactive.

ME: I suppose this explains the feelings that we get about getting in contact with someone, or talking to someone when we see them for the first time. We sort of get a feeling that we are being drawn to them in some way, that we must do something with them.

SE1: That is one way of putting it, yes. Note that this is nothing to do with the romantic side of attraction, which is purely a function of an agreement between Aspects before becoming incarnate.

ME: You just mentioned that there are different types of attraction between entities or beings and that these different types create the attraction to the entity or being that needs to be interacted with. Can you identify what they are?

SE1: Yes, of course. I just want to say at this point that the subsignatures associated with the different types of attraction are specific to working together for a purpose and not to affect an individualized change.

- Attraction to give forgiveness

- Attraction to create an environmental change

- Attraction to work together on a common subject or experience

- Attraction to assist in an aspect of a life plan

- Attraction to assist in a life plan in totality

- Attraction to create a change in thought process of a group of incarnates (small or large)

- Attraction to another to address a karmic link or debt

- Attraction to another to create a link that starts in one life but continues in many other lives

- Attraction to another to terminate a link that started in one life, continued in many other lives, but now needs to be finalized

- Attraction to another to receive inspiration or leadership

- Being attractive to another to give inspiration or leadership

- Attraction to another for educational purposes

- Being attracted to another to be educated

This list is not exhaustive and there are subsections to these headings, but it does give you an idea.

Again, note that each of these types of attraction has a different subsignature that draws entities or beings together to interact in a way which is specific to their life plan and any karmic links. There can of course be subsignatures within the subsignatures.

ME: I suppose that this would be relative to when an entity or being has many experiences to experience or has chosen a complicated or difficult incarnation.

SE1: Yes, and all of the things in between as well.

It's time to fully focus on the physical universe and specialize on those environments that are in the lowest frequencies, using the Earth as an example.

ME: Ah!! I can just hear the readers thinking "about time!"

The Caretakers—of the Physical Universe

SE1: A Caretaker is the overall name for those entities that work specifically within the frequencies of the physical universe. This is where most of the entities that incarnate mankind has knowledge about, such as Elementals (nature spirits) and so-called Angels, reside. It includes the Attractionists above and the roles in the subsections below.

The Vehicle Creators

SE1: **The Vehicle Creators** are those entities that design and create the vehicles used for experiencing the lowest frequencies of the multiverse that we call the physical universe. They design the incarnate vehicle specific to the frequential and planetary, or other environment that they are to operate within and in the way it is supposed to be experienced. That means that an incarnating entity experiences resistance, lack of functionality, and connectivity in all frequencies of the physical universe relative to that frequency.

ME: Are these Curators the ones that we talked about in *The History of God*? Are they not really Curators but TES or Aspects of TES that worked on the design of the human form when the possibility of incarnating with individualized free will was introduced?

SE1: Well, although the Vehicle Creators are a genre of Creator, their role is not totally occupied by Curators.

ME: You mean that there are some Vehicle Creators that are not Curators?

SE1: The Vehicle Creators can and do include members of those entities or beings that are in the evolutionary cycle and use the incarnate vehicles created by the Vehicle Creators themselves. The group of Vehicle Creators that developed the human vehicle also included a small group of those TES, via their Aspects, that specialized in gaining evolutionary content by incarnating into the Earth environment as incarnate mankind.

There is a group of these entities comprising Curators and entities or beings in the evolutionary cycle, that are the collective creational mind, so to speak, for every vehicle that allows a level of incarnate interaction to be achieved within the environment they were designed for. This obviously includes all of the twelve frequencies associated with the physical universe and the frequential representations of the vehicles created for those frequencies.

ME: What incarnate vehicles are used on the Earth other than the human form?

SE1: From the perspective of mankind's understanding, all types of flora and fauna can be used for incarnate experience. However, the genre of TES and therefore Aspect that incarnates into flora and fauna are different to those that incarnate into the human form.

ME: How are they different? Ah! Don't tell me, they are of a different level of sentience.

SE1: You nearly said evolutionary level then.

ME: Yes, but I realized that it is the sentience that creates the difference in genre of an entity or being and not the evolutionary level.

SE1: And this is because?

ME: Testing me, are you?

SE1: Just seeing what has stayed in your mind.

ME: Within each of the genres of TES and Aspect there is an opportunity to evolve. However, the evolutionary progression attained is specific to the genre of TES and its projected Aspects and not evolution in a general sense. And so, the evolutionary level of a TES that is only able to occupy the incarnate vehicle of the level of fauna via its projected Aspect, although it may be high, would not be as high as a TES that occupies a human vehicle via its projected Aspect, although it may be low, for example. Evolutionary level is therefore specific to the level of individualized sentience that is assigned to a body of energy and not evolution itself.

SE1: Good, good, good.

ME: So if this is correct, does the group of entities or beings that are in the evolutionary cycle and that are part of the creative group that developed and maintain the human vehicle also include the genre of TES or Aspect that can only incarnate into fauna or flora?

SE1: No, the level of sentience that this genre of incarnating entities and beings has does not support such capability.

If you remember the information about what genres of entity or being can incarnate into what vehicle, you will know that the genre of entity or being that can incarnate into the human form and those incarnate vehicles of various types that support the same genre of entity or being in the rest of the physical universe can also incarnate into any flora or fauna—animal, vegetable, or mineral vehicle that they choose, but they don't generally because there is little evolutionary content to be gained from such an exercise.

ME: Yes. I also remember that the genre of entity or being that can only incarnate into fauna, can also incarnate into any flora, vegetable or mineral vehicle that they choose. However, they cannot incarnate into the vehicles that support the genre of entity or being that are classified as a TES or the Aspect of a TES.

SE1: Correct.

ME: I also note that the genre of entity or being in the rest of the physical universe that can only incarnate into flora can also incarnate into any mineral vehicle that they choose, but not in the incarnate vehicles that support the genre of TES and Aspect that the vehicle incarnate humankind supports or those that support the genre of TES or Aspect that can incarnate into the animal vehicle. This is the same downstream for that genre of TES and Aspect that can only incarnate into the mineral; it can't incarnate into the vehicle that a higher level of sentience can incarnate into.

SE1: Good. So now you can see that the Vehicle Creators would only be able to work with entities and beings that were of the same genre of TES and Aspect sentience that allows incarnation into the type of vehicle that is similar to, or the same quality as, the human vehicle—in terms of its ability to support a quotient of sentience, that is.

ME: How does that work with the Shard of an Aspect? A Shard has a significantly reduced level of sentience in comparison to its Aspect.

SE1: As you know, a Shard can incarnate into a human vehicle or any other vehicle of the same quality because it is a smaller individualization of an entity or being of a higher genre or sentience and as such, it carries the signature of that level of overall sentience and not the sentience quotient that is assigned to it.

ME: The Vehicle Creators that created the human vehicle then only have help or assistance from those entities or beings that are of the highest level of individualized sentience, those that are capable of incarnating into the human form and its equivalents within the physical universe and its frequencies.

SE1: That's right.

ME: And this group of entities or beings that we discussed in *The History of God* is the same group that helped the Vehicle Creators to develop the human vehicle and its various updates?

SE1: Yes. Focusing back to that Event Space, I see that we discussed the creation of the human form in a way that suggested that the group of entities or beings that assisted the Vehicle Creators actually did the work of developing the human form. This is not the case, although they did have a large part to play.

ME: What was the most important role that they had to play then?

SE1: As with all entities and beings that work with the Vehicle Creators, they test out the use of the incarnate vehicles that they are developing for and on behalf of the Vehicle Creators and more importantly, those entities and beings that are in the evolutionary cycle and that will be using these incarnate vehicles to accelerate their evolutionary quotient and potential.

ME: So they gain essential feedback from those who use the vehicles?

SE1: Yes. This is a most important exercise and it has to be done on a regular basis as it allows the ability to modify the vehicles according to a number of factors.

These factors are:

- The changes in frequency of the environment that they are working in.

- Physical changes in the environment that they are working in.

- The ability to move from one environment to another when things such as interplanetary, intergalactic, or interfrequential travel is achieved.

- Resistance to atmospheric changes.

- Adaptability to changes in sentience of the entity or beings, i.e., the Aspect, incarnating into the vehicle.

ME: Changes in sentience of the entity or being? Why would the vehicle have to cope with that?

SE1: If you can remember from *The Anne Dialogues* the quotient of sentience that is assigned by a TES to the projected Aspect can range from 2.5 percent to 30 percent of overall TES sentience depending upon the total number of Aspects projected and the amount of sentience the TES decides is appropriate for a specific Aspect and its tasks/experiences when incarnate. A Shard can be as low as 2.5

percent of the 2.5 percent or as high as 30 percent of the 2.5 percent of the TES sentience assigned to an Aspect. The incarnate vehicle therefore has to be capable of accepting a maximum of 30 percent of TES sentience and a minimum of 2.5 percent of 2.5 percent of TES sentience and still function correctly. [*A Shard can therefore be a minimum of 0.0625 percent of TES sentience and a maximum of 0.75 percent of TES sentience.—GSN*]

A similar function that deletes the use of the Shard is also used for those vehicles that are used for the flora, fauna, and minerals that are designed for use on a planetary body and are associated with the lower quality genres of entity or being.

ME: The Vehicle Creators also create the flora, fauna, and mineral vehicles then?

SE1: Yes, they can. Each of these vehicles has the capability of being occupied by a TES or an Aspect of a TES. Note, though, that the Vehicle Creators generally specialize in the creation of complex vehicles, those that need rapid forms of animation or ambulation and they would only create a flora or mineral vehicle if a complex version was required.

And …

Just before your readers ask the question about insects, a single TES Aspect would be in control of a whole hive and not one specific insect.

ME: Ah! Now that's interesting. Why does it require a whole TES sentience to work with an insect hive and not an Aspect?

SE1: In general, and at the level of experiential ability of the individual insect vehicle, the hive is the best way to experience a collective mind constructed of autonomous, but not individualized, components in a fully integrated and collective sense. This means that a TES would assign its sentience to the total population of hive components of a certain genre or family of insects and not just the population associated with a single hive. In this way, the TES is experiencing the collective mind of the genre or family of insects associated with a planetary body in totality.

ME: I assume then that, in the example of a bee, the TES associated with a specific genre of bee is experiencing every aspect of the function and experience of a bee from an individual bee in one hive, to the collective functions of all bees in a specific beehive to the total collective functions of all bees in all hives on a planetary body.

SE1: That's correct. Each different genre or family of bees, in this example, would have a different TES, in control of and experiencing through all bees and hives of that genre or family. The TES involved in a hive mind would, however, be of the genre associated with an animal vehicle.

A similar function is used for the occupation of the collective sentience associated with tree and plant collectives. Tree collectives can spread beyond one particular planetary body to many others and the TES associated with them would be in control of all of those in the same genre or family on all of the planetary bodies that they occupy, such as Maple, Elm, or Oak.

ME: What about the different vehicles used in the physical universe in totality? How many vehicle versions or body form factors are there?

SE1: The Vehicle Creators create a plethora of vehicles available for every environmental condition associated with a particular frequency and/or planetary body and other nonplanetary environments.

ME: Give me an example.

SE1: Well, the Earth is an excellent example of the vast number of form factors that are available for an entity or being to incarnate into, discounting of course the quality of sentience associated with a TES or Aspect and the limitations in the various form factors that that quality of sentience allows.

ME: You are suggesting then that there are at least as many variations of form factor that we have on the Earth available for incarnate evolutionary experience in the rest of the physical universe?

SE1: At least a hundred and twenty times as many, and that's only in the Gross Physical levels. There are many more on the levels above the first three frequencies.

ME: How are the incarnate vehicles constructed?

SE1: The Vehicle Creators have three main templates that they use in the physical universe. This is concurrent with all animated vehicles that are used for housing an Aspect or Shard, irrespective of the quality of sentience that is projected into it.

One: the representation of the vehicle in the environment and frequency of operation—its form and relative energetic templates. Two: the supporting energetic structure that allows animation and ambulation of the vehicle and the ability for the Aspect to integrate with it while still being connected to its TES—the energy distribution system. Three: the method of generation of energy to support the perpetuation of the vehicle—the number of energy receptors or chakras and/or ingestion of solid materials. Ingestion of solid materials is, however, used mainly in the lowest of the frequencies—the Gross Physical.

The energetics associated with an incarnate vehicle have the following variations as a result of the base frequency of operation for the incarnate vehicle. Note that the higher up the frequencies the incarnate vehicle is, the lower levels of construction are no longer necessary to support the vehicle's continued existence, so are therefore not required, and are subsequently not included in the construction of the vehicle.

- The **Gross Physical** has seven energetic templates, seven energy distribution systems, and seven chakra groups for the vehicles that are used in the first three frequencies of the physical universe.

- The first **Spirituo-Physical** level has four energetic templates, four energy distribution systems, and four chakra groups for the vehicles that are used in the fourth frequency of the physical universe.

- The second **Spirituo-Physical** level has three energetic templates, three energy distribution systems, and three chakra groups for the vehicles that are used in the fifth frequency of the physical universe.

- The third **Spirituo-Physical** level has two energetic templates, two energy distribution systems, and two chakra groups for the vehicles that are used in the sixth frequency of the physical universe.

- The fourth **Spirituo-Physical** level and the energetic levels have one energetic template, one energy distribution system, and one chakra group for the vehicles that are used in the seventh frequency and above, up to the twelfth, of the physical universe.

SE1: Just to make things clearer for your readers, I will describe the frequencies of the multiverse, those that apply to the physical universe, that are relevant to the Gross Physical and Spirituo-Physical aspects of the incarnate vehicle that are created by the Vehicle Creators.

The **Gross Physical** level relates to the first three frequencies of the multiverse. This is the physical form that you see as the human body right now.

The **first Spirituo-Physical** level relates to the fourth frequency level and is sometimes referred to as the astral level. This can also be classified as the lower astral.

The **second Spirituo-Physical** level relates to the fifth frequency level. This can also be classified as the upper-lower astral.

The **third Spirituo-Physical** level relates to the sixth frequency level. This can also be classified as the lower-upper astral.

The **fourth Spirituo-Physical** level relates to the seventh frequency level. This can also be classified as the upper astral.

It is these levels that the Aspect generally traverses through when the Gross Physical body is regenerating during the normal sleep cycle. It is also where normal transcendental meditation techniques allow the Aspect to traverse the frequencies above the Gross Physical in a conscious sense.

ME: Which vehicle is the most prolific in the physical universe? We seem to focus on variations upon the human body theme in science fiction films and books.

SE1: The human form and its variants are a very useful and flexible form to use and is quite well distributed in the lower frequencies of the physical universe. However, it is what you would call a "mantoid" [*the mantis-based form—GSN*] form that is the most prolific.

ME: Why is that?

SE1: Simply because it is more capable of being used in the frequencies above the Gross Physical. They are available across the physical universe from the fourth frequency right up to and including the seventh frequency. It is quite an accomplished form and is one that is naturally good at manipulating energies on all of the levels it operates within.

ME: I would have thought that the human form is best because of the dexterity of the hands?

SE1: The manipulation of energies by a combination of the incarnate vehicle and the use of pure intention is a better method of creativity.

ME: So whatever the vehicle form factor, the method of creation uses the three main templates you just described.

SE1: Yes. Do note, though, that the higher up the frequencies the vehicle is, the less complicated it is for the Aspect to incarnate into it, and the more energetic functions are retained. Vehicles that are created for use in the first three frequencies of the multiverse are the most complicated specifically because there is normally a need to create a vehicle that has a metabolism of some sort to generate low-frequency energy and needs to make use of a gas that is in the atmosphere of the environment to assist in the metabolic function.

ME: How do the Vehicle Creators know which incarnate vehicle is required for which planetary environment?

SE1: They work very closely with the Habitation Creators and I suppose this is a good opportunity to describe the work of this genre of Caretaker.

The Habitation Creators

SE1: **The Habitation Creators** deal with the maintenance of the ability for the environment to support the perpetuation and reproduction of the incarnate vehicles created for a specific environment or environments. They understand the work of the Atmospherisists due to be described later and introduce existing flora and fauna or suggest the creation of new flora and fauna to the Vehicle Creators as appropriate. The flora, and in some respects fauna, exists to support the balance of the environment in an automatic way, but this isn't always the case. The Habitation Creators also include the Habitation Specialists. Don't forget that the Vehicle Creators generally specialize in the creation of complex vehicles, those that need rapid forms of animation or ambulation, and although they do create flora vehicles, this is only generally for more complicated flora.

ME: The Habitation Creators work on a planetary environment from a general basis then?

SE1: They are the initial creators of the environment, if you wish, and the overseers of the environment, with the Habitation Specialists doing the main work of the maintenance. We will discuss the Habitation Specialists in a moment.

ME: Which comes first then, the development of the incarnate vehicle with the environment modified to support the perpetuation of the incarnate vehicle, or does the creation of the environment come first and then the incarnate vehicle is developed to suit the environment?

SE1: It's a mixture of both in reality. There are environments on planets or the moons of planets that exist naturally where, with a minor level of modification, they will support an existing incarnate vehicle form factor or sometimes an existing incarnate vehicle form requires minor modification to work with that environment.

There are environments that need to be introduced to support a specific incarnate form factor that is required to be introduced into a certain spatial location. There are also environments where a new incarnate form factor needs to be developed to allow it to be a useful location for evolutionary progression of a different incarnate type.

ME: I remember being told that the Earth's environment has had a number of incarnate human form factors transplanted into it?

SE1: Yes, there have been three such transplants but that was only after the human incarnate vehicle had been fully developed and was in use in other frequential and spatial locations in the physical universe. Most of the diversity of human forms is due to them being modified to work with certain frequential states on the Earth, and then, as the Earth dropped down the frequencies as a result of the incarnating Aspects becoming addicted to low-frequency thoughts, behaviors, and actions, new modifications were made to support the lower base frequencies. However, some of the versions adapted to the lower frequencies naturally through what you might call "Darwinian" evolution, adding to the diversity.

Getting back to main theme of this dialogue, though, the Habitation Creators look at the location that is to be used as an environment for evolutionary progression via incarnation and establish what is naturally occurring versus what needs to be added and which incarnate vehicle type/s can be used. If you like, they create a checklist.

ME: What would that checklist look like or contain?

SE1: They look at a number of things. I will list them for you in order of importance and action by the Habitation Creators. They need to liaise with the Atmospherisists to achieve some of these checklist items. Also, some of these items only apply to planetary or other locations in the Gross Physical aspect of the physical universe.

The frequency of the location.

1. Is the location a planetary body or a moon?

2. What base elements are available, or required?

3. Is a light and heat source close by or required? This can be a sun or a nebula.

4. Does the location have an atmosphere?

5. Is an atmosphere required?

6. If an atmosphere is available, what elements is it made from?

7. Is the atmosphere self-perpetuating/generating or does it need maintenance of some sort?

8. Does the atmosphere need regenerating through a metabolic process of some sort? Does it need flora to do this or another process?

9. Does the atmosphere have the qualities or elements desired for an incarnate vehicle that has a metabolic process that requires the use of a gas?

10. Does the atmosphere have a "weather" system? Does it need a weather system to be created? How would it be maintained or perpetuated?

11. Does the location have a hard, soft, or liquid surface?

12. Does the surface have the ability to support flora if required?

13. What currently existing flora can be used? Is new flora required? Is the flora self-perpetuating?

14. Does the location need fauna to assist in the perpetuation of the flora?

15. What fauna is available that can self-perpetuate in the current or desired atmosphere?

16. Can the fauna metabolize the flora if it needs to?

17. What is the optimal combination of flora and fauna for the location and its atmosphere and surface type/s?

18. What currently available incarnate vehicle can be supported by the desired eco-structure of the location? Does it need modification? Is a new design required?

19. Is the location to support an existing incarnate civilization or to allow one to develop in its own way?

20. If an existing incarnate civilization is to occupy the location, can it be employed to assist in the development of the location?

21. Which Habitation Specialists are required to support the ongoing maintenance of the environment? How many are needed? How many are available?

ME: This is quite a lot to consider!

SE1: It's not an exhaustive list by any means either.

ME: And all of this and more is required to be able to support the perpetuation and reproduction of an incarnate vehicle or vehicles?

SE1: In the main, yes, although the higher the frequency of the location, the less physical support from an eco-structure is required to assist in the perpetuation and reproduction of an incarnate vehicle.

ME: How many planets have the diversity of flora and fauna of the Earth?

SE1: Not many. The Earth, being pan-frequential within the physical universe, is a very complicated environment. Remember the Earth supports three types of sentient entities or beings of the quality that can incarnate in the human form. Two different form factors for incarnation are available for two of the sentient entities or beings. The third is energetic and therefore doesn't require an incarnate vehicle.

Most locations—planets, moons, or nebulae—have very simple eco-structures and as a result limited flora and fauna. Some of the atmospheres of the locations that are used by incarnate vehicles are aggressive to put it mildly. In fact, some of them are similar in chemical composition to sulphuric acid or caustic soda! Having said that, there are two environments that are similar to those just described that have quite a diversity of flora and fauna. The Populationists [*see later—GSN*] are very good at placing the right flora and fauna in the environment that they are working on.

Most planetary or moon-based environments that are used in the Gross Physical, the first three frequencies, need a good quality environment that is rich, but not necessarily diverse, in eco-structure. This is predominantly required for those incarnate vehicles and the incarnate Aspects that are or have a desire to be interdependent with the location of the incarnate activity and its environment.

ME: Does the dependency on eco-structure change with the level of frequency? For example, the higher up the frequencies, the less eco-structure is required?

SE1: No, there is no difference as there are flora and fauna that are available right up to the twelfth frequency. However, looking into your mind for a moment, I see that you had an assumption that as the location of incarnation increases in frequency, the need for an eco-structure reduces.

ME: I was thinking that, yes.

SE1: Well, what I just said should answer that question. However, what I will say is that there are many planets or moons that appear to be barren at the Gross Physical frequency level but that have fully populated eco-structures full of flora and fauna on the higher levels of frequency. There are also planets or moons that are barren on all levels of frequency associated with the physical universe but that are used as a focal point for the work of incarnate entities or beings who work independently of an eco-structure.

ME: Would these be like bases or outposts?

SE1: Sometimes, it depends if they are travelers or not, but in a lot of examples the focus of the entities or beings who work with a planet or moon that is barren throughout the frequencies is to either work together in an area of low frequency on a common project, or simply to experience low-frequency experience, or to assist the Habitation Creators, if requested, to create an eco-structure on a barren planet or moon.

When incarnate humankind can experience for themselves the higher frequencies associated with the physical universe, they will see that things are not as they seem, that everything is occupied and used in some way, shape, or form for the benefit of accelerating their evolution by working with low-frequency environments and is not just unoccupied or dead.

ME: It looks like the physical universe is a valuable commodity.

SE1: It is and will be for some time to come. There is much to be gained from working in low-frequency environments, provided one doesn't get addicted to the thoughts, behaviors, and actions associated with it.

I had it in mind to change the order of dialogue to allow the flow from the Habitation Creators to go to the Atmospherisists, but I have someone you know tapping on my energetic shoulder, so to speak. Someone who loved the Habitation Specialists and communicated with them on a regular basis while incarnate with you.

A: Hello—It's me!!!!

I felt the familiar energy that was Anne. It had been nearly two and a half years since I last worked with Anne on The Anne Dialogues *and I quickly remembered that one of her parting comments was that she would make a guest appearance in this book. I have to be honest, I was expecting an earlier entrance and even a comment or two from The Origin, but to date neither had shown up on my energetic radar, until now, that is.*

The Habitation Specialists

SE1: I will let you two reacquaint yourselves before I get involved with this dialogue again.

ME: Will you return?

SE1: Yes, once Anne has worked with you on the Habitation Specialists.

This was to be Anne's guest appearance then, describing the roles of this genre of Caretaker and therefore Curator.

A: I wanted to get involved when you were focusing on the Earth as an example of the work of the Curators in the Gross Physical.

ME: Well, I have to say that when incarnate you were very interested in nature and the Elementals so it feels very appropriate that you take part in this book at the point where we describe them.

Shall I introduce the Habitation Specialists or will you?

A: I will let you do that then I will take over!

ME: **The Habitation Specialists** are the entities that incarnate mankind calls nature spirits or Elementals. They have a very specialized function and they can be aligned to a single plant or microbe family or type.

Just to be clear here, that even though animals and plants are classified as incarnate vehicles for the use of certain genres of TES Aspect or unprojected TES (those TES that have either no currently projected Aspects or have not generated any Aspects to project), they would still be in need of care and attention from the Habitation Specialists—specifically those that are populated with TES of a genre that have a lower quotient of sentience than those that project Aspects into the animal vehicles.

It also has to be noted that in some instances the TES who projects an Aspect or Aspects into the animal vehicle may be working directly with or under the direction of the Habitation Specialists. This is because ultimately the flora and fauna are a function of environmental eco-structure while also providing incarnate-based evolutionary progression, and as such, the Habitation Specialists are responsible for their maintenance.

A: Very well put—to quote The Source—very well put!

ME: Thank you. It's an honor to be able to work with you again. I expect it is difficult to work on this level again after being back in the energetic for so long?

A: Let's just say that low frequencies are a discomfort, but only a minor one if you protect yourself. And, yes, it's nice to be able to work with you again in this way.

ME: How many different types of Habitation Specialists are there?

A: Well, that's an interesting question because there are as many as are required to support the environment that they are working in.

ME: OK, wrong question. Can you describe some of them that we have here on Earth?

A: Yes, of course. I think the best thing to do is to describe the main genres of Habitation Specialist that work with the Earth because, as you alluded to a moment ago, there can be a Specialist for a type of bacteria, and as you are aware, there are many types of bacteria.

I will give you a general list first and then we can focus on them in more detail as we carry on. Before I carry on, though, I want to make a point of reference. What are described as Angels are not nature spirits—Habitation Specialists. Angels are generally recognized as being an incarnate's Guide—its guardian angel is a common term used on Gross Physical Earth but I would suggest that the use of the words "incarnate Guide" or simply "Guide" is more appropriate in today's level of education.

There are however Habitation Specialists that manifest a "form" to check on the physical representation of the work that they have done. It is not uncommon for them to be described in terms of being an Angel, as Guides are, specifically as the energies that they use to surround and protect themselves are represented in the iridescent gold, silver, white, and red spectrum of the frequencies that the human eye can detect. The human religious education process provides the memory-based imagery that is used to translate what is seen or perceived as being energetic into something that is recognizable as divine or supposedly understood as being divine, rather than what it actually is. In fact, any entity or being that projects a protective energy around themselves so that they can work with the Gross Physical but not be affected by its low frequencies can be described as angelic in representation.

Based upon this, if something is seen as, or described as, angelic, it is used to describe anything that is considered as being pure or divine and a recognizable image, usually one that is associated with an existing image that is associated with that description used, irrespective of its correctness.

ME: Are you suggesting that the term "angelic" or "angel" is no longer appropriate?

A: It served a purpose, that purpose being a label to use to describe a phenomenon that was observed by lowly educated people in an Event Stream where simple descriptions were necessary and a means of fear-based guidance was prevalent, more prevalent than in the current Event Stream.

Let's move on to my real work with you. I just wanted to put the story straight because, in the summary toward the start of this book, you referred to Angels as being a Habitation Specialist Curator.

ME: Got it.

A: Right, moving on then.

There is a Habitation Specialist for each of the families of flora and each of the families of fauna. They tend to work in the frequency directly above that where their flora or fauna of responsibility reside but they can also work in all of the frequencies associated with the physical universe, starting at the fourth frequency. Those that work on the Gross Physical frequencies therefore operate in the fourth frequency and outside of the normal visual range of the human eye.

Before I move on, I also want to say that the use of the labels or names to describe these entities as fairies, pixies, gnomes, elves, leprechauns, gremlins, demons, etc., cannot be used as a descriptor of their genre of specialism or the work that they do. These are simply labels given to the images of these entities in the event that a Habitation Specialist is observed by an incarnate human and how the Habitation Specialist decides to present their image to the observing incarnate human, or how the observing human decides to translate what they see in terms of previous education on the subject.

ME: I can understand the function of translation of the image of the Habitation Specialists by the incarnate in terms of the received imagery and adapted or acceptable imagery, but why do they feel the need to change their image from what they really are to one that is more acceptable to the incarnate human?

A: It is simply about two things. First, incarnate humankind, in general, is not ready to accept the real form factors used by these Curators because they would be considered abhorrent. And secondly, there are times when a Habitation Specialist does not want the attention of an incarnate human.

ME: Why would we consider them as being abhorrent?

A: Their form is multipoluous, having no specific form other than that which is required to work with the energies they need to work with to manage and maintain the flora and fauna of the environment that they are working within. A multipoluous form is nondescript while also being, at times, descript. Those times when they are descript may show their form to be acceptable to the incarnate human mentality, but more often than not it isn't, which causes a level of mental shock and psychiatric disturbance to the uneducated or unexpansive observer.

ME: They change their appearance to one which is acceptable to the observing incarnate human then?

A: Yes. In essence, they are gentle entities and are affected by the fear expressed by incarnate humans when they observe their real form. As a result, they scan the mind of the incarnate, see if they are presenting a translated image to themselves and if not, change their form to one that is within the range of acceptability to the observer.

ME: I would guess that this is where we get the more popular imagery of pixies and elves and fairies from?

A: In most versions, yes—goblins and demons imagery being the far end of the tolerable spectrum. Most of the time they work and like to work unobserved and prefer it to stay that way.

ME: Why are they affected by the fear of an incarnate observer?

A: Fear is a low-frequency emotion. It is a low-frequency thought, behavior, and action and as such creates an area of low frequency around the incarnate human that is in fear. Low frequencies, when expressed in this context, have the ability to block the work of the Habitation Specialist.

ME: Block? How does that work? I would have expected the work of a Curator to be unaffected by any energies or frequencies that an incarnate human can project.

A: Block is possibly the wrong word to use. Filter or slowdown is a better way of putting it.

Have you noticed how flowers thrive in the presence of some people but struggle in the presence of others?

ME: Yes, I have. We call those that flowers thrive with as having green fingers.

A: Yes, you do. These people are generally in tune with the higher frequencies associated with the Habitation Specialists and the flora that they work with. These people, should they observe a Habitation Specialist doing its work, would either see it in an acceptable translated image of some sort or would tend to ignore the image that they are seeing in preference to focusing on the environment that they are comfortable with, their garden or flowers, etc.

ME: Are you saying that people turn a blind eye to that which they are seeing, even though it is real and part of the greater energetic reality?

A: Tuning out, so to speak, is what most incarnate humans do. Tuning out is performed on a daily basis and is not specific to observing a Habitation Specialist doing its work.

ME: OK, so incarnate humans either receive a tailored image of what the Habitation Specialists are, create a translated image, or tune out of what they are seeing.

A: Yes, that's right. Don't forget that what incarnate humans see is a function of frequential reception by the physical eyes and energetic perception. Based upon this, the perceived imagery is received first and the frequential second, the functionality being the incarnate entity's sentience automatically separating out that which is perceived and can be seen from that which is perceived and cannot be seen, creating a condition where what is seen/perceived is either seen and perceived or perceived and can be seen but should not be seen and is therefore tuned out.

ME: Who sees them mostly?

A: Most adult incarnate humans operate in the "perceived and can be seen but is tuned out" condition. However, it is the young incarnates, children that see them the most.

ME: And they see/perceive them as they are supposed to be seen?

A: Not normally. They tend to have an image projected to them by the Habitation Specialist that is being observed once that Habitation Specialist has scanned the mind of the observing child.

ME: Hence the plethora of stories where children have seen the Habitation Specialists as fairies, etc.

A: Correct. They are cute images, though, aren't they?

ME: I suppose they are the most benign images one can make. You mentioned that they prefer to not be seen/observed. How do they manage to stay covert?

A: Bearing in mind that most of the time they are not being observed or perceived, they go about their work unhindered and without the need to do anything about their appearance. In general, though, when they note that there is an incarnate human close to them, they create an image of the local topography that surrounds them so that they are shielded visually (frequentially) and energetically from most observers.

ME: When I was writing *The History of God* I used to meditate in the back garden before going to work and I noticed that there was a nature spirit/Elemental—a "Habitation Specialist" working with the local energies. I noticed that it was working with a small vortex of energy that was on the land. It saw me and was delighted to be noticed in its real form and that I was not frightened of it, indeed I was delighted to be able to see it.

A: Yes, I remember that on another occasion you were even more delighted when a group of other Habitation Specialists realized that you were observing them and that you were interested in what they were doing. I recall you were in complete joy at what you were seeing/perceiving.

ME: Yes, I was. I sent them lots of high-frequency energy and love and they revelled in it. They all gathered around me and held (made contact with) my hands. They surrounded me and gave me so much loving energy back that I can feel that energy now and the emotion supporting it. It was wonderful.

A: Yes, it is, isn't it? Imagine what the Earth would be like if everybody responded in a similar way to these entities. The Earth would be a significantly higher frequency and the population of flora would be much, much higher as a result.

An Image of a Habitation Specialist

ME: Can you provide the readers with a general image of a Habitation Specialist?

A: I think that you are best to provide that. You can use the memory of the image you have of the one in the back garden.

ME: Was that Habitation Specialist indicative of their general unfiltered appearance?

A: It's close enough. I would like to point out that the two separate experiences you had were of two different genres of Habitation Specialist.

ME: I got the feeling that they were different entities at the time I experienced the second interaction with the Habitation Specialists but I didn't quite understand why. I would like to defer the honor of describing them, and just elaborate what I saw and let you add additional detail if you feel it necessary, please.

A: OK, I am happy with that.

ME: What I saw was a ball of black and gray misty energy that glided along the ground, the grass. It appeared to have flecks of electricity, sparks, floating around it. It just moved over the ground until it found the area of the garden that it needed to work on. It looked like it was working on the Elderberry tree we had. It must have had some disease or other because part of the Habitation Specialist seemed to solidify, to separate out from the main body of energy of this entity, and move toward the area of interest on this tree. It looked like it was going to create an arm and a hand at first but it stayed in a sort of undulating spiky form which changed to be a totally smooth appendage which then surrounded the area of interest. As this appendage surrounded the area of a particular branch, it turned blacker, then yellow and then red before going to a neutral gray color. I got the impression that it was working on the etheric energies of the tree that were relative to that branch. When the work was finished the appendage moved away from the tree returning to its undulating spiky form, and then reintegrated back into the main body of energy.

Thinking back to that Event Space, I remembered what was happening to the form and appearance of the Habitation Specialist when it was doing its work. I would have thought that its form and appearance would have stayed motionless but it didn't. As the work was being performed, its external form changed to be a mixture of random fractals of spikes and subtle and strong geometric forms. Its appearance followed similar colors to that seen in the etheric energies being worked on with the tree. Its form was therefore different to that part of it which surrounded the branch of the Elderberry tree.

I wonder what was happening there.

A: The Habitation Specialist was harmonizing with the area of disease and transferring the energies associated with the disease from the tree to itself and then converting them back to its normal energy set and balance. It created an energy that was sympathetic to those of the tree and the disease, and swapped them so that the tree's energy stayed in balance and the energy of the disease was moved away. The Entity then absorbed the diseased energy by sympathizing with it and then changing it back to those energies that were its normal energy set.

ME: So in summary, it took the illness away from the tree by taking it upon itself, backfilling its energies to make sure the tree's energies were whole again, and then converted the energy of the disease back into its own energy.

A: That's about the size of it.

ME: What do they do for the trees/plants and animals? How many different types are there?

A: I think that the best way to answer that question is to list them out and explain what they do and are responsible for in summary. What I will say, though, is that the work they do for animals is limited, for want of a better word, to those that are capable of accepting only limited sentience, or are in existence for environmental functionality only and as a result, they will be limited to insects and small animals.

The Different Habitation Specialists

A: This list is not exhaustive and clearly there are types of flora that fill in the gaps between these examples, but it will give the reader enough to work with in terms of the variations of Habitation Specialists and their roles.

The **Bacterial Worker's** role is divided into two main roles. The first is specialized in working with all aspects and variations of bacteria from a physical perspective in terms of their ability to grow in different environments. These environments range from being in the atmosphere to being attached in an internal and/or external way to a "host," such as minerals, plants, and incarnate vehicles of all sizes and capabilities of housing sentience. The second is specialized in the effect each bacteria has with its interaction with the environment and its "hosts" in terms of being detrimental or beneficial. Every bacterium has a detrimental and beneficial role, and the Bacterial Worker uses this knowledge to assist in the overall balance of the eco-structure of a planet and its flora, fauna, and incarnate vehicles—which include the sentient quotient of the flora and fauna.

The **Algae Worker** specifically focuses on maintaining the balance of proliferation of algae versus dependency. They ensure that there is just enough algae from a planet-wide perspective to sustain those forms that use it as food—specifically marine-based fauna. Additionally, they ensure that the algae maintains its efficiency in creating the gas it is designed to create to assist in the maintenance of the atmosphere. On the Earth, your most important gas is oxygen. It must be noted that without an optimal balance of the population of algae, the atmosphere cannot support the current diversity of flora, fauna, and incarnate vehicles.

The **Tuber Worker** is aligned to those plants whose roots are the fruit that can be ingested and digested as a form of Gross Physical energy. Tubers such a potatoes, beetroot, parsnip, yams, and carrots, etc., provide essential Earth energies, and it is the role of these entities to ensure that tubers can hold an optimal level of base Earth energy associated with their genre.

The **Root Workers** focus on the development of the root system of all flora relative to the environment that they are expected to exist within. In essence, they work on the adaptation of the root system, and its ability to absorb and distribute minerals and nutrients to the main plant system relative to its environment. For example, whether a plant can exist in the four main environmental types, just one, or a combination of types such as on a rock face, in soil, in sand, or in water and the variations of rock, soil, sand, and water.

The **Herb Worker** has a very special role because herbs are specifically available for the correction of energetic and Gross Physical dysfunction/illness. The Herb Worker therefore has the responsibility of developing the herb genome to cope with existing and new physical issues that the incarnate vehicles attract through association with the lower frequencies. Although some herbs can be considered detrimental to the human vehicle, this is due to a lack of understanding to their higher functions and so-called dosage. Like oxygen—enough is good for you, too much or not enough is detrimental. The fact that herbs are eaten on a regular basis suggests that they are used as a constant state of unconscious medication by those that eat them.

The **Shrub Worker** works only on those plants that are classified as shrubs or bushes. Of course there are many shrubs, and their genres are based upon their adaptation to different environments. The role of the shrub is to create and sustain the integrity of the soil-based environment that they are in and protect it from some of the more detrimental energies that are received by the Earth from the Sun. In essence, they ensure that a land-based environment does not become a desert.

The **Creeper Worker** is specialized in maintaining and perpetuating the protective habitat-creating ability of all genres of creeper. Creepers are fast-growing, invasive, and pervasive and are particularly good at integrating with existing flora. They provide a wealth of protection for smaller flora and fauna ensuring that larger fauna is not able to destroy areas of the environment that are difficult to maintain or that need a certain level of accurate balance to perpetuate its existence.

The **Tree Worker** is responsible for all genres of trees that are found within the physical universe. They are effective transplanters of trees and adapt trees from one planetary location and frequency to exist in another planetary location of the same frequency. In some cases of demand, they can also adapt a tree to exist in a different frequency as well. Because trees are capable of interplanetary communication, the Tree Worker also works on the communication mediums used by a transplanted tree ensuring that communication is maintained between the trees at its previous location and those of its same genre in its new location.

The **Liverwort Worker** specializes in all flora that is required to exist in locations of high humidity, moist air, and water. They specifically work on the creation of new genres of liverwort that are exposed to areas where rooting is not possible. Liverworts are especially good at stabilizing loose ground and the gas-partial pressures of an environment by storing the basic components of the atmosphere.

The **Moss Worker** looks after the function of a moss as a sort of natural battery for large areas of flora such as forests. Mosses absorb water and ensure that water and essential nutrients are not lost to evaporation, ensuring the flora it is part of is maintained at a consistent level in all atmospheric conditions. It is the role of the Moss Worker to adjust and modify the absorption capabilities of the mosses and their ability to exist in different environments. They ensure that this function is kept in an optimal condition to enable them to support all the types of flora, and some small fauna, in the area that they are required in. Their function is therefore area- and flora-dependent.

The **Fern Worker** is responsible for the use of these plants to repair and medicate damaged or once-barren ground. They are the main tool in the Habitation Specialists' toolbox for the regeneration of ground after natural and incarnate human-made disasters. They are also introduced when an area of ground has become naturally depleted of nutrients by being subjected to overpopulation of a certain type of flora.

The **Succulent Worker** specializes with those plants that are designed to exist as arid or barren areas of land with little or no land-based irrigation possibilities. The Succulent Workers use these plants as a prelude to establishing a fertile land out of an arid environment. They are used to establish and reestablish flora in an area that has been subjected to dramatic atmospheric changes from cold or tepid to hot and/or dramatic land-based changes derived from volcanic and tectonic events.

The **Insect Worker** works with all of the Habitation Specialists and the TES associated with the insect genre it interacts with. In effect, this Worker is a go-between ensuring that the work of the insects as a collective is in accordance with the maintenance of the flora that they exist within. They communicate with the TES in control of the insect hive to relay what they want it to perform based upon the synergetic requirements of the Habitation Specialists working within the area of the hive. Insects are rarely out of synergy with their natural environment, and that includes locusts whose role at times is to sterilize an area of flora.

The **Small Animal Worker**—This covers land, sea, and air. The Small Animal Worker looks after those animals that are too small for an Aspect to incarnate into but are animated by a single TES in a way that is similar to but not the same as an insect hive mind. Notice how a flock of birds or a school of fish work and move together in unison and harmony? Notice how land-based animals work in communities? This is the function of the TES operating as a collective mind while allowing a minor level of individuality.

Insects don't have this minor level of individuality, although it may appear that they do. The Small Animal Worker, in conjunction with the animating TES, ensures that there is synergy between the animals and its environment making sure that the population is maintained at an optimal level for the environment used. What this means is that the population is kept to a level where the environment is naturally self-sustaining and is not placed under strain through overpopulation and overactivity in one specific area. The Earth could use this function to control the total population of the incarnate human vehicle were it not a necessary requirement to have the existing population, and more, to provide enough incarnate vehicles for those that wish to accelerate their evolutionary progression by incarnating on Earth at these frequencies.

One of the ways in which the Habitation Specialists affect essential maintenance or regeneration of a plant/tree is by temporarily replacing its energetic template with its own by mimicking the template of the plant until the original plant energy template assumes the correct structure of the plant/tree by copying that of the mimicked template.

The Habitation Specialists are my favorite genre of Curator. They have wonderful loving energy and are only concerned with the well-being of the flora or fauna they are responsible for.

ME: So, if they are so loving, why do they avoid incarnates?

A: They don't avoid all incarnates—they love those that incarnate into the animal vehicles. Have you noticed how cats and dogs are drawn to things that you cannot see?

ME: Yes, I have, on a regular basis.

A: Well, that's because they are communicating with the Habitation Specialist that they have seen. Habitation Specialists don't shy away from animals because they are generally pure of heart.

ME: You mean they don't have any hidden agendas or addictions to low-frequency thoughts, behaviors, and actions?

A: No. Even those animals that are trained by incarnate humans to be vicious or angry become passive when in the presence of a Habitation Specialist. You see the TES associated with plants and animals are a lower level of sentience than that of incarnate humankind and therefore cannot work with individualized free will. They work together in a way that an incarnate with individualized free will cannot understand. However, it is understood by the Habitation Specialists and so there is a natural affinity. The level of sentience incarnate humankind has creates both wonderful and devastating things and low-frequency existence provides a need to understand things in a low-frequency way. This means that that which is not Gross Physical cannot be explained and is therefore something to be feared.

ME: How do the Habitation Specialists become associated with the flora or fauna they are responsible for?

A: They choose to work with that which they are drawn to work with, that which they resonate with.

ME: You mean they have a natural affinity for a certain frequency or the frequency of certain flora or fauna?

A: Yes, quite literally that which is of the same frequency as they are interested in or feel that they are in harmony with. It's a bit like when incarnate humans have an affinity of preference for either cats or dogs or certain plants or trees.

ME: And they are allowed to choose the flora or fauna that they want to work with?

A: Yes, of course. It makes for a better relationship with the flora/fauna and Habitation Specialist and the response to the work of the Habitation Specialist.

ME: Is there any time when a type of flora or fauna does not have a Habitation Specialist to maintain them?

A: No, never. There is always a Habitation Specialist to maintain them. There are never any gaps in coverage. I do have to say, though, that there are some times when a Habitation Specialist covers two types of flora or fauna but it does have to be of the same family or same genre.

ME: Why is that? I almost expected that a Habitation Specialist could turn their energies to look after any flora or fauna.

A: The answer is in their name—"specialist." Don't forget that they work on incredible levels of detail when they interact with the flora or fauna that they are responsible for.

ME: Just how many Habitation Specialists are working with the Earth at this moment?

A: Open your eyes and see.

Just for your information, dear reader, I am sitting on the roof of our country house in Crete and am looking at a wonderful vista of hills, mountains, and olive trees. It's Easter here (April 2018) and there have been many celebrations and lighting of fireworks. This doesn't seem to stop the local insects and animals from going about their daily business, though. The birdsong is wonderful. I cast my energetic vision (my third eye) around me and see the energies of pine martins, mice, cats, badgers, rats, and all the insects that live in and on the land around me. They are all industrious and in harmony with their environment. I send them my love and they respond by sending me love back. I change my focus and look around again. I am amazed to see that the whole hillside leading up to the mountains in front of me is full of Habitation Specialists. It's teeming with them. From what I can see, there is almost one Habitation Specialist for one tree. Sometimes there are two or more Habitation Specialists tending to the needs of a tree. How could that be? I expected there to be significantly less than what I am seeing. I decided to ask Anne what was happening here.

A: No need to ask. I can tell you straight away.

ME: No, no need. I can see it now.

A: Go on. I want to see if you have fully understood what you are perceiving.

ME: OK, I expected to see just a few Habitation Specialists but what I am seeing is myriad. But this is not myriad Habitation Specialists. This is myriad versions of the same Habitation Specialist. It very much feels like a Habitation Specialist can divide itself into many versions of itself to allow it to work on as many items of flora or fauna that it is responsible for. But why did I just see one in our garden all those years ago?

A: What distracted you is what you saw in your garden. You saw just one of the possible divisions of a local Habitation Specialist and so considered them as just one entity for just one job or role. They never work in this way in entirety; only sometimes do they work in the undivided way. Most of the ways they work are in the divisible method. This is the only way in which they can perform their role and be successful, such is the volume of individual flora and fauna that they work with.

ME: Based upon this, when we see a Habitation Specialist we should not think of them as one, but moreover as a division of one.

A: That is a good way to think about it, yes.

I suddenly had a feeling, it was one that was creeping up on me that Anne was about to go soon and that I would be left to work on the rest of the book with The Source. I was, however, delighted to receive another feeling that my expectation was more aligned to another day and not just yet.

A: I have decided to stay a while with you. The final Caretaker genre, as a subgenre of the Curators, that you were supposed to discuss was the Populationists, but I have been given authority to bring the discussion on those Caretakers forward so that it dovetails in with the discussion on the Habitation Specialists that we have just enjoyed.

ME: Why have you been given authority to stay and discuss the Populationists when they are not the genre of Caretaker that you have decided to work with me with?

SE1: It made more sense for Anne to work with you and describe the work of these Caretakers as well simply because the work that they do is aligned to the work of the Caretakers that Anne has an affinity for. I therefore decided that I would finish the book with you by describing the work of the Atmospherisists.

ME: Well, I am always open to a surprise and this is a nice one for me. Thank you for being so considerate.

SE1: Good. Now move on to the Populationists.

ME: Will do!

The Populationists

SE1: I will let Anne deliver the summary.

A: What a treat to work in this extended way again, thank you. Here we go!

The Populationists distribute the flora and fauna that are available to whichever location they are needed within the physical universe. They have various levels of responsibility but in essence each is specialized according to the environment they are working with. The environment can be universal, galactic, system, planetary—includes moons or nebulae-based habitat. They work in close harmony with the Atmospherisists, who provide the details behind the atmosphere they are creating or are able to create with the materials they have. The Populationists then create or assign the basic vehicles that are used for those entities that are incarnate solely for the purposes of being a "living" functional aspect of the atmosphere.

ME: OK, I have a question straight away.

A: Go ahead.

ME: I understand that the flora and fauna of a planet have a role in terms of supporting the continuation of the habitability of the environment that they are in from the perspective of supporting the incarnate vehicles that are used by high-sentience TES (that genre that incarnate mankind are part of), but I don't quite understand that they can provide a living functional aspect of the atmosphere.

A: The Populationists have a vast catalogue, so to speak, of flora and fauna that contribute to the maintenance and functionality of an atmosphere-based environment. If they can't supply the right sort of flora and fauna from the catalogue of existing flora and fauna, they create what they need either by modifying existing flora or fauna that are close to the existence and contributory requirements of the atmosphere that they are destined for, or they create a new bespoke flora and/or fauna.

ME: What creates the need for fauna to support and maintain an atmosphere?

A: Simply put, the metabolic process.

ME: Go on.

A: If the atmosphere is not totally regenerating, and not many are that are in the Gross Physical aspect of the physical universe, then there needs to be some functionality within the flora and fauna that contributes toward the regeneration of that atmosphere that they are to work with.

In terms of the flora, it is relatively sensible to assume that there is a symbiotic relationship between the planet, its atmosphere, and the flora that exists within it. In general, the flora of a planet exists by using the elements within and without the planet for sustenance and growth. One of the byproducts of this relationship is that the flora removes from the atmosphere any elements (gasses and the like) that are not useful to the continued function of the atmosphere and wider environment. This includes the metabolic function of the fauna and incarnate vehicles for those high-sentience entities that incarnate into the planetary environment for experiential and evolutionary purposes, especially those that require the use of certain gasses or elements to support their continued metabolic functionality by respiration.

ME: So the flora can, as we know here on Earth, provide a regenerative and cleaning function. The Populationists therefore populate a planet with those aspects of flora that not only perpetuate the original atmosphere but also regenerate it and even augment it to allow for the expansion of high-sentience incarnate vehicle population.

A: Yes. But more often than not, they choose the flora that can change the atmosphere from one that does not support the incarnate vehicle type that is required or desired to be used on a certain planet to one that will support the desired or required vehicle type. They also introduce those flora that take any metabolic functions that result in pollution of the desired atmosphere, that being, changing it in some way from what it was, or desired to be, to one where there is a percentage of undesired gasses or elements within that atmosphere.

The Importance of Plant Life

ME: The Populationists include flora that acts as a filter as well?

A: Yes, of course. In fact, there are many such plants used to maintain the elemental balance of Earth's atmosphere, chickweed is one of them, pine trees are another. Other flora is specialized in removing carbon dioxide that is produced as part of the metabolic function of most of the fauna and incarnate vehicles that are used in the Earth's atmospheric environment.

ME: The fauna has a function in the maintenance of the atmosphere as well, though.

A: Yes, they do. With respect to certain floras, which exist by changing a gas from one element to another, they need to be maintained in an atmosphere where there is an equal but opposite function by another necessary aspect of flora or fauna. Using the Earth as an example again, this would be the byproduct of the respiration of most of the fauna, including the incarnate vehicles that incarnate humankind use to experience, learn, and evolve on the Earth. With the more advanced incarnate vehicles used, including those classified as fauna, a byproduct of the respiration process is the use of oxygen and the generation of a waste product. This waste product is carbon dioxide. On other atmosphere-based planets, it's other gasses or elements. In the instance of the Earth, though, most of the flora have been designed with the function of absorbing carbon dioxide and producing oxygen as a waste product of their own metabolic process. Another gas that is created as a byproduct is methane. Methane is quite destructive.

ME: The Earth has a rather unique balance then, one where there must be enough flora to cope with the need to maintain its natural atmosphere through natural attrition of the flora itself, and by refreshing that which has been used by the fauna and turned into another element as part of their metabolic process.

A: That's right, and incarnate humankind is not very good at understanding this. Incarnate humankind creates a detrimental effect to this precarious balance in two ways. First, it has allowed itself to procreate without thought for how the environment it exists within can support it. Second, as a result of this expansion, it has justified the need to reduce the flora, and some fauna, in order to make habitats for the increased number of incarnate vehicles.

ME: Basically then, there are more incarnate human vehicles than the Earth can support with the current level of flora.

A: That's about the size of it. A responsible incarnate civilization would spot the need to support the balance of this symbiotic relationship and act accordingly and with maturity of thought and action. Incarnate humankind is intoxicated with its own low-frequency importance and therefore disguises the issues in several political ways, securing political advantage at the detriment of the Earth and its flora/fauna-based atmospheric balance.

Fauna That Produce Atmospheric Balance

A: It's not always the flora that provides the balance by creating a sustainable atmosphere that incarnate vehicles can be used within.

ME: Go on.

A: There are many planets in the Gross Physical frequencies of the physical universe that need fauna to maintain the atmospheric balance of a planet. On these planets, the fauna does the work of filtering or changing the waste products of an incarnate vehicle that uses inspiration of one or more gas elements of the planetary atmosphere that it is aligned to. In this instance, the flora may be either limited in population or in functionality that support the continued balance of the atmosphere, and so the Populationists introduce a genre of fauna, modify a genre of fauna, or create a new genre that supports the regeneration requirements of the atmosphere that the existing fauna cannot create or needs help with.

ME: Are there any such animals on the Earth that contribute toward the balance of the atmosphere?

A: Not in the Gross Physical frequencies, no. There are three special genres of fauna in the fourth and fifth frequencies that inspire higher frequency gasses that are rare from the perspective of the Gross Physical and expire high-frequency oxygen, but you will only see these when you are collectively working in the fourth frequency and above as a minimum frequency in the physical universe. I would, however, like to advise you that an animal called *Loriciferans* was discovered in 2010 and that it did not need oxygen to support its continued existence, so there are animals that operate outside of the normal balance of the Earth's atmosphere.

ME: At the start of this dialogue, and included in the summary at the start of this book, you mentioned that there are flora and fauna found in planetary systems, galaxies, nebulae, and gas giants. What did you mean by this?

A: Incarnate humankind will not accept this yet but there are areas within nebulae that are inhabited by both flora and fauna.

ME: I would have thought that both flora and fauna and incarnate vehicles need an area of locally low frequency, a planetary body, to incarnate into. Surely this is the only way to create and maintain an atmosphere?

A: Nebulae are highly populated areas of the physical universe, and that includes the Gross Physical frequencies as well. It's not a necessary requirement for incarnate existence to be located on a planet, and it's certainly not a necessary requirement for the existence of flora or fauna.

ME: But nebulae aren't frequentially solid—are they?

A: No, they are not. I will explain. A fish does not live on the surface of the Earth, it exists in a higher frequency aspect of the Earth, the water that is part of the surface but that is not frequentially attached to it.

ME: Oh! Are you suggesting that nebulae are a bit like seas in space?

A: That's a nice way of putting it and it's a good thought process, but no. Nebulae are simply energetic elements that are not attracted to each other in a way that creates a lower frequency object from the coupling together of a group of higher frequency objects like a planet is. The flora and fauna that exist within them exist in a way that is not centrally located, in a way a bit like the fish in your sea-in-space idea. The flora exists within certain desirable groups of energies relative to those that maintain their existence. In some areas, they also group together. The fauna and incarnate vehicles move around the energies and elements of the nebulae by using the forces of attraction and division. They take sustenance from the energies and elements and some of the fauna. Their metabolic process does not require the respiration of a gas but the attraction of certain elements of a desired frequency level to metabolize flora that has been absorbed energetically and turn it into energies that sustain their form. The incarnate vehicles operate in the same or a similar way. Think of it as being in an energetic and elemental soup that is not soup.

ME: What about planetary systems?

A: The Populationists analyze all of the planet's moons and the sun/s and establish what flora and fauna form factors fit in with the environments available on these bodies, whether modifications of the form factors is necessary or if new form factors are required. They also analyze the possibility of using the same genre of form factor across all possible environments in the planetary system.

ME: Why would they try to keep the same form factor on all planets within a planetary system?

A: They just like to keep things simple. Sometimes all planets in a system have the same form factors, sometimes it's just one or even two that have the same form factor. Sometimes it's only the moons that can be populated.

ME: How many incarnate vehicles of the humanoid type are in the Earth's planetary system?

A: Only those that are on Earth. There are other incarnate vehicle form factors on other planets but they are positioned in a higher frequency.

ME: How many planets or moons are populated then?

A: Just five, which includes the Sun.

ME: And how many incarnate form factors are on these five bodies?

A: Twenty-seven all together. Two are on Earth. The others are not all in the same frequency so a great number of these incarnate vehicles exist independently of each other.

ME: But I thought that the Earth was in a quarantined part of the Galaxy?

A: It is from the perspective of the third frequency. From the perspective of the remaining frequencies of the physical universe, it's not.

ME: Do gas giants have flora and fauna?

A: Yes. The Populationists use a similar, but not same, genre of flora and fauna to that used in the population of nebulae. Gas-based planets and nebulae are similar energetically and so it is possible to use similar forms in both environments. As I stated before, the Populationists like to keep things simple.

ME: Does this not stop or reduce the diversity of experience for those entities and beings in the evolutionary cycle?

A: No, because there are many other galaxies where there is a plethora of form factors used.

ME: Are you suggesting that each galaxy in the physical universe is populated in a different way?

A: It's no suggestion, they are. The Populationists work with all of the sets of galaxies that manifest in the frequencies associated with the physical universe. Some of these galaxies are pan-frequential; this means that they manifest in all frequencies of the physical universe from the third frequency upward. Others are mono-frequential, which means that they only manifest in one frequency.

In some galaxies, the Populationists ensure that they are populated with only one incarnate form factor, whereas others are populated with all of the genres of incarnate form factors. Such is the availability of galaxies versus incarnate form factor that there are enough galaxies available to have a galaxy per incarnate form factor—that being of the genre that accepts the TES with the same sentience quotient as that of incarnate humankind.

ME: I expect then that there are galaxies that are populated in many different ways, with all different possible combinations of incarnate vehicle form factor being used as well as just one?

A: Of course, all permutations are used. But remember, even though they work closely with the Atmospherisists, they can and do work independently from them.

ME: And I expect that this is when an incarnate vehicle has to work in an atmosphere that is challenging in some way?

A: Yes. In general, the Populationists know which incarnate vehicle form factor to use in a certain environment, but as I stated before, there are those that need respiration to assist the metabolic functions of some forms and those that metabolize without respiration but nevertheless still need to work within an atmosphere of some sort.

It's time for me to go and for The Source to finish off this dialogue about the Curators with the Atmospherisists. Don't forget that I will be helping you out every now and then with your next book on energetic/vibrational healing and psycho-spiritual issues.

ME: Thank you. It has been an honor and a delight working with you again.

And with that, I felt a little sadness as I felt the energy of the OM that was incarnate as Anne fade away to the frequency where it resides.

SE1: Now that you feel full, let's get on with the remaining Curator, the Caretaker that is an Atmospherisist.

ME: OK, we are on the home straight!

The Atmospherisists

SE1: **The Atmospherisists** work with the stability of the wider environment, planetary or otherwise, and how it is used by the incarnate vehicle and supporting infrastructure it is designed for. They modify and manipulate the functions of the atmosphere and its periods of change relevant to the location of the planet or environment. It should be noted that a planet is not the only location for incarnate vehicles to work within, and neither is there a need for respiration to ensure bodily function within the location and frequency it resides within.

ME: So these Curators create atmospheric environments then.

SE1: Yes, but as you know, not everywhere.

ME: I will start with an easy question, I hope. When is an atmosphere not created?

SE1: When there is either no need or requirement for an incarnate vehicle that is dependent upon respiration to exist, where there is no need for an atmosphere to be used for the absorption of any elements to sustain the incarnate vehicle or if the location is to be populated by high-frequency incarnate vehicles such as in the tenth, eleventh, and twelfth frequencies, or by purely energetic entities or beings.

ME: Where are atmospheres created?

SE1: In reality, the Atmospherisists can create an atmosphere in any location where there is an area or volume of attractivity that can support an acceptable level of containment of that atmosphere. A low-frequency planet [*solid—GSN*] is a good example of one such area, a gas giant or gas-based planet is another.

ME: Would volumes of space such as nebulae have an atmosphere?

SE1: If it is required, yes, of course. Have you forgotten that flora and fauna populate nebulae as well?

ME: Well, I am just being complete in my questioning.

SE1: Good recovery. Again, yes, atmospheres are available in many nebulae. In fact, there is at least 34 percent of all nebulae in the third frequency [*the Gross Physical—GSN*] that have an atmosphere of some level. One thing that you need to note is that an atmosphere is simply a collection of gas elements and supporting frequencies that can support one or more of the available incarnate vehicles that need an atmosphere to perpetuate their metabolism. The metabolic process of an incarnate vehicle can be achieved with and without respiration. Such is the flexibility of the metabolism of those incarnate vehicles that are available that many can exist within the atmospheric conditions that are sustained within the volume of a nebula. It is not necessary to have a planetary body to contain the gas elements that support low-frequency incarnate vehicles. For example, the Atmospherisists have created over forty thousand nebulae that are carbon dioxide- and oxygen-based.

ME: So the incarnate human vehicle that we have on Earth could exist within one of these nebulae without being inside the contained environment of a spaceship then?

SE1: Well, it may be able to breathe but it may need protection from some of the radioactive elements that also exist in some of these nebulae.

ME: OK, but it would be possible to exist in some of them?

SE1: Yes, not every part of a nebula is totally gaseous. There are some areas of locally low density that could be used as a natural habitat within the nebula. Incarnate humankind is sort of "ground-centric." You need to feel something solid under your feet. However, the variant of incarnate human vehicle that is found in areas of nebulae that do not support an area of local low frequency is not of the two-legged variety, it has four arms instead.

ME: No legs?

SE1: No legs, just four arms. You see in areas of nebulae where there are no gravity-based locations, there is no need for legs and so the human vehicle has been designed with arms only. It's a most efficient form factor. Think about it a moment. Do you see astronauts making much use of their legs in a zero-gravity environment? No. They are not necessary. In fact, there are variants of the human form that have six arms—and of course no legs.

ME: Will we ever see them? [*I was thinking of some Hindu images of Shiva.—GSN*]

SE1: Maybe in a few thousand years, when the Earth version of incarnate humankind has matured and is allowed to venture beyond the local space that they are held within.

ME: Getting back to the work of the Atmospherisists, how do they create an atmosphere?

SE1: They work with the Attractionists to ensure that the gas elements that they need to use are both able to be attracted to each other and repelled by each other in certain conditions such as heat, radiation, gravity, and frequency changes. Clearly, the attraction and repulsion functions are more important in a nebula than on a planet because gravity is more capable of containing gas elements in a planetary environment, whereas, in a nebula-based environment, the gasses have to use attractivity rather than have the assistance of gravity to stay in a cohesive state.

ME: It's simply a case of deciding what gas elements are required for the location to support the incarnate vehicle/flora and fauna that is destined to populate that location then?

SE1: Thinking in limited terms, yes. But don't forget that planets, suns, and moons can and are moved around to support a required or desired environmental system. The Curators can and do assemble and disassemble planetary and nebula-based systems in the Gross Physical. The sizes, density, elemental, frequential, gravitational, and attractional conditions of areas of locally low frequency—planets, moons, and suns—are at times selected to make bespoke solar or other habitation systems.

ME: And suns are centers of habitation as well?

SE1: If you remember our dialogue in *The History of God*, then you will know that the answer is a very firm "yes."

ME: So what defines if an area or volume of space is an atmosphere?

SE1: In terms of a planet, it is an area or volume of space in and around an area of locally low frequency which other elements are attracted to, but not absorbed by, that area of locally low frequency. In terms of a nebula, it is a volume of space where there is a density or collection of gas elements that are both attracted to and repulsed from each other to the point where their spatial location remains in a generally static condition.

In general, though, an atmosphere can be described as an area or volume of space where there is a collection of gaseous elements.

ME: We have weather systems on planets as a function of the atmosphere's interaction with the surface of the planet. On the Earth, the seas and mountains have a big part to play. Does this happen in a nebula?

SE1: As you well know, weather systems are created as a function of the movement of those gaseous elements around the environment of their location. Areas of dense collation of similar or same elements in different frequencies can affect those areas of less dense collation. This causes attraction and repulsion, compression and decompression of those gasses causing movement in and around the surface of a planet or denser gaseous body or its other areas or volumes of dense collated gasses. Movements of these gasses can cause funneling effects and the subsequent accelerated movement of the gasses in certain directions causing flow or what you call winds. These, as you are aware, can and are multilayered and can and do move in different directions to each other.

ME: So "weather" systems are created by allowing collections of elements (seas) to come and go (collate and uncollate) and create changeable atmospheric conditions through attractivity, repulsion, temperature, frequency, and elemental transformation.

SE1: Yes. The Atmospherisists kick off the creation of gas movement by introducing changes to the density of the gasses in the atmosphere and/or generating etheric squeeze. If you like, they do this by making a system of exchange between densities of gasses by using slightly higher frequencies. They use those in the etheric which are components of the first frequency to create imbalances in density and squeeze those gasses of the atmosphere that are in an area or volume of density in between higher frequency gasses thereby reducing the volume available to the dense gasses. This further creates one of two things, either an area of greater density and therefore pressure, changing the forces of interaction between those areas of now greater density and those other gasses that are near or surround them in whatever levels of density they are, or, gasses are ejected as a result of compression created by the squeeze. In some instances, these gasses are superheated changing their frequential state to one of a higher level. Once started, the process of movement is self-perpetuating—in most instances. In essence though, the Atmospherisists create weather systems, if required, relative to the gaseous elements of the area being used for evolutionary experience. This is one of their goals in creating an atmosphere and its working attributes.

ME: That's how winds are created on a planet; how are they created in a nebula?

SE1: In very much the same way except that they are not created in the location of an area of locally low density—a planet. In the instance of the nebula, the topography of the planet is not available, but there are areas of gas of varying localized densities and these are equivalent in function to having mountains to move around or being squeezed by etheric frequencies. Seas of very dense gasses are also available to create exchanges of gaseous state and density change. The movement of gasses within a gas giant or nebula are, for want of a better word, more aggressive in their movements in and around the volume of space that is called a nebula.

ME: How are atmospheres perpetuated or maintained?

SE1: In all cases, the Atmospherisists keep analyzing the functions of the atmosphere, its desired interactions and interdependent entities/beings, and upon seeing the potential for a drop in its efficiency, they make changes to its functionality by using one of the following methods of change:

- Introduce new gasses

- Reduce the gas content of one or more gasses

- Increase the gas content of one or more gasses

- Swap out gasses

- Introduce more of the same gasses equally

- Reduce the same gasses equally

- Apply etheric squeeze in certain locations of weather movement

- Change the density of an area or volume of density (of the planet or in terms of a nebula, the gas)

- Change the density of a local area of gas

- Change the frequency of certain areas within the atmosphere

- Move the planet closer to a sun

- Move a moon of the planet closer to the planet

- Change the direction of flow of the gasses (change wind direction)

- Change the speed of flow of the gasses

- Change the temperature of the gasses either in localized areas or in the total atmospheric volume

- The use of electricity-based attraction and repulsion (thunderstorms on Earth)

- Changes to the magnetic field (magnetosphere) of a planet

- Changes to the direction of rotation of the molten core of a planet (if it has one)

- Changes in pressure of the molten core of a planet (volcanoes)

- Changes to the angle of planetary axis

- Changes of direction to the jet stream

- Changes of direction to the stratostream

- Changes in direction to the magnetostream

ME: There is a magnetostream?

SE1: Yes, the magnetosphere has its own magnetic flow/s as well—hence a magnetostream.

ME: I suppose that makes sense. A scientist reading these lines will be interested, I have no doubt.

SE1: Yes, when you are using transportation systems that travel within the magnetosphere, you will notice how it affects that mode of transport.

ME: We should discuss this in another book.

SE1: That will be for the scientists to work on, not you. Getting back on track, the list above is also how the Atmospherisists change an atmosphere from one condition to another. Using the Earth as an example, you are all experiencing the work of the Atmospherisists right now. Have you ever thought how the jet stream changes its direction of travel so dramatically giving a number of locations colder and wetter conditions?

ME: Don't tell me, the Atmospherisists used etheric squeeze to change the actual direction and route of flow from what it was to another, the one we now have.

SE1: You are quick today—and accurate as well. Yes, that is exactly the methodology that they used.

The Atmospherisists work in a number of different weather systems that are part of a planet's atmospheric function. Weather systems can be in one function for as little as a few minutes to greater levels of existence such as from hours to days, to weeks, to months, to years, to decades, to centuries, to millennia. They can change an atmosphere from one condition to another in a matter of a few hours, and this means that even weather systems of atmospheres that have been in static existence for centuries or millennia can be changed to something else in a few hours.

ME: I guess the reaction from the Earth's perspective would be a change from an ice age to a tropical age.

SE1: A change of such magnitude takes a little longer than a few hours. I would say a number of days but no more than a month. You have examples, old stories of sudden weather changes, do you not?

ME: They are myths. One such example would be the story of Noah.

SE1: It's not a myth; it's a true event—weather-wise. Look for more in the depth of your mythology, there are many more. Also look into taking deep ice core samples and analyzing them. You will see more evidence of slow, rapid, and normal weather and atmospheric changes in the core samples as well.

I suddenly felt a change in the energy of The Source, and just as I was contemplating this feeling, The Source confirmed my feelings.

SE1: We have reached the end of the digestible information relating to the work of the Curators. You need to work on editing these texts and contemplate working on the new book.

I suddenly felt another energy, in fact, more than one!

O: Yes, you have an easier book to write first and then we will get together again. This will be your holiday, so to speak.

I was surprised at The Origin suddenly appearing in my mind.

O: Why are you surprised? I could hear you wondering why I had not participated in this dialogue! You are quite telepathically loud when you want to be.

ME: I have to admit that I felt a little disappointed that you did not make a guest appearance.

O: Isn't that what I am doing now? No. There was no need. You were doing just fine with Source Entity One. I will work with you in the two books to follow the next.

ME: I guess these will be *Beyond the Origin* and *The OM, The Uncreated Creations*?

O: Those are the ones. For the next book, book number eight, you will work by yourself and Anne—where appropriate. This you already know. You have already worked with me on a book specifically about me [The Origin Speaks—*GSN*] so the book on the OM should be book number nine. The book with me will be book number ten. You already know the content you will deliver for books eleven and twelve.

ME: Yes, they are on the purpose of significant figures in history—including so called anti-Christ personalities, and one that illustrates when, where, and how religious processes and texts fit in with my work. This book will explain the true common source of our modern religions.

O: Good, you are set. No more disappointments about when I appear in your mind—this is ego.

ME: Yes, I know. All OK now.

O: Good. Then it's time to sign off.

SE1: Yes, it's time to wish you well. I will make a number of guest appearances in the book on the OM and in books eleven and twelve.

O: In the book on the OM, you will be working mostly with the OM so don't expect too much interaction with Source Entity One or me.

A: And I will only be helping with issues relating to healing that create a bridge with the book that we worked on [The Anne Dialogues—*GSN*].

ME: And what areas will that be?

A: Impatient, aren't you? Mmm, OK, I will tell you in summary. I will work with you on the subject of the way in which we incarnate affect the incarnate vehicle, healing with the help of other entities, and some of the psycho-spiritual issues. Having said that, though, it will be mostly based upon your own healing work over the last fifteen years.

ME: Thank you.

O, SE1, & A: It's time for you to take a little rest now. Editing will be a good rest for you; you won't have to be connected.

Don't forget to stay as ego-free as you can and be considerate to others.

And with that, the collective energies that were The Origin, Source Entity One, and Anne faded away. Of course, it was only just The Origin and individualizations of sentience that was part of the myriad functions of The Origin that I was communicating to; it's just that they have different roles and responsibilities, different energy signatures or personalities, different names!

I sat at my computer and sighed a little. I may as well stay here for a moment and absorb the energies that still lingered around me. I had a little tear in my eyes as I started to contemplate writing the afterword.

Afterword

Well, I am here again. (*Didn't I say this at the start of the book?*) The text of another book finished, but not the work supporting its publication I note—the editing. There is a certain level of relief that follows from such a realization, a taking in of a second breath and a moment of relaxation. I just need to get down to working with the two lovely ladies that work with editing the manuscript in total and adding, where appropriate, a glossary of terms. Many, I thought, will be carried over from previous books, but of course in any new dialogue, there are new concepts to be described and new terminology to explain.

One of the things that I notice now is a complete lack of detailed reference to the use of the word "Angel." I very much feel that this will disappoint those readers who expected it to dominate these texts. I also feel that this term and the understanding surrounding it was a function of a lack of education, and therefore lack of understanding, of higher and deeper subjects resulting from observations of various genres of Curator or main Guide and Helpers by those unable to assimilate, in an accurate way, that which they are observing.

Hierarchies of Curator explained by religious texts and illustrated in the first part of this book, are in my mind, only clearly explained in a way that is concurrent with the level of education, technology, and expansivity of incarnate humankind at the time of teaching, which, of course, was limited to say the least. The desire to perpetuate these teachings without distortion or dilution has resulted in a kindergarten level of understanding that perpetuates even to this day. I hold them in the same light as using a parable to teach a way to live in a karma-free or reduced way, or a nursery rhyme to describe a medieval illness. Although reasonable at the time, it now only creates confusion and misinformation. Indeed, such is the level of understanding or difference in terminology today that I nearly removed that part from the book as a whole. The only reason it stayed in was to illustrate a moot point, that being, that this is what was a previous level of understanding, an understanding that had little if no detailed description to support it, and therefore has no place in today's metaphysical thesaurus whereas we are a more mature and higher frequency incarnate race now and so can be exposed to more detail and higher concepts surrounding the Greater Reality we exist within and its functionality.

This book is therefore here to help open up and expand the thought processes of readers by exposing them to different and more accurate [*for the moment that is—I expect deeper concepts and more accurate information to be broadcast by those who come after me—GSN*] information and understanding concepts surrounding the multiversal environment we exist within.

I encourage you, dear reader, to use this book as a way to make you ask more questions about yourself, the environment you incarnate into, and the greater multiversal reality our physical universe is part of. More importantly, it is important to recognize that there are vast numbers of entities in service to the maintenance and perpetuation of this multiversal environment that The Source created to help expedite its evolutionary progression, who in the process of performing their role, support those that are in the evolutionary cycle—US!

These entities are called …

"The Curators!"

Guy Steven Needler
15th April 2018

Glossary

Acid Test—A way of testing if gold is real or not by the use of acid to remove a layer of gold exposing the underlying metal as either a substrate or real gold. In this instance, it is a way of exposing the truth.

Akashic Records—An eternal past present and future record of each of humankind's actions and subsequent evolution.

Alternative Reality—A personal or group-based perception or desire for a certain experiential environment within a known environment relative to their thoughts, behaviors, and actions and the desire to ignore that which one doesn't desire to interact with.

Aspect—An Aspect is a smaller part of the TES that is used to experience the minute detail of the environments within the multiverse. It is used to experience the lowest frequencies of the multiverse presented by the physical universe through the process of incarnation. A maximum of twelve Aspects can be projected by the TES at any one time.

Being—An individualized unit of sentience that has developed independently by the function of similar, same, or sympathetic energy/ies collecting together and evolving over a period.

Big Bang—The current popular scientific explanation of how the universe started. The Source Entity stated in earlier dialogues with me that it was far from the truth—that it simply created our multiverse and, as such, it "winked" directly into existence. Whether this created a big bang is unclear from my dialogues.

Billennia—A multiple of a million (a millennia is a thousand).

Black Hole—A black hole physically is an area of local gravitational density and spiritually is an area of stable dimensional instability, a dimension within a dimension. A spiritual explanation is that a black hole is a small galaxy whose role is to collect lower frequency material into one place—within itself.

Bone of Contention—A way of describing a discussion point where there are mixed beliefs or levels of agreement.

Carrier Wave—Telecommunications terminology. A sinusoidal waveform modulated with an input signal for the purpose of transmitting information. It is usually a higher frequency than the input signal (the data being transmitted). The purpose of the carrier wave is usually either to transmit the information through space as an electromagnetic wave (as in radio communication) or to allow several carriers at different frequencies to share a common physical transmission medium by frequency, division, multiplexing (as is used in, for example, a cable television system). (Source: Wikipedia, http://en.wikipedia.org/wiki/Carrier_wave.)

Chakra—An energy center in the human body.

Cimension—A single dimension that has all the faculties of the first three lower dimensions we call up, down, left, right, forward and backward (3D), including other dimensions, without them needing to be singularly represented.

Coadunate—A telepathically connected collection of civilizations that are all collectives in their own right and are congregated together as a larger collective.

Collation—The grouping together of similar or same energy/ies.

Continuum—A continuum is a body that can be continually subdivided into infinitesimal elements with properties being those of the bulk (body) material.

Core Star— The point or location of the division of sentience and energy of the incarnate Aspect within the human vehicle. The energy used to animate the human vehicle coalesces in the Tan Tien (located two inches below the navel and three inches in towards the centre of the body) with the sentience coalescing in the Soul Seat (located close the point where the front and rear aspects of the heart chakras are joined or located - close to the thymus). The Core Star is often mistaken for the Tan Tien as it is so close to the Core Star. The Core Star is positioned two inches (5cm) above the navel (belly button) and three inches (7.5cm) in toward the center of the human vehicle from the navel.

Counterclockwise—That is to say, it is an object with "handedness" (right-handed or left-handed).

Curved Ball—A way of saying that someone answers a question with a question, or simply puts something in the way so as not to answer the question.

Demarcation between Event Spaces—The line of noninteraction drawn between one Event Space and another. Note, though, that an insufficient demarcation line can result in lack of integrity of an Event Space and therefore create an alternate reality instead. Sufficient demarcation results in a robust Event Space.

Dimensiate—An effect of being pan-dimensional (across many dimensions simultaneously).

Dimensional Mechanics—A method of creating a dimension within a dimension.

DNA—Deoxyribonucleic Acid Dysfunction—out of specification functionality Energy levels—the distance between each level that is consistent with the difference between the frequencies in the human auric levels.

Dragon Entity/Byron—A 27th level energy being.

Dualistic—A condition where two realities are in existence concurrently due to the possibility of an alternative reality being created when a choice of two directions is available.

End of Event—Event Space can allow any changes to have its own "end of event," even when there appears to be no real end. An end is therefore also not a temporal position; it is a function of finalization of an individualized experiential direction.

Entity—An individualized unit of sentience, given a body of energy/ies by the division of sentience away from a higher entity, by that higher entity.

Event Space—An area or volume of space within The Origin and therefore the Source Entity that exists as a parallel function of space. It is space overlapping space or space within and without a space. Everything exists in terms of events and not in terms of time.

Event Space Horizon—When all events that are concurrently represented in the same space are observed by an entity, the collective images of the environments created by those Event Spaces appear to be a white horizon on a white background. This effect is created when the entity cannot divide the different environments represented by the different Event Spaces into separate images, creating sensory overload and the "white on white" effect. The use of the words Event Horizon to describe the periphery of a black hole, or wormhole, as we would call them, is therefore no surprise because everything blends into one.

Event Stream—The expected direction of a series of natural events within an Event Space are identified as an Event Stream.

Event Stream Bubble—Where each event is a bubble of interaction between an entity/being and the environment it is working within. The bubbles (events) can grow and explode into another bubble or shrink and implode into nothingness. Bubbles that grow sometimes explode into another bubble that is nearby creating a new but combined bubble. They can explode into a new bigger bubble allowing them to cope with an expansion of event fractals that are still combined together in the space, the Event Space, which was created for the original and static Event Stream. Those bubbles of events that shrink and implode either disappear totally, thus representing an end of that particular Event Stream, or they implode and reappear within another event. When a bubble has naturally ended its usefulness, it implodes back into its originating Event Stream bubble.

Exponential Growth and Exponential Decay—This occurs when the growth rate of a mathematical function is proportional to the function's current value. In the case of a discrete domain of definition with equal intervals, it is also called geometric growth or geometric decay (the function values form a geometric progression). (Source: http://en.wikipedia.org/wiki/Exponential_growth.)

Fluidic Space—Space that is constantly changing in every way, from dimension to frequency.

Frequential—Sequentially based frequencies in frequentic space.

Frequential Plane—A singular sequential frequency.

Frequentic/ial—A multifrequency space.

Geometric Progression/Growth—In mathematics, a geometric progression, also known as a geometric sequence, is a sequence of numbers where each term after the first is found by multiplying the previous one by a fixed non-zero number called the common ratio. (Source: http://en.wikipedia.org/wiki/Geometric_progression.)

Gestalt Mind—A collection of entities that share a single mind function, such as ants or trees and most other energy-based beings within this universe.

Global Reality—A further dissection of the overall theme of reality. It is relative to an area within a universal reality that affects a large but not significant number of entities within the universal environment. The global reality can therefore be described in universal terms as being akin to an area the size of a galaxy.

God Head—The Hindu word/descriptor for the TES.

Hara Line—The energetic link from the True Energetic Self (TES) to the incarnate vehicle. It links the Aspect projected into the human vehicle with the vehicle and the frequencies associated with the physical universe. It is the power and communication source of the human vehicle. The hara line is positioned in the center of the human form from the center of the top of the head, splitting into two at the Tan Tien and continuing earthward down the legs. (See Barbara Brennan's *Hands of Light*.)

Higher Self—A spiritual word/descriptor for the TES.

Holographic—A three-dimensional rendering.

Hot Swap—A computer peripheral term used to describe the removal or plugging in of a peripheral without the power being turned off. In the spiritual, this relates to the swapping in/out of a soul from/to a physical human body without the body needing to die or be born. This is sometimes called a walk-in.

Human Aura—The energy fields associated with the physical and astral components of the human body.

Hyperspace—A moment of frequential and dimensional phase that is different from the normal graduations of phase that allows movement between dimensional and frequency based environments.

Individualized Reality—The reality that entities with individualized free will choose to create around them. In some instances, the fully individualized reality can create full separation from the greater reality.

Intelliate—Intelligence-based communication.

Join the Dots—A way of saying that one "understands" through logical means, or lateral thinking, the process of going from one level of understanding to another via known steps.

Light Particle—A particle of light is known as a photon. A photon travels at the speed of 186,000 miles per second. The theoretical particle, the tachyon, is supposed to travel faster than the speed of light.

Local Reality—The official start of convolution within realities. This is a reality within a reality within the universal reality. Local realities can vary in size and number of interactive entities. Local realities are normally created when a group of entities choose to not only change the function of their interaction with the overall reality, but actively choose to disassociate any previous knowledge of the former reality.

Locally Individualized Reality—Relative to small groups of entities within a local reality, such as those living within a certain country. This occurs when entities are aware of the local reality but are unable to change the reality that has been changed for them by more influential entities.

Loci/Locus—The center or source of an object/entity. Mathematically speaking, it is the set of all points or lines that satisfy a given requirement. In Source Entity Three's environment, it represents the location of the majority of the entities concerned.

Logarithmic Growth—In mathematics, logarithmic growth describes a phenomenon whose size or cost can be described as a logarithmic function of some input. For example, $y = C\log(x)$. Note that any logarithm base can be used since one can be converted to another by a fixed constant. Logarithmic growth is the inverse of exponential growth and is very slow.

Lossy—A computer term used to describe a conversion function that results in a reduction of some sort due to an either incorrect conversion factor or a specific function of the process used. Certain "losses" are sometimes considered acceptable, but this is only the case where the output is not critical; e.g., converting an image to JPEG is a lossy conversion function.

Macro-universe—A complete universe where our own universe would serve to be the subatomic levels.

Magnetosphere—The outer region of a planet where the magnetic field of the planet controls the motion of certain charged particles.

Magnetostream—Magnetic flow within the confines of a magnetosphere of a planet.

Matter—(The elements) in the body is continuously distributed and fills the entire region of space it occupies. (Source: http://en.wikipedia.org/wiki/Continuum_mechanics.)

Metaconcert: The linking together of minds, either energetic based or thought based, to create a collective that has a synergetic effect in the ability to process information, a task, or some creative function.

Micro Event Space—A microscopically small Event Space that is specific to the needs of an individual entity, being, or environment.

Micro-universe—A complete universe at the scale of the subatomic.

Minor-verse—A universe of lesser content in terms of dimension and frequency and habitation, one of lower importance.

Monoversal—A local environment. More than one locality can be classified as monoversal, but within the space that is universal or multiversal (more than one universal environment).

Multipolous—A multiple of a multiple of a multiple. For example, X cubed, cubed, cubed ($X^{3,3,3}$).

Multiversal Reality—The experiential condition that is created by the governing entities responsible for a specific multiversal environment within a specific Source Entity. It is a generalized function of reality and is subject to change both by the Planners, other Curator functions, and the interactions of the incumbent entities/beings that are working within that environment.

Multiverse—An environment housing myriad universes.

Nova—A star that increases in brightness by many thousands of times its usual brightness, gradually fading to its original brightness. The last stages of the life of that star.

Null Space—The space in between universes for travel between universes.

The Om—Energy-based beings not indigenous to Earth. The Origins uncreated creations.

Omniciate—Omniscience-based communication.

Omnifunctional—To be able to operate, as if in an individualized way, within all environments, spaces, and events, irrespective of structural conditions and parallelized versions, concurrently.

Omnipresent—To be located within all environments, spaces, and events, irrespective of structural conditions and parallelized versions concurrently.

Omniscient—To be focused within one's sentience that is located within all environments, spaces, and events, irrespective of structural conditions and parallelized versions, concurrently.

Orgone—The visual representation of cosmic "free" energy.

The Origin—The creator of the twelve Source Entities who exist within the Origin, the greater God, an entity of pure sentient energy.

Overall Reality—The experiential condition that is created by the existence of the sentience that is The Origin. It contains all of its personal experiences, growth, realizations, creations, and explorations of self. It is the only reality that can be considered static in function and observation.

Overdrive—A way of saying that someone or something's performance has increased. The overdrive was a semiautomatic secondary gearbox added on to the manual gearbox of classic sports cars or performance automobiles in the 1960s and 1970s in the UK.

Over Soul—The Quantum Healing Hypnosis Technique (QHHT) word/descriptor for the TES. QHHT was a hypnosis-based healing technique taught by Dolores Cannon.

Parallel Condition—The duplication of Event Space. It is the creation or generation of a new but similar Event Space when a choice can be made and that choice or the possibility of the choice or the possible possibility of that choice results in a large enough downstream differential to create a new series of experiences that are self-contained and independent of the Event Space they separated from. The overall size of the Event Space is a function of the inclusion of other entities or beings that interact with the initiating and subsequent downstream experiences generated from the initial choice.

Polyomniscient—A multiple aspect of omniscience. A condition that will be achieved by The Origin as it expands into those areas of itself that are beyond its current area of sentient self-awareness.

Primary Incarnation—A descriptor for the incarnate functionality of an Aspect if a secondary incarnation is employed.

Psychometry—Gaining spiritual information about an object or person via tactile contact.

Quadrulistic—A condition where four realities are in existence concurrently due to the possibility of alternative realities being created when a choice of four directions is available.

Readings or Reader—Acting as a medium for a client or clients who want to know more information about themselves from spirit, but who are unable to ask for themselves during meditation or any other means. A "Medium" gives a "Reading."

Reality—An environment and interactive condition we create as a desire function of an Event Space or Event Stream. It is an entity—or being—generated perception-based condition.

RNA—Ribonucleic Acid Simulacrum—similar or in the same likeness.

SCUBA—An acronym for Self-Contained Underwater Breathing Apparatus.

Secondary Incarnation—A descriptor for the incarnate functionality of an Aspect that uses a significant percentage of its sentient energies to have an incarnation in a lower frequency within the physical universe. This is not a Shard but an incarnation within an incarnation because the Aspect in the primary incarnation continues while the secondary incarnation is in action. In the event that the primary incarnation is placed in stasis for the duration of the secondary incarnation the primary incarnation will re-commence once the secondary incarnation is finished.

Sentiate—Sentience-based communication.

Shard—A Shard is a smaller part of the Aspect that is used to experience the minute detail of the environments within the multiverse. It is also used to experience the lowest frequencies of the multiverse presented by the physical universe through the process of incarnation. As with the TES a maximum of twelve Shards can be projected by the Aspect at any one time.

Skewed Distribution: An effect in standard distribution where the classic "bell curve" is pulled to one side of the graph of distribution in lieu of being "normally" distributed.

Soul—The Christian and spiritual word/descriptor for the Aspect or Shard. The Soul is considered to be individualized in totality and not part of a larger being. It is also generally related with the human body and no other incarnate vehicles.

Soul Seat— This is where the sentience of the Aspect resides. It is the personality of what we, as a projected Aspect of our TES are, "it is our sentience". Its position is close to where the front and rear Aspects of the heart chakra join - close to the thymus.

The Source Entity—What we call God, the creator of our multiverse. A smaller individualization of The Origin's sentience.

Space—The area or volume within the Source (and ultimately The Origin) where everything exists.

Spaced Out—A term I used to describe being close to fainting.

Speed of Light—The speed of light is currently understood as being 186,000 miles per second.

Spirituo-physical—The level where the gross physical and energetic/spiritual frequency levels meet and mix.

Spliced Undulation of Dimension—One or more dimensions linked together as a result of them being close together or overlapping in some part of their areas.

Start of Event—Event Space can allow any changes to have its own "start of event," even when there appears to be no real start. A start or beginning is therefore not a temporal position, it is simply a function of a change of experiential direction to create a new individualized experiential direction.

Stickle Brick—A child's building block similar to a Lego block but with spikes to join them together—like a Bristle Block.

Stratostream—The flow of wind or air at stratospheric or very high altitude within the atmosphere of a planet.

Subincarnation—A descriptor for the incarnate functionality of a Shard.

Supernova—An exploding star caused by gravitational collapse.

Synergy—The effect experienced where the sum of the whole is more than the sum of the individual units creating the whole when treated in isolation.

Tan Tien—This is where the energy of the Aspect spreads out into the energy network that contains the energy template and the chakras. It ends up being a focus of tremendous energy. It is positioned two inches (5cm) below the navel (belly button) and three inches (7.5cm) in toward the center of the human vehicle from the navel.

Telekinesis—Levitation of an object or person by application of pure thought.

Teleportation—The ability to dissolve and materialize the physical body at will while changing location in the process.

Triangulation: A method used in surveying to measure position and distances between positions by the use of a triangle and the angles relating to the position of other positions or locations being surveyed. Mathematically it is a method of proving a mathematic assumption by the use of three different mathematical methods to gain the same answer.

Trilistic—A condition where three realities are in existence concurrently due to the possibility of alternative realities being created when a choice of three directions is available.

True Energetic Self—(TES) what we truly are—an entity of pure sentience with a given or commandeered body of energy.

UFO—Unidentified Flying Object.

Universal Reality—A smaller representation of the multiversal reality insomuch as it starts out to be that when a multiverse and its universal components are first introduced as a medium for evolutionary progression. The universal reality can only be changed as a result of all entities within that environment choosing to change the reality as a total collective.

Walk-In—The swapping in and out (one for another) of Aspects (souls) within a single incarnate vehicle. There are many variations upon this theme.

Wormhole—Physically an area where two frequencies connect with each other. It is possible to use wormholes to jump up through the frequencies.

About the Author

Guy Needler MBA, MSc, CEng, MIET, MCMA initially trained as a mechanical engineer and quickly progressed on to be a chartered electrical and electronics engineer. However, throughout this earthly training he was always aware of the greater reality being around him, catching glimpses of the worlds of spirit. This resulted in a period from his teenage to early twenties where he reveled in the spiritual texts of the day and meditated intensively. Being subsequently told by his guides to focus on his earthly contribution for a period he scaled back the intensity of spiritual work until his late thirties where he was re-awakened to his spiritual roles. The next six years saw him gaining his Reiki Master and a four year commitment to learn energy and vibrational therapy techniques from a direct student of the Barbara Brennan School of HealingTM, which also included a personal development undertaking (including psychotherapy) as a course prerequisite using the PathworkTM methodology described by Susan Thesenga with further methodologies by Donovan Thesenga, John and Eva Pierrakos. His training and experience in energy based therapies have resulted in him being a member of the Complementary Medical Association (MCMA).

Along with his healing abilities his spiritual associations include being able to channel information from spirit including constant contact with other entities within our multi-verse and his higher self and guides. It is the channeling that resulted in "The History of God" and produced his other books. It continues to produce further work.

As a method of grounding Guy practices and teaches Aikido. He is a 6th Dan National Coach with 36 years experience and is currently working on the use of spiritual energy within the physical side of the art.

Guy welcomes questions on the subject of spiritual physics and who and what God is.

Other Books by Ozark Mountain Publishing, Inc.

Dolores Cannon
A Soul Remembers Hiroshima
Between Death and Life
Conversations with Nostradamus,
    Volume I, II, III
The Convoluted Universe -Book One,
    Two, Three, Four, Five
The Custodians
Five Lives Remembered
Jesus and the Essenes
Keepers of the Garden
Legacy from the Stars
The Legend of Starcrash
The Search for Hidden Sacred Knowledge
They Walked with Jesus
The Three Waves of Volunteers and the
    New Earth
Aron Abrahamsen
Holiday in Heaven
Out of the Archives – Earth Changes
Justine Alessi & M. E. McMillan
Rebirth of the Oracle
Kathryn/Patrick Andries
Naked in Public
Kathryn Andries
The Big Desire
Dream Doctor
Soul Choices: Six Paths to Find Your Life
    Purpose
Soul Choices: Six Paths to Fulfilling
    Relationships
Patrick Andries
Owners Manual for the Mind
Dan Bird
Finding Your Way in the Spiritual Age
Waking Up in the Spiritual Age
Julia Cannon
Soul Speak – The Language of Your Body
Ronald Chapman
Seeing True
Albert Cheung
The Emperor's Stargate
Jack Churchward
Lifting the Veil on the Lost Continent of
    Mu
The Stone Tablets of Mu
Sherri Cortland
Guide Group Fridays
Raising Our Vibrations for the New Age

Spiritual Tool Box
Windows of Opportunity
Patrick De Haan
The Alien Handbook
Paulinne Delcour-Min
Spiritual Gold
Michael Dennis
Morning Coffee with God
God's Many Mansions
Carolyn Greer Daly
Opening to Fullness of Spirit
Anita Holmes
Twidders
Aaron Hoopes
Reconnecting to the Earth
Victoria Hunt
Kiss the Wind
Patricia Irvine
In Light and In Shade
Kevin Killen
Ghosts and Me
Diane Lewis
From Psychic to Soul
Donna Lynn
From Fear to Love
Maureen McGill
Baby It's You
Maureen McGill & Nola Davis
Live from the Other Side
Curt Melliger
Heaven Here on Earth
Henry Michaelson
And Jesus Said – A Conversation
Dennis Milner
Kosmos
Andy Myers
Not Your Average Angel Book
Guy Needler
Avoiding Karma
Beyond the Source – Book 1, Book 2
The Anne Dialogues
The Curators
The History of God
The Origin Speaks
James Nussbaumer
And Then I Knew My Abundance
The Master of Everything
Mastering Your Own Spiritual Freedom

For more information about any of the above titles, soon to be released titles,
or other items in our catalog, write, phone or visit our website:
PO Box 754, Huntsville, AR 72740
479-738-2348/800-935-0045
www.ozarkmt.com

Other Books by Ozark Mountain Publishing, Inc.

Sherry O'Brian
Peaks and Valleys
Riet Okken
The Liberating Power of Emotions
Gabrielle Orr
Akashic Records: One True Love
Let Miracles Happen
Victor Parachin
Sit a Bit
Nikki Pattillo
A Spiritual Evolution
Children of the Stars
Rev. Grant H. Pealer
A Funny Thing Happened on the
    Way to Heaven
Worlds Beyond Death
Victoria Pendragon
Born Healers
Feng Shui from the Inside, Out
Sleep Magic
The Sleeping Phoenix
Michael Perlin
Fantastic Adventures in Metaphysics
Walter Pullen
Evolution of the Spirit
Debra Rayburn
Let's Get Natural with Herbs
Charmian Redwood
A New Earth Rising
Coming Home to Lemuria
David Rivinus
Always Dreaming
Richard Rowe
Imagining the Unimaginable
M. Don Schorn
Elder Gods of Antiquity
Legacy of the Elder Gods
Gardens of the Elder Gods
Reincarnation...Stepping Stones of Life
Garnet Schulhauser
Dance of Eternal Rapture
Dance of Heavenly Bliss

Dancing Forever with Spirit
Dancing on a Stamp
Manuella Stoerzer
Headless Chicken
Annie Stillwater Gray
Education of a Guardian Angel
The Dawn Book
Work of a Guardian Angel
Blair Styra
Don't Change the Channel
Who Catharted
Natalie Sudman
Application of Impossible Things
L.R. Sumpter
Judy's Story
The Old is New
We Are the Creators
Jim Thomas
Tales from the Trance
Nicholas Vesey
Living the Life-Force
Janie Wells
Embracing the Human Journey
Payment for Passage
Dennis Wheatley/ Maria Wheatley
The Essential Dowsing Guide
Maria Wheatley
Druidic Soul Star Astrology
Jacquelyn Wiersma
The Zodiac Recipe
Sherry Wilde
The Forgotten Promise
Lyn Willmoth
A Small Book of Comfort
Stuart Wilson & Joanna Prentis
Atlantis and the New Consciousness
Beyond Limitations
The Essenes -Children of the Light
The Magdalene Version
Power of the Magdalene
Robert Winterhalter
The Healing Christ

For more information about any of the above titles, soon to be released titles,
or other items in our catalog, write, phone or visit our website:
PO Box 754, Huntsville, AR 72740
479-738-2348/800-935-0045
www.ozarkmt.com